Descriptive Taxonomy

The Foundation of Biodiversity Research

In an age when biodiversity is being lost at an unprecedented rate, it is vital that floristic and faunistic information is up-to-date, reliable and easily accessible for the formulation of effective conservation strategies. Electronic data management and communication are transforming descriptive taxonomy radically, enhancing both the collection and dissemination of crucial data on biodiversity.

This volume is written by scientists at the forefront of current developments of Floras and Faunas, along with specialists from applied user groups. The chapters review novel methods of research, development and dissemination, which aim to maximise the relevance and impact of data. Regional case studies are used to illustrate the outputs and impacts of taxonomic research. Integrated approaches are presented which have the capacity to accelerate the production of Floras and Faunas and to better serve the needs of a widening audience.

Abstracts for each chapter are available for download at www.cambridge.org/ 9780521761079.

MARK F. WATSON is Head of the Major Floras research programme at the Royal Botanic Garden Edinburgh (RBGE), where he leads the Flora of Nepal team. He is a taxonomic botanist and expert in floristic research in the Sino-Himalayan region, with over 23 years' experience at RBGE in floristics, fieldwork and biodiversity informatics.

CHRIS H.C. LYAL is a researcher at the Natural History Museum in London, with over 40 years' experience in insect taxonomy, including fieldwork in many countries. He has worked on the digitisation of taxonomic literature to address the 'taxonomic impediment' – the shortage of taxonomists and taxonomic tools that hinders work in other areas of biodiversity research and management.

COLIN A. PENDRY is an Editor for the Flora of Nepal at RBGE and has a background in ecology as well as in both floristic and monographic taxonomy. He has extensive experience of fieldwork in the UK, SE Asia, Latin America, the Caribbean and Nepal and maintains an active programme of plant collecting in Nepal.

The Systematics Association
Special Volume Series

SERIES EDITOR

DAVID J. GOWER

Department of Life Sciences, The Natural History Museum, London, UK

The Systematics Association promotes all aspects of systematic biology by organising conferences and workshops on key themes in systematics, running annual lecture series, publishing books and a newsletter, and awarding grants in support of systematics research. Membership of the Association is open globally to professionals and amateurs with an interest in any branch of biology, including palaeobiology. Members are entitled to attend conferences at discounted rates, to apply for grants and to receive the newsletter and mailed information; they also receive a generous discount on the purchase of all volumes produced by the Association.

The first of the Systematics Association's publications, *The New Systematics* (1940), was a classic work edited by its then-president Sir Julian Huxley. Since then, more than 70 volumes have been published, often in rapidly expanding areas of science where a modern synthesis is required.

The Association encourages researchers to organise symposia that result in multi-authored volumes. In 1997 the Association organised the first of its international Biennial Conferences. This and subsequent Biennial Conferences, which are designed to provide for systematists of all kinds, included themed symposia that resulted in further publications. The Association also publishes volumes that are not specifically linked to meetings, and encourages new publications (including textbooks) in a broad range of systematics topics.

More information about the Systematics Association and its publications can be found at our website: www.systass.org

Previous Systematics Association publications are listed after the index for this volume.

Systematics Association Special Volumes published by Cambridge University Press:

78. *Climate Change, Ecology and Systematics* (2011)
    Trevor R. Hodkinson, Michael B. Jones, Stephen Waldren and
    John A. N. Parnell
79. *Biogeography of Microscopic Organisms: Is everything small everywhere?* (2011)
    Diego Fontaneto

THE SYSTEMATICS ASSOCIATION SPECIAL

VOLUME 84

Descriptive Taxonomy

The Foundation of Biodiversity Research

EDITED BY

MARK F. WATSON
Royal Botanic Garden Edinburgh

CHRIS H. C. LYAL
Natural History Museum, London

COLIN A. PENDRY
Royal Botanic Garden Edinburgh

THE
Systematics
ASSOCIATION

CAMBRIDGE
UNIVERSITY PRESS

CAMBRIDGE
UNIVERSITY PRESS

University Printing House, Cambridge CB2 8BS, United Kingdom

Cambridge University Press is part of the University of Cambridge.

It furthers the University's mission by disseminating knowledge in the pursuit of education, learning and research at the highest international levels of excellence.

www.cambridge.org
Information on this title: www.cambridge.org/9780521761079

First published 2015

Printed in the United Kingdom by TJ International Ltd. Padstow Cornwall

A catalogue record for this publication is available from the British Library

Library of Congress Cataloguing in Publication data
Descriptive taxonomy : the foundation of biodiversity research / edited by Mark
F. Watson, Royal Botanic Garden, Edinburgh, Chris Lyal, Natural History Museum,
London, Colin Pendry, Royal Botanic Garden, Edinburgh.
    pages   cm. – (The systematics association special volume series ; 84)
ISBN 978-0-521-76107-9 (hardback)
1. Biodiversity – Mathematical models.   2. Variation (Biology) – Mathematical
models.   3. Conservation biology.   4. Nature conservation.   5. Sustainable
biodiversity.   I. Watson, M. F. (Mark Francis), editor.   II. Lyal, Christopher H. C.,
editor.   III. Pendry, Colin A., editor.
QH75.D465   2015
333.95–dc23
                                                                    2014025973

ISBN 978-0-521-76107-9 Hardback

Additional resources for this publication at www.cambridge.org/9780521761079

Contents

Colour plate section appears between pages 158 and 159

Contributors

A. L. Allcock Ryan Institute for Environmental, Marine and Energy Research, National University of Ireland Galway, Ireland

M. V. Angel National Oceanography Centre, Southampton, UK

G. A. Boxshall Natural History Museum, London, UK

S. Bridgewater Royal Botanic Garden Edinburgh, UK

S. J. Brooks Department of Life Sciences, Natural History Museum, London, UK

S. J. Chambers National Museums of Scotland, Edinburgh, UK

B. Collen Centre for Biodiversity and Environment Research, University College London, UK

J. B. Connor Timber Press, Portland, Oregon, USA

D. V. P. Conway Marine Biological Association of the United Kingdom, Plymouth, UK

J. Dick Centre for Ecology and Hydrology, Edinburgh, UK

S. Fielding National Oceanography Centre, Southampton, UK

A. G. Gutierrez US Army Center for Health Promotion and Preventive Medicine, MD, USA

M. Hall Royal Botanic Garden Edinburgh, UK

D. J. Harris Royal Botanic Garden Edinburgh, UK

L. C. Hastie University of Aberdeen, Aberdeen, UK

C. L. Häuser Museum für Naturkunde, Leibniz Institute for Research on Evolution and Biodiversity Berlin, Germany

S. J. Hay Fisheries Research Services, Aberdeen, UK

D. Hopkins Natural History Museum, London, UK

R. Hyam Royal Botanic Garden Edinburgh, and Department of Botany, Natural History Museum, London, UK

A. Ingvarsdottir University of Aberdeen, Aberdeen, UK

A. W. G. John Sir Alister Hardy Foundation for Ocean Science, Plymouth, UK

S. L. Jury School of Biological Sciences, University of Reading, UK

D. W. Kirkup Royal Botanic Gardens, Kew, UK

S. KNAPP Department of Life Sciences, Natural History Museum, London, UK

S. G. KNEES Royal Botanic Garden Edinburgh, UK

C. H. C. LYAL Department of Life Sciences, Natural History Museum, London, UK

P. MALCOLM Royal Botanic Gardens, Kew, UK

A. G. MILLER Royal Botanic Garden Edinburgh, UK

S. E. MILLER National Museum of Natural History, Smithsonian Institution, Washington, DC, USA

S. P. MILLIGAN Centre for Environment, Fisheries and Aquaculture, Lowestoft, UK

A. MINELLI Department of Biology, University of Padova, Italy

D. W. MINTER BioNET-International, Egham, UK

J.-M. MOUTSAMBOTÉ Institut de Développement Rural, Université Marien Ngouabi, Republic of Congo

A. L. MULFORD National Museums of Scotland, Edinburgh, UK

A. PATON Royal Botanic Gardens, Kew, UK

C. A. PENDRY Royal Botanic Garden Edinburgh, UK

G. J. PIERCE University of Aberdeen, Aberdeen, UK

M. R. PULLAN Royal Botanic Garden Edinburgh, UK

J. RASMUSSEN Fisheries Research Services, Aberdeen, UK

K. RIEDE Zoologisches Forschungsmuseum Alexander Koenig – Leibniz Institute for Terrestrial Biodiversity, Bonn, Germany

M. SHAW Centre for Environment, Fisheries and Aquaculture, Lowestoft, UK

R. SMITH Centre for Ecology and Hydrology, Edinburgh, UK

V. S. SMITH Department of Life Sciences, The Natural History Museum, London, UK

R. WADSWORTH Centre for Ecology and Hydrology, Lancaster, UK

M. F. WATSON Royal Botanic Garden Edinburgh, UK

A. L. WEITZMAN National Museum of Natural History, Smithsonian Institution, Washington, USA

M. WOOTTON Sir Alister Hardy Foundation for Ocean Science, Plymouth, UK

A. H. WORTLEY Royal Botanic Garden Edinburgh, UK

Introduction

M. F. Watson, C. H. C. Lyal and C. A. Pendry

We are living in an age where biodiversity is being lost at an unprecedented rate, with the well-documented problems of habitat destruction being compounded by the largely unknown future effects of climate change. High-quality, accurate and reliable biodiversity data are needed by biologists, conservationists and environmental modellers to understand and assess the ecosystems in which they work, to produce effective conservation strategies, and to feed computer-generated models, which predict what environments and habitats we might face in the future. Descriptive taxonomy – the collection, characterisation, description and naming of biological organisms – has been a cornerstone for the provision of authoritative data for these purposes, in addition to its general primary purpose of developing a taxonomic understanding of the biota. The chapters in this book explore changes to the traditional methodology of descriptive taxonomy, how new technologies are being embraced and how new requirements are being met.

Floras and Faunas, and their equivalents in other biological kingdoms, present data on organisms occurring within a geographical region. In addition to monographs, which focus on a taxon at the global scale, they have been a major output from taxonomists. They establish a regional classification bringing order to past works, provide tools for identification and inventories through keys and descriptions, and record data on distribution ranges, ecology and conservation status. These works have long been acknowledged as critical for understanding the organisms of a region and,

Descriptive Taxonomy: The Foundation of Biodiversity Research, eds M. F. Watson, C. H. C. Lyal and C. A. Pendry. Published by Cambridge University Press.
© The Systematics Association 2015

in recent years, as fundamental to the formulation of conservation strategies. Electronic data management and dissemination has the potential to transform floristic and faunistic projects radically and diversify the users of these data. Online dissemination enables unparalleled access to, and offers novel means of presenting, data in a variety of formats tailored to specific user requirements.

This book is based on the theme of the Sixth Biennial Conference of the Systematics Association, held at Royal Botanic Garden Edinburgh, 28–31 August 2007. It brings together scientists working on floristic, faunistic and mycological projects, including those producing field guides, and representatives from other user groups. The intent is to discuss novel areas of research and to help create a more outward looking, integrated approach, which better serves the needs of the end users. The book is arranged in five parts: the first addressing the issues of the current and potential users of descriptive biodiversity data and the relevance to diverse audiences; the second looks at the outputs and impacts of descriptive taxonomic products through a series of regional case studies; the third takes a closer look at field guides and applications of floristic and faunistic works; the fourth assesses the influence of new technologies on the gathering and management of data and collections in the field; and the fifth covers the impact of technological advancements in data location, dissemination and integration, and the new field of DNA barcoding.

Part I: The widening audience

Traditionally Floras, Faunas, Mycotas and the like have been intended for natural historians, in the wider sense, and for taxonomists. Their aim, as pointed out in several papers in this section, has primarily been to enable users to identify organisms within a geographical area and, secondarily, to act as a published repository for a wide range of related information, including taxonomic, systematic, morphological, behavioural, biological, ecological and phenological. They have ranged from the scholarly and academic to the illustration-rich and text-light field guide to simple lists of species with minimal additional information. Each of these products has its place, but this place is not always recognised by the users. The first three chapters in this section explore how the contents of Floras and Faunas have been and can be used by conservationists, ecologists and others to address questions that were perhaps outside the intent of the original compilers. Each of them also makes recommendations for future developments in floristic and faunistic studies, in terms of content, increasing use of digital tools and in collaboration across disciplines. The development of new methodologies in compilation, and highlighting valuable content types, are valuable for the preparation of Floras and Faunas, but must be considered in the context of publication; unless a product is to be completely digital (and see later chapters for examples of this idea) it will need to be published. As discussed in Chapter 4, while publishers are considering digital products in this area, they are for their main market of paper-based publications constrained by market requirements for content and delivery style, and those engaged in the preparation of any new Fauna or Flora needs to take this into account.

Part II: The products of descriptive taxonomy

While many Floras and Faunas are nationally based there is, perhaps increasingly, a requirement for regional studies also. In many cases these can be built on previous work, although bringing that work together can have its challenges. A first step is to determine just what species are known from a region, and how they are distributed. This deceptively simple task has posed significant problems in some projects, and is still an issue for some users. For example, transnational control of pests, or management of genetic resources under the Nagoya Protocol require that all parties are using the same names for the same organisms. An attempt to address the problem of harmonising names and constructing a list is discussed in Chapter 5. Building on earlier experience, the management of the project was of critical importance, and particularly guiding and facilitating the work of contributors across Europe. The importance of sustaining activity after funding for a particular project comes to an end is stressed in Chapter 5, and is also a theme of Chapter 6. The development of the work that compiled the *Flora Europaea* through Euro+Med PlantBase is described. Again, there is a mixture of technological solutions and facilitating and encouraging the work of a cadre of taxonomists to update, discover and deliver information. The next two chapters in this section also cover regional approaches with a digital approach. Chapter 7 focuses on making available in digital format the great quantity of work that has been done on African Floras. Currently inaccessible to many, digitising the legacy literature in a controlled fashion and delivering it in a simple manner has made access very much simpler to a wide audience. The approach used XML markup – something that is returned to in Chapter 19 – to effectively turn the literature content into a database that could be queried with a set of predetermined questions, prioritised because of the likely use of the content. This has taken already published regional Floras to a new readership and, importantly, laid the groundwork for future work on African plant diversity. It is an example of reuse of published work – an area that has to be a priority given the huge volume of study available in libraries but with relatively limited accessibility. Chapter 8 discusses a different approach, to making information available, although this time there are several strands to the information: literature, nomenclature and taxonomy, distributions and associations, and biographical about mycologists. Two of these strands are available in multiple languages, enabling the system to function in the context of national and regional websites elsewhere. As with other case studies in this section, the use of digital media has increased access and flexibility of use of resources, and enabled use of the resources in a number of different contexts.

The final chapter in this section, Chapter 9 on the Zooplankton Identification Manual for North European Seas (ZIMNES) project, takes the digital argument a little further and into a different domain, that of marine environments. In this case the compilation is for a digital system that features a web-based identification guide, but which also will be available in PDF format. Users are expected to encompass both specialists and non-specialists, a trend that is continued in the next section.

Part III: Outputs and impact: field guides and applications

While the more academic 'end' of Floras and Faunas is aimed at professionals and overlaps with other forms of academic taxonomic literature, there is a large constituency that needs Floristic and Faunistic treatments that are explicitly intended to assist in identification in the field – field guides. Such tools need to be very strongly tailored to their users and the ways in which those users access information. The most common type of field guide is a 'standard' handy-sized volume with illustrations and text. The precise format is of importance to users, and this is addressed in some detail in Chapters 10, 11 and 12. With regard to the images presented, care must be taken to ensure that the illustrations truly capture the organism in the manner in which people are likely to observe it. Chapter 10 provides a case study in which the execution of the guide relied not so much on formulaic 'traditional' images but much more on images presented to aid identification of the living organism. This approach is perhaps antithetical to the concept of an all-inclusive Fauna or Flora as being discussed in the first section of the book, but equally valid and with a very clear user base. Chapters 11 and 12 consider field manuals for quite restricted groups of users, in the context of particular projects and particularly for assessment and collecting purposes, and associated with training. In these cases the developers of the guides have been able to work closely with the users, getting feedback from them and being able to incorporate this into redesign. In the case study in Chapter 11 the developers focussed, as with the dragonfly work in Chapter 10, on the aspects of the organisms that will be most apparent to the user. In the case of plants this largely excluded reproductive structures, as the majority of times that people come into contact with plants, perhaps particularly in tropical work, the plants are not in a reproductive phase. The project discussed in Chapter 12 addressed this problem in a slightly different manner, by stressing phenological data in the products, so that the users could time their work in the ecosystems covered to maximise the likelihood of finding identifiable material, something that was particularly important for the Seed Bank collectors. The emphasis of working with the users is taken a further step in Chapter 13, which is explicitly about training and recognition of the most effective 'shortest route' to effective field identification through selection of characters and hands-on experience with collecting and preparing plants. This feeds back to the discussions in earlier chapters on character selection, and also provides insights into how field guides are actually used, and the types of learning reinforcement that can assist users.

The final chapter in this section takes us in a different direction. As is discussed in Chapter 22, the use of DNA in identifications is a growing trend. In most cases, however, this is done in the laboratory and some time after field collection. However, there are situations where rapid field identification of critical species is required, and DNA might be the most effective way of achieving this. In Chapter 14 we have an example of such a scenario and tools developed to facilitate this. Two tools are discussed: comparison of a specimen with a three-dimensional image displayed by a wearable computer, and a portable DNA laboratory for use in the field. In this case study, the concept of a field guide has been translated into a small suite of high-tech. tools that are tightly focussed on meeting the needs of particular users in a particular set of circumstances – perhaps the opposite end of the spectrum from the large-scale scholastic tomes.

Part IV: The influence of technology on data gathering in the field

The previous section took us to the field use of Faunas and Floras. The other side of the same equation is the gathering of data in the field to support an understanding of biodiversity, and how the collections made are managed and used. Traditionally collectors used to operate in a fairly simplistic manner – go to a place, search for organisms, kill them, bring them back and then sort out the information they provide back at the laboratory. This methodology is increasingly outdated. Of course, most collectors learned particular methods to locate target groups, but with advances in technology these have, in some cases, become both more refined and standardised. This is a theme of Chapters 15 and 16, where a range of techniques is addressed, and Chapter 17 where the implementation of novel technologies in a very challenging environment for discovering biodiversity – marine systems – are discussed. Other technological solutions are discussed in all chapters in this section, in particular digital capture of information in the field. Particular attention is paid to digital photography in all chapters, ideally linked to global positioning system recording. This is linked to the selection of just what to collect, and what to preserve in collections; increasingly it is important to understand the collecting biases that led to what is preserved and accommodate that in analyses – issues that had previously been discussed in terms of contents of Floras and Faunas in Part III. It is also important to collect efficiently, so that images and samples for DNA analysis are all that is required, rather than entire specimens. Data capture in the field may be more efficient than retrospective searching for data, and the ways in which such data capture can be brought into a more efficient workflow are touched on in Chapter 16 and explored further in Chapter 18.

Part V: New technologies: their current use and future potential

The impact of novel technologies unsurprisingly is a component of many chapters in the volume, and is taken further in this section. Chapter 19 focuses on the transformation of texts to XML documents, which allows direct querying of their content, as well as extraction and reuse. The example discussed in Chapter 7 gives some idea of the power of this approach, but in Chapter 19 the concept is taken further. Such a system would allow users to effectively compile bespoke Faunas and Floras from published works. While the concept of bringing together information from different sources and uniting it sounds, if not simple, at least practical, it brings with it a host of problems. The issue of agreeing which names to use for species across different countries has been discussed in Chapter 5, but this is even more of an issue when one is attempting to bring together information not only from different countries but also from different authors and compiled at different times. Names are, if not invariant, at least possible to track through variations of spelling as taxonomists change their systematic position to reflect new understanding of the species' relationships. However, there is no such easy link to the species concept employed by the authors, especially if we are attempting to semi-automate the process. Chapter 20 explores this issue through the application of globally unique identifiers, an increasingly important element in the biodiversity informatics aspect of floristic and faunistic work. An indication of the rate of change in this area is in numbers; when the chapter was written the Global Biodiversity Information Facility mediated some 140 million occurrence records linked to names, a figure that, in 2014, has now risen to 416 242 316. Chapter 21 also calls for rapid change, pointing out that descriptive taxonomy is a slow labour intensive process, and identifying the need for tools to accelerate the process. In Chapter 12 a methodology was discussed that produced an average of three field guides per month; in Chapter 21 further tools are discussed for use in a wider context. Since the chapter was written in 2010 a great deal has changed and tools that are discussed as necessary are now appearing. For example, the development of a smooth online workflow for the whole life cycle of a manuscript, from writing to submission to peer review to publication and dissemination, is now a reality in the *Biodiversity Data Journal.*

The final chapter in the book brings us back to species and species concepts, but again seeking the most rapid and effective way of assessing what is in an area and, thus, what is to be covered in faunistic and floristic work. In areas that are very poorly known, and for taxa that pose taxonomic problems, a traditional solely morphological approach is extremely time-consuming. The addition of the use of DNA barcodes to the process, again tied to an efficient workflow, demonstrably both speeds the process and, tied to morphological examination, can provide a far more accurate and detailed understanding of the biota.

Overall, the chapters in this volume demonstrate the wide range of uses of descriptive taxonomy and how to overcome some of the problems in applying it beyond how the original authors anticipated their publications would be used. Novel techniques are discussed, both to access legacy material and also to collect, prepare and publish new information. The importance of understanding the purpose of each part of the process and how it contributes to meeting the needs of the user is highlighted and, most significantly, workflows to maximise efficient discovery, compilation and delivery are presented.

PART I

The widening audience

Floras yesterday, today and tomorrow

A. G. Miller, M. Hall, M. F. Watson, S. G. Knees,
C. A. Pendry and M. R. Pullan

1.1 Floras past

Frodin (2001) masterfully traces the history of Floras from their origins to their present form, offering both historical analysis and insightful critique. The current paper will draw substantially upon this authoritative work, *Guide to standard Floras of the world*, to frame the discussion of the role and purpose of the modern Flora. It does so by examining some of the important historical influences on our understanding of a Flora's purpose. Frodin roughly characterises the historical purpose of descriptive Floras as being twofold. Broadly speaking, the first purpose of Floras is for *identification* of plant species, achieved (hopefully) by the provision of keys, descriptions and illustrations. The second (often opposed) purpose of Floras is *archival* or *encyclopaedic*, with the Flora acting as a repository of comparative, descriptive, taxonomic data, such as extensive synonymy and specimen information.

Frodin (2001) considers the *Flore française* of J. B. de Lamarck and A. P. de Candolle (1805–1815) as the first modern Flora. This pioneering work was, in effect, the third edition of Lamarck's *Flore françoise* (1778), a publication that is highly significant in a historical discussion of Floras for two principal reasons: it was the first floristic work to contain Lamarck's analytical, dichotomous keys for species identification, and (of particular significance for this paper) because it contains some of the earliest, explicit views of the purposes of Floras. For Lamarck, Floras

Descriptive Taxonomy: The Foundation of Biodiversity Research, eds M. F. Watson, C. H. C. Lyal and C. A. Pendry. Published by Cambridge University Press.

were not scholarly works for consumption by other taxonomists. In his opinion, there was no purpose in Floras being elegant, encyclopaedic, library volumes. Rather, their purpose was to be a practical tool for the identification of plant species. Lamarck's opinion on the purpose of descriptive Floras translated into his concise descriptive style, which he employed in *Flore française*, along with the consistent use of dichotomous keys, and notes on distribution and habit. Lamarck's use of concise descriptions in vernacular language, the use of vernacular names and the absence of much synonymy and specimen citation was part of its orientation to more popular, practical (as well as scholarly) use.

This concise, pragmatic approach to Flora writing is also characteristic of a series of colonial Floras produced by Kew in response to Britain's desire to document the plant wealth in its colonies. J. D. Hooker's *Flora of British India* (1875–1896) is a significant example of a concise, utilitarian Flora. Before the *Flora of British India* the only Flora ostensibly covering India up to the mid nineteenth century was that of Roxburgh, published complete only in 1832. There were other impressive works such as those of Wight (1831) (exceptional in being heavily illustrated), but Hooker's is notable for taking a radical and sweeping approach, both to species concepts and nomenclature (postulating the 'Kew Rule'). In the preface, Hooker (1875) makes it very clear that in his *Flora of British India* conciseness is paramount:

> An exhaustive Flora would be a work of many years and many volumes; and it is as a handbook to what is already known, and a pioneer to more complete works, that the present is put forward … the adoption of as concise a style and phraseology as is consistent with clearness, and the avoidance of repetition in the descriptions and remarks on each species will enable me to compress the whole into a portable form.

Not only are concise descriptions clearer, they enable the Flora to be more compact. Hooker was clearly aware that a more compact Flora is produced more quickly and cheaply. However, a problem with this concise approach was that, although the species are usually grouped with shared characters, the descriptions are often not particularly diagnostic and frequently not usable by themselves to separate similar species. In many cases, accurate identification is only achievable with reference to a comprehensive, well-curated herbarium. This is compounded by the fact that only synoptic (not dichotomous) keys are included. Nevertheless, the *Flora of British India* was a revelation for a descriptive Flora in English. Although much of the taxonomy has been subsequently refined, it is a good example of the benefits of producing a usable product 'warts and all'. In the absence of an alternative (until very recently) it has been much used and copied by later workers.

A concise, pragmatic approach to writing Floras was also championed by another British colonial botanist, George Bentham. At the beginning of his *Flora hongkongensis*, Bentham (1872) espoused the principles of writing a concise Flora, which were subsequently repeated in a number of the other great colonial Floras such as *Flora australiensis* (1863–1878) and Bentham's *Outlines of elementary botany as introductory to local Floras* (1861). These principles are expressed as aphorisms – for brevity, these can be summarised by the following points (Frodin, 2001):

- the principle object of a Flora is to afford the means to identify any plant growing in its area;
- a Flora should have good descriptions;
- a Flora should be concise and accurate;
- a Flora should not be overloaded with technical terms;
- plants should be arranged in a natural system; and
- artificial keys should be provided.

Bentham's aphorisms have much in common with the ethos of the first modern Flora, Lamarck and de Candolle's *Flore française*. Bentham is clear; a Flora is not a repository of knowledge for the taxonomic community, but is a tool for effecting identifications of plants, both by specialists and non-specialists alike.

Frodin (2001) contrasts this floristic approach taken by the so-called 'French School' and 'British School', with that of the 'Central European School'. During much of the nineteenth century the Floras emerging from Central Europe were constructed as encyclopaedias – detailed repositories of information about the plants of an area. This is considered to be a legacy of the Linnaean approach to Flora writing, a legacy that ensured that detailed descriptions and notes, as well as extensive synonymy and specimen citations, were all included. The influential botanical centre of Berlin saw the production of a number of encyclopaedic Floras in late nineteenth and early twentieth centuries; such as Ascherson and Graebner's *Synopsis der mitteleuropäischen Flora* (1896–1939), Reichenbach's *Icones florae Germanicae et Helveticae* (1837–1914) and Hegi's detailed *Illustrierte Flora von Mittel-Europa* (1906–1931).

Indeed, the lack of concise Floras as a whole in Central Europe must partly be a function of the relative importance of monographical work over floristic work in early twentieth-century German botany. Emphasis on large-scale, time-consuming monographical projects, such as Engler and Prantl's *Die natürlichen Pflanzenfamilien* (1849–1893), meant that Floras came to be seen as a secondary consideration. Even the iconic floristic work of this Central European School, *Flora brasiliensis* (Martius et al., 1840–1906), was almost monographical in approach. Frodin (2001) highlights the pervasive significance of this Flora by stating that it 'established the tradition – still with us – of large scale, multi volume, descriptive regional Floras .... They came to be seen as suitable vehicles for submonographical studies .... Most remain more or less encyclopaedic, and as well retain an aura of prestige: a form of institutional "cachet" '.

1.2 Floras present

This brief historical background forces us to question the current purpose of Floras, and we are pushed to consider how effective Floras are in fulfilling their ascribed role. Heywood (1995) notes that in the nineteenth century, world exploration (and exploitation) and building of empires by the European powers led to a need for colonial Floras. Post World War II, the desire for reconciliation and cultural integration led to the creation of the *Flora Europaea* project, which in turn acted as stimulus in other parts of the world (see Chapter 6, Jury, in this volume). Heywood argues that in the last 10–25 years an intensification of Flora writing is attributable, in large part, to the conservation movement, and highlights the need for basic floristic inventory assessments as a basis for resource management, conservation and other biological activities.

Recent, high-profile cases have been made for a strong link between taxonomy and conservation (House of Lords, 1992, 2002; Mace, 2004; Wilson, 2004). Clearly, in the age of a Sixth Great Extinction Crisis (Wilson, 1992), one of a Flora's most important roles is facilitating biodiversity conservation. Although this received wisdom is seemingly self-evident, in a discussion of a Flora's purpose it is important to investigate these purported links between writing a Flora and the conservation of plant species. Such probing will help clarify the needs of Flora users and can feed into discussions of a Flora's design and orientation.

Mace (2004) argues that taxonomy has something of a dual role in its contribution to biological conservation. Firstly, taxonomy must necessarily identify, circumscribe and inventory biological diversity. In any area of vegetation, we must know what exists before we can attempt to preserve its existence (Mace, 2004). In this respect, floristic projects can often be at the forefront of conservation efforts, identifying new species, mapping species distributions and 'Red Listing' plant species that are threatened with extinction (Secretariat of the Convention on Biodiversity, 2002). Floristic taxonomists also have an important role to play in identifying potential sites for conservation, for as Prance (1995) argues 'it is systematists who hold most of the data about centres of endemism and who can locate hotspots accurately'.

This link between taxonomy and conservation can be expanded using the *Flora of the Arabian Peninsula and Socotra Archipelago* (FAPSA; Miller and Cope, 1996–ongoing) as a case study. Flora projects such as FAPSA are often the first point of call for those within a country or region, such as government bodies or research institutes, or international non-governmental organisations (NGOs) (e.g. the World Conservation Monitoring Centre) wishing to obtain authoritative data on plants. Much of this is related to assessing the conservation status of particular areas or species. For example, FAPSA supplied much of the southwest Asian data to two major global conservation initiatives; *Global biodiversity – status of the earth's living resources*

(Groombridge, 1992), which was the first comprehensive inventory of the of the status of the earth's living resources, and the *Centres of plant diversity* project (Davis, 1994), which gives accounts of nearly 250 major sites for the conservation of plant diversity worldwide. Within the period 2006–2007, the FAPSA research team was involved in a wide variety of regionally and globally important conservation initiatives, such as:

- Supplying plant distribution data and advising policy makers with respect to biodiversity access agreements, conservation zoning plans.
- Addressing the 2010 targets of the Convention on Biological Diversity – Global Strategy for Plant Conservation, through work with the Arabian Plant Specialist Group (International Union for Conservation of Nature (IUCN) – Species Survival Commission). This involves compiling checklists, IUCN Red Listing and identifying Key Biodiversity Areas/Important Plant Areas. All this activity is orchestrated towards establishing a regional protected area network.
- Campaigning to prevent road building through protected areas on Socotra – using valuable data on plant distribution.
- Consulting on the establishment of *ex situ* conservation initiatives such as the development of the Oman Botanic Garden.

Clearly, Floras cannot be considered in isolation. Floras are institutional projects, not simply compilations of plant descriptions and associated data. As Blackmore (1997) stated, 'a new Flora is not simply a book, but a means of structuring and delivering botanical information'. So, it is important to note that floristic projects generate a great variety of spin-off projects, which in turn lead to a wide range of collaborations both within the partner institutes and worldwide. As the above examples from Arabia show, these collaborations often revolve around the provision of up-to-date, accurate, voluminous data. In response to the biodiversity crisis, these collaborations between taxonomists and conservation professionals are increasingly being demanded (Gotelli, 2004; Pendry et al., 2007).

Collaborative efforts allow taxonomists to appreciate the needs and demands of non-taxonomists. Whilst conservationists need data that plant taxonomists hold, they also need the ability to identify species in the field. As Mace (2004) writes, 'Taxonomy and conservation go hand in hand. We cannot necessarily expect to conserve organisms that we cannot *identify*, and our attempts to understand the consequences of environmental change and degradation are compromised fatally if we cannot *recognise* and describe the interacting components of natural ecosystems'. The ability to name and identify is fundamental to the oft-repeated link between taxonomy and the conservation of species. Accurate identification of species is fundamental to the initial 'observations of the species or populations that indicate [conservation] attention is needed' (Mace, 2004).

Whilst conservation professionals require accurate taxonomic data coupled with reliable identifications, the notion of a *taxonomic impediment* throws into question whether these services are being adequately delivered by floristic projects and their institutions. In most biodiversity rich countries, serious biological research is often limited by the ability to map the distributions of species and also to identify them. A number of reasons have been identified for this impediment, including the under-funding of systematic research (House of Lords, 2002), a diminishing number of trained taxonomists (House of Lords, 2002) and the funding of phylogenetic research over floristic taxonomy (Wheeler, 2004). Whilst these factors undoubtedly all have a role to play, in a discussion of the effectiveness of Floras, perhaps it is appropriate to also consider the argument of Wheeler et al. (2004), that taxonomists must pay attention to revising their practices. In a floristic context it is important to ask: 'Are the methods of production of a Flora contributing to the taxonomic impediment?'

Nearly 70 years ago, Corner (1946) highlighted that the design, conception and production of Floras may actually be failing their users. Set against the backdrop of the rapid disappearance of the southeast Asian forests, Corner wrote that 'thus contrary to my early belief, I found the systematic work on Malayan, if not Asiatic, flowering plants to be incomplete and unreliable and so unsuited to the identification and study of the living plants that nothing could be accepted without personal identification'. Corner reasoned that a number of these problems stemmed from inadequate taxonomic descriptions, and summarised these problems as follows:

- ignorance of vegetative characters;
- ambiguous descriptions (characters which change from living to dried specimens – hair colour; leaf arrangement – opposite versus spiral);
- faulty synonymy and nomenclature; and
- error – copying of family and generic characters from other works without careful definition for the subject flora.

Based upon his experiences with the Malayan flora, Corner (1946) understood that such problems were systemic in taxonomic practice and argued that 'nearly every tropical Flora is fundamentally unsuited to its subject ... they not merely discourage the aspirant by so aggravating his difficulties, but they expose their authors to unlearned ridicule'.

From our own experience of participating in biodiversity studies in the Arabian Peninsula, the unsuitability of Floras for identifying living plant species is neither historical nor limited to the wet tropical regions of the world. Using the FAPSA as an example, although we could claim that it is of great use to other taxonomists, it would be stretching the truth to say that it is widely used by conservationists, ecologists and environmental impact assessors to identify plants in the field. In fact, the Flora has little practical field-use to these environmental professionals. Although there are a number of factors at play here, we contend that the conception and execution of floristic production has a significant role.

As well as those identified by Corner (1946), a number of problems exist with the production of a Flora. Floras are written far too slowly. This is particularly true of encyclopaedic Floras, which aim to be a repository of taxonomic information, but, as Heywood (1984) remarks 'even serial, research Floras, such as *Flora Malesiana*, *Flora Zambesiaca* (see Chapter 7, Kirkup et al., in this volume), *Flora Iranica*, which are not markedly encyclopaedic or archival, are planned in such a way that they are not completed within a reasonably short timescale'. Such striving for scholarly perfection not only slows down Flora writing, but in turn it often renders the finished product inaccessible to conservationists working within the target country. As Corner (1946) remarked, this exclusion is compounded by the ambiguous, convoluted, overly technical descriptions. Concomitant problems are that Floras are often too large to use in the field; they often lack the language of the target country (*Flora Iranica*; Rechinger, 1963–ongoing) – original text in Latin, commentary in German – is a wonderful example of this trend) and that the huge time investment involved often results in publications of great expense and therefore limited circulation.

Many of the problems with Floras emerge from their design, which in turn spring from a confused conception and orientation. As a number of authors, including Jarvie et al. (1998), Heywood (1995), Palmer et al. (1995), Schmid (1997), Wilken et al. (1997), Frodin (2001) and Wheeler (2004) have emphasised, Floras need to be carefully oriented towards the needs of carefully identified user groups. Heywood (1995) and Frodin (2001) emphasise that there may be more than one target audience, each with differing, and sometimes conflicting needs. However, in a biodiversity crisis in which it is estimated that up to 30% of plant species are at risk of extinction (Secretariat of the Convention on Biodiversity, 2002; Thomas et al., 2004), it is perhaps prudent that the priority for floristic research should be producing Floras and disseminating taxonomic data that are able to be used accurately and efficiently by the conservation community.

1.3 Flora futures

With this priority in mind, we are faced with the convergence of two historical trends. If Floras are to be at the forefront of plant conservation activities, they need to be both *encyclopaedic* and *concise*. Ecologists, climate modellers, environmental scientists and land managers require detailed data on distribution, morphology and physiology. They also require concise, speedy, accessible means to effect accurate species identifications. If they are to warrant Wheeler's (2004) call for a funding shift away from phylogenetics, floristic research must find ways to cope with these synergistic demands. Floras must find ways to combine the Central European thirst for taxonomic detail with the Bentham-like need for conciseness, speed and cost effectiveness.

In his wide-ranging article, Wheeler (2004) has identified the opportunities for floristic projects offered by high-speed internet access and emerging digital technologies. These web-based opportunities for a 'revolutionised' descriptive taxonomy include:

- cyber taxonomic research and education platforms;
- virtual monographic/floristic tools;
- a visual data Morphobank analogous to GenBank;
- high-resolution images of type and other specimens;
- online open library with all published species descriptions;
- image recognition software with applications for species identifications and search engines for a morphology image data bank; and
- sophisticated interactive identification keys.

Whilst Wheeler (2004) applied these to taxonomy as a whole, a number of these opportunities are of particular relevance for floristic research. For several years, the FAPSA project has been revising its working practices to increasingly incorporate digital photography and web-based databases. In this respect, FAPSA has been responding to the recommendations set down by Godfray (2002), Bisby et al. (2002) and Wheeler (2004) to revolutionise taxonomic practice using internet-based informatics.

The development of the Royal Botanic Garden Edinburgh's floristic database Padme has begun to radically alter the nature of the FAPSA project. As Frodin (2001) noted, with the advent of sophisticated taxonomic databases, the debate about the appropriate amount data to be included in Floras is becoming increasingly academic. Heywood (1984) criticised Floras for not recording much of the information used in the decision-making process. Comparing Floras to icebergs, he contended that only the tip of the information was visible, whilst the vast majority remained out of sight. Whilst in the past the detailed taxonomic data was not published (either for conciseness or through lack of space), a floristic project is now able to make these data available through web-accessible databases. These allow the most detailed floristic information to be supplied to taxonomic users in a structured format, at high speed and at little cost. Crucially, this enables this information to be constantly revised and updated to reflect new taxonomies, changes in extinction threat and expanded geographical distributions. Therefore, web-based databases allow floristic projects to fulfil one of their major roles in this biodiversity crisis; the rapid provision of accurate floristic data to conservation professionals.

For the FAPSA project, the Padme database is also crucial to fulfilling the other major role of floristic projects – providing usable, accessible identification tools to the plants of a designated region. Padme is critical for this on a number of levels. Fundamentally, by storing more detailed, *encyclopaedic* taxonomic information on a web-platform it allows the printed Flora to become increasingly concise and geared towards the *identification* of plant species. On another level, it provides the development of interactive identification keys and automated identification systems which, along with DNA barcoding (see Chapter 22, S. E. Miller, in this volume) may in the future actually usurp the printed Flora as the primary means of plant identification (Gaston and O'Neill, 2004). Continuing technological innovations for structuring, exchanging and integrating information and falling costs of cyber-publishing may eventually transform the Flora into an entirely web-based entity. Used on a handheld level, such electronic identification guides may provide a powerful complement to the drift towards DNA-based identification.

By orientating their efforts to producing concise, speedy species descriptions, floristic projects will massively increase their effectiveness at providing accurate species identification for non-specialists. Rather than being based on textual descriptions, these identification guides (either as printed or electronic works) will be much more powerful if based on digital images. For FAPSA, the Padme database has allowed the practice of Flora production to become increasingly based upon the digital image. Recent work in Arabia has focussed on developing appropriate fieldwork methods for compiling digital image databases. These have centred on the rapid digital profiling of all available characters on an individual plant, which effectively creates digital specimens of the living plants. Importantly, these are numbered in the same sequential system as other records and so are immediately available for taxonomic work. Not only does this maximise the level of species recording whilst in the field, but also it allows rapid transfer of taxonomic material between participating institutions. Thus, digital plant specimens from field material meet the needs of Agosti and Johnson (2002) who call for increased data access for taxonomists.

The recent publication of a new species of *Barleria* from Oman has demonstrated that digital photographs taken in the field are able to provide excellent taxonomic illustrations of new species, at a fraction of the traditional time and cost (Knees et al., 2007). Not only are these images able to illustrate traditional taxonomic accounts and print-based Floras, they can also form the basis of electronic, multimedia identification tools. The benefits of using digital images as the basis of the 'identification content' of floristic projects are manifold. Fundamentally, illustrations are often far more effective than descriptions in conveying information about plants and their characters. Whilst print-based publications may struggle with visually representing the species concepts based upon single specimens, the accumulation of digital specimens will allow electronic tools to represent the huge variation in plant form that faces the field botanist. Thus, we are in strong agreement with Wheeler (2004) in saying that:

> The advent of digital imaging is a technological breakthrough for morphology. Digital images are to morphological knowledge what the Gutenberg Press was to the written word, and morphology is about to explode into the twenty-first century. Digital libraries of morphology will make structural knowledge as readily searchable and accessible as GenBank has for molecular sequence data.

Instead of compressing plant morphology into language, images allow the variation in plant form to be visualised directly. Images thus allow a direct encounter with 'living' plants, in equal measure for professional taxonomists and more popular users. Structured compilations of digital images (such as interactive visual keys, or field manuals) thus allow increased access to species identifications and abide by several of Bentham's aphorisms, including the need for concision, accuracy and simplicity. Images taken in the field, such as those of *Barleria samhanensis* (Knees et al. 2007), have the advantage of recording the living plant. This allows the 'specimen' and taxonomic accounts to incorporate vegetative characters, thus mitigating Corner's complaints against the ignorance of non-flowering/fruiting characters in Floras. Digital profiles of living plants also reduce ambiguity in text-based descriptions, allowing increased brevity, and reducing the possibility of reiterating previous taxonomic errors. All this amounts to the production of more effective, more inclusive tools for the identification of plant species. Once incorporated in the taxonomic database, a compilation of images allows identification tools to be produced more quickly. If Bentham had a new aphorism for Floras, it would surely be for the increased use of illustrations, particularly digital images, in floristic works.

1.4 Concluding remarks

In conclusion to this brief discussion, it is important to stress that shifting floristic research to a basis of digital images has a significant further advantage. Once digital plant specimens are compiled in Padme, one of the many potential uses of this resource is to produce a series of low-cost, practical photographical guides to specific groups of plants on the Arabian Peninsula. These guides will play a crucial role in developing botanical education programmes in the region, which in many respects circumvent the important problems of exclusivity. Whilst previously this may have been seen as a 'spin-off' project, in the understanding of Blackmore (1997) that a Flora is not simply a book, but a project whose role is delivering structured botanical information, then combating the decline in botanical education in developing, biodiversity-rich countries must surely be one of a Flora's core goals (Samper, 2004). In programmes across the Arabian region (including reconstructive initiatives in Iraq), there is great potential for using digitally produced plant profiles and interactive identification guides as a major resource for a series of training programmes aimed at building capacity in plant taxonomy (particularly plant identification), for taxonomy students, ecologists, environmental impact assessors and conservationists. This use of floristic research for capacity building in botanical expertise is crucial if biodiversity studies and conservation initiatives are to flourish in biodiversity-rich but financially poor countries.

References

Agosti, D. and Johnson, N. F. (2002). Taxonomists need better access to published data. *Nature*, **417**: 222.

Ascherson, P. and Graebner, K. O. R. P. P. (1896–1939). *Synopsis der mitteleuropäischen Flora*, 12 volumes. Leipzig: Engelmann, Borntraeger.

Bentham, G. (1861). *Outlines of elementary botany as introductory to local Floras*. London: Lovell and Reeve.

Bentham, G. (1863–1878). *Flora australiensis*, 7 volumes. Melbourne and London: Lovell Reeve.

Bentham, G. (1872). *Flora hongkongensis*. London: Reeves and Co.

Bisby, F. A., Shimura, J., Ruggiero, M., Edwards, J., and Haeuser, C. (2002). Taxonomy, at the click of a mouse. *Nature*, **418**: 367.

Blackmore, S. (1997). Aspects of the design for a Flora of Nepal. Presented at International seminar-cum-workshop on the Flora of Nepal, April 15-16, 1997, Kathmandu, Nepal.

Candolle, A. P. de and Lamarck, J. B. A. P. M. de (1805-1815). *Flore française*, volumes 1–5. Paris: Desray.

Corner, E. J. H. (1946). Suggestions for botanical progress. *New Phytologist*, **45**: 185–192.

Davis, S. D. (ed.) (1994). *Centres of plant diversity: a guide and strategy for their conservation. Volume 1: Europe, Africa, South West Asia and the Middle East*. Cambridge: IUCN Publications Unit.

Engler, H. G. A. and Prantl, K. A. E. (1849-1893). *Die natürlichen Pflanzenfamilien*. Leipzig: Wilhelm Engelmann.

Frodin, D. G. (2001). *Guide to standard floras of the world: an annotated, geographically arranged systematic bibliography of the principal floras, enumerations, checklists and chorological atlases of different areas*. Cambridge: Cambridge University Press.

Gaston, K. J. and O'Neill, M. A. (2004). Automated species identification: why not? *Philosophical Transactions: Biological Sciences*, **359**: 655–667.

Godfray, H. C. J. (2002). Challenges for taxonomy. *Nature*, **417**: 17–19.

Gotelli, N. J. (2004). A taxonomic wish-list for community ecology. *Philosophical Transactions of the Royal Society of London B*, **359**: 585–597.

Groombridge, B. (ed.) (1992). *Global biodiversity – status of the Earth's living resources. A report compiled by the World Conservation Monitoring Centre*. London: Chapman and Hall.

Hegi, G. (1906–1931). *Illustrierte Flora von Mittel-Europa*, 7 volumes. Munich: Lehmann.

Heywood, V. H. (1984). Designing Floras for the future. In *Current concepts in plant taxonomy*, pp. 275–288. Systematics Association Special Volume no.25, V. H. Heywood and D. M. Moore (eds). London: Academic Press.

Heywood, V. H. (ed.). (1995). *Global biodiversity assessment. United Nations Environment programme.* Cambridge: Cambridge University Press.

Hooker, J. D. (1875–1896). *Flora of British India*, volume 1. London: L. Reeve and Co.

House of Lords (1992). *Systematic biology research. Select Committee on Science and Technology, first report.* HL Paper 22-I. London: Stationery Office.

House of Lords (2002). *What on Earth? The threat to the science underpinning conservation. Select Committee on Science and Technology, third report.* HL Paper 118(i). London: Stationery Office.

Jarvie, J., Ermayanti, H. and Mahyar, V. W. (1998). Techniques used in the production of an electronic and hard copy Flora for the Bukit-Baja Bukit-Raya area of Kalimantan. In *Plant diversity in Malesia III*, M. Dransfield, J. E. Coode and D. A. Simpson (eds). Richmond: Royal Botanic Gardens, Kew, pp. 129–143.

Knees, S. G., Laser, S., Miller, A. G. and Patzelt, A. (2007). A new species of Barleria (Acanthaceae) from Oman. *Edinburgh Journal of Botany*, **64**: 107–112.

Lamarck de, J. B. (1778). *Flore française.* Paris: d'Imprimerie Royale Agasse.

Lamarck de, J. B. and Candolle de, A. P. (1805–1815). *Flore française*, 6 volumes. Paris: Agasse.

Mace, G. M. (2004). The role of taxonomy in species conservation. *Philosophical Transactions of the Royal Society of London B*, **359**: 711–719.

Martius, C. F. P. von, Eichler, A. W. and Urban, I. (1840–1906). *Flora brasiliensis.* Leipzig: Wein.

Miller, A. G. and Cope, T. (1996–ongoing). *Flora of the Arabian Peninsula and Socotra Archipelago.* Edinburgh: Edinburgh University Press.

Palmer, M. J., Wade, G. L. and Neal, P. R. (1995). Standards for the writing of floras. *BioScience*, **45**: 339–334.

Pendry, C. A., Dick, J., Pullan, M. R., Knees, S. G., Miller, A. G., Neale, S., and Watson, M. F. (2007). In search of a functional flora – towards a greater integration of ecology and taxonomy. *Plant Ecology*, **192**: 161–167.

Prance, G. T. (1995). Systematics, conservation and sustainable development. *Biodiversity Conservation*, **4**: 490–500.

Rechinger, K. H. (ed.) (1963–ongoing). *Flora iranica.* Graz: Akademische Druck u. Verlagsanstalt.

Reichenbach, H. G. L. (1837–1914). *Icones florae Germanicae et Helveticae*, 25 volumes. Leipzig: Hofmeister.

Roxburgh, W. (1832) *Flora Indica.* Serampore: W. Thacker.

Samper, C. (2004). Taxonomy and environmental policy. *Philosophical Transactions of the Royal Society of London B*, **359**: 721–728.

Schmid, R. (1997). Some desiderata to make floras and other types of works user (and reviewer) friendly. *Taxon*, **46**: 179–194.

Secretariat of the Convention on Biodiversity (2002). *Global strategy for plant conservation.* Quebec: Secretariat of the Convention on Biological Diversity/Botanic Gardens Conservation International.

Thomas, C. D., Cameron, A., Green, R. E., Bakkenes, M., Beaumont, L. J., Collingham, Y. C., Erasmus, B. F. N., de Siqueira, M. F., Grainger, A., Hannah, L.,

Hughes, L., Huntley, B., et al. (2004). Extinction risk from climate change. *Nature*, **427**: 145–148.

Wheeler, Q. D. (2004). Taxonomic triage and the poverty of phylogeny. *Philosophical Transactions of the Royal Society of London B*, **359**: 571–583.

Wheeler, Q. D., Raven, P. H. and Wilson, E. O. (2004). Taxonomy: impediment or expedient? *Nature*, **303**: 285.

Wight, R. (1831). *Illustrations of Indian botany*. Glasgow: Curtt and Bell.

Wilken, D., Whetstone, D., Tomlinson, K. and Morin, N. (1997). Considerations for producing the ideal Flora. In *Floristics for the twenty-first century*, N. Morin, D. Whetstone, D. Wilken and K. Tomlinson (eds.). St Louis: Missouri Botanical Garden.

Wilson, E. O. (1992). *The diversity of life*. London: Allen Lane.

Wilson, E. O. (2004). Taxonomy as a fundamental discipline. *Philosophical Transactions of the Royal Society of London B*, **359**: 739.

2

Current uses and future perspectives for conservation biology

B. Collen

2.1 Introduction

Conservation science is a discipline which has been born in response to the simple fact that biodiversity is declining at never before seen rates (Millennium Ecosystem Assessment, 2005). Background extinction rates are being dramatically exceeded, and models of future scenarios predict that this rate will only increase (Fig 2.1), perhaps by an order of magnitude, unless preventative action is taken (Regan et al., 2001). The reasons for this decline are at least well known, if not well understood. Land clearance reduces available habitat; exploitation removes healthy animals from the population; introduced predators and diseases impact 'naïve' species, and, ultimately, extinction breaks down ecological networks – Diamond's evil quartet (Diamond, 1989). Increasingly, climate change is enhancing the negative impacts of this list of threats (IPCC, 2002; Thomas et al., 2004). The problem and its effects are so pressing that it has been framed under international legislation, and more than 190 countries signed up to a target set to achieve a significant reduction in biodiversity loss by 2010 (UNEP, 2002), a target that was not met (Butchart et al., 2010). Effective action to achieve such a target requires detailed information, and Floras and Faunas often provide much of the data that underpin priority-setting decisions derived from biodiversity data. While the key taxonomic issue to be faced by biodiversity conservation remains the under-description of species (May, 1988; Wilson, 2003), a growing issue that

Descriptive Taxonomy: The Foundation of Biodiversity Research, eds M. F. Watson,
C.H.C. Lyal and C.A. Pendry. Published by Cambridge University Press.

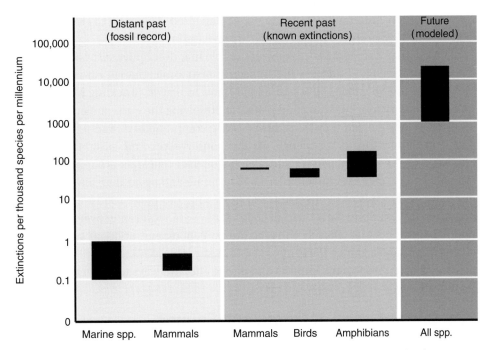

Figure 2.1 Variation in rate of extinction over time. Distant past = average extinction rates estimated from fossil record. Recent past = calculated from known extinctions (lower estimate) or known plus 'possibly extinct' species (upper bound). Future = model derived estimates including species-area, rates of shift between threat categories, probability associated with IUCN threat categories, impact of projected habitat loss and correlation of species loss with energy consumption. Redrawn from the Millennium Ecosystem Assessment (2005)

threatens to complicate, and perhaps undermine, conservation planning is taxonomic inflation (Isaac et al., 2004; Mace, 2004).

Throughout this chapter I primarily refer to species conservation, as species are often considered the natural taxonomic rank to form the basis for both conservation assessments and management. There are of course habitat-based conservation alternatives that are also possible. Informative conservation science relies on accurate, high-quality data that feeds into conservation decisions at all levels, particularly in species conservation. Species are of great importance to conservation in many different ways. Species form both a means of measurement to gauge human impact on biodiversity, and a target for action – the way in which we manage biodiversity. Species have a resonance with the public, and policy makers; it is arguable that the majority of conservation funding is derived from species level or species-focussed conservation projects. They are the subject of national legislation; species are used at the national level in law, for example the US Endangered Species Act, or the UK Biodiversity Action Plans. Species are also subject to international legislation, for example, multilateral environmental agreements such as the

Convention on International Trade in Endangered Species (CITES) and the Convention in Migratory Species (CMS) are species focussed.

In this chapter I undertake a review of the role that descriptive taxonomy plays in conservation biology. I address the impact of taxonomic change on conservation biology, and the role that Floras and Faunas have to play in providing baseline data for conservation priority setting and planning. Resolving the current elevated rate of biodiversity decline can only be achieved using comprehensive and representative data and with intricate knowledge on the conservation and sustainable use of biodiversity. The increasingly wide availability of electronic data are revolutionising our ability to provide ever larger volumes of accurate and up-to-date information on the status and trends of biodiversity, and from which to make robust conservation management decisions. New types of collaboration are required between conservation biology and systematics to enhance the availability and utility of such data, to enable robust and accurate measures of biodiversity. This framework will allow better prediction of anthropogenic impacts and devise effective ways to mitigate them.

2.2 Current uses of Floras and Faunas

With a critical shortage of biodiversity information with which to address challenges to conservation, Floras and Faunas are often one of the first providers of data. The production of Floras and Faunas is clearly still a popular endeavour. A survey of the *Zoological Record* on BIOSIS from 1989 to 2007 showed that using the search term 'Fauna of*', in excess of 1000 volumes were published during the period. A brief search through the Zoological Society of London library catalogue, founded in 1826, one of the world's most comprehensive zoological libraries, contains records of 131 Faunas of India alone. Clearly this does not represent the Floras published in this period as well.

Identifying concentrations of species richness, diversity or endemism is a central theme of many conservation studies (Gomez de Silva and Medellin, 2001). Floras and Faunas might be used in conservation biology in the first instance, for generating species lists for a given area or location. These species lists may then form the basis of many conservation actions, including protected area location, priority area selection algorithms (Pressey and Cowling, 2001) and perhaps even monitoring data (Roberts et al., 2007). There are, however, several sources of uncertainty or instability in species list generation which, left unchecked or unaccounted for, may adversely impact conservation. Taxonomic coverage and the effect of cryptic species are particularly problematic; however, change in the use of species concepts (Isaac et al., 2004), the effect of which I will return to later, is of growing concern in certain vertebrate groups in particular. Gomez de Silva and Medellin (2001) point out, for example, that limits to the use of existing species lists for conservation are primarily due to their compilation by an array of field observers, with varying level of skill, and different goals. The resulting heterogeneous data across a given area means that missing species from species lists are likely to be a non-random subset of the total assemblage in many cases, particularly when original goals are highly varied, and when single studies focus on a particular issue. Incompleteness of lists and heterogeneous data can lead to misleading results (e.g. see Kodric-Brown and Brown, 1993). Also further information may still be required, even when comparing two areas based on species lists alone. For example, abundance may matter if the underlying incomplete lists do not accurately reflect the ecological character of a given area (Balmer, 2002).

Even within some of the most species-rich countries, certain groups have been recently seen to almost double over a very short period of time (e.g. Sri Lanka: Meegaskumbura et al., 2002). In another example, recognised alpha diversity has increased by up to 6 times in Bolivian amphibians during a 15-year period (Padial and De la Riva, 2006). For conservation biology this is unfortunate, since mastering species numbers may be crucial to discerning the changing patterns of global diversity. Further, instability in species lists is likely to be more prevalent in local and national level lists, due to localised population extinction processes, or expansion in range through colonisation or reintroduction. A distinction must be made though between fluctuations in numbers of species caused by extinction (and colonisation) and those caused because taxonomy is not complete. The two issues will require very different solutions.

Conservation biology often requires more fundamental data than simple species lists, some of which might be provided by Flora and Fauna publications. The next logical step is to use basic information from Floras and Faunas to inform conservation assessments, such as the IUCN Red List of Threatened Species (herein 'Red List'; IUCN, 2009), as these give far greater information to conservation biologists (Mace and Lande, 1991). However, they require more detailed knowledge of species' ecology, life history and geographical information from Floras and Faunas, combined with population-trend information and data on threatening processes, to build a comprehensive dataset to give robust conservation assessments.

In a broader context, a key aspect for conservation biology is the trade off between simple lists of species and something that may be more informative to conservation, such as the relationships described in Fig 2.2A – Green et al. (2005) use the same model as another application of a similar principle. For the purposes of this chapter, I adopt their model for the following hypothetical example. You are trying to decide on the status of species within an area. You may ask several questions about how you might go about this, but the decision should account for two main factors: fitness for purpose of the techniques you are intending to use and the resources available. In this example, we will consider two options: firstly, to generate a species list or inventory for the area and, secondly, to generate some sort of conservation assessment for those species.

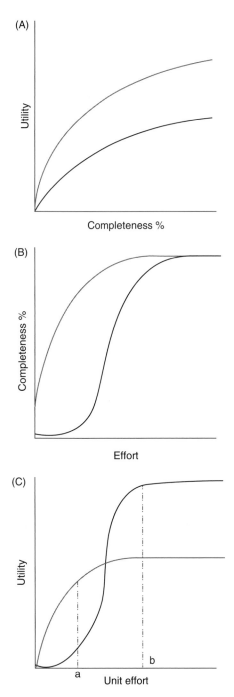

Figure 2.2 (A–C) Hypothetical relationships between utility, effort and completeness for species inventory (grey curves) and conservation assessment (black curves). Figure adapted with permission from Green et al. (2005).

Step 1 in Fig 2.2A shows that however much work is put into a species inventory it will never be as useful to conservation biology as the conservation assessment; but the assessment will take longer to complete, though both techniques become more accurate as they progress. Figure 2.2B evaluates completeness against effort needed to complete each of the techniques. The advantage of the species inventory is that it can be completed with less effort. Figure 2.2C combines steps 1 and 2 and addresses what you would do if you had 'a' units of effort to expend, against what would you do if you had 'b' units. The model formalises decisions to use informative datasets that can be most readily gathered – the 'low hanging fruit' (*sensu* Raven and Wilson, 1992). It is important because temptation may often be to gather the easiest to obtain data, regardless of limited use (failure to consider Fig 2.2A), or the efficiency of adding to any existing data (failure to consider Fig 2.2B). Working together in this manner and considering this framework, Floras and Faunas can complement the more stringent data demands of biodiversity data for conservation biology. Knowing the shapes of these curves would ultimately benefit decision-making in conservation biology.

2.3 Taxonomy underpinning biodiversity

In all areas of species-based conservation, taxonomy underpins our appreciation of biodiversity, and plays a fundamental role (Geeta et al., 2004). However, the incomplete and non-random coverage of species description continues to be an issue in biodiversity conservation. In 1992, Raven and Wilson set out a 50-year plan for biodiversity surveys to catalogue the Linnean shortfall (Raven and Wilson, 1992). So 20 years on, how are we doing? Raven and Wilson estimated that there were 1.4 million species known in 1992; approximately 15% of the actual total. Two major taxonomic federations, Species 2000 and Integrated Taxonomic Information System (ITIS), are producing a Catalogue of Life[1], and released a series of annual checklists. The 2013 *Annual Checklist* (Roskov et al., 2013) contains 1 352 112 species, which they estimate to be around two-thirds of the world's known species – so progress remains slow, even for the known species.

While we cannot necessarily expect to conserve organisms that we cannot identify, several attempts at conservation shortcuts have been made to prioritise action amongst the species we do know. All recognise that the available resources for conservation are insufficient to prevent the loss of much of the world's threatened biodiversity. Conservation planners have been forced to prioritise which species and areas should receive the most protection, in the context of great uncertainty – this has become known as 'the agony of choice'. Several tools have been developed to aid them in prioritising conservation actions. One of the most highly cited is that

---

[1] http://www.catalogueoflife.org

which weights areas of high species richness and high rate of degradation most strongly – Biodiversity Hotspots (Myers et al., 2000). However, there are many others (for a review, see Brooks et al., 2006).

Of particular relevance to systematics and conservation is the concept of incorporating measures of phylogenetic diversity into conservation selection algorithms (May, 1990; Vane-Wright et al., 1991; Faith, 1992). Species do not represent equal components of evolutionary history; rather they differ in the amount of phylogenetic diversity they represent, reflecting the tempo and mode of divergence across the phylogenetic tree. It is, therefore, implicit that the extinction of an old, monotypical or species-poor clade would result in the loss of a greater proportion of biodiversity than that of a comparatively young species, or one with many close relatives (May, 1990; Mace et al., 2003). Figure 2.3 demonstrates how using

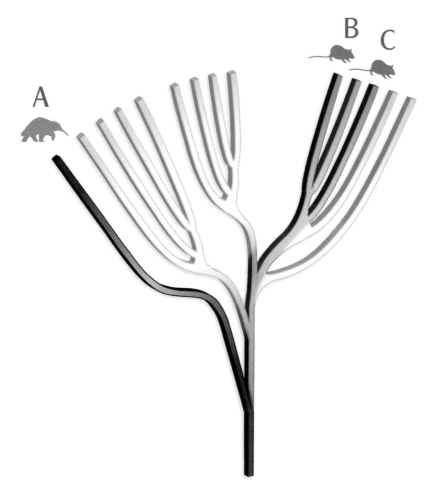

Figure 2.3 Hypothetical phylogenetic tree (www.edgeofexistence.org; Isaac et al., 2007).

evolutionary-branch length as a measure of independent evolution, the extinction of Species A, would result in the loss of a far greater amount of evolutionary history than if Species B or C were lost, the inference being that the loss would be felt more keenly. Given that extinction risk appears to be clustered (Purvis et al., 2000), this might matter. Combining branch-length data from a recent publication on the relationships of all mammals (Bininda Emonds et al., 2007) with threat evaluations from the Red List (IUCN, 2009) has resulted in a technique intricately tying two key areas in which Floras and Faunas, descriptive taxonomy and systematics can contribute to conservation biology (Isaac et al., 2007).

2.4 Measuring species level trends in biodiversity

As signatories to the Convention on Biological Diversity (CBD) 2010 target, almost all nations were compelled to assess progress towards reducing biodiversity loss. Seven focal areas have been outlined by the CBD in order to direct the development of headline indicators of biodiversity change under the CBD framework (see Table 2.1; UNEP, 2006). Information from Floras and Faunas fed into baseline data for the focal areas 'Trends in abundance and distribution of selected species' and 'Change in status of threatened species', which include indicators such as the Living Planet Index (Loh et al., 2005; Collen et al., 2009a) and the Common Bird Index (Gregory et al., 2005; Pan-European Common Bird Monitoring, 2006) and the Red List Index (Butchart et al., 2004, 2007). The CBD framework and existence of the target motivated further development in some indicators (Mace and Baillie, 2007: e.g. see Butchart et al., 2004, 2007; Loh et al., 2005). Nevertheless, taxonomic coverage is still limited.

Geographical range distributions can provide improved resolution for conservation strategies allowing better spatial mapping of key areas for conservation. All bird, mammal and amphibian distributions are mapped (Stuart et al., 2004; Cardillo et al., 2005; Orme et al., 2005), and are revealing a great deal about the patterns of species' geographical range; not least that while overall distribution between vertebrate taxa might be similar, congruence between groups might be low, in particular amongst rare taxa (Grenyer et al., 2006). We still do not know, though, how representative these groups are of broader biodiversity, which may yet prove to be a problem for conservation strategies and biodiversity targets. In all these processes, the user groups require robust, accurate and high-quality data in order to make the best decisions. Certain approaches, such as a sampled approach to Red Listing, are set to broaden coverage (Baillie et al., 2008; Collen et al., 2009b); however, Floras and Faunas can play an increasingly important role on collating and disseminating key biodiversity data for taxa not yet included.

Table 2.1 Focal areas identified in the Convention on Biological Diversity framework[2]

Focal area	Indicator
Status and trends of the components of biological diversity	Trends in extent of selected biomes, ecosystems and habitats Trends in abundance and distribution of selected species Coverage of protected areas Change in status of threatened species Trends in genetic diversity of domesticated animals, cultivated plants and fish species of major socioeconomic importance
Sustainable use	Area of forest, agricultural and aquaculture ecosystems under sustainable management Proportion of products derived from sustainable sources Ecological footprint and related concepts
Threats to biodiversity	Nitrogen deposition Trends in invasive alien species
Ecosystem integrity and ecosystem goods and services	Marine Trophic Index Water quality of freshwater ecosystems Trophic integrity of other ecosystems Connectivity/fragmentation of ecosystems Incidence of human-induced ecosystem failure Health and well-being of communities that depend directly on local ecosystem goods and services Biodiversity for food and medicine
Status of traditional knowledge, innovations and practices	Status and trends of linguistic diversity and numbers of speakers of indigenous languages Other indicator of the status of indigenous and traditional knowledge
Status of access and benefit-sharing	Indicator of access and benefit-sharing
Status of resource transfers	Official development assistance provided in support of the Convention Indicator of technology transfer

[2] http://www.cbd.int/2010-target/framework/indicators.shtml

2.5 Taxonomic inflation

By impacting the very unit that many conservation actions are determined by, taxonomic inflation threatens to undermine conservation (Isaac et al., 2004; Mace, 2004). Two conflicting explanations of this phenomenon have been put forward. The first is that the problem is geopolitical (Harris and Froufe, 2004), owing to a strong geographical bias in the early work on DNA sequence data. DNA variation between the species assessed was very low because of the relatively low genetic diversity in northern species in comparison to their tropical relatives. The second is that increased use of the phylogenetic species concept (PSC), rather than the biological species concept (BSC) is responsible, at least amongst larger charismatic species groups (Isaac et al., 2004: see Fig 2.4). However, in the more species-rich groups, such as insects or fungi, drivers of change are likely to be different (Knapp et al., 2004) and, with the particular species concept applied rarely being adequately documented, the effect of species concept on description rates is difficult to assess. In seed plants in particular, new descriptions on the whole are thought to represent new species discovery rather than circumscription (Knapp et al., 2004).

Nonetheless, the magnitude of the effect is likely to be large for vertebrates at least. Agapow et al. (2004) estimate that adoption of the PSC over the BSC would give rise to an increase of 48% in species richness, with an associated reduction in

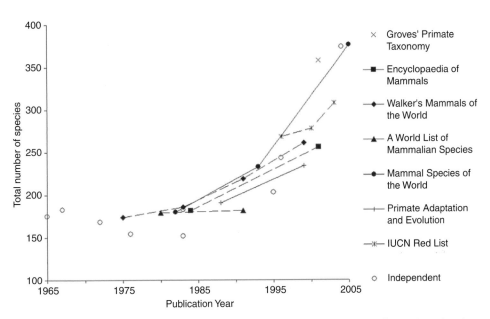

Figure 2.4 Change in primate species numbers between 1965 and 2005 (reproduced with permission from Isaac et al. (2004).

average population size and geographical range. In combination with threatening processes, such changes are likely to lead to an increased number of threatened species under-threat classification schemes, such as the Red List, with 11% moving from the Vulnerable category to the higher risk Endangered category (Agapow et al., 2004). What is less clear on a global scale is where that species richness would show up geographically. The implications are not insignificant. Conservation might experience a negative impact by spreading already restricted funding ever more thinly, due to species classified as threatened having small ranges and being in threatened habitats requiring a greater share of the available resources. Under widespread taxonomic change, it is not clear whether the areas selected by some priority-setting algorithms, such as hotspots based on species richness, might change. Accumulating lines of evidence suggest amongst certain groups at least, changes could be dramatic (Peterson and Navarro-Sigüenza, 1999).

2.6 Areas of new species discovery

It is estimated that just 1.5–1.8 million of the approximately 14 million extant species (Wilson, 2003) have been described, and there is still considerable uncertainty how many species exist (Godfray, 2002). If the description of species is inherently non-random, with species in some taxa more likely to be described than those in others, then views of diversity are correspondingly distorted, and so are our conservation actions that we base on them. This matters if, for instance, conservation policies are based on skewed reflections of true diversity patterns. Across higher taxa, studies consistently show that the probability of description is not equal for all species within a taxon (Gaston, 1991; Allsop, 1997; Cabrero-Sanudo and Lobo, 2003; Collen et al., 2004). Broad-scale comparisons among lower taxa have suggested that certain groups may receive a greater degree of taxonomic scrutiny (May, 1988), perhaps because they appeal to us more (Purvis et al., 2003), and that some taxa have a higher chance of observation due to larger size (Gaston, 1991). Even within taxa, accumulating evidence suggests that some species are more likely to be described than others, though explanations are more subtle and vary among groups (Reed and Boback, 2002; Collen et al., 2004).

Figure 2.5 shows that if the traits that predispose carnivores and primates to being described more recently are examined, the overwhelmingly most significant predictive trait is geographical range size. But this is the trait that is prized so highly in many area-selection algorithms; so the species that are most likely to receive conservation attention (restricted range) are least likely to have been described. While global-level studies might point to general patterns, more targeted regional-scale analyses might provide target areas for renewed research efforts. For example, in a study of the taxonomic description of anurans in the Brazilian Cerrado,

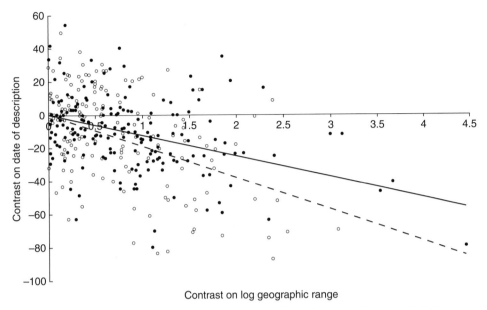

Figure 2.5 Relationship between contrasts of date of description and geographical range, after Collen et al. (2004). Solid circles denote carnivores (solid line is regression line); open circles denote primates (dotted line is regression). An ANCOVA (not reported) showed a significant effect of order.

Diniz-Filho et al. (2005) are able to note the likely effect on reserve-system design, as well as aligning them with areas most likely to contain new species.

2.7 Biodiversity data coverage

A further issue that limits the usefulness of current outputs is the extent of species coverage. Biodiversity data are biased towards the large and charismatic species, and the process of conservation assessment has in the past been opportunistic and sporadic. With rare exceptions, we can surmise that biodiversity data are lacking for many plants, the majority of insects and all microorganisms (Balmford and Bond, 2005). This creates many problems, as when trying to address human impact on biodiversity, we are attempting to talk broadly; in reality the data are still very restrictive. The biodiversity crisis is undeniably in large part an insect crisis (Dunn, 2005). Taking Red List coverage as an indication of available biodiversity data and data that are extremely useful for many different conservation actions (Lamoreux et al., 2003), an examination of the 2007 Red List shows coverage is incomplete for many groups (Fig 2.6; though see Baillie et al., 2008).

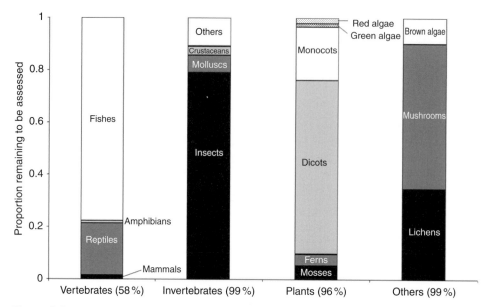

Figure 2.6 Species groups remaining to be assessed for the IUCN Red List (data from IUCN 2009). Values in brackets are the percentage of species within each group which have not yet been assessed by IUCN. Note all birds have been evaluated.

Descriptive taxonomy might be able to further influence conservation by aiding in the issue of reclassifying Data Deficient (DD) species on the Red List. The DD category is applied to a species when the available information is not sufficient for a full assessment of conservation status to be made. In reality, there are three reasons why a species might be classified as DD:

1. Unknown provenance, e.g. a species only from one specimen with extremely uncertain locality information.
2. Insufficient information, e.g. lack of relevant data on population, trend or geographical range to apply criteria.
3. Uncertain taxonomic status, i.e. we are unable to understand the unit to be assessed.

For this final reason, there is a clear role for descriptive taxonomy in clarifying these species dilemmas. With 5590 species classified on the Red List as DD (IUCN, 2009), the problem is not insubstantial.

In contrast, well over half of the 1000+ publications of Floras and Faunas identified by the survey were on invertebrates. However, the biogeographical coverage is dramatically skewed towards the Palaearctic (Fig 2.7). Combining the two endeavours is critical for biodiversity conservation. Initiatives such as a sampled approach

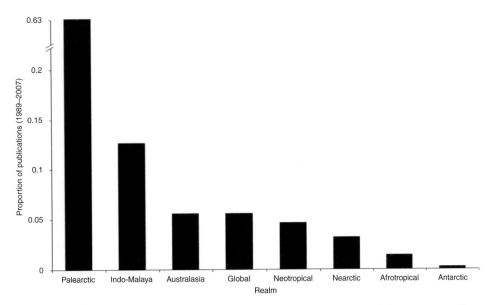

Figure 2.7 Proportion of Faunas published between 1989 and 2007 and their associated biogeographical realm (data from Zoological Record search of term 'fauna of*').

to Red Listing (the Red List Index sampled approach: Baillie et al., 2008; Collen et al., 2009), provide a step in the right direction, though results take time, and can be costly. Developing inexpensive methods that are simple to implement might improve the coverage of some groups. For example, Roberts et al. (2007) use independent datasets to demonstrate that simple species lists might be used to monitor bird populations. It is imperative with such techniques that repeat sampling occurs though, something that is being aided in many cases by web-based initiatives.

2.8 Biodiversity on the World Wide Web

Many examples of best practice come from new web-based initiatives. There are several notable projects, the first of which is from the New South Wales Parks and Wildlife service (2007). This web-based database of floral and faunal records from the region draws together more than one-million recorded sightings, using data from historical reports, the Department of Environment and Conservation staff, survey data from major projects, consultants and the general public. The user can also generate distributions for the species, as well as a number of other features.

These types of data may then have a number of positive influences on conservation. Recording threatened species occurrences encourages additional data to be gathered, and therefore better conservation decisions to be made on enhanced datasets. They provide many avenues for research, including a test case for parameterising new advances such as the Red List's 'Possibly Extinct' category (Butchart et al., 2006), the potential for niche modelling and base information for planning.

A second example is provided by the Atlas of Australian Birds[3]. The stated aims are:

- To collect and analyse data on the distribution and relative abundance of Australia's bird species.
- To compare the distribution and abundance of bird species to the previous Atlas.
- To collect information on rare and threatened bird species.
- To involve the community in the conservation and monitoring of birds.

Much like the US Christmas Bird Counts[4], the general public are used to produce the data. Practical conservation is aided by providing the opportunity and the tools for large numbers of people to monitor, providing a more extensive monitoring network, which raises awareness, and provides data that feeds back into conservation research (e.g. interpreting trends), and could feed back into refining taxonomy (e.g. if decisions are based on sympatry/allopatry with little distributional data).

From all projects, the overriding message is that quality is paramount, as exemplified by the American Museum of Natural History SPIDA (SPecies Identified Automatically)[5] project. By providing the facility for expert identification online, it takes away observer bias and recognises that we are probably not all going to become spider taxonomists. The lack of trained systematists is particularly problematic in relatively small and inconspicuous organisms, which compromise the majority of biodiversity.

One warning sign though is that all of these examples of best practice are in developed countries. Initiatives such as the Global Biodiversity Information Facility[6] and the Encyclopedia of Life[7] aim to put biodiversity data on the World Wide Web, thus making it more accessible to developing nations. Both these projects, however, require that primary biodiversity data are collected, the majority of which reside in the tropics, in countries least able to provide the data. Repatriating data that originated in less developed countries, but which are currently held in developed country institutions, should be a key aim of any such project.

---

[3] http://birdata.com.au/about_atlas.vm   [4] http://www.audubon.org/bird/cbc
[5] http://research.amnh.org/invertzoo/spida/common/index.htm
[6] http://www.gbif.org   [7] http://www.eol.org

2.9 Conclusions

Conservation biologists must weigh the obligation to keep pace with developing taxonomic knowledge with the necessity to accurately measure biodiversity depletion. In order to be successful in tackling the biodiversity crisis, predictive conservation science must move beyond just recognising lists of species, to monitoring, modelling, predicting and managing biodiversity based on those outcomes. In the future, conservation science requires three things from descriptive taxonomy:

1. That a solution is found to the problems posed by taxonomic inflation or change, and that this solution might be different for the generation of species lists and the units used for conservation management. Taxonomic and nomenclatural changes (be they rank, circumscription or new species) must be presented in such a way as to allow users to manage biodiversity effectively.

2. That Floras and Faunas feed into monitoring programmes, which might in the future be incorporated into forecasting tools.

3. That the baseline coverage for biodiversity data is broadened, to include the species and groups that represent the majority of biodiversity.

Acknowledgements

I am grateful to one anonymous reviewer, John Ewen, Kate Jones, Sam Turvey, Nick Isaac and Georgina Mace for discussion, data and comments, and Marie Hitchcock for her help in accessing the Zoological Society of London's library catalogue. This work was funded through grants from the Rufford Foundation and the Systematics Association.

References

Agapow, P.-M., Bininda-Emonds, O. R. P., Crandall, K. A., Gittleman, J. L., Mace, G. M., Marshall, J. C. and Purvis, A. (2004). The impact of species concept on biodiversity studies. *Quarterly Review of Biology*, **79**: 161–179.

Allsop, P. G. (1997). Probability of describing an Australian scarab beetle: influence of body size and distribution. *Journal of Biogeography*, **24**: 717–724.

Baillie, J. E. M., Collen, B., Amin, R., Akcakaya, H. R., Butchart, S. H. M., Brummitt, N., Meagher, T. R., Ram, M., Hilton-Taylor, C. and Mace, G. M. (2008). Towards monitoring global biodiversity. *Conservation Letters*, **1**: 18–26.

Balmer, O. (2002). Species lists in ecology and conservation: abundances matter. *Conservation Biology*, **16**: 1160–1161.

Balmford, A. and Bond, W. (2005). Trends in the state of nature and their implications for human well-being. *Ecology Letters*, **8**: 1218–1234.

Bininda Emonds, O. R. P., Cardillo, M., Jones, K. E., MacPhee, R. D. E, Beck, R. M. D., Grenyer, R., Price, S. A., Vos, R. A., Gittleman, J. L., Purvis, A. (2007). The delayed rise of present-day mammals. *Nature*, **446**: 507–512.

Brooks, T. M., Mittermeier, R. A., da Fonseca, G. A. B., Gerlach, J., Hoffmann, M., Lamoreux, J. F., Mittermeier, C. G., Pilgrim, J. D., Rodrigues, A. S. L. (2006). Global biodiversity conservation priorities. *Science*, **313**: 58–61.

Butchart, S. H. M., Stattersfield, A. J., Bennun, L. A., Shutes, S. M., Akçakaya, H. R., Baillie, J. E. M., Stuart, S. N., Hilton-Taylor, C. and Mace, G. M. (2004). Measuring global trends in the status of biodiversity: Red List Indices for birds. *PLoS Biology*, **2**: e383.

Butchart, S. H. M., Stattersfield, A. J. and Brooks, T. M. (2006). Going or gone: defining 'Possibly Extinct' species to give a truer picture of recent extinctions. *Bulletin of the British Ornithologists' Club*, **126A**: 7–24.

Butchart, S. H. M., Akcakaya, H. R., Chanson, J. S., Baillie, J. E. M., Collen, B., Quader, S., Turner, W. R., Amin, R., Stuart, S. N. and Hilton-Taylor, C. (2007). Improvements to the Red List Index. *PLoS ONE*, **2**: e140. DOI:110.1371/journal.pone.0000140.

Butchart, S. H. M., Walpole, M., Collen, B., van Strien, A., Scharlemann, J. P. W., Almond, R., Baillie, J. E. M., Bomhard, B., Brown, C., Bruno, J., Carpenter, K. E. Carr, et al. (2010) Global biodiversity: indicators of recent declines. *Science*, **328**: 1164–1168.

Cabrero-Sanudo, F. J. and Lobo, J. M. (2003). Estimating the number of species not yet described and their characteristics: the case of the Western Palaearctic dung beetle species (Coleoptera, Scarabaeoidea). *Biodiversity and Conservation*, **12**: 147–166.

Cardillo, M., Mace, G. M., Jones, K. E., Bielby, J., Bininda Emonds, O. R. P., Sechrest, W., Orme, C. D. L. and Purvis, A. (2005). Multiple causes of high extinction risk in large mammal species. *Science*, **309**: 1239–1241.

Collen, B., Purvis, A., Gittleman, J. L. (2004). Biological correlates of description date in carnivores and primates. *Global Ecology and Biogeography*, **13**: 459–467.

Collen, B., Loh, J., Holbrook, S., McRae, L., Amin, R. and Baillie, J. E. M. (2009a). Monitoring change in vertebrate abundance: the Living Planet Index. *Conservation Biology*, **23**: 317–327.

Collen, B., Ram, M., Dewhurst, N., Clausnitzer, V., Kalkman, V., Cumberlidge, N. and Baillie, J. E. M. (2009b). Broadening the coverage of biodiversity assessments. In *Wildlife in a changing world: an analysis of the 2008 IUCN Red List of Threatened Species*, J. C. Vie, C. Hilton-Taylor and S. Stuart (eds). Gland: IUCN, pp. 67–75.

Diamond, J. (1989). Overview of recent extinctions. In *Conservation for the twenty-first century*, D. Western and M. C. Pearl (eds). New York: Wildlife Conservation International, pp. 37–41.

Diniz-Filho, J. A. F., Bastos, R. P., Rangel, T. F. L. V. B., Bini, L. M., Carvalho, P. and Silva, R. J. (2005). Macroecological correlates and spatial patterns of anuran description dates in the Brazil Cerrado. *Global Ecology and Biogeography*, **14**: 469–477.

Dunn, R. R. (2005). Modern insect extinctions, the neglected majority. *Conservation Biology*, **19**: 1030–1036.

Faith, D. P. (1992). Conservation evaluation and phylogenetic diversity. *Biological Conservation*, **61**: 1–10.

Gaston, K. J. (1991). Body size and probability of description: the beetle fauna of Britain. *Ecological Entomology*, **16**: 505–508.

Geeta, R., Levy, A., Hoch, J. M. and Mark, M. (2004). Taxonomists and the CBD. *Science*, **305**: 1105.

Godfray, H. C. J. (2002). Challenges for taxonomy. *Nature*, **417**: 17–19.

Gomez de Silva, H. and Medellin, R. A. (2001). Evaluating completeness of species lists for conservation and macroecology: a case study of Mexican land birds. *Conservation Biology*, **15**: 1384–1395.

Green, R. E., Balmford, A., Crane, P. R., Mace, G. M., Reynolds, J. D. and Turner, R. K. (2005). A framework for improved monitoring of biodiversity: responses to the World Summit on Sustainable Development. *Conservation Biology*, **19**: 56–65.

Gregory, R. D., van Strien, A., Vorisek, P., Meyling, A. W. G., Noble, D. G., Foppen, R. P. B. and Gibbons, D. W. (2005). Developing indicators for European birds. *Philosophical Transactions of the Royal Society of London B*, **360**: 269–288.

Grenyer, R., Orme, C. D. L., Jackson, S. F., Thomas, G. H., Davies, R. G., Davies, T. J., Jones, K. E., Olson, V. A., Ridgely, R. S., Rasmussen, P. C., Ding, T.-S., Bennett, et al. (2006). Global distribution and conservation of rare and threatened vertebrates. *Nature*, **444**: 93–96.

Harris, D. J. and Froufe, E. (2004). Taxonomic inflation: species concept or historical geopolitical bias? *Trends in Ecology and Evolution*, **20**: 6–7.

IPCC (2002). *Climate Change and Biodiversity. IPCC Technical Paper V.* Geneva, Switzerland: Intergovernmental Panel on Climate Change. Available at: www.ipcc.ch/pub/tpbiodiv.pdf.

Isaac, N. J. B., Mallet, J. and Mace, G. M. (2004). Taxonomic inflation: its influence on macroecology and conservation. *Trends in Ecology and Evolution*, **19**: 464–469.

Isaac, N. J. B., Turvey, S. T., Collen, B., Waterman, C. and Baillie, J. E. M. (2007). Mammals on the EDGE: Conservation priorities based on threat and phylogeny. *PLoS ONE*, **2**: e296. DOI:210.1371/journal.pone.0000296.

IUCN (2009). *2009 IUCN Red List of Threatened Species.* Available at: www.iucnredlist.org.

Knapp, S., Nic Lughadha, E. and Paton, A. (2004). Taxonomic inflation, species concepts and global species lists. *Trends in Ecology and Evolution*, **20**: 7–8.

Kodric-Brown, A. and Brown, J. H. (1993). Incomplete datasets in community ecology and biogeography: a cautionary tale. *Ecological Applications*, **3**: 736–742.

Lamoreux, J., Akcakaya, H. R., Bennun, L., Collar, N. J., Boitani, L., Brackett, D., Brautigam, A., Brooks, T. M., de Fonseca, G. A. B., Mittermeier, R. A., Rylands, A. B., Gardenfors, U., et al. (2003). Value of the IUCN Red List. *Trends in Ecology and Evolution*, **18**: 214–215.

Loh, J., Green, R. E., Ricketts, T., Lamoreux, J. F., Jenkins, M., Kapos, V. and Randers, J. (2005). The Living Planet Index: using species population time series to track trends in biodiversity. *Philosophical Transactions of the Royal Society of London B*, **360**: 289–295.

Mace, G. M. (2004). The role of taxonomy in species conservation. *Philosophical Transactions of the Royal Society of London B*, **359**: 711–719.

Mace, G. M. and Baillie, J. E. M. (2007). The 2010 biodiversity indicators: challenges for science and policy. *Conservation Biology*, **21**: 1406–1413.

Mace, G. M. and Lande, R. (1991). Assessing extinction threats – toward a reevaluation of IUCN Threatened Species categories. *Conservation Biology*, **5**: 148–157.

Mace, G. M., Gittleman, J. L. and Purvis, A. (2003). Preserving the Tree of Life. *Science*, **300**: 1707–1709.

May, R. M. (1988). How many species are there on Earth? *Science*, **241**: 1441–1449.

May, R. M. (1990). Taxonomy as destiny. *Nature*, **347**: 129–130.

Meegaskumbura, M., Bossuyt, F., Pethiyagoda, R., Manamendra-Arachchi, K., Bahir, M., Milinkovitch, M. C. and Schneider, C. J. (2002). Sri Lanka: an amphibian hot spot. *Science*, **298**: 379.

Millennium Ecosystem Assessment (2005). *Ecosystems and human well-being: biodiversity synthesis*. Washington DC: World Resources Institute.

Myers, N., Mittermeier, R. A., Mittermeier, C. G., Fonseca, G. A. B. and Kent, J. (2000). Biodiversity hotspots for conservation priorities. *Nature*, **403**: 853–858.

New South Wales Parks and Wildlife Service (2007). *Atlas of New South Wales wildlife*. Available at: http://wildlifeatlas.nationalparks.nsw.gov.au/wildlifeatlas/watlas.jsp.

Orme, C. D. L., Davies, R. G., Burgess, M., Eigenbrod, F., Pickup, N., Olson, V. A., Webster, A. J., Ding, T.-S., Rasmussen, P. C., Ridgely, R. S., Stattersfield, A. J., Bennett, P. M., et al. (2005). Global hotspots of species richness are not congruent with endemism or threat. *Nature*, **436**: 1016–1019.

Padial, J. M. and De la Riva, I. (2006). Taxonomic inflation and the stability of species lists: the perils of ostrich's behaviour. *Systematic Biology*, **55**: 859–867.

Pan-European Common Bird Monitoring (2006). *European common bird index: population trends of European common birds 2005 update*. EBCC (European Bird Census Council).

Peterson, A. T. and Navarro-Sigüenza, A. G. (1999). Alternate species concepts as bases for determining priority conservation areas. *Conservation Biology*, **13**: 427–431.

Pressey, R. L. and Cowling, R. M. (2001). Reserve selection algorithms and the real world. *Conservation Biology*, **15**: 275–277.

Purvis, A., Agapow, P.-M. Gittleman, J. L. and Mace, G. M. (2000). Nonrandom extinction and the loss of evolutionary history. *Science*, **288**: 328–330.

Purvis, A., Cardillo, M., Grenyer, R. and Collen B. (2003). Correlates of extinction risk: phylogeny, biology, threat and scale. In *Phylogeny and Conservation*, A. Purvis, T. M. Brooks and J. L. Gittleman (eds). Cambridge: Cambridge University Press, pp. 295–316.

Raven, P. H. and Wilson, E. O. (1992). A fifty-year plan for biodiversity surveys. *Science*, **258**: 1099–1100.

Reed, R. N. and Boback, S. M. (2002). Does body size predict dates of species description among North American and Australian reptiles and amphibians? *Global Ecology and Biogeography*, **11**: 41–47.

Regan, H. M., Lupia, R., Drinnan, A. N. and Burgman, M. A. (2001). The currency and tempo of extinction. *American Naturalist*, **157**: 1–10.

Roberts, R. L., Donald, P. F. and Green, R. E. (2007). Using simple species lists to monitor trends in animal populations: new methods and a comparison with independent data. *Animal Conservation*, **10**: 332–339.

Roskov Y., Kunze T., Paglinawan L., Orrell T., Nicolson D., Culham A., Bailly N., Kirk P., Bourgoin T., Baillargeon G., Hernandez F., De Wever A. (eds) (2013). *Species 2000 and ITIS Catalogue of Life, 2013 Annual Checklist*. DVD. Reading: Species 2000. Availiable at: http://www.catalogueoflife.org/annual-checklist/2013/info/ac.

Stuart, S. N., Chanson, J. S., Cox, N. A., Young, B. E., Rodrigues, A. S. L., Fischman, D. L. and Waller, R. W. (2004). Status and trends of amphibian declines and extinctions worldwide. *Science*, **306**: 1783. DOI:10.1126/science.1103538.

Thomas, C. D., Cameron, A., Green, R. E., Bakkenes, M., Beaumont, L. J., Collingham, Y. C., Erasmus, B. F. N., Siqueira, M. F. D., Grainger, A., Hannah, L., Hughes, L., Huntley, B., et al. (2004). Extinction risk from climate change. *Nature*, **427**: 145–148.

UNEP (2002). *Report on the sixth meeting of the Conference of the Parties to the Convention on Biological Diversity (UNEP/CBD/COP/20/Part 2) Strategic Plan Decision VI/26*. Available at: http://www.cbd.int.

UNEP (2006). *Report on the eighth meeting of the Conference of the Parties to the Convention on Biological Diversity*. Available at: http://www.cbd.int.

Vane-Wright, R. L., Humphries, C. J. and Williams, P. H. (1991). What to protect – systematics and the agony of choice. *Biological Conservation*, **55**: 235–254.

Wilson, E. O. (2003). The Encyclopedia of Life. *Trends in Ecology and Evolution*, **18**: 77–80.

3

The present and future value of Floras for functional ecologists

J. Dick, R. Smith and R. Wadsworth

3.1 Introduction

Ecology is the scientific study of the distribution and abundance of living organisms, and how the distribution and abundance are affected by interactions between the organisms and their environment. The discipline of ecology clearly relies upon the ability of ecologists to correctly identify the organisms under study, and ecologists frequently rely on Floras for this purpose. Floras (treatises describing and listing all the plants of a region or time) may appear as books or, more frequently these days, in electronic formats. Floras are used by ecologists to identify plants, but also as a rich source of species-specific information including morphology, phenology, habitat niche, associated species and geographical distribution. Floras usually include further information on the distribution and habitat preferences, although this may range from 'dot maps' to vague descriptions, e.g. 'widespread', 'occasional', etc., and may include information on local names, uses and even folklore. In recent years, such information has also been used to assign plants to functional types or groups (see review by Petchey and Gaston, 2006).

However, Floras are not contructed to fully describe all the characteristics of the plants they include, as they concentrate primarily on the distinguishing features to aid identification. In this paper we will explore the value of Floras to functional ecologists considering:

Descriptive Taxonomy: The Foundation of Biodiversity Research, eds M. F. Watson, C. H. C. Lyal and C. A. Pendry. Published by Cambridge University Press.

1. The problems that arise if the organism is not correctly identified to the level of species.

2. Using Floras as the primary source of data to establish functional similarity between groups of species, i.e. the identification of plant functional types or functional groups.

3. Comparing the accuracy of information contained in different Floras.

We will conclude by listing some simple measures that Flora writers might consider in order to make their products more useful to functional ecologists, and how ecologists could assist taxonomists by contributing data to web-based datasets.

3.2 Functional ecology

In this paper the phrase 'functional types' and 'functional groups' are used in a similar sense to 'functional attributes' (Gillison and Carpenter, 1997), 'vital characteristics' (Noble and Gitay, 1996; Roberts, 1996), 'vital attributes' (Noble and Slatyer, 1980) and possibly 'ecological guilds' (Brzeziecki and Kienast, 1994); the term has been defined as 'those biotic components of ecosystems that perform the same function or set of functions within the ecosystem' (Smith et al., 1997).

As pointed out by Petchey and Gaston (2006), in their review of functional diversity, this subdiscipline of ecological science has grown exponentially over the last decade, but the term 'functional diversity' is not yet well-defined. Over 50% of the 238 articles they reviewed did not provide or cite a definition of functional diversity within an ecosystem. We take 'functional ecology' to be broadly concerned with the way that individual organisms, through their behaviour, evolution, physiology or other characteristics, affect the way an ecosystem functions (the pattern of features and fluxes of material and energy). In this chapter we refer specifically to the measurement and analysis of functional traits of taxa to define biological diversity of an area. We use the term phi diversity (φ-diversity) to distinguish this method of analysing functional diversity and so avoid confusion. We feel this term is appropriate as it complements the existing 'diversity' terms (Whittaker, 1972):

- Alpha (α) diversity – species 'richness' within an ecosystem.

- Beta (β) diversity – species 'richness' between ecosystems.

- Gamma (γ) diversity – species 'richness' at a geographical or regional scale.

The three terms (α-, β- and γ-diversity) are already defined in the literature and consider the species (taxa) present in a specific area at different spatial scales. Phi diversity is complementary to these by defining the biodiversity of an area by the functional processes associated with the taxa that are present. The species in a specific area are grouped by the traits they exhibit there, and taxa are not restricted to a single functional grouping. For example, two tree species may be in the same resource-use group (upper canopy) on one functional axis, but in different seed-dispersal groups on another functional axis. These groupings of taxa along various functional axes become the fundamental units for calculating the φ-diversity of an ecosystem. Unlike the other three measures of biodiversity, which are based on the presence of individual taxa, φ-diversity is a composite measure of biodiversity focusing on the diversity of function, through biological processes or ecystem services, of the combination of all species present within a specific area.

In this next section we demonstrate the difficulty of calculating φ-diversity when the component taxa of an ecosystem could not be correctly assigned to species.

3.3 Species identification

The ability to use Floras as a data source to assign species to functional groups, and thereby calculate φ-diversity, relies on the correct identification of species in an ecosystem. For example, Dick et al. (2000) attempted to determine the φ-diversity of mature undisturbed lowland Dipterocarp forest. They used datasets provided by the BPK Samarinda Clearing House, BPK, Samarinda, for 38 unlogged plots in 3 forests located in Kalimantan and the 16 functional groups identified by Lawson et al. (2000). Lawson and co-workers determined what they considered a simple, but commercially meaningful, classification based on four height classes and four wood-density classes. Wood density was used as an analogue for species light requirement for seedling establishment and growth. Maximum height of a species, as defined by Floras, was considered to reflect the species final position in the canopy and possibly its competitive ability (Weiher et al., 1999). When trees were only identified to genus in the dataset, the authors used local knowledge and assigned the tree to the functional group to which they considered most of the genus belonged.

Over 80% of the 21 860 trees recorded across all 3 sites were assigned to a functional group. All three forests showed the typically negative exponential distribution of stem diameter class distributions associated with mature forests (Uuttera et al., 2000) and apparently had similar climate, soil and topography. It was therefore hypothesised that the forests would be functionally similar. A principal coordinates analysis, however, indicated that there was significant difference in φ-diversity between the three forests despite the apparent functional similarity of all three forests.

When investigating the difference between the forests, one forest had a much higher incidence of trees in Lawson's 'upper canopy – light wood' functional type and this contributed to the noticeable difference in φ-diversity between the three forests.

Further investigation revealed that 63% of the individuals in this functional type belonged to the genus *Syzygium* and had not been identified to species but were assigned by Lawson to the 'upper canopy' using expert local judgement. However, *Plant resources of South-East Asia* (Lemmens et al., 1995) describes 32 *Syzygium* species found in Kalimantan and Borneo, and their height data would put only 28% of species in the 'upper canopy', 17% would be 'emergent' and 55% in the 'lower canopy', showing that the genus included trees with substantially different functional niches. Dick and co-workers concluded that the lack of botanical identification to species level made it difficult to know if the trees had been assigned to the correct functional group and whether the three forests were significantly different.

3.4 Flora as primary data sources for establishing functional similarity between groups of species

In order to create functional types using data contained within Floras we have explored two basic approaches: text analysis and data matrix analysis. We will illustrate the advantages and disadvantages of both approaches with Floras for East African trees. Our analysis sought to produce a functional gradient to aid selection of species for restoration in Mabira Forest Reserve, Uganda and the Mau Forest Complex, Kenya, as part of an European Union-funded project, FOREAIM[1]. The species list for the Mabira Forest Reserve was obtained from the 1996 biodiversity report (Davenport et al., 1996). A total of 284 species of trees and shrubs were recorded by the inventory and a further 28 species were reported to be known from previous studies (total 312). It was not possible to create a full data matrix of parameters for all 312 species as the information had to be collated from printed Floras. As we were conducting a functional analysis to aid species selection for restoration ecology, we concentrated on 'useful' trees and shrubs as defined in the Floras of Katende et al. (1995) and Maundu and Tengnas (2005). The analysis was conducted on 131 species from the Mabira Forest Reserve (42%). A total of the 65 most abundant species were selected for study in the Mau Forest Complex, Kenya, on the basis of their abundance in the forest. A Flora published by the Museum of Kenya (Beentje, 1994) was also utilised to obtain information on the trees from the Mau Forest Complex.

3.5 Text analysis

Natural language processing (NLP) of botanical texts is a complex (and possibly intractable) problem. The two multi-Flora projects have been extremely useful in

---

[1] http://foreaim.cirad.fr

defining the exact nature of the problem. In contrast, text-mining is less ambitious and searches for patterns in unstructured or natural language texts; as opposed to data-mining that searches for patterns in structured data (such as tables and data-bases) (Miller and Han, 2001; Witten and Frank, 2005). An overview of a range of text-mining techniques and objectives was provided by Feldman and Sanger (2007) and techniques related to bioinformatics by Ananiadou and McNaught (2006). We applied the methodology described by Wadsworth et al. (2006), whose central concept is that if two descriptions use many words in common they are likely to be discussing the same issue and, therefore, to be semantically close. This approach to text-mining is very similar to 'information retrieval', where the objective is to rank documents based on their similarity to a key word or phrase (e.g. as used by the internet search-engine Google). The description of each species is treated as a separate 'document' and its similarity to all other documents assessed. Interest in text-mining is evident from the establishment of the world's first National Centre For Text-Mining[2] in the UK in 2004 (Ananiadou et al., 2005). There is an extensive and growing literature on text-mining in the bioinformatics community, such as the BioCreAtIvE contest (Hirschman et al., 2005), but unfortunately this is much more concerned with genetic and molecular studies than 'whole organism ecology'.

The textual overlap between *Useful trees and shrubs for Uganda* (Katende et al., 1995) and *Useful trees and shrubs for Kenya* (Maundu and Tengnas, 2005) (and hence the 'similarity' between the species included) was initially calculated using all of the available text. Principal component analysis (PCA) was used to visualise the matrix of similarities. Unfortunately the dominant influence on the amount of overlap was the source of the text (Fig 3.1); the Kenyan descriptions form a distinct group in the lower left of the figure with only a limited amount of overlap with the Ugandan descriptions.

Both Floras were structured in a very similar manner and the vocabulary was also similar, so the dominance of the source of information in the PCA was initially rather surprising. Part of the description of each species was the list of common names in the local languages, as the languages used in Katende et al. (1995) and Maundu and Tengnas (2005) are different, the repeated use of the language iden-tifiers generated a significant overlap between species in each Flora. In addition, several of the descriptions in Maundu and Tengnas included extensive descriptions of related species, while this was not provided by Katende and co-workers. The style of the Flora, therefore, significantly influenced the analysis.

After reducing the text description to the four common elements of ecology, categorised as basic description, uses, management and remarks, the difference between the languages in the two Floras was minimised. Species collated from Maundu and Tengnas (2005) are still a recognisable group within the larger number

---

[2] http://www.nactem.ac.uk/

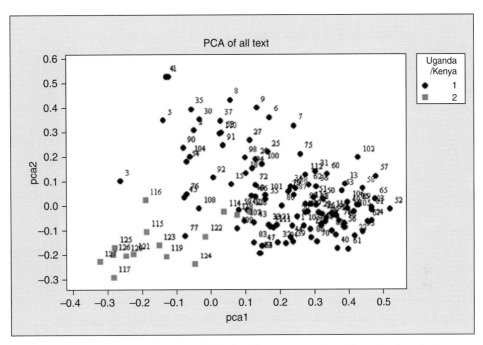

Figure 3.1 PCA based on all text available for all species; circle = Ugandan descriptions and square = Kenyan descriptions, see text for detail.

of Ugandan species; however, this is now because the Kenya Flora was used to fill in for species not described in the Flora of Katende and co-workers (Fig 3.2). These species tend to be the ones that grow in drier environments and so were not included in Katende et al. (1995).

This second analysis revealed the underlying and implicit ecological structure in the dataset. The primary environmental gradient runs from lower left to upper right on the PCA visualisation; to the left are spiny shrubby species of semi-arid environments, while species in the upper right are larger trees commonly found in wetter environments. Along the second axis of the PCA the large species restricted to rain forest have a high score (at the top of the PCA diagram) (*Bombax buonopozense, Funtumia elastica, Entandrophragma utile*). More versatile and domesticated species are at the right-hand side (*Schrebera arborea, Celtis mildboreadii, Holoptelea grandis*). For the shrubs, the most arid scrubby species are at the left of the PCA diagram (*Flueggea virosa, Rhus vulgaris, Capparis tomentosa*) and shrubs of wetter conditions have a low second axis score and are opposite the rain forest trees (*Croton macrostachyus, Maytenus undata, Dichrostachys cinerea*).

This analysis demonstrates the value of using text analysis of Floras to gain an understanding of the principal concerns of the authors of the Floras and of the main environmental gradients within a region. Although PCA has been used to visualise

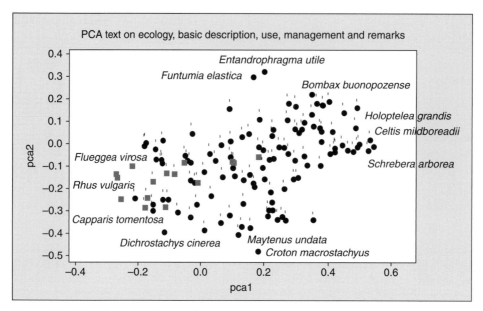

Figure 3.2 PCA of text detailing ecology, basic description, uses and management.

the similarities the matrix of semantic overlaps, it is amenable to many other types of classification and visualisation. It is recognised that a potential limitation to the method is its sensitivity to the style of the language used.

3.6 Data-matrix analysis

A data matrix can be compiled from the information within a Flora by manually extracting information from each description. In contrast to the automatic text-mining described above, this is a time-consuming task as Floras are predominantly text descriptions. Further, when compiling a data matrix manually, the inconsistencies between Floras in what is recorded and how the data are presented are unavoidable. This has to be positively addressed at an initial stage of data analysis. There may be a benefit in the long run as the exercise will retrieve more useful data for analysis than an automated procedure, but the use of text recognition and matching procedures within this data matrix construction phase is sensible.

We created a data matrix of 44 functionally useful parameters for the 131 species of Mabira Forest, Uganda, using Katende et al. (1995) and Maundu and Tengnas (2005). It was only possible to complete the data matrix for 7 out of the 44 parameters using the Floras alone, as some of the parameters (e.g. maximum size of the fruit) were only reported for 11 of the 131 species (Table 3.1). This level of incompleteness is typical of many Floras as the author is primarily concentrating on

Table 3.1 Characteristics extracted from Katende et al. (1995) and Maundu and Tengnas (2005) showing the percentage of the 131 species list reported for each characteristic

Variable	No. species	Species %	Variable	No. species	Species %
Family	131	100	Flower length	99	76
Growth form	131	100	Maximum altitude	98	75
Ecological type	131	100	Leaf retention	94	72
Young shoots not green	131	100	Coppice/pollarding	88	67
Leaf type	131	100	Growth rate	84	64
Leaf type2	131	100	Fruit remakes	83	63
Fruit shape	131	100	Below leaf texture	80	61
Flower sex	130	99	Minimum altitude	73	56
Inflorescences	130	99	Bark type	66	50
Tree sex	129	99	Wood density	65	50
Habitat	128	98	Fruit seed dispersal	58	44
Fruit colour	128	98	Bark defence	53	41
Maximum average height	124	95	Flower smell	52	40
Flower shape	124	95	Fruit minimum length	50	38
Multi-stemmed	122	93	Maximum number seed per kilogram	47	36
Bark colour	121	92	Functional category	44	34
Bark texture	121	92	Minimum number seed per kilogram	27	21
Flower colour	121	92	Propagation	24	18
Buttressed	115	88	Seed length	23	18
Fruit maximum length	113	86	Fruit protection	12	9
Upper leaf texture above	110	84	Fruit maximum width	11	8
Trunk shape	99	76	Fruit minimum width	10	8

reporting distinguishing features rather than faithfully reporting information on the same character set for all of the species. The data compiler is then uncertain, without further sources of information, as to whether the lack of reporting indicates a trait that never occurs (genuinely missing, e.g. species does not produce fruit), does not commonly occur (unobserved by the Flora compiler) or is just not useful for species separation. It is common for studies clustering species in functional groups to use many sources of data. For example, Willby et al. (2000) report that they consulted over 200 published works and online databases in order to construct a 58-trait matrix of 120 species of European hydrophytes.

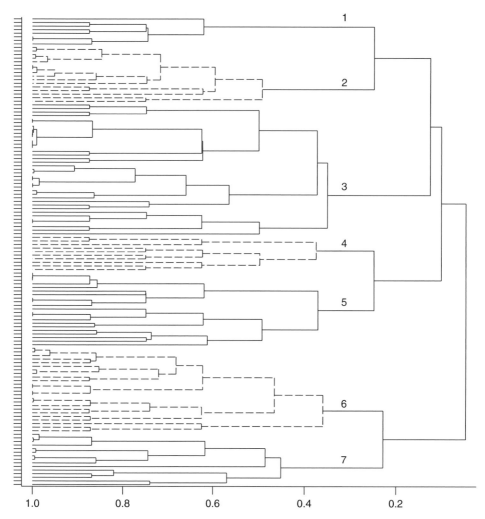

Figure 3.3 Dendogram of clustering analysis for 131 tree species of the Mabira Forest Uganda (reference line at 30% similarity using complete linkage shown) dataset.

Cluster analysis is a robust methodology often used to create groups of species with similar function (Valerio and Sosinski, 2003; Petchey and Gaston, 2006). However, missing data can affect the resulting groupings. Analysis of traits relevant to the life strategy of the tree, e.g. average maximum height, growth rate, presence or absence of buttress and multi-stemmed characteristic, give a simple illustration of the problems of substantial numbers of missing values when conducting this type of analysis. The resultant dendrogram along this functional axis shows clear separation into 7 groups at 30% similarity using a complete linkage method that encourages the formation of compact groups (Fig 3.3).

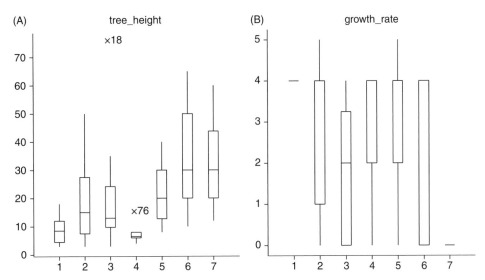

Figure 3.4 (A,B) Box plots of tree height and growth rate for the seven groups identified by cluster analysis for 131 tree species from the Mabira Forest Uganda. Groups 1–7 arranged left to right in each box plot. Growth rate scored 1–5 with 1= very slow and 5 very fast; 0 score = data missing).

The resultant groups appear to be discriminated on height (Fig 3.4A) with trees in groups 1 and 4 having lower average maximum height compared with the other groups. All the species in group 1 were also classed as fast growing (Figure 3.4B). Members of this group included *Vernonia auriculifera*, *Phytolacca dodecandra* and *Turraea robusta*, which were all classed as pioneers by the Floras used. However, tree height was not discriminatory between groups 6 and 7; rather it was the fact that there was no information in the data matrix on growth rate which distinguished group 7. Growth rate was missing for 64% of the species and this was a discriminatory feature in the dataset.

3.7 Comparing the accuracy of information contained in diffent Floras

In addition to missing data the differences in the data reported between Floras was investigated. We compared the robustness of information reported by Maundu and Tengnas (2005) and Beentje (1994). For example, a simple regression between the maximum heights reported for 65 Kenyan trees reveals a fairly good, but a far from perfect, correlation (Figure 3.5). This is reassuring in two senses: the fitted line indicates a reasonable correspondence between the same trait recorded in the two Floras with some discrepancy, which may reflect the different performance of

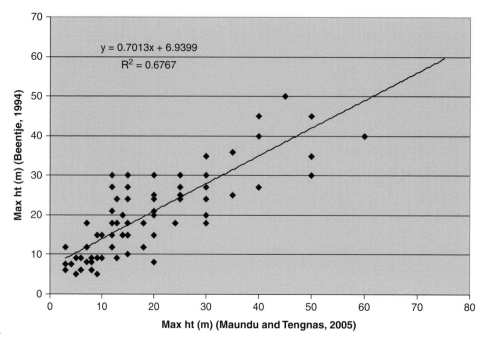

Figure 3.5 Comparison of maximum height quoted in two Floras for 65 tree species found in the Mau Forest Complex, Kenya (see text for details).

the trees in the two countries, and the less than perfect correlation indicates that the Flora compilers were using different sources of information so we are getting genuine extra data on the recorded traits. Therefore, the use of a second Flora to gap fill can be justified, but it can also give more information on ranges and uncertainty of traits reported in both Floras and so provide a better analysis.

An important point for ecologists working with several Floras is to be certain how much of the data extracted is genuinely independent, rather than being derived from the same observations. In this case there was no difficulty in confirming independence, but as more extensive Floras are constructed and compared it is worth tracking the original data source as well as the data values.

3.8 Conclusion

At present Floras are valuable sources of ecological information. However, historically ecologists have complained that using Floras was difficult because of:

1. Inconsistent naming of taxa; when a revision occurred it was often years before all ecologists became familiar with the new taxonomic name for a species causing confusion in the literature.

2.   Data-delivery formats that are complex and not easily read; as in all branches of science taxonomy has specialised terminology, but this can hinder access for ecologists.

3.   Incomplete reporting of characteristics (morphological, habitat, etc.), as only distinguishing features that separate species are reported.

4.   A primary focus on the single species; ecologists study many organisms in an ecosystem and, therefore, have to consult many sources of data to create a data matrix for the community they are studying.

The functionality, and so usability and relevance, of future Floras will, we believe, increase with the use of digital databases and photographs (Pendry et al., 2007). Such databases will allow many of the problems with historical Floras to be overcome as web-based Floras are created and become interlinked in projects like the Global Biodiversity Information Facility (GBIF), the Biological Access Service for Europe (BioCASE) and, more recently, the Encyclopedia of Life project. The historically static approach to presenting floristic information will be superseded by a dynamic exchange of data and knowledge between taxonomists and ecologists worldwide. Ecologists will also have a real opportunity to contribute their knowledge to such databases.

Currently, Floras hold very little physiological information, data which is important when studying the function of a species in an ecosystem. There is scope with the new web-based database approach to integrate data from all branches of science. For example Diaz et al. (2004) studied 12 key traits associated with the establishment and regeneration processes of 640 vascular species from Argentina, England, Iran and Spain, in a collaborative ecology project. Five of the traits (leaf size, canopy height, life span, seed mass and seed shape) are commonly reported in Floras, while six of the other traits could be provided to a central database by taxonomists or ecologists with little additional effort (specific leaf area, leaf toughness, in-rolling of lamina, leaf thickness, woodiness and shoot phenology). The twelfth trait (mean distance between ramets connected below ground or at ground level) is a more challenging trait to collect.

In conclusion, taxonomists and ecologists have historically worked together, with Floras as the primary meeting point, but we believe that the integration of these two disciplines will be even stronger in the near future as new web-based databases come online.

Acknowledgements

The authors are indebted to all our colleagues, taxonomists and ecologists, who have discussed the ideas contained in this paper, and especially to our partners in

Kenya and Uganda who took the time to explain their forests to the lead author – particularly Florence Muindi who tragically died of meningitis during the FOREAIM project. We are also grateful to three anonymous referees for their useful comments.

References

Ananiadou, S. and McNaught, J. (eds) (2006). *Text mining for biology and biomedicine*. Boston and London: Artech House.

Ananiadou, S., Chruszcz, J., Keane, J., McNaught, J. and Watny, P. (2005). The national centre for text-mining: aims and objectives. *Ariadne*, **42**, June 2005. Available at: http://www.ariadne.ac.uk/ issue42.

Beentje, H. (1994). *Kenya trees shrubs and lianas*. Kenya: National Museums of Kenya.

Brzeziecki, B. and Kienast, F. (1994). Classifying the life-history strategies of trees on the basis of the Grimian model. *Forest Ecology and Management*, **69**: 167–187.

Davenport, T., Howard, P. and Baltzer, M. (1996). *Mabira Forest Reserve: biodiversity report*. Uganda: Forest Department.

Diaz, S, Hodgson, J. G., Thompson, K., Cabido, M., Cornelissen, J. H. C., Jalili, A., Montserrat-Marti, G., Grime, J. P., Zarrinkamar, F., Asri, Y., Band, S. R., Basconcelo, S., et al. (2004). The plant traits that drive ecosystems: evidence from three continents. *Journal of Vegetation Science*, **15**(3): 295–304.

Dick, J. McP., Smith, R. I. and Lawson, G. J. (2000). *Functional and botanical classification of three forests in Kalimantan, Indonesia*. Part 3 of CEH Final Technical Report as part of the DFID Forest Research Programme 'Growth and Yield Frameworks' Project, April 1999–June 2000.

Feldman, R. and Sanger, J. (2007). *The text-mining handbook. Advanced approaches in analyzing unstructured data*. Cambridge: Cambridge University Press.

Gillison, A. N. and Carpenter, G. (1997). A generic plant functional attribute set and grammar for dynamic vegetation description and analysis. *Functional Ecology*, **11**(6): 775–783.

Hirschman, L., Yeh, A., Blaschke, C. and Valencia, A. (2005). Overview of BioCreAtIvE: critical assessment of information extraction for biology *BMC Bioinformatics* 2005, **6**(Suppl. 1). DOI: 10.1186/1471-2105-6-S1-S1.

Katende, A. B., Birnie, A. and Tengnäs, B. (1995). *Useful trees and shrubs for Uganda. Identification, propagation and management for agricultural and pastoral communities Regional Soil Conservation Units (RSCU)*. Sweden: Swedish International Development Cooperation Agency (SIDA).

Lawson, G. J., Friend, A. D., Smith, R. I., and Dick J. (2000). *Functional classifications, physiological ecology and options for parameterising and modifying the hybrid forest model for application to Indonesian TMF*. Edinburgh: Centre for Ecology and Hydrology.

Lemmens, R. H. J. J., Soerianegara, I. and Wong, W. C. (1995). *Plant Resources of South-East Asia No. 5(2)*. Bogor, Indonesia: PROSEA.

Maundu, P. and Tengnas, B. (2005). *Useful trees and shrubs for Kenya*. World

Agroforestry Centre, Eastern and Central Africa Regional Programme.

Miller, H. J. and Han, J. (eds) (2001). *Geographic data mining and knowledge discovery*. London: Taylor and Francis.

Noble, I. R. and Gitay, H. (1996). A functional classification for predicting the dynamics of landscapes. *Journal of Vegetation Science*, **7**(3): 329–336.

Noble, I. R. and Slatyer, R. (1980). The use of vital attributes to predict successional changes in plant communities subject to recurrent disturbances. *Vegetation*, **43**: 5–21.

Pendry, C. A., Dick, J., Pullman, M. R., Knees, S. G., Miller, A. G., Neale, S. and Watson, M. F. (2007). In search of a functional Flora – towards a greater integration of ecology and taxonomy. *Plant Ecology*, **192**(2). 161–167. DOI: 10.1007/s11258-007-9304-y.

Petchey, O. L. and Gaston, K. J. (2006). Functional diversity: back to basics and looking forward. *Ecology Letters*, **9**: 741–758.

Roberts, D. W. 1996. Landscape vegetation modeling with vital attributes and fuzzy-systems theory. *Ecological Modelling*, **90**(2): 175–184.

Smith, T. M., Shugart, H. H. and Woodward, F. I. (eds) (1997). *Plant functional types: their relevance to ecosystem properties and global change*. International Geosphere–Biosphere Programme Book Series 1. Cambridge: Cambridge University Press.

Uuttera, J., Tokola, T. and Maltamo, M. (2000). Differences in the structure of primary and managed forests in East Kalimantan, Indonesia. *Forest Ecology and Management*, **129**, 63–74.

Valerio, P. D. and Sosinski, E. E. (2003). An improved method for searching plant functional types by numerical analysis. *Journal of Vegetation Science*, **14**: 323–333.

Wadsworth, R. A., Comber, A. J. and Fisher, P. F. (2006). Expert knowledge and embedded knowledge: or why long rambling class descriptions are useful. In *Proceedings of the 12th International Symposium on Spatial Data Handling*, A. Riedl, W. Kainz and G. Elmes (eds). Berlin: Springer, pp. 197–213.

Weiher, E., van der Werf, A., Thompson, K., Roderick, M., Garnier, E. and Eriksson, O. (1999). Challenging Theophrastus: a common core list of plant traits for functional ecology. *Journal of Vegetation Science*, **10**: 609–620.

Whittaker, R. H. (1972). Evolution and measurement of species diversity. *Taxon*, **21**: 213–251.

Willby, N. J., Abernethy, V. J. and Demars B. O. L. (2000). Attribute-based classification of European hydrophytes and its relationship to habitat utilization. *Freshwater Biology*, **43**: 43–74.

Witten, I. H. and Frank, E. (2005). *Data mining: practical machine learning tools and techniques*. San Francisco: Morgan Kaufman.

4

A publisher's perspective: making biodiversity information available and relevant to a wide audience

J. B. Connor

4.1 Introduction: the publishing triangle

For over three decades, Timber Press has published books on plants, including encyclopaedias, horticultural monographs[1], field guides and the occasional Flora. Timber Press's market and authors are international, and many of its books are translated into and from other languages. It is not an academic or institutional publisher, neither is it geared to publishing for the mass market. Timber Press is a mid-range, commercial publisher of information-rich books on plants, and it is from that perspective that the present chapter is written.

Book publishing is a triangular set of relationships between author, publisher and end user, each party with different, sometimes conflicting, priorities. With botanical and horticultural books, in general, the key consideration for authors is content. They are knowledgeable and passionate about their subject, and their book is often their life's work. They want to communicate what they know, and credibility, comprehensiveness and currency of information are what are most important to

---

[1] The term horticultural monograph or monograph used in this chapter refers to books on a genus or group of plants intended for a horticultural and botanical audience, as distinct from a scientific monograph intended for an academic readership.

Descriptive Taxonomy: The Foundation of Biodiversity Research, eds M. F. Watson, C. H. C. Lyal and C. A. Pendry. Published by Cambridge University Press.
© The Systematics Association 2015

them. Authors want their book to enhance their reputation and advance their career. The market may be less of a consideration than a favourable response from peers and reviewers, and while they would like to be financially rewarded for their work, that is not usually their primary motivation.

For most publishers, the overriding consideration is who is going to buy the book. The market needs to be clearly defined and as broad as possible. The price must be right for the market, the economics of that particular book must be viable, and these commercial considerations are often what define the form the book takes. When publishers are considering a proposal, it is usual to identify the market, look at the appropriateness of the content for that market, evaluate the economics, and then work with the author to tailor the content and the presentation as much as possible to fit these requirements. Financial considerations are not the only ones, however. While the realities of business underpin what commercial publishers do, most people in publishing are motivated by the desire to publish worthwhile books by reputable authors, and see them enjoy a positive response from reviewers and readers, and flourish in their intended market.

End users of botanical and horticultural books are primarily interested in the usefulness of the book, which means that the content should be appropriate to their needs. They may be looking for broad geographical coverage rather than depth of locally specific information. For some, the author's interpretation may be more valuable and interesting than detailed factual information and identification keys. For others, comprehensiveness, authority and currency will be more appealing than accessibility and an engaging style. Price is definitely a consideration, as are presentation and packaging, particularly when it comes to illustrations and portability.

4.2 Levels of information

Information on the flora and fauna of a region has traditionally been published at several levels of complexity. A selection of plant books from North America's Pacific Northwest shows such a hierarchy.

Level 1: At the top level is the most comprehensive botanical publication for the region, the five-volume Flora, *Vascular plants of the Pacific Northwest* (Hitchcock et al., 1959–69). Its authority is conveyed by its extensiveness and also by its austere packaging, without title or illustration on the front cover.

Level 2: At the next level of comprehensiveness are two smaller Floras, one of which is a condensed version of the five-volume work, *Flora of the Pacific Northwest: an illustrated manual* (Hitchcock and Cronquist, 1973) and the other an identification guide (consisting mostly of keys) to the plants of a slightly smaller geographical area: *Plants of western Oregon, Washington and British Columbia* (Kozloff, 2005).

Level 3: Horticultural monographs, at the third level, bring together information on a genus or group of plants, drawing on Floras from around the world as well as the expertise and experiences of naturalists and horticulturists. Examples of these that Timber Press has published include books on *Penstemon* (Nold, 1999), *Calochortus* (Gerritsen and Parsons, 2007), *Lewisia* (Davidson, 2000), *Trillium* (Case and Case, 1997) and *Vaccinium* (Trehane, 2004) – all genera relevant to the Pacific Northwest region. Horticultural monographs move beyond being purely descriptive of plants in botanical terms, to include cultivation and propagation, hybrids and cultivars, the history of the genus and taxonomic debates; the best of these are anecdotal and resonate with the author's passion for the subject. Colour photographs and illustrations of plants in the wild, as well as in cultivation, are usually a feature. The readership is much broader than for higher-level, more-technical botanical works, extending from botanists to nursery professionals, amateur naturalists and gardeners.

Level 4: Monographs, such as those indicated at level 3, depend on Floras as a source of information, and in turn they inform many other kinds of books, both plant identification and horticultural, at a professional and popular level. These 'popular books' are ranked at level 4, and include field identification guides to wildflowers and other plants, and a major encyclopaedia for gardeners. For example: *Wetland plants of Oregon and Washington* (Guard, 1995); *Wildflowers of the Columbia Gorge* (Jolley, 1988); *Plants of the Pacific Northwest coast: Washington, Oregon, British Columbia & Alaska* (Pojar and MacKinnon, 2004); *Wildflowers of the Pacific Northwest* (Turner and Gustafson, 2006); *Wildflowers of the western Cascades* (Ross and Chambers, 2005); *Pacific states wildflowers* (Niehaus and Peterson, 1998); *Encyclopedia of Pacific Northwest native plants for gardens and landscapes* (Robson et al., 2008); and *Wildflowers of Washington* (Lyons, 2000).

While the content of Floras may be directed primarily at an academic or professional botanical audience, it has important implications for publications further down the line, with information disseminating into the world of horticulture as well as natural history – and not just to books but websites, blogs and apps.

The retail price of a book and the numbers sold tend to reflect the complexity and accessibility of information at these different levels. More-technical, comprehensive books cost more and sell fewer copies. For example, in 40 years, the five-volume Flora (Hitchcock et al., 1959–69) at US$375 has sold fewer than 5000 copies. In a little less time, the condensed Flora, at the next level down, at $60 has sold 10 times as many. *Plants of the Pacific Northwest coast* (Pojar and MacKinnon, 2004), on the fourth level, was intended for a broad market, as the back-cover copy states: ' . . . residents who want to know more about their natural surroundings; students, scientists and resource specialists who require an up-to-date reference . . . and travellers who need a relatively simple and easy-to-use guide'. Covering a more limited geographical area than the Flora, and priced at $20, it has sold more than 100 000 copies in 13 years.

The presentation and usability of a book are also often indicative of the complexity of information and the intended audience. A detailed identification manual, presented mostly in the form of keys with some line illustrations and photographs in a section, is clearly aimed at an advanced reader. A photographic field guide, by contrast, with a colour-coded structure, brief descriptions and range maps, will be more accessible and relevant to an amateur audience.

4.3 What do end users want, and are publishers able to deliver this?

The priority for end users is the usefulness of the book, but how can this be defined? In a small, informal survey, a short questionnaire (Appendix 4.1) was sent to a number of Timber Press authors and readers, who can be roughly grouped as professionals (botanists, horticulture professionals, ecologists) and amateurs (natural history enthusiasts and serious gardeners). The survey asked what was most useful to them in plant information, whether from published books or electronic sources. In their responses, they were clear about their preferences, which matched my own observations after nearly 30 years publishing in this field.

Professionals said they looked for breadth and depth – as much information as possible in whatever forms are available, whether a Flora or a field guide, a book or online resource. Illustrations are desirable, but less essential than authoritative, descriptive text. The publishing process and the reputation of the publisher are very important for higher-level users. They acknowledge that editing can improve the accuracy and enhance the 'palatability' of information; that design and layout can make the difference between a book that is a pleasure and one that is a frustration; and that the reputation of the publishing company can validate the work – particularly when it's the author's first book. These users are looking for the same authority and credibility from online sources – and often not finding it.

Amateurs, on the other hand, want information that is immediately applicable to them, and that often means that it is synthesised and localised. They are looking for interpretation and ideas in addition to descriptions, and they value highly the writer's ability to make the information accessible and relevant. In general, they prefer books to online sources, and illustrations are very important, particularly colour photographs.

Publishers want and need to satisfy their market, but delivering what end users want is not always feasible for unsubsidised, commercial publishers. For Timber Press, field guides, plant encyclopaedias, and plant books with knowledgeable and engaging authors are generally successful and profitable. However, there are three kinds of information that readers want, but publishers like Timber Press find challenging to deliver:

1. breadth and depth of biodiversity information for professionals, such as in Floras;
2. horticultural monographs focused on a particular genus or group of plants; and
3. localised biodiversity information.

It may not be long before printed Floras are a thing of the past. The long gestation means they may be outdated before they are finished. The high editorial cost and often vast extent mean they are expensive to produce, their rate of sale is slow, and so publishers these days cannot afford to make the large, long-term investment required. Electronic delivery appears to be an obvious solution, but nobody except libraries is willing to pay for this and, until they are, publishers like Timber Press cannot provide it.

While there is a proliferation of online biodiversity information from institutions, groups and individuals, many of these sites are unsustainable in the long term. They often start with great zeal and countless hours of volunteer time, but subsequently peter out, with many existing sites incomplete or not regularly updated and maintained. Openness and flexibility are two great advantages of online delivery, but one downside is that these projects tend to be open-ended in terms of both time and expense. Many sites are driven by the enthusiasm and commitment of people with demanding jobs who simply do not have the time to devote to them. The information frequently lacks what users say they value highly – the editorial scrutiny, peer review and validation that publishers provide. If online biodiversity information sources are to be truly sustainable, there is a need to develop cooperative strategies to integrate and rationalise the numerous repositories and to bring to them the kinds of review and discipline that have always been so crucial in publishing.

The second challenging area, particularly for publishers like Timber Press, is horticultural monographs – an important link in the chain of published information that starts with Floras and continues with more popular books such as field guides and gardening books. Horticultural monographs have been at the heart of Timber Press's publishing programme since its inception, but are increasingly becoming less viable. The challenge is that they sell on average fewer than 1600 copies worldwide in the first year and sometimes not many more beyond that. There is a future for monographs, however, because they lend themselves to being published as print-on-demand or short-run digital-print books. In this form, they can be kept up to date, and the investment is limited to editing and layout, without the huge burden of printing and storing thousands of copies. With a limited market through normal book-trade outlets, it's logical for publishers to sell directly to end users via the internet. With no booksellers or wholesalers to take 50% of the price, monographs in limited runs may be no more expensive than a conventionally printed book.

The third area that poses a challenge for publishers is localised biodiversity information, whether for professionals or amateurs. The more geographically limited an area, the smaller the market and, therefore, the less appealing and viable for a publisher. However, it is precisely this depth and richness of localised information that will awaken people to the importance of a region or an ecosystem and inspire further research and conservation efforts. A book is more useful than an online source because it is portable and can be taken into the field. One appealing solution may be for publishers to have an archive of text and images that can be combined to make customised, localised field guides that can be printed in small runs.

4.4 New directions for plant books

While some of these newer publication models may offer solutions to the challenges facing publishers of biodiversity information, there will always be a demand for books in their traditional form. In order to keep their programmes dynamic and profitable, specialist publishers need to broaden their scope. At Timber Press, new topics come under the general heading of sustainability. Leading horticultural authors are now focusing on topics such as: how gardeners can encourage biodiversity; garden ecology; naturalistic landscape design and planting; low-maintenance, sustainable planting; and green roofs and rain gardens. For example: *Rain gardens* (Dunnett and Clay, 2007); *Planting green roofs and living walls* (Dunnett and Kingsbury, 2004); *Insects and gardens* (Grissell, 2006); *Teaming with microbes: a gardener's guide to the soil food web* (Lowenfels and Lewis, 2006); *Green roof plants: a resource and planting guide* (Snodgrass and Snodgrass, 2006); and *Bringing nature home: how native plants sustain wildlife in our gardens* (Tallamy, 2007).

Authors of traditional field guides and plant encyclopaedias have looked to Floras as key sources, but will the writers of these new-generation books also find Floras useful resources? What can the authors of higher-level publications include that would be useful and enriching to authors and readers of books aimed at a wider audience? This was one of the questions asked in the informal survey, and a common request – from ecologists, horticulturists, landscape architects and gardeners – was for descriptive plant information to be set in a broader ecological context. For instance, what is the importance of a particular plant in supporting biodiversity and, thus, the health of the ecosystem? Which insects and other animals depend on the plant, directly or indirectly? How can plants be used in the garden to best help the dependent animals?

Reforestation and landscape rehabilitation specialists, and landscape architects and gardeners designing naturalistic, low-maintenance plantings often group species that grow together in nature, so details of which species associate naturally is valuable. So too are clues about a particular habitat of a species. Does it grow in a mass or as a solitary plant? Does it occur on forest edges, in riparian corridors or on steep banks? What conditions allow a particular plant or community to thrive – or just survive, particularly with regard to water and soil type?

4.5 Conclusion

Descriptive biodiversity information is an early, sometimes the first, step in a chain of information that reaches increasingly widely into the community. Authors of Floras and higher-level publications can contribute to the relevance and usefulness of books at all levels by including more information about the ecological context of plants. Satisfying the authors' and end-users' needs and desires for information at many levels presents challenges for publishers like Timber Press, whose publication lists must be dynamic and forward looking while remaining commercially viable. While most are not yet embracing the electronic delivery of biodiversity information, publishers will continue to explore the possibilities and also look for viable ways to deliver what readers want in book form.

Appendix 4.1

The intention of the small, informal survey was to solicit comments and opinions from end users of botanical and horticultural information to support or challenge my own observations and round out my 'publisher's perspective'. It is neither rigorous nor stands up to scientific scrutiny. The following list of questions was sent to the people listed below. Some responded by email, others by phone or in person.

1. What level of plant information is most relevant to your interests? Flora, genus- or family-specific monograph, highly illustrated plant encyclopaedia aimed at horticulturists and gardeners, field guide?
2. Would you prefer to have access to this as a book or online?
3. Would you be willing to pay for this online?
4. How important is it to you that sources you use have been 'filtered' or validated by the publishing process, in particular editing?
5. How important is the reputation of a publisher in establishing the credibility of information, and organising and presenting it?
6. How important are illustrations? Do you prefer colour photographs or line drawings?
7. What do you want from descriptive plant/biodiversity information? Do you get it? What could be added to make it more widely useful?

8. Have you seen plant/biodiversity information presented in ways that are particularly interesting, novel, or useful – either published or online?

9. What do you consider an exemplary flora or presentation of plant/biodiversity information?

Respondents to the questionnaire were:

Allan M. Armitage: horticulture professional, academic, plant breeder, author.

Rick Darke: horticulture professional, landscape design consultant, ecologist, natural history enthusiast, serious home gardener, author.

Mark Fishbein: academic, ecologist, natural history enthusiast.

Lane Greer: horticulture professional, natural history enthusiast, serious home gardener, author.

Ann Littlewood: natural history enthusiast, serious home gardener.

John Long: horticulture professional, natural history enthusiast, serious home gardener.

Karen Suher: horticulture professional, natural history enthusiast, serious home gardener.

Douglas Tallamy: academic, ecologist, natural history enthusiast, serious home gardener.

References

Case, F. and Case, B. (1997). *Trilliums*. Portland, OR: Timber Press.

Davidson, B. L. (2000). *Lewisias*. Portland, OR: Timber Press.

Dunnett, N. and Clay, A. (2007). *Rain gardens: managing water sustainably in the garden and designed landscape*. Portland, OR: Timber Press.

Dunnett, N. and Kingsbury, N. (2004). *Planting green roofs and living walls*. Portland, OR: Timber Press.

Gerritsen, M. and Parsons, R. (2007). *Calochortus: mariposa lilies and their relatives*. Portland, OR: Timber Press.

Grissell, E. (2006). *Insects and gardens: in pursuit of a garden ecology*. Portland, OR: Timber Press.

Guard, B. J. (1995). *Wetland plants of Oregon and Washington*. Vancouver, BC: Lone Pine.

Hitchcock, C. L. and Cronquist, A. (1973). *Flora of the Pacific Northwest: an illustrated manual*. Vancouver, BC: University of Washington Press.

Hitchcock, C. L., Cronquist, A., Ownbey, M. and Thompson, J. W. (1959–69). *Vascular plants of the Pacific Northwest*, 5 volumes. Vancouver, BC: University of Washington Press.

Jolley, R. (1988). *Wildflowers of the Columbia Gorge: a comprehensive field guide*. Portland, OR: Oregon Historical Society

Kozloff, E. N. (2005). *Plants of western Oregon, Washington, and British Columbia*. Portland, OR: Timber Press.

Lowenfels, J. and Lewis, W. (2006). *Teaming with microbes: a gardener's guide to the soil food web*. Portland, OR: Timber Press.

Lyons, C. P. (2000). *Wildflowers of Washington*. Vancouver, BC: Lone Pine.

Niehaus, P. and Peterson, R. T. (1998). *Pacific states wildflowers*. New York, NY: Houghton Mifflin.

Nold, R. (1999). *Penstemons*. Portland, OR: Timber Press.

Pojar, J. and MacKinnon, A. (2004). *Plants of the Pacific Northwest coast: Washington, Oregon, British Columbia & Alaska*. Vancouver, BC: Lone Pine.

Robson, K. A., Richter, A. and Filbert, M. (2008). *Encyclopedia of Pacific Northwest native plants for gardens and landscapes*. Portland, OR: Timber Press.

Ross, R. A. and Chambers, H. L. (2005). *Wildflowers of the western Cascades*. Portland, OR: Timber Press.

Snodgrass, E. and Snodgrass, L. (2006). *Green roof plants: a resource and planting guide*. Portland, OR: Timber Press.

Tallamy, D. W. (2007). *Bringing nature home: how native plants sustain wildlife in our gardens*. Portland, OR: Timber Press.

Trehane, J. (2004). *Blueberries, cranberries and other vacciniums*. Portland, OR: Timber Press.

Turner, M. and Gustafson, P. (2006). *Wildflowers of the Pacific Northwest*. Portland, OR: Timber Press.

PART II

The products of descriptive taxonomy

Lessons learned from two projects, the Fauna Europaea and the *Checklist delle specie della fauna italiana*

A. MINELLI

5.1 Introduction

The Fauna Europaea[1] electronic database was completed around September 2004, crowning a four-year project financed by the European Union. The idea had been floated from at least 1995, when the *Checklist delle specie della fauna italiana* ('the Italian Checklist') of the animal species of Italy (Minelli et al., 1993–1995) was approaching completion, this offering a reference against which to evaluate the problems anticipated in a corresponding venture at a continental scale.

The Italian project had covered all metazoan groups, terrestrial, freshwater and marine (and also the protist taxa traditionally treated as 'animals' from a nomenclatural point of view), listing 57 468 species in total. Marine animals were excluded from Fauna Europaea as they had been covered by a different project, the European Register of Marine Species. The list eventually produced by the latter was released electronically[2] and in print (Costello et al., 2001) when the Fauna Europaea project was in its first year of activity.

---

[1] http://www.faunaeur.org   [2] http://www.marbef.org/data/erms.php

Descriptive Taxonomy: The Foundation of Biodiversity Research, eds M. F. Watson, C. H. C. Lyal and C. A. Pendry. Published by Cambridge University Press.

A long preparatory phase, largely developed with generous help from the Linnean Society of London, culminated in 1998 with the identification of three core institutions to which the leadership of Fauna Europaea was eventually entrusted: the Zoological Museum of the University of Amsterdam, the Zoological Museum of the University of Copenhagen and the Muséum National d'Histoire Naturelle in Paris. Success with the European Union application led to 4 years of intense activity, between 2000 and 2004, during which more than 400 specialists were involved in producing an updated, critical species list and collating information about distribution.

5.1.1 Fauna Europaea coverage

Information returned from the Fauna Europaea website covers taxonomy, nomenclature and geographical distribution. Users access the database through a very simple interface allowing a search by scientific name at the genus and/or species level. The information retrieved includes synonyms (with bibliographical reference to the work where the synonymy was first proposed) and the list of all subordinate taxa in the database. For species-level taxa, geographical distribution is given as presence/absence in individual countries (or major subunits of countries, especially when large islands or isolated archipelagos are involved). In its current version, the Fauna Europaea database includes entries for some 125 000 species and the genera into which they are grouped.

Originally, the Fauna Europaea project aimed at covering all non-marine species of metazoans in Europe. At the time of the first release, it was estimated that a few thousand species entries had still to be added, the largest missing set being a subgroup of the staphylinid beetles. I will briefly outline below some critical steps in the history of the Fauna Europaea project, as a background for a subsequent discussion of the most important lessons we learned from this work.

To be sure, Fauna Europaea did not grow on bare ground. Neither did it simply grow by establishing or tightening up a network of lower-scale, perhaps national, previously existing databases of animal species. There was no chance, indeed, of establishing such a network, for the simple reason that the vast majority of European countries did not possess a comprehensive species list for their national fauna. However, as such a list was available for one country, i.e. Italy, it was sensible to use this product as a blueprint for the larger project to be developed at European scale. Nevertheless, two big problems had to be studied anew. One was the geographical framework for the new database; the other was its informatics infrastructure.

As for geography, we needed (a) to decide whether to follow the geographical (physical) boundaries of Europe strictly, or to allow for some exceptions; (b) to adopt a sensible and definitely agreed list of geographical units for each of which to record the presence of the individual species and, last but not least; (c) to use updated but also (so far as possible) uncontroversial names for these (political) units. The eventual result of lengthy discussion and negotiation was a standard list of geographical names (see Guidelines for contributors[3]).

This chapter is not the best place to illustrate the computer science aspects of the project. I will only mention that the Amsterdam team successfully developed a very sophisticated import tool, through which the individual contributors were able to check their spreadsheets for internal consistency and completeness quite easily by themselves, and eventually to correct them, before submitting the data to the technical staff of Fauna Europaea.

On other topics, decisions were largely similar to those previously adopted for the Italian Checklist. In particular, we decided to include the following categories of species:

- *Indigenous*, operationally defined as the species recorded after 1600 as naturally belonging to the area, either permanently or as regular (seasonal or occasional) migrants.

- *Adventitious*, including organisms that have become naturalised in existing eco-systems, invasive organisms that successfully tend to disrupt existing ecosystems and synanthropic organisms that can only establish spontaneous, viable populations in 'man-made' habitats.

- *Cryptogenic*, i.e. widespread species not demonstrably indigenous or adventitious in the area.

Whereas excluded were:

- *Domesticated* or sub-domesticated, exotic and other species that do not establish spontaneous, viable populations out of human captivity.

- Exotic imports or *casual intruders* that for climatic or other reasons cannot establish spontaneous, viable populations.

- *Fossil* species, including species that have suffered regional extinction before 1600.

5.2 Taxonomic scope and arrangement

Contributors were allowed to distinguish subspecies, but no real effort at a complete coverage of intraspecific taxa was attempted for all groups. Synonyms were included, but in this case too the database was not expected to register all accepted synonyms, but only those that had been in use as valid names within the last few decades. The database aimed to be authoritative for genus- and species-level

---

[3] http://www.faunaeur.org/documents/FaEu_Guidelines_v4.0.1.pdf

taxonomy and nomenclature, but not for suprageneric taxa. Nevertheless, a large effort was made to place all genera covered by Fauna Europaea within a searchable consensus tree inclusive of taxa between the phylum and each family included. A comprehensive taxonomic framework had also been provided to the users of the Italian Checklist, but in this respect there are major differences between the approach eventually adopted in this work and the different choice followed in Fauna Europaea. The main difference is not so much in the degree of completeness of the hierarchical tree made available to the users of either database (more detail is available from Fauna Europaea), as in the way this information is actually accessible. In Fauna Europaea, taxa of the same rank within an immediately higher taxon are only retrievable in alphabetic order. For example, a query for the full list of European mammals will return a list opening with the members of the Bovidae, with 11 species listed alphabetically, as follows:

Ammotragus lervia (Pallas, 1777)

Bison bonasus (Linnaeus, 1758)

Bos primigenius Bojanus, 1827

Capra aegagrus Erxleben, 1777

Capra ibex Linnaeus, 1758

Capra pyrenaica Schinz, 1838

Ovibos moschatus (Zimmermann, 1780)

Ovis aries Linnaeus, 1758

Rupicapra pyrenaica Bonaparte, 1845

Rupicapra rupicapra (Linnaeus, 1758)

Saiga tatarica (Linnaeus, 1766)

One may object to the listing of *Bison* and *Bos* between *Ammotragus* and *Capra*, but this is arguably a minor shortcoming. I would expect many users to be unhappy if this taxonomic mix derived from alphabetic listing extended to families within the whole of the mammals (and beyond). In fact, next to the 11 members of the family Bovidae, the query's return from Fauna Europaea will list the European representatives of Canidae, Castoridae, Cercopithecidae, Cervidae, Dipodidae, Equidae, Erinaceidae, Felidae, Herpestidae, Hystricidae, Leporidae, Macropodidae, Molossidae, Muridae, Mustelidae, Myocastoridae, Myoxidae, Ochotonidae, Odobenidae, Phocidae, Procyonidae, Pteropodidae, Rhinolophidae, Sciuridae, Soricidae, Suidae, Talpidae, Ursidae, Vespertilionidae and Viverridae, in this order. There is of course a rationale behind the choice of avoiding any ordering criteria but the alphabetic. Why should we list arthropods before chordates, but next to molluscs? Why do we usually put mammals, rather than birds or teleosts, at the end of the list of vertebrate taxa? Support for such a use comes from tradition (or cultural inertia) rather than from nature (or progress in phylogenetic knowledge).

Nevertheless, I see a big advantage in keeping such ordering available (with sensible updates now and then) compared to a 'hypotheses-free' alphabetic listing as in the mammal example just provided. I will give here only one, but in my opinion serious, argument in favour of conserving a consolidated sequence – although often a phylogenetically inadequate one – in listing the taxa. This argument is provided by the use of taxonomic lists in arranging specimens in a museum collection. Recently, when paying my first visit to the Museum für Naturkunde in Stuttgart, I asked Dr. Wolfgang Schawaller, who was kindly showing me through the insect collections, about the criteria they have followed in arranging the beetles. He told me that the collection had been arranged according to the classic, multi-volume *Coleopterorum catalogus* (Junk and Schenkling, 1910–1940). That is, in the traditional order. No guarantee of phylogenetic standards, to be sure, but something much more informative than plain alphabetic order. On this basis alone, it took me one minute to find out the couple of drawers containing one of my favourite genera (*Sagra*, Chrysomelidae), without any help from electronic databases and, of course, from any previous knowledge of the local insect collection, holding 1.5 million beetle specimens. In the drawers close to those containing specimens of *Sagra* there were, as expected, representatives of other chrysomelid taxa one might wish to have immediately available for comparison. This was much better than having, close to *Sagra*, alphabetical neighbours such as specimens of *Sagrina* (Foraminifera) or *Sagriva* (Hemiptera), or the alphabetically closest genus names within Coleoptera, or Chrysomelidae, depending on the level of name pooling.

5.3 Lessons learned

Perhaps a costly but eventually rewarding strategy would be to enter species names in the database accompanied by an appropriate set of metadata that would allow a future user to choose among a set of alternative listings, including phylogenetic, traditional classificatory and plain alphabetical.

To preserve the traditional order in listing taxa, in the Italian Checklist we added a numerical code to the individual taxon name that allows immediate association of a genus, or species, with its traditional 'relatives'. The coding system was made flexible to allow subsequent addition of new entries. These codes were provided in the original printed version of the Italian Checklist, produced in the years 1993–1995, before realising what meagre use the average reader can make of them. However, the basic choice not to discard traditional listing order in favour of the alphabetical order was and, in my opinion still remains, important to be taken into account when planning a new taxonomic database, especially one whose scope is broader than a single animal or plant family.

Of the other important lessons learned in developing the Fauna Europaea database, I will briefly mention the primacy of sound taxonomic background over the simple mining and collation of distribution data, and the need for long-term investment of human and material resources. I will discuss in more detail another aspect: how to assemble an international team for such a venture and to steer it towards the common target.

Common experience with discussion lists on the internet may suggest that an active community can evolve easily by self-assembly. Let's float a question and a lot of interested people will offer comments, criticism and insight. Membership will fluctuate, but may eventually stabilise, especially if the debate is sensibly moderated. Thus, if we want to build up a database of, say, all the animal species known to exist in a country, an active working group will coalesce easily, as soon as the project is flagged via the internet. I do not think that this is a viable option. Self-assembly requires a good degree of homogeneity among the elements (in this case, people) expected to gather together spontaneously. But homogeneity is an unlikely property of the kind of community required to cooperate in a project like Fauna Europaea. There are many reasons for that.

First, among taxonomists there are both professionals and amateurs. Proportions among these two components are very different according to the taxa involved, but a comprehensive project like Fauna Europaea will necessarily include the professionals working, say, on nematodes and mites, together with the non-professionals among which we must recruit the specialists for several families of beetles, moths or flies. Attitudes of professionals and amateurs, when facing the opportunity to join a project like Fauna Europaea, can be profoundly different. One aspect is money. From the perspective of a professional taxonomist, working for the database can be just a part of his/her paid job, but an amateur may refuse to offer nontrivial help without financial reward. Other, not necessarily minor, difficulties may derive from the requirement to share unpublished information, especially if individual contributions to the multi-authored project are not likely to be distinctly acknowledged.

Another heterogeneity within the community of potential contributors to a project like Fauna Europaea is between 'true' taxonomists and people with good experience in identifying specimens and in producing accurate faunal lists, but largely insensitive to the taxonomic problems continuously emerging even in the traditionally best investigated groups. Thus, we cannot take for granted that all contributors will use the same names for the same taxa, or mine the literature for distribution data in the same way. Other differences can be expected from people educated in different national traditions, as some communities, e.g. in the Eastern European countries, have long inclined towards 'splitting', and others, especially in Western Europe, towards 'lumping'; some agreement must necessarily be obtained before data provided by all of them are eventually released for public access.

Finally, there are different attitudes in respect to the codes of nomenclature. When acting as managing editor for the Italian Checklist, I discovered to my amazement that dozens of my 274 authors had never seen a copy of the *International code of zoological nomenclature* ('the Code'; International Commission on Zoological Nomenclature, 1999), so that hundreds of entries had to be individually checked for agreement with the Code, and often needed be corrected. But the problem with nomenclature is not only the existence of the knowledgeable and the ignorant, but also the presence of communities, as among the lepidopterists, that are explicitly critical of some of the Code's provisions and obstinately refuse to accept them. A typical example of this 'rebellious' attitude concerns the grammatical agreement in gender between the genus name and the specific epithet. Many lepidopterists refuse to follow Article 31.2 of the Code, which prescribes gender agreement, and conserve the original spelling of the epithet unchanged, even if the species is moved to a different genus whose grammatical gender is different from the original. Clearly, disagreement on these rules causes a problem of consistency within the database.

This manifold lack of homogeneity within the taxonomic community should not, and cannot, be ignored. To some extent, its very existence contributes critical ideas and invites steady refinement of the ongoing work. But this is something we cannot expect to happen without guidance. The working community needs continuous, careful steering. The project must proceed towards a fixed deadline, which must be taken seriously by all partners. On the other hand, difficulties must be expected and solutions must be adopted. This is only possible if problems are revealed in a timely manner, in advance of the project's deadline. But we cannot expect that a contributor experiencing problems will immediately flag them, and ask for help or replacement. In a self-assembled, autonomously evolving community, such a partner would simply disappear from the discussion, but the problem will remain, perhaps unnoticed, for a long while.

A mildly moderated website may offer a suitable environment for a friendly, constructive discussion, but ventures like Fauna Europaea and the Italian Checklist are of a completely different nature. These are projects rather than umbrellas and, as such, require leadership – intelligent, friendly, but also firm leadership. Especially in large-scale projects, we cannot take anything for granted. We cannot read a contributor's silence about his/her work as a proof that he or she is regularly progressing, without problems, with his/her share of work. Neither can we wait until the project's deadline before checking, informally at least, how things are actually going on. We cannot take for granted that the taxonomic scope of each contributor's work has been defined unambiguously; this can always be questionable, because of the changing nature of classification. A set of genera recently moved from family A to family B may fail to be listed simply because the specialist for family A adopts the updated circumscription of this taxon whereas the specialist for family B follows a less recent classification. This happens, indeed, but a project manager should be able to discover the problem in time. With the Italian Checklist, I got the list of nemerteans from a marine biologist who failed to include one genus, because this lives in fresh water rather than in the sea. A dipterist without training in applied entomology provided an otherwise good list for the psychodids, but omitted the genus *Phlebotomus* which is traditionally studied by medical entomologists. The copepods were contributed by several people, three of them respectively listing the marine planktonic, the benthonic and the parasitic or otherwise host-associated forms and another two contributing the list of the freshwater taxa; all of this eventually resulted in the total omission of one small family.

Summing up, if the traditional tools for archiving and retrieving nomenclatural and taxonomic information were badly inadequate to serve our current needs, neither does modern information technology offer an automatic solution to our problems, especially those deriving from the idiosyncrasies of the social and intellectual structure of our community of both producers and users of taxonomic information.

Acknowledgements

I am very grateful to Chris Lyal and an anonymous reviewer for their useful suggestions on a previous version of this article and to the Systematics Association for encouraging and supporting my participation in the Edinburgh meeting.

References

Costello, M. J., Emblow, C. and White, R. (eds) (2001). *European Register of Marine Species, a check-list of the marine species in Europe and a bibliography of guides to their identification (Patrimoines naturels 50)*. Paris: Muséum National d'Histoire Naturelle.

International Commission on Zoological Nomenclature (1999). *International code of zoological nomenclature*, Fourth Edition. London: International Trust for Zoological Nomenclature.

Junk, W. and Schenkling, S. (eds) (1910–1940). *Coleopterorum catalogus*. Berlin: W. Junk.

Minelli, A., Ruffo, S. and La Posta, S. (eds) (1993–1995). *Checklist delle specie della fauna italiana*. Bologna: Calderini.

6

Flora Europaea and Euro+Med

S. L. JURY

6.1 *Flora Europaea*

Flora Europaea was a project originally proposed by Werner Rothmaler, but to cover a larger area, including the Caucasus, Transjordan and parts of North Africa (see preface to the first edition, Tutin et al., 1964; Anon., 1977; Jury, 2006). However, no formal proposal was accepted at a session of the eighth International Botanical Congress in Paris in 1954, and so it was taken up by a group of British and Irish senior university botanists who decided to go it alone. They had a difficult start and, for several years, little success in obtaining funding from research councils. Sponsorship by the Linnean Society of London gave scientific credibility and provided a meeting place, but no funding. It was a project many people said could not be done, and others said that, if it was, it would lead to a significant downturn in taxonomic research. Undaunted, this initial group formed an Editorial Committee in 1956 of six leading botanists, under the Chairmanship of Professor Tom Tutin and with Professor Vernon Heywood as Secretary. The members of the Editorial Committee, Messrs Tutin (Leicester), Heywood (Liverpool, later Reading), Alan Burges (Liverpool, later Ulster), David Valentine (Durham, later Manchester), Max Walters (Cambridge) and David Webb (Trinity College Dublin), were encouraged by the late Maybud Campbell, who provided morale-boosting claret at strategic low points and significant financial contributions at crucial moments. They were

Descriptive Taxonomy: The Foundation of Biodiversity Research, eds M. F. Watson, C. H. C. Lyal and C. A. Pendry. Published by Cambridge University Press.

all remarkable in the way they doggedly persisted with the project until significant financial support was forthcoming from the UK science-funding body, DSIR (Department for Scientific and Industrial Research, a forerunner of the present day Research Councils).

Flora Europaea was innovative in a number of important aspects. The generic accounts were written by their respective taxonomic experts, whenever possible and wherever they were based, although it should be noted that many were authored by the editors. Fifty-one botanists contributed to volume one, with a total of 187 contributors for the completed five volumes (Webb, 1978: 9). The draft accounts were then subjected to a rigorous review process. 'Externally authored' manuscripts were circulated around the Editorial Committee as a 'Stage One' manuscript. Editorial comments and corrections (mainly concerned with style) were incorporated and the whole retyped onto off-set lithography stencils before duplicating as a 'Stage Two' manuscript to be circulated to a team of 31 Regional Advisors (representing all the *Flora Europaea* territories) and nine Advisory Editors. The late J. E. Dandy, of the then British Museum (Natural History), was an Advisory Editor who checked the place of publication for every species, resulting in the discovery of many nomenclatural errors. This wide circulation was important, for it not only resulted in a large number of corrections being made, but it also gave the work a Europe-wide dimension and stamp of approval. Controversial decisions, including the use of English (as opposed to Latin) and Engler's classification (out-dated at the time, but in widespread use across the European continent) have proved to have been correct, even if they were hotly contested at the time (D. A. Webb, pers. comm.). The choice of format, especially that of adopting two-letter codes for the territories, has proved popular and been copied in many other Floras that followed (e.g. *Flora Meso-Americana* and *Flora Iberica*). The *Flora Europaea* rules were set at the Leicester Editorial Committee meeting in 1956 and published by Heywood (1958), with a supplement two years later (Heywood, 1960). All new taxa and new combinations were published separately in a series of 20 *Notulae* (the last with a later Addendum) in *Feddes Repertorium* and the *Botanical Journal of the Linnean Society*. These were later reprinted, without change of pagination, in a single volume with an introduction and index (Heywood, 1986).

The persistence of the Editors paid off and a series of grants enabled the project to be completed with the fifth and final volume delivered to Cambridge University Press in 1977, and published in 1980. Throughout this effort, the Editorial team remained the same, except for the addition of Professor David Moore (Reading) for work on volume two and later volumes. Editorial Assistants changed during the project but Arthur Chater (Leicester, later Reading) remained throughout. By the time the final volume was completed, the Editorial Committee realised that the earlier volumes were somewhat out-of-date, because, far from suppressing the taxonomic research of European plants, *Flora Europaea* seemed to have significantly stimulated the discipline. Many new European taxa had been described and needed evaluation before incorporation into the *Flora Europaea* dataset. Volume one was not only the most out-of-date, but as it had numerous errors and lacked the consistency and rigor of the later volumes, the Editorial Committee decided it must be revised. Although the main project had been funded though grants, the volumes had been published commercially by Cambridge University Press, who had paid royalties into the *Flora Europaea* Trust Fund managed by the Linnean Society. This resulted in a significant sum of money accruing, enough to employ Dr John Akeroyd to revise volume one in 1983.

Akeroyd, with minimal secretarial support, did a remarkable job. A good, all-round taxonomist who had specialised in the Mediterranean, he had a good knowledge of not only the plants, but also the active taxonomic botanists of Europe. Akeroyd can claim some pretty impressive statistics for the new edition of volume 1, with approximately a 10% increase in taxa: 250 extra species and 150 subspecies added (Akeroyd and Jury, 1991). For example, the first edition enumerated 166 species of *Silene*, including a further 34 species mentioned in 'observations'. After revision this increased to 194 species with 16 in 'observations'. The task proved to be much more substantial than originally envisaged, and if the Editors had realised just how much work was needed, it is questionable if the revision would have ever gone ahead. One of the main concerns of the Editorial Committee was that it had not been possible to implement the full *Flora Europaea* revisionary process with its Regional Advisors scrutinising the various stages of the manuscripts, and, thus, the work lacks the European *imprimatur et nihil obstat*. However, the Council of Europe adopted the *Flora Europaea* nomenclature and so it has been used in its legislation. After the revision was published (Tutin et al., 1993), the revision of further volumes was considered (Cambridge University Press even raised this issue with the *Flora Europaea* Residuary Body in 2008); however, no funding body appears to want to support such a venture.

Two outstanding successes of *Flora Europaea* are the bringing together of Europe's botanists to work and collaborate in a way previously unimagined, and the stimulation of taxonomic research to solve taxonomic problems highlighted in the volumes (Jury, 2006). The *Flora Iberica* project has so far published 17 volumes (18 if you count the 2 large parts of volume 7 dealing with the *Leguminosae*) of a proposed 21 and work continues apace on the remainder with 2 volumes at proof stage (Castroviejo, 1986–2012). Two volumes of *Flora Hellenica* (Strid and Tan, 1997, 2002) out of a total of about 10 have so far been published. These two areas represent two of the Mediterranean, and indeed European, hotspots, that still lack complete, high-quality, modern floristic works. Both projects have resulted in numerous new taxonomic discoveries and the publication of many new taxa and combinations; Castroviejo (2006) gives data from *Flora Iberica*. Also, numerous monographical works have been published for groups in the Euro–Med region (the combined *Flora Europaea* and *Med-Checklist* areas), e.g. that of Diaz Lifante (1996) for *Asphodelus* where the total 5 species with 6 taxa included in *Flora Europaea* has increased to 12 species and about 21 taxa, with 25 in the whole Euro+Med area.

6.2 ESFEDS

In 1981, Heywood led the way forward for European floristics by setting up an electronic system, known by its acronym ESFEDS (European Science Foundation European Documentation System) with support from the European Science Foundation (Heywood et al., 1984; Packer and Kiger, 1989; Jury, 1991). An Oracle database system was set up on a mini-computer that contained all the *Flora Europaea* nomenclature using a system of colour codes for accepted names, synonyms, etc. This was novel at the time and resulted in a considerable amount of computer science research in addition to the botanical. It comprised the *Flora Europaea* data, with corrections, although considerable effort was made to update the ferns with help from Clive Jermy of the Natural History Museum, London. Since the revision to *Flora Europaea* volume one was published after the completion of ESFEDS, the taxonomy and nomenclature of the revision had not been incorporated. Although the main aim of ESFEDS had been the production of a published checklist, funding for the project, through the European Science Foundation Country Consortium, failed and this product was never produced. However, a checklist of European pteridophytes was generated from the relational database and published (Derrick et al., 1987). This was the first comprehensive checklist of European pteridophytes with full synonymy and distribution information for the 329 accepted taxa. ESFEDS was a project ahead of its time and has been criticised for having had to spend too much time struggling to solve problems relating to computer science rather than concentrating on botanical aspects (Jury, 2006).

6.3 Euro+Med PlantBase

In 1988, the Linnean Society set up a 'Pan-European Flora and Database Initiative' discussion group as part of its Bicentenary celebrations. This kindled discussions amongst European botanists, and a few years later a steering group approached the European Union with an ultimately unsuccessful 'Concerted Action' to fund a Europe-wide floristic database project. As this group had become dormant, a new 18-member group was convened in Reading in October 1996 under the heading 'The Pan-European Initiative in Plant Systematics', sponsored by the *Flora Europaea* Trust Fund (Jury, 2006). A Steering Group of Vernon Heywood, Stephen Jury, Franco Raimondo and Benito Valdés was elected and the 'Euro-Mediterranean Initiative in Plant Systematics' was born, later to become 'Project

Sisyphus' and finally 'Euro+Med PlantBase'. International meetings were held in Palermo, June 1997, and Seville, June 1998, which resulted in a successful application for funding to the European Union Commission, Framework V, in June 1999. Euro+Med PlantBase was funded for 3 years from 1999.

The ESFEDS database provided the starting point for the Euro+Med PlantBase project. The late Richard Pankhurst developed Pandora software to add in the updates of the second edition of *Flora Europaea* volume one and to merge this with the data from the three published *Med-Checklist* volumes (Greuter et al., 1984–1989) and the fourth edition of the *Flora of Macaronesia: checklist of vascular plants* (Hansen and Sunding, 1993). The project also added additional names accepted in over 100 standard Floras for the Euro+Med area, published after *Flora Europaea* or *Med-Checklist* (or from the corresponding families not yet covered by *Med-Checklist*). This 'appending' process was carried out by Euro+Med partners with regional responsibilities (the 'Input Centres') in Seville (Western Europe and North and West Africa), Bratislava (Central and Northern Europe), Palermo (Southern Europe, Egypt, Libya and the Middle East) and Sofia (Eastern Europe), using software written by Pankhurst. All these data were merged and family reports produced for editing by a team of Editors, after which the equivalent of the *Flora Europaea* Regional Advisors (now over 70) scrutinise the data for their territories.

It was recognised at the outset that the editing would have to be done by a truly international team, not confined to just two countries as *Flora Europaea* had been. Only Spain could claim enough trained taxonomists, but they were heavily engaged on their own *Flora Iberica* and other regional projects (Castroviejo, 1986–2012). Walter Berendsohn and his team in Berlin developed the software for a web-based editor that can access the central database remotely through the internet and allow editorial changes to the database (Geoffroy et al., 2004). This allows dispersed taxonomists to take responsibility for their areas of expertise. The European Union-funded European Distributed Institute of Taxonomy (EDIT) programme has developed a significantly improved version, which allows larger-scale editing and is more user-friendly. Euro+Med PlantBase has transferred its database from Pandora to the Berlin Taxonomic Information Model, which was already being used by a number of other large plant-based projects[1]. It is now part of the Pan-European Species directories Infrastructure (PESI) project, which was funded by the European Union, Framework 7 Capacities Work Programme[2].

Euro+Med had also been concerned to link its verified synonymic core data to other databases with additional information. So far, Euro+Med has worked with Pertti Uotila and the Atlas Florae Europaeae project in Helsinki, Finland, the PhytoKaryon database of cytological information in Patras, Greece, and the

---

[1] http://www.bgbm.org/biodivinf/docs/bgbm-model/software.htm
[2] http://www.emplantbase.org

University of Bern, Switzerland and their contractors, Verlag für interactive Medien, Gaggenau for information on conservation. It has looked for additional funding to develop these further and add other data sources. These 'beads' of Euro+Med verified data also link on to other websites. This was an idea developed by Heywood to obtain maximum usefulness for the greatest number of people.

The second main objective of the project was to produce new taxonomic revisions for the whole Euro+Med area. Groups were chosen to represent different areas of interest (e.g. plants important for conservation and listed by sites, crop wild relatives, critical taxa, etc.). These included: *Acis*, *Galanthus*, *Leucojum* (*Amaryllidaceae*), *Anthriscus*, (*Apiaceae*), *Launaea* (*Asteraceae*), *Brassica*, *Cardamine* (*Brassicaceae*), *Erodium*, *Geranium* (*Geraniaceae*) and *Asphodelus* (*Liliaceae*). Sixteen authors in six countries were involved in their production.

As of August 2013, Euro+Med PlantBase provides access to information on 154 plant families, corresponding to 91% of the European flora of vascular plants.

References

Akeroyd, J. R. and Jury, S.L. (1991). Updating 'Flora Europaea'. *Botanika Chronika*, **10**: 49–54.

Anon. (1977). Brief history of the *Flora Europaea* project. In *Flora Europaea Final Symposium Cambridge, 31 August – 4 September 1977*. Cambridge: Cambridge University Press.

Castroviejo, S. (ed.) (1986–2012). *Flora Iberica*, volumes **1–8**, **10**, **11–15**, **17**, **18** and **21**. Madrid: Real Jardín Botánico, CSIC.

Castroviejo, S. (2006). Taxonomy, Floras and conservation. In *Taxonomy and Conservation*, E. Leadlay and S. L. Jury (eds). Cambridge: Cambridge University Press, pp. 96–100.

Derrick, L. N., Jermy, A. C. and Paul, A. M. (1987). A checklist of European pteridophytes. *Sommerfeltia*, **6**: i–xx, 1–94.

Diaz Lifante, Z. (1996). Revisión del género Asphodelus L. (Asphodelaceae) en el Mediterráneo Occidental. *Boissiera*, **52**: 1–189.

Geoffroy, M., Güntsch, A. and Berendsohn, W. G. (2004). Teleworking for taxonomists – The Berlin Model Internet Editor. In *Abstracts and Programme, International Scientific Symposium 'Botanic Gardens: Awareness for Biodiversity'*, E. Zippel, W. Greuter and A.-D. Stevens (eds). Moraga, CA: International Scientific Symposium, pp. 54–55.

Greuter, W., Burdet, H. M. and Long, G. (eds) (1984, 1986, 1989). *Med-Checklist*, vols **1**, **3** and **4**. Genève: Conservatoire et Jardin Botanique de la Ville du Genève; Berlin: Botanic Garden and Botanical Museum Berlin-Dahlem.

Hansen, A. and Sunding, P. (1993). Flora of Macaronesia. Checklist of vascular plants, Fourth Edition. *Sommerfeldia*, **17**: 1–295.

Heywood, V. H. (ed.) (1958). *The presentation of taxonomic information: a short guide to contributors of Flora Europaea*. Leicester: Leicester University Press.

Heywood, V. H. (ed.) (1960). *The presentation of taxonomic information: a short guide to contributors of Flora*

Europaea, supplement. Leicester: Leicester University Press.

Heywood, V. H. (ed.) (1986). *Flora Europaea Notulae Systematicae ad Floram Europaeam Spectantes.* Koenigstein: Koeltz Scientific Books.

Heywood, V. H., Moore, D. M., Derrick, L. N., Mitchell, K. A. and Scheepen, J. Van (1984). The European taxonomic, floristic and biosystematic documentation system. In *Databases in systematics,* R. Allkin and F. A. Bisby (eds). London: Academic Press, pp. 79–89.

Jury, S. L. (1991). Some recent computer-based developments in plant taxonomy. *Botanical Journal of the Linnean Society,* **106**: 121–128.

Jury, S. L. (2006). Good networks: supporting the infrastructure for taxonomy and conservation. In *Taxonomy and conservation,* E. Leadlay and S. L. Jury (eds). Cambridge: Cambridge University Press, pp. 305–314.

Packer, J. G. and Kiger, R. W. (1989). *Flora Europaea* and the European documentation system. In *Floristics for the twenty-first century,* N. Morin, R. D. Whetstone, R. D. Wilken and K. L. Tomlinson (eds). St Louis: Missouri Botanical Garden, pp. 8–10.

Strid, A. and Tan, K. (eds) (1997). *Flora Hellenica,* volume **1**. Koenigstein: Koeltz Scientific Books.

Strid, A. and Tan, K. (eds) (2002). *Flora Hellenica,* volume **2**. Ruggell: A. R. G. Gantner Verlag K. G.

Tutin, T. G., Heywood, V. H., Burges, N. A., Moore, D. M., Valentine, D. H., Walters, S. M. and Webb, D. A. (1964–1980). *Flora Europaea,* volume **1**. Cambridge: Cambridge University Press.

Tutin, T. G., Burges, N. A., Chater, A. O., Edmondson, J. R., Heywood, V. H., Moore, D. M., Valentine, D. H., Walters, S. M. and Webb, D. A. (1993). *Flora Europaea,* volumes **1–5**, Second Edition. Cambridge: Cambridge University Press.

Webb, D. A. (1978). *Flora Europaea*: a retrospective. *Taxon*: **27**: 3–14.

7

Increasing the utility of the regional African Floras

D. W. Kirkup, P. Malcolm and A. Paton

7.1 Introduction

The *Flora of tropical East Africa* ('FTEA'; Beentje et al., 1948–2012) and *Flora Zambesiaca* ('FZ'; Pope et al., 1960–onging) are comprehensive regional projects that deal with the nomenclature, identification, description, geographical distribution, ecology and ethnobotany of vascular plant species. Begun almost 50 years ago and now nearing completion, they were conceived primarily as a platform for further detailed monographical research, just as they themselves may be based on earlier accounts in the *Flora of tropical Africa*. Although very useful for the identification of species, these Floras were designed to be used by taxonomists in the herbarium. The sheer physical bulk of the works (FZ currently stands at 53 volumes containing c. 8000 species), which is a consequence of the level of detail they contain, effectively limits their use in the field.

Half a century after their inception, the world is a very different place from the one in which these Flora projects were conceived: the pace of habitat and biodiversity loss has accelerated to levels that would have been unimaginable then; man-induced climate change is an accepted reality now that few would have entertained even 20 years ago; and there has been a technological revolution in the way in which we communicate and share information. Against this background, we might ask

Descriptive Taxonomy: The Foundation of Biodiversity Research, eds M. F. Watson, C. H. C. Lyal and C. A. Pendry. Published by Cambridge University Press.

what is the relevance of these 'monographic' Floras, which fill our library book-shelves, to today's needs?

It might be assumed that the works have a broad usage but they are hardly accessible. A simple nomenclatural query could prove extremely difficult for a non-expert to resolve from a poorly indexed, multi-volume hard-copy text, partic-ularly if the original text exists only in a few libraries. Even potential user-groups of professionals have failed to engage with the works; for example, it is widely held (amongst taxonomists at least) that ecologists hardly ever use Floras for identifica-tion, in particular shying away from using the keys.

Yet in our present day quest for understanding our rapidly changing environ-ment, taxonomic information has never been at such a premium: species identi-fication, the attachment of the correct name to an organism, underpins ecological research and ethnobotanical study as much as it does systematics, and it is the gateway to all literature concerning that organism. Even though the content of the Floras is largely governed by their original intended purpose (i.e. largely taxonomic research), the *prima facie* case seems that the information contained in Floras is greatly under-utilised: the contention is that the potential readership is far broader than taxonomy alone, extending to ecologists, economists and the education sector.

In 2000 at Kew we began to explore ways of making the African Floras mentioned above more accessible, primarily by capture of the hard copy information and making it searchable via the internet. Two key uses of floristic information were identified through discussion with various institutions and individuals. These uses can be summarised as:

1. A 'checklist' query which seeks to enable a user to find out about plants which match selection criteria, e.g. 'Which species of a particular plant family occur in Northern Malawi?'

2. A 'nomenclatural' query allows a user to establish the accepted name for a plant and its synonyms and thus enable the user to find out all available information concerning a particular species.

In this chapter we describe how we approached the digitisation of Kew's African Floras: focusing on FZ and FTEA, but including *Flora of tropical Africa* ('FTA', Oliver, 1868–1902), *Flora Capensis* ('FC'; Harvey and Sonder, 1860–1933) and *Flora of west tropical Africa* ('FWTA', Hutchinson et al., 1927–ongoing). We high-light what we see as the particular strengths of content of a Flora that we can build upon for production of a range of outputs, which will make possible further work on the plant diversity Africa.

7.2 The Floras

The characteristics of the regional African Floras are described in Kirkup et al. (2005). They are largely complementary in geographical scope apart from FTA which overlaps with the three newer (more or less contemporaneous) tropical Floras FWTA, FTEA and FZ. The temperate Southern African FC covers the same area as (and is the basis for many of the accounts contained in) the modern *Flora of South Africa*.

Rather unsurprisingly, each Flora contains essentially the same sorts of information, but varies in their individual format and layout, and in the level of detail presented. Given the long time span over which these projects have run, and the variety of contributors that have been involved, there is often variation in presentation to be found between the earlier and later volumes within the same Flora.

The sequence of families in each Flora is based on the Bentham and Hooker classification system (1862–1883). The accepted scientific names below family level are followed by their authority and references to relevant literature. For taxon at species rank and below, the place of publication and date are also cited. Synonymy is given for names at genus level and below, which is quite extensive in the case of FTA and FZ, but less so for FWTA, and in any case is largely limited to the area under review and adjacent regions. As comprehensive research Floras, both FTEA and FZ cite type material for the accepted names of species, giving the collector name, locality, and the names of the herbaria where the material is housed (FTEA also provides the types of synonyms).

Dichotomous keys, either of the bracketed or indented type, provide a means of identification to all taxa in the Flora area from family level down to infraspecific rank. Descriptions of the taxa generally cover the range of morphological variation as found within the Flora area and are intended to be concise and diagnostic rather than comprehensive or comparative, their aim being to serve as a check on the keyed out taxa. In the 'excursion flora' format of FWTA, much of the descriptive information is included within the keys, the actual species descriptions themselves being very condensed.

The geographical distribution of the species in the area covered is summarised according to the particular system of geographical or botanical division adopted in the Flora. In FWTA, FTEA and FZ the primary division is at geographical country level. For FTEA and FZ below this there is further division into 'Flora' districts, which seem partly to be based on administrative boundaries, but also may relate to botanical regions. The older FTA, which covers a much larger area than any of the individual Floras mentioned above, generally employs larger territories, some of which equate to modern-day countries, but many of which have no modern geopolitical equivalent. Even in the more modern FWTA, changes that have occurred in the country names and boundaries since the publication of the Flora means that summarising the species distributions in terms of the modern country names or other geographical units (e.g. the Taxonomic Databases Working Group (TDWG) geographical categories) can be difficult.

In each of the Floras specimens are cited. This usually takes the form of the locality (sometimes with the altitude) and the collector's number (sometimes with the date of collection). For species with numerous collections, selected representative specimens are chosen which cover the distributional (in a geographical and ecological sense) range of the taxon. A small amount of ecological data is given, which usually includes the altitudinal range and the habitat, although the latter can be difficult to summarise for widespread species, which might occur in a variety of habitats. The geographical distribution of the species outside the area of the Flora is also summarised, typically with decreasing accuracy the further one moves away from the area treated by the Flora. The presentation of this information is rather variable: sometimes a list of countries is given, alternatively, the boundaries of the geographical range might described (i.e. 'From ... extending to ...' or, 'Between ...', etc.); often there is a mixture of both forms.

7.3 Digitisation methods

As described above, early considerations of the desired outputs that a digitised African Flora should yield were the capacity to answer 'checklist' and 'nomenclatural' type queries, with reusability of the data for further work also being a major consideration. These criteria effectively ruled out, *a priori*, any approaches to digitisation which did not involve the capture of digital text (such as creating facsimiles of the pages such as TIFF images or PDF image files), since their content would not be searchable.

'Image over text' approaches, where the complete scanned text is indexed, does allow searching, but it does not provide specific enough contexts (typically the context would be by page) in which to unambiguously answer the queries. For example, scientific names may occur in many different contexts within the Flora, such as an accepted name, a synonym, within the habitat or other notes. A feature, if not a strength of the 'image over text' approach, is that the converted text is generally not required to be proofread, since it is left to the reader to resolve any mismatches or omissions in query results by viewing the original page image(s). The digitisation costs are relatively cheap and such a system might be suitable for queries involving a single search criterion, which return one or only a few names, but we did not deem it robust enough to cope with queries that are based on several search criteria and which would commonly return a large lists of results (e.g. 'checklist' type). The uncritical acceptance of the reliability of such results would lead to errors, whereas the burden of having to verify each record individually we felt would be unacceptably high. A system based on this approach would therefore be limited, and through the inevitable frustration of its users, it would also run the danger of falling into disrepute.

In order to reliably answer 'checklist' and 'nomenclatural' queries we felt it would be necessary to restrict searches to very narrow contexts within the text, much like fields in a database. In addition, the more finely 'particulate' the data could be made, the more flexibility it would give for feeding into other projects. In order to tag the context of information within the digitised text we devised a simple method using standard desktop MS Office software. The procedure entails the use of format and regular expression matching in order to identify first the broad contexts, then to iteratively work within these to tag ever narrower contexts using extensible mark-up language, XML. The procedure is described in full in Kirkup et al. (2005).

The initial intent was to concentrate on tagging only the information that we needed to answer our specific queries, but we found that with little extra overhead it was possible to tag documents according to the full schema. On average it takes two days to tag 200 pages of text with another 2–3 days to proofread the content of the tags that are used in the searches (i.e. the nomenclature and geography). To date, all of FWTA (together with its companion work the *Useful plants of west tropical Africa* (UPWTA; Dalziel, 1937)), and the published volumes of FTEA, FZ, FTA and FC have been processed.

7.4 Outputs

From the outset of the project the imperative has been to enable querying of the digitised Floras via the internet since it was felt that this would give the widest possible dissemination. The early prototypes of the web-based system at Kew (c. 2002) were built using extensible stylesheet language templates (XSLT) to query the XML tagged text directly via an XSLT parser, which was run as a Java servlet. However, even with a relatively small sample of FZ, the performance of the system was found to be poor because it required that entire documents needed to be loaded into the computer memory in order to run the queries. In addition, there were difficulties in managing multiple documents which could only worsen as more volumes were added: in short, it was felt that this system could not satisfactorily be scaled-up for the whole Flora. Given the capabilities of the technology, and the expertise that was available at that time, this architecture based on direct query of the XML documents was abandoned in favour of one based on the much more familiar relational database.

The digitised FZ is stored in a MySQL database[1]. This online version provides easy search access to the 32 published volumes of the Flora, covering approximately

---

[1] http://www.kew.org/efloras

27 000 plant names. Simple forms are used to perform the 'nomenclatural' query to search for accepted names and synonyms across the whole Flora by entering the whole or part of the name. The complete Flora entry for a taxon can be viewed by clicking a name in the returned list. The Full Search form allows more powerful searches on accepted names, and the ability to make a 'checklist' query to generate a list of species from a particular geographical division or country.

The above queries are run against what is essentially the unaugmented text of the Flora. The original intent of the project was that no new or updated information would be added (with the exception of some minor corrections, all of which are documented on the website). However, some extra work was carried out to flag endemic status, to code habit and habitat with controlled vocabularies, and to calculate the maximum and minimum values for the altitudinal range. This interpretative information extends the functionality of the interface to make possible the creation of lists of endemics, lists of species that match a particular habit, and of species that occur at a specific altitude, so we may ask 'Which trees endemic to Northern Malawi occur above 1000 m altitude?'

As well as these search capabilities, FZ online also features a taxon browser to steer the user through the taxonomic hierarchy, and each of the dichotomous keys contained in the Flora are presented in an easy navigable form featuring onward links to key couplets, to taxon pages or to subkeys as applicable. FZ is also now available through the African Plants content area of the Aluka website[2]. This is a subscription-based service, which also hosts FWTA, UPWTA and FTEA, with FTA and FC to follow once they have been digitised. In the Aluka system, the content of the Floras is associated with other sources of African plant information such as illustrations and digital images of type specimens.

7.5 Analysis of FZ online system logs

The usage of Kew's FZ online website has been logged as a feature of the FZ online system since its launch in early 2004. The system logs record each type of query, the search terms used and the details of the taxon information retrieved, as well as user information such as the IP address and the URL of the referring web page. By analysis of the logs it is possible to build a picture of who the users are, the route through which they are arriving at the FZ online website and the kinds of questions that they are asking. The underlying trends for the 4-year period beginning at the start of 2004 up to the end of 2007 are summarised in Fig 7.1, through seasonal decomposition of the time series using the R statistical software package 'Stats'

---

[2] http://www.aluka.org

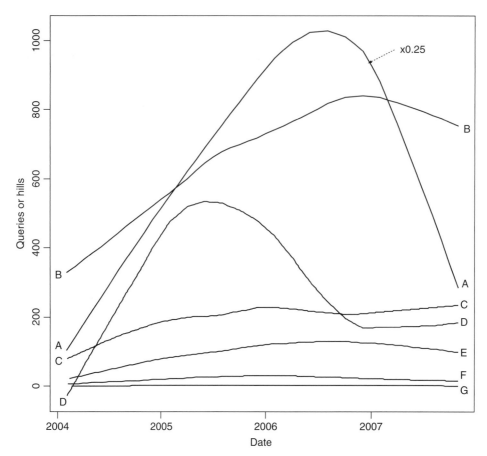

Figure 7.1 Trends in the usage of *Flora Zambesiaca* online – February 2004 to November 2007 with seasonal component removed. (A) 'Detail' searches or browsing (note Y axis scale × 0.25). (B) Simple 'lookup' or 'nomenclatural' type queries. (C) Referrals from Kew's electronic Plant Information Centre (ePIC) search engine. (D) referrals from Google. (E) 'Advanced' or 'checklist' type queries. (F) 'Advanced' queries originating from European countries. (G) 'Advanced' queries originating from African countries.

(Cleveland et al., 1990; Ripley, 2007). These summaries exclude as far as possible the records of usage by staff within Kew and those arising from the internet search engine Indexing Robots.

Out of the total of 186 634 log records for the study period, the overwhelming majority (97%) are simple searches to retrieve taxon details. These searches (Figure 7.1A) are referred either through the name search query pages (39%) or via the taxon browse and key pages (17%). A large proportion of these would seem to be systematic downloads of the complete Flora, either manually, or partly or wholly automated (there is no evidence in the patterns of usage of the key pages to suggest that the keys are being used for identification, rather they just provide a convenient route to the taxon details pages). About 13% of the simple searches originate from other search engines external to the FZ online system. These include Kew's ePic search facility (6%) and internet search engines such as Google and Ask (7%). Figure 7.1C,D shows that trends in such referrals reached a peak (of c. 3000 records per quarter) during the year 2005. Throughout 2006 these figures declined steadily reaching a low (of c. 700 records) for the first quarter of 2007; since then there has been a steady rise back to towards the levels of the 2005 peak. A further 28% of the log records result from a miscellany of sources, which include some direct links to taxon details from special-interest groups developed within sites such as Wikipedia (e.g. for Euphorbia and Cucurbitaceae).

Of the information accessed through the FZ online query interface, the advanced queries (i.e. the 'checklist' type, Figure 7.1E) are much less frequently used than simple lookups (Figure 7.1B). At 5563 records they only account for about 3% of the total logged and have remained at a low if not declining level since the system went live.

The number of terms included in the advanced queries is shown in Table 7.1. There is a (descending) monotonic relationship to the rank popularity, so that the highest proportion (58%) of the advanced queries included only a single term. The most popular of these (in descending order) are queries based on the genus name, followed by those with the family name, then by plant habit and lastly, by country. A further 32% of the advanced queries comprise two terms, by far the most popular of which combines genus+species terms, followed next by genus+country and then family+country. After these, searches combining terms for country+ endemic status and for habit+habitat closely follow. Much further down the rankings are searches on habit+endemic status and family+habit. Queries containing three search terms account for about 6% of the total of all advanced queries. Those ranked in the top 30 are, in order of popularity, combinations of genus+species+ country, genus+country+district, genus+species+habit habit+country+habitat and genus+habit+habitat.

Although it is difficult to be absolutely certain of the geographical location of the users of the system, the location of host computers with IP addresses that have been traced geographically, together with the numbers of each query type gives a reasonable basis for a breakdown of usage by region. The single geographical group with the largest representation in the logs is formed by the European countries, which account for c. 28% of all queries. The USA (if taken to comprise all the dot.com, dot.net and dot.edu registered hosts) together with Canada are a close second with c. 26%, whereas all the African countries taken together, although ranked next in third place, only account for 3% of usage of the system, which is just a little ahead of Australia. The European and African countries are compared graphically in Fig 7.1F,G.

Table 7.1 Usage statistics of search terms included in 'Advanced Queries' on FZ online, February 2004 to November 2007

Rank	Family	Genus	Species	Habit	Country	District	Endemic	Non-endemic	Habitat	Altitude	Counts
1	0	1	0	0	0	0	0	0	0	0	2404
2	0	1	1	0	0	0	0	0	0	0	1540
3	1	0	0	0	0	0	0	0	0	0	884
4	0	0	0	1	0	0	0	0	0	0	593
5	0	1	0	0	1	0	0	0	0	0	322
6	1	0	0	0	1	0	0	0	0	0	242
7	0	1	1	0	1	0	0	0	0	0	186
8	0	0	0	0	1	0	0	0	0	0	126
9	0	0	0	0	1	0	1	0	0	0	69
10	0	1	0	0	1	1	0	0	0	0	58
11	0	0	0	1	0	0	0	0	1	0	48
12	0	1	1	1	0	0	0	0	1	0	41
13	0	1	1	1	0	0	0	0	0	0	30
14	0	1	0	0	0	0	1	0	0	0	22
15	0	0	0	1	1	0	0	0	0	0	21
16	0	0	0	1	1	0	0	0	1	0	20
17	0	1	0	1	0	0	0	0	0	0	19
18	0	1	0	1	0	0	0	0	1	0	18
19	0	1	1	0	0	0	1	0	0	0	18
20	0	1	0	0	1	0	1	0	0	0	18
21	0	1	1	0	0	0	0	1	0	0	17

7.6 Discussion

Analyses of the usage logs for FZ online seems broadly to support our original thinking as to which queries would be of most value to users of an online Flora, although the number of advanced searches ('checklist' type) is much lower than we probably would have expected compared with the number of simple queries ('nomenclatural' type). To this extent the advanced query interface may be viewed as a qualified success. Of the 'checklist' type queries, the species lists that are obtained from genus, habit and country-based search terms appear to be particularly useful. As we envisaged, this checklist generating function provides a significant extension of the utility of the information contained in the Flora far beyond what is practicable with the hard-copy format. From the origins and the types of questions being asked, it also seems reasonable to assume that the user group extends beyond the taxonomic community. However, system usage to date also suggests that the effort spent in coding some classes of information (such as elevation ranges and habitat types) may not be justified and should be given more thought.

Part of the reason for the relatively high numbers of the simple query types is due to the systematic and/or automated downloading of the (more or less) complete database. This isn't something that the FZ online system facilitates particularly well (because it was not designed to) and it is clearly a tedious and time-consuming process to do manually. The fact that people are prepared to do this strongly suggests that there is a need for users to have access to the complete local copy of the species information. The scale of this is something that we had not anticipated, although we have responded to individual requests for copies of the data, the database acting as an effective 'shop window'. This strongly promotes the Flora as a basis for further (monographic) revisionary work, but has also been used to support ecological research; for example, the classification of plant functional types (see Chapter 3, Dick et al., in this volume).

Another area that we did not fully anticipate is the degree to which referral from the major internet search engines (for example Google, Ask, etc.) acts as an important route to the species information pages. Roughly 10% of usage is via this route (excluding referrals as from Kew's ePic system). A feature of these searches is that they bypass the FZ online query interface altogether. As a consequence of this, it would seem important to ensure that appropriate keywords are included in the metadata that describe the both content and the function of the FZ online website. In this way it may be possible to guide people towards the more complex functions of the website. Given that downloads of taxon pages are important to users, the adoption of a standard format for taxon information such as Taxon Concept Schema (TCS) would be of benefit since this would also allow access via specialist search tools (such as GBIF/TDWG TAPIR).

The readership of FZ online has, after a peak of activity in 2005, now seemed to have reached a steady state of about 3000 log records per quarter. The vast majority of usage is from the developed world (especially Europe and North America), a level that is an order of magnitude above that of Africa. African stakeholders are not engaging with the project. Why this is so is not clear, perhaps because of a lack of reliable internet connections, or competition from other initiatives (such as Aluka or the online Flora of Zimbabwe). If it is that problems lie with the online format, then there may be justification for an offline version of the Flora, which could be distributed either by download, on CD-ROM or DVD; existing interactive key software could prove a suitable medium for such a product and might also incorporate identification tools such as an Interactive Key To African Plants.[3]

The new World Wide Web technologies underpinning social networking also hold great promise for furthering community involvement, both in the development and the use of the African online Flora (Mayo et al., 2008). One such tool, 'Scratchpad', developed through the European Distributed Institute of Taxonomy (EDIT; Roberts et al., 2007), allows easy creation of information portals to which the entire community are able to contribute. The Gateway to African Plants[4] is a community website based on a Scratchpad that comprises a standard checklist of plant names, plant descriptions, an illustrated glossary and an online key. It is intended to enable the identification of species of plants found in sub-Saharan Africa and Madagascar, and to find further information about them. The resources contained are also intended to help contributors to the project develop and refine the identification tools.

References

Beentje, H. J., et al. (ed.) (1948–2012). *Flora of tropical East Africa*. Richmond: Royal Botanic Gardens, Kew.

Bentham, G. and Hooker, J. D. (1862–1883). *Genera plantarum*. London: Lovell, Reeve and Co.

Cleveland R. B., Cleveland W. S., McRae J. E. and Terpenning I. (1990). STL: a seasonal-trend decomposition procedure based on loss. *Journal of Official Statistics*, **6**: 3–73.

Dalziel, J. M. (1937). *Useful plants of west tropical Africa*. Richmond: Royal Botanic Gardens, Kew.

Harvey, W. H. and Sonder, O. W. (1860–1933). *Flora capensis*. Dublin, London and Cape Town: Hodges, Smith and Co.; Lovell Reeve and Co., Robertson.

Hutchinson, J., et al. (ed.) (1927–ongoing). *Flora of west tropical Africa*. Richmond: Royal Botanic Gardens, Kew.

Kirkup, D., Malcolm, P., Christian, G. and Paton, A. (2005). Towards a digital African Flora. *Taxon*, **54**: 457–466.

Mayo, S. J., et al. . (2008). Alpha e-taxonomy: responses from the systematics

[3] http://www.kew.org/science/directory/projects/IntKeyAfricanPlants.html
[4] http://gateway.myspecies.info

community to the biodiversity crisis. *Kew Bulletin*, **63**: 1–16.

Oliver, D. (ed.) (1868–1902). *Flora of tropical Africa*. London: L. Reeve.

Pope, G., et al. (ed.) (1960–ongoing). *Flora Zambesiaca*. Richmond: Royal Botanic Gardens, Kew.

Ripley, B. D. (2007). *The R Stats Package*, Version 2.5.1.

Roberts, D., Rycroft, S. D., González, M. and Smith, V. S. (2007). Scratchpads: what are they? *European Distributed Institute of Taxonomy News*, pp. 8–11.

8

Cybertruffle: an online resource for mycology

D. W. MINTER

8.1 Introduction

This chapter describes the development of the various websites on the Cybertruffle server[1], which are the result of long-term collaboration between mycologists in over 20 countries (Argentina, Armenia, Austria, Brazil, Bulgaria, Chile, China, Cuba, Czech Republic, Dominican Republic, France, Georgia, Germany, India, Mexico, Poland, Puerto Rico, Slovakia, Trinidad and Tobago, UK, Ukraine, USA, Venezuela). This collaboration had its beginnings in the 1980s, but became much more active after 1992 as a result of a series of projects funded mainly through the UK Darwin Initiative: Fungi of Ukraine (1993–1996), Fungi of the Caribbean (1997–2000), Biodiversity in the former Soviet Union – the millennium opportunity (1998–2001), Biodiversity conservation in Cuba (2001–2004), Recovering Ukraine's lost steppe (2002–2005), and Conservation of Microfungi – a voice for unprotected and vulnerable organisms (2007–2010).

From the outset, as much information as possible was handled through a computer database rather than on paper or in word-processor files. Although this involved a large initial investment in time and effort, in retrospect it was far-sighted, because it permitted data to be used for a much wider range of purposes. Although

---

[1] http://www.cybertruffle.org.uk

Descriptive Taxonomy: The Foundation of Biodiversity Research, eds M. F. Watson, C. H. C. Lyal and C. A. Pendry. Published by Cambridge University Press.
© The Systematics Association 2015

each of the first two Darwin Initiative projects had the objective of producing a paper publication (Minter and Dudka, 1996; Minter et al., 2001), they were produced almost entirely as an output from that database. Enlargement of the database continued during the next three Darwin Initiative projects, and during that time the first digital publications arising from the database were made, in the form of CD-ROMs and simple websites (Minter, 1996; Minter et al., 2002, 2003; Gvritishvili et al., 2003, 2007; Pérez et al., 2006a, 2006b). Based on these products, a decision was made late in 2005 to make the accumulated information available online. In 2006 an internet server (the Cybertruffle server) was acquired, and a copy of the database was transferred to that server. Work then began on the programs and interfaces necessary to make the database usable as an online resource. The present chapter describes that work, and discusses how this database and the websites that give access to it can be used, particularly for biodiversity research.

8.2 The Cybertruffle server and component databases

The Cybertruffle server is used principally to provide information about fungi and their associated organisms. It uses LINUX as an operating system, and hosts a wide range of websites. The computer database that stores the data uses MySQL software. The design of the database follows specifications described by Minter (1996), but modified and slightly simplified for fast online use. All Cybertruffle websites conform to a design brief, so that they have a consistent and predictable appearance and that the results pages from database interrogations can be used in connection with a wide range of websites. The database is interrogated using SQL requests generated through custom programs written in PERL. There are four main Cybertruffle websites:

1. *Cyberliber – electronic library for mycology.* Provides access to bibliographical information and scanned images of pages of mycological literature published in a wide range of languages. The website itself (menus, header pages etc.) functions only in English.

2. *Cybernome – nomenclator for fungi and their associated organisms.* Provides nomenclatural and taxonomic information about fungi and their associated organisms. This website is fully functional in Chinese, English, French, Georgian, German, Polish, Portuguese, Russian, Spanish and Ukrainian.

3. *Robigalia – biological records of fungi and their associated organisms.* Provides information about when, where and with what fungi and their associated organisms can be observed. This website is fully functional in Chinese, English, French, Georgian, German, Polish, Portuguese, Russian, Spanish and Ukrainian.

4. *Valhalla – past mycologists.* Provides biographical information about mycologists of the past. This website functions only in English.

8.2.1 Cyberliber

At the time of writing, the website provides access to nearly 60 000 database records, each with bibliographical information about an individual mycological work or publication. In addition, the website makes available more than 198 000 scanned images of pages of mycological publications. About 25 000 of those pages are shown courtesy of LibriFungorum[2] through a cooperative arrangement to share resources. Cyberliber is currently growing rapidly, and these numbers are likely to rise. Cyberliber provides access to scanned images of the great thesauri of early mycological literature (Lindau and Sydow, 1908–1909, 1913; Ciferri, 1957–1960). These volumes are a huge resource on early mycological literature. All of the main catalogues and thesauri for mycology have been scanned and images of individual pages are available through the website. In addition to the above, they include *Index of Fungi* (volumes 1–4, and its supplements), Lamb's *Index Nominum Lichenum*, *Petrak's Lists* (volumes 1–8), Saccardo's *Sylloge Fungorum* (volumes 1–26) and Zahlbruckner's *Catalogus Lichenum Universalis* (volumes 1–10). Significant journal holdings include *Acta Mycologica* (volumes 35–42), *Grevillea* (complete), *Michelia* (complete), *Mycologia* (volumes 1–20, 35–44), *Mycotaxon* (volumes 1–85) and *Sydowia* (volumes 1–10). As this, and the other three main datasets, is a major international collaborative effort, all the contributors are listed and supporting organisations acknowledged in all cases.

8.2.2 Cybernome

At the time of writing, the website provides access to almost 550 000 database records of scientific names of organisms and their taxonomic position. All biological kingdoms and a very wide range of ranks are represented. The aim is to provide basic nomenclatural and taxonomic information about organisms which appear on the Robigalia (biological records) website, with onward links where possible to standard nomenclators. The taxonomic information is, thus, generally conservative. This database is now increasing in size rather slowly, with names being added only when required as a result of new entries appearing in Robigalia. Work continues, however, to improve the quality of individual records.

8.2.3 Robigalia

At the time of writing, the website provides access to over 68 000 database records of where, when and with what fungi and their associated organisms occur. Currently the following countries are best represented (figures are for fungi only): Ukraine (76 117 records), Cuba (44 859 records), Venezuela (36 676 records), Georgia (31 330 records), UK (20 396 records), Puerto Rico (19 146 records), Russia

---

[2] http://www.librifungorum.org/

(15 435 records), Brazil (11 555 records), Chile (9345 records), Slovakia (8985 records), USA (8742 records), Dominican Republic (6381 records), India (6342 records) and Trinidad and Tobago (5191 records). There are multiple ways of accessing the biological record data, with viewing fungi within a country (with or without their associated organisms), and viewing the fungi associated with a particular organism, being particularly useful.

8.2.4 Valhalla

At the time of writing, the website provides access to biographical information about around 2900 mycologists of the past. Each mycologist has a separate page which, in the current version, is fixed (i.e. not produced dynamically).

8.3 Intended audience

The main Cybertruffle websites are aimed at people who need information about fungi – a very wide potential audience. This includes those with interests in biodegradation, biodeterioration, biodiversity, biogeography, biological control, biological recording, bioprospecting, bioremediation, climate change, conservation, ecology, ethnomycology, history of mycology, industrial mycology, invasive species, medical and veterinary mycology and plant pathology. Because the websites, Robigalia in particular, are so strong in their handling of organisms associated with fungi, they are likely to be valuable to people working with any of the main biological kingdoms (animals, chromistans, fungi, monerans, plants and protists). People with such interests include scientists (amateur and professional), civil servants, nature reserve wardens, non-government organisations, administrators, lawyers, politicians, students of natural history and educated laypeople worldwide. The Cyberliber and Valhalla websites are considered to be of more limited interest, mainly restricted to scientists, while the Cybernome and Robigalia websites are of more general appeal. Whilst a familiarity with written English can now be expected from most scientists, not all other users will be able to read English fluently, if at all. The Cybernome and Robigalia websites are thus designed to provide all of their information in a wide range of languages, and all four websites are intended to be usable by the educated layman. The Cybertruffle specialist Mycota websites (described below) are aimed at users who speak either English or the native language(s) of their country. In accordance with perceived user needs, all websites covered by the present work aim to provide information in as simple and accessible a format as possible. Pop-up advertisements and moving logos, etc. are avoided. The websites are designed to be easy to use, rapid to download, with flexible, fast searching and browsing facilities. The facility for direct machine-access to information on the Cybertruffle server is useful for interoperation with other internet biodiversity websites.

8.4 Cybertruffle as a contribution to Mycotas

A Mycota is a descriptive catalogue of the fungi found in a defined area or with a defined associated organism. Mycotas are critical for understanding the biology of that area or associated organism, and for the formulation of conservation strategies. They may establish a regional classification bringing order to past works, provide tools for identification through keys and record data on each organism covered by the work. Mycota typically include information about the name of each taxon, a description, one or more illustrations, text describing the range, abundance, habitat, associated organisms and substrata, a list of source material including specimens examined, and a list of bibliographical references. There may also be maps showing the geographical distribution of taxa, and there are often keys enabling identifications to be made. Conservation status evaluations are now starting to appear in Mycotas. There is usually some introduction, often with notes about the country in question.

The Cybertruffle database contains many of the elements of a typical Mycota in a highly structured form, and so it is very useful as a component of online Mycotas. As a result, in addition to the four main websites, various specialist mycota websites are being developed on the Cybertruffle server to provide access to particular parts of the database (most bilingual, one trilingual), and completed parts are already available online. These include Fungi of Brazil / Fungos do Brasil, Fungi of Chile / Hongos de Chile, Fungi of Cuba / Hongos de Cuba, Fungi of the Dominican Republic / Hongos de la República Dominicana, Fungi of Puerto Rico / Hongos de Puerto Rico, Fungi of Trinidad and Tobago, Fungi of Ukraine / Гриби України / Грибы Украины and Fungi of Venezuela / Hongos de Venezuela, Fungi on Eucalyptus / Hongos de Eucalyptus, Fungi on Pines / Hongos de Pinos, Fungi on Quercus / Hongos de Quercus. Each of these has its own set of menus and header pages, but uses a range of additional custom programs to access data in Cybertruffle's four main databases.

8.5 Value for biodiversity research

The Cybertruffle database and main websites are the only large-scale internet resources for mycology that are truly global in outlook and which provide information in more than one language. Within a year of the beta versions becoming available, there were already on average about 500 different users accessing the site daily and the number was rising. While the value of the Valhalla website is limited for biodiversity research (it can help to identify historical mycological explorers of a region), the other three websites are tremendously useful in that field.

8.5.1 Access to literature

Outside Europe and North America biodiversity research is severely hampered by lack of access to the necessary scientific literature. Much of that relevant literature is taxonomic, and so relates to publications with a long, useful life. Many still relevant taxonomic works are now out of copyright, and in mycology this is true for much of the biodiversity literature relating to Africa, parts of Asia and South America. The Cyberliber website is an attempt to deal with this problem by providing biblio-graphical references so that users can see what literature exists, and by making key publications openly available online. The following aspects of the design of the Cyberliber website have made it popular with users:

- The ability to browse generally without specifying a particular interest (author name, journal, topic, etc.).
- The detailed contents pages provided for journal volumes make it easy for the user to locate an individual work.
- The small JPG-format images used to display key publications are quick to download, which is important for users who do not have a fast internet connection.
- The same JPG images can easily be referenced from external websites (in this respect, the website is an example of best practice) through a simple and pre-dominantly predictable system of folder and file names.

Each book or serial publication has its own folder with a unique number as the name; volumes and parts are stored in subsidiary folders, each with a name derived from the volume or part number; the name of an individual page file can be derived from the page number of the original document in more than 99% of cases. This has led to extensive use of Cyberliber resources by external websites such as IndexFungorum, and currently Cyberliber is probably the largest single resource specifically for mycological literature on the internet.

8.5.2 Access to scientific names

People working with fungal diversity, including systematics, need information about the scientific names not only of their fungi but also of the organisms with which they are associated. Mycological libraries with complete runs of Saccardo's *Sylloge Fungorum*, Petrak's *Lists*, *Index of Fungi* and its supplements, Zahlbruckner's *Catalogus Lichenum Universalis*, and Lamb's *Index Nominum Lichenum* are rare outside Europe and North America, and there can be very few libraries anywhere in the world with full collections of nomenclatural catalogues for all groups of organisms. Under these conditions, online nomenclators are critically important. Cybernome is unique among mycological online nomenclators, because (while specialising in the fungi) it seeks to provide information about all taxonomic ranks for all kingdoms of organisms and, having entered the system, that information is openly available by browsing, not limited in access through having to specify interest in a particular single organism. The user can see the author(s) and place of publication of a particular species then (instead of having to start a new search) can browse to see what other species there are in the same genus. Furthermore, the information is available in a wide range of languages, making Cybernome an example of best practice in this respect. Cybernome does not aim to be a definitive nomenclator, but it does provide, as much as possible, links to such websites.

8.5.3 Access to information about where, when and with what fungi and their associated organisms occur

In any work with biodiversity, climate change, ecology and similar subjects, questions very soon arise. Where does this organism occur? When was it first/last seen? What time of the year can it be observed? What does it grow on? There are several online resources for fungi providing information which can be used to answer such questions. Usually the information provided is in the form of individual records of specimens in reference collections or of published reports or of field observations. To make sense of these, the user has to view each one and assess them individually. The Robigalia website, however, uniquely permits the user to see a synopsis of information from all sources, and to refine or expand the search criteria used to generate that synopsis. Thus, the user can move easily from viewing all records of a fungus with all associated organisms worldwide, to just the records from one country or one subnational unit, or to just the records worldwide with a particular associated organism, or to just the records with that associated organism from a particular country or subnational unit. At all points, the user has access to all the individual records making up that summary. Significantly, when viewing a fungus with a particular associated organism, it is possible to change the display to a view of the associated organism with that fungus. From there, it is a short step to viewing all fungi associated with a particular organism, with distribution maps showing where fungi have been collected in association with that organism, and all of this information is available in a wide range of languages.

8.5.4 Ecological associations

Many online resources for biodiversity provide few or no facilities for viewing information about associated organisms: typically they rely on large numbers of single records of single observations of single organisms. Such systems are of limited use for work in biodiversity, climate change, ecology and similar subjects (obtaining information from such systems usually entails data-mining of a range of different 'ecosystem' or 'ecological notes' fields). Animals, chromistans, fungi, monerans, plants and protists do not, however, exist in a vacuum. They are associated with each other. The flexibility in handling such associated organism information distinguishes the Robigalia website. The site is particularly effective in highlighting communities which simply cannot be detected by conventional 'fauna and flora' websites. The Scots pine (*Pinus sylvestris*), for example, is known to be associated with over 1000 different fungi, more than 200 of which are known only in association with that plant. How can one evaluate the biodiversity of native Scottish pine forests without taking such information into account? The importance of associated organisms is too easily forgotten and can lead to questionable conservation initiatives. The value of an enormous seed bank, for example, no matter how well those seeds are preserved, is immediately limited if there are no equivalent latter day Noah's Arks for the pollinators, mycorrhizal fungi and other symbionts which those plants need.

8.6 Problems

For the Cybertruffle server and its websites to survive and grow, several problems must be resolved.

8.6.1 Continuity

In mycology, online resources of this sort have only developed under very specific conditions. It is necessary to have as the driving force someone with a combined long-term interest in mycology, computers, databases, the internet and computer programming. The great mycological websites of IndexFungorum, Landcare New Zealand[3], Mycobank[4] and the US Department of Agriculture (USDA)[5] are all examples where this has happened. Ideally, the mycologist responsible for developing such sites should have a stable environment and long-term control of the resources necessary for delivering the product. That, however, is not always the case, with the result that some websites lead a precarious existence: only one person understands how they work, and there is no understudy (see also Chapter 4, Connor, in this volume).

8.6.2 Bottlenecks

The process of acquiring new records is simple compared with the job of editing those records and ensuring that they are of a sufficient quality for incorporation in the database. The value of a database lies less in the individual records, and more in the quality of the links between the various data items. Skilled editors are in short supply. The result is that, for the biological records tables in the database (used for

[3] http://nzfungi2.landcareresearch.co.nz/   [4] http://www.mycobank.org
[5] http://nt.ars-grin.gov/fungaldatabases

Robigalia), for example, there is a backlog of records waiting to be processed, and the queue (already several hundred thousand records long) is growing in size.

8.6.3 Record quality

One result of seeing the first versions of the Cybertruffle websites going live on the internet has been to realise that there are many areas where the quality of the data could be significantly improved. In the years since the first versions began to operate, new standards have been developed, particularly for citing locality information, but the retrospective application of those standards would be an enormous task.

One possible solution to the three previous problems might be to make the internet version of the database the master copy, and to introduce a system of online editing and updating for qualified collaborators. Although ideal in many ways, the resources needed to make such a change do not exist, and nor are there experts with time available to prepare secure editorial interfaces. At present, these problems are chronic rather than acute. The solution in general lies in much financial resources, but at present those are far from certain.

8.7 Future development

Although already providing a great deal of online information about fungi, the main Cybertruffle websites can still be enhanced in many aspects. In particular, they fall significantly short of being true online Mycotas, and would benefit from the addition of conservation assessments, morphological descriptions and illustrations of individual taxa, and keys to aid identification. Indexes of individual journal volumes, and cumulative indexes of journals and other serial publications, together with indexes of books are a huge and largely untapped resource. This is being incorporated into Cybertruffle as this, and the linking to digitised publications, would greatly simplify biodiversity work and conservation status evaluations. The fungal community has led the way making the registration of nomenclatural novelties a requirement for valid publication. IndexFungorum is the *de facto* world nomenclator for the fungi, and is the main registration authority. The Cybertruffle server, with its multilingual websites, might be an ideal site for another registration point.

8.8 Concluding remarks

The Cybertruffle websites and Mycotas have an important and increasingly valuable role to play in biodiversity research: they not only provide critically important missing ecological links to and between the other biological kingdoms, but also inform users about the fungi of an area, reminding them of a group of organisms too frequently forgotten. Too many large internet initiatives use words like 'biodiversity', 'climate change' or 'ecology' in their titles without ensuring that their coverage of the theme is as complete as their name suggests. The major botanical and zoological institutions setting up those initiatives rarely think to ensure fungi are properly represented. In the long-term, this is damaging to the initiatives themselves, but it also misleads politicians and other funding bodies into thinking the job has been done, when it has not. The result is that when mycologists then apply for funding to cover the biodiversity, climate change or ecology of fungi in the same area, the response is sometimes less than positive. Mycologists are reluctantly forced to seek their own solutions when such flagship projects pass them by, while the limitations inherent in those flagship projects may themselves be treated as a cogent argument for pluralism: a variety of different internet sites providing similar but not identical services is likely to be more robust and more useful in the long-term than a single monolithic site.

References

Ciferri, R. (1957–1960). In *Thesaurus Literaturae Mycologicae et Lichenologicae Supplementum 1911–1930*, 4 volumes, G. Lindau and P. Sydow (eds). Cortina, Italy: Papia.

Gvritishvili, M. N., Hayova, V. P., Kryvomaz, T.I. and Minter, D. W. (2003). *Electronic distribution maps of Georgian Fungi*. [CD-ROM] Isleworth, UK: PDMS Publishing, ISBN 0-9540169-6-3.

Gvritishvili, M. N., Hayova, V. P., Kryvomaz, T. I. and Minter, D. W. (2007). *Electronic distribution maps of Georgian Fungi*. Available at: http://www.cybertruffle.org.uk/gruzmaps [website, version 1.10].

Lindau, G. and Sydow, P. (1908–1909). *Thesaurus Litteraturae Mycologicae et Lichenologicae*, volumes 1–2. Lipsiae, Germany: Fratres Borntraeger.

Lindau, G. and Sydow, P. (1913). *Thesaurus Litteraturae Mycologicae et Lichenologicae ratione habita praecipue omnium quae adhuc scripta sunt de mycologia applicata 3 (complectens corrigenda, supplementum, enumerationum alphabeticam titulorum annorum 1907–1910)*. Lipsiae, Germany: Fratres Borntraeger.

Minter, D. W. (1996). Recording and mapping fungi. In *A century of mycology. British Mycological Society Centenary Symposium*, B. C. Sutton (ed.). Cambridge: Cambridge University Press, pp. 321–382.

Minter, D. W. (ed.) (2003). *Mycology in Ukraine, a CD commemorating the XIV Congress of European Mycologists, Katsiveli, Yalta, Crimea, 22–27 September 2003*. [CD-ROM] Isleworth, UK: PDMS Publishing.

Minter, D. W. and Dudka, I. O. (1996). *Fungi of Ukraine. A preliminary checklist*. Egham, UK and Kiev, Ukraine: International Mycological Institute and M. G. Kholodny Institute of Botany.

Minter, D. W., Rodríguez Hernández, M. and Mena Portales, J. (2001). *Fungi of the Caribbean – an annotated checklist*.

Isleworth, UK: PDMS Publishing, ISBN 0-9540169-0-4.

Minter, D. W., Mena Portales, J., Rodríguez-Hernández, M., Iglesias Brito, H., Camino Vilaró, M. and Mercado Sierra, Á. (2002). *Electronic distribution maps of Caribbean Fungi/ Mapas de Distribución Computarizados de los Hongos del Caribe.* Available at: http://www.biodiversity.ac.psiweb. com/carimaps [website version 1.00].

Minter, D. W., Mena Portales, J., Rodríguez-Hernández, M., Iglesias Brito, H., Camino Vilaró, M. and Mercado Sierra, Á. (2003). *Electronic distribution maps of Caribbean Fungi/ Mapas de Distribución Computarizados*

de los Hongos del Caribe. [CD-ROM] Isleworth, UK: PDMS Publishing, ISBN 0-9540169-4-7.

Pérez, J.-M., Rodríguez Hernández, M., Areces Berazaín, F., Minter, D. W. and Minter, W. J. K. (2006a). *Plants of Viñales – a pictorial guide / Plantas de Viñales – guía ilustrada.* Available at: http://www.cybertruffle.org.uk/vinales/ eng [website, version 1.10].

Pérez, J.-M., Rodríguez Hernández, M., Areces Berazaín, F., Minter, D. W. and Minter, W. J. K. (2006b) *Plants of Viñales – a pictorial guide / Plantas de Viñales – guía ilustrada.* [CD-ROM] Isleworth, UK: PDMS Publishing, ISBN 0-9540169-9-8.

9

Zooplankton Identification Manual for North European Seas (ZIMNES)

L. C. Hastie, J. Rasmussen, M. V. Angel, G. A. Boxshall,
S. J. Chambers, D. V. P. Conway, S. Fielding, A. Ingvarsdottir,
A. W. G. John, S. J. Hay, S. P. Milligan, A. L. Mulford,
G. J. Pierce, M. Shaw and M. Wootton

9.1 Background

The ecological importance of marine zooplankton cannot be overestimated. Throughout the world's oceans, plankton species abundance and diversity impact, determine and drive global cycles, food-web structure and ecosystem stability (Banse, 1995; Sommer, 1996; Lindley et al., 2003). Plankton communities mediate transfer of organic matter from the productive photic zone to deep waters, and biogeochemical processes that drive the carbon cycle (Russell-Hunter, 1970). Plankton species form the foundation for productivity and the harvest of the seas and monitoring data on these species are important to inform marine management (Brander et al., 2003; Reid et al., 2003; Stevens et al., 2006). We know that anthropogenic influences, together with climatic factors and changes affect their diversity, distribution and dynamics in marine ecosystems (Molinero et al., 2005, 2008).

Marine research projects, surveys and monitoring programmes often require routine taxonomic identification of marine zooplankton (Bottger-Schnack et al., 2004). This work requires taxonomic skills and knowledge that are nowadays very scarce. Critical reference texts, keys and other relevant information are sometimes

Descriptive Taxonomy: The Foundation of Biodiversity Research, eds M. F. Watson,
C. H. C. Lyal and C. A. Pendry. Published by Cambridge University Press.
© The Systematics Association 2015

difficult to find. Many of the species monographs and papers required are out of print and access to these is often restricted to a few libraries. Since revisions of taxonomic groups and general taxonomic changes may be published at any time, it is important for up-to-date information to be accessed. There is a general requirement, therefore, not only to consolidate and preserve expertise, but also to provide accessible, up-to-date information on zooplankton taxonomy (Harris et al., 2000). There is a specific need for an accessible and authoritative taxonomic guide to marine zooplankton, suitable for use by scientists and students working with marine zooplankton samples, in government laboratories, university research departments and other marine institutes in the UK and Northern Europe.

An electronic system for the identification of zooplankton could offer a range of distinct benefits to marine ecologists. These include greater accessibility, clarity and flexibility (for revision and updating), as well as providing a platform for the sharing of information and expertise. However, a web-based zooplankton guide would, by necessity, be generalised in nature. As such, it should be considered to support, rather than replace traditional paper-based formats, particularly in highly specialised taxonomic studies.

Here we describe a National Environment Research Council (NERC)-funded Knowledge Exchange project that aimed to prepare an illustrated, electronic media-based manual containing taxonomic descriptions and illustrated explanations of the diagnostic features necessary to identify zooplankton species, along with life-cycle stage descriptions for key species, plus brief notes and key references on ecology, abundance and distribution. The aim was to make the manual clear and user-friendly for both specialists and non-specialists, whilst also being suitable for training purposes.

9.2 ZIMNES website

The marine area covered is the northeast Atlantic, from surface waters to 200 m depth. A list of c. 250 key zooplankton species was selected for inclusion. Criteria for inclusion include occurrence in the study area, abundance, ecological importance and availability of specimens and data. Material from plankton specimen collections held at participating institutes was used to prepare diagrams and photographs along with text on morphology, distribution, abundance and general ecology. The main sources of information utilised were published literature, personal materials, bench manuals and additional materials (photographs/drawings).

As draft species accounts were collated and compiled, the material was adjusted to fit standardised presentation formats. This should ultimately be available as both online pages and PDF files, ready for web-based publication and easily translated into hard copy.

The ZIMNES website was developed with open-source tools and offers a model which could be made available for people interested in developing hierarchical information websites (code-structure and database, not actual content).

The website system is database driven (MySQL) to allow for continued updates and new content to be added, and the front-end design is developed through a template system that separates the code (php) from the visual design (HTML and CSS). The central information is a list of taxonomic 'entities' (ranging from phyla to species), which are interlinked in a flexible table structure. Currently no rules on linkage are enforced as the primary use of the moment is for applied sample analysis, but users familiar with the php language can easily add such a feature.

All additional information is connected to this entity list, and allows the addition of information such as literature, images and text at any taxonomic rank using the same editing tools. This modular structure should allow other users of the platform to develop their own tools or modules to link directly into a species list.

The website structure is built to be utilised without having to register users or logging in to access information. Editors and administrators can edit pages directly through a permission-based editing system directly when navigating the site. Registered users who are not editors or administrators cannot edit any content directly on the site.

At present, the ZIMNES website[1] has 1013 interlinked entities (372 species, 267 genera), and descriptive text for c. 200 entities is available. A set of c. 400 images has been uploaded. Some work has been undertaken on debugging and optimising usage of the system. Additional features listed include a glossary, news system, help pages and web links.

It is planned to establish linkage between texts and glossary, improve the tree-structure for navigation and create a user discussion forum. Other ideas that may be developed in future include the possibilities of providing video demonstrations, a user 'virtual microscope', physiological/ecological rates and measures of important species and more defined geographical ranges.

The ZIMNES project is currently unfunded and the authors welcome suggestions for, and collaboration in, future developments.

Acknowledgements

The ZIMNES project was funded by a NERC Knowledge transfer grant. The ZIMNES website is hosted by SAHFOS. We are extremely grateful to Darren Stevens (SAHFOS) and Dan Lear (MBA), who helped to set up the ZIMNES website, to Tanya Jonas and Chris Reid (SAHFOS), and to John Fraser and Maria Pan (FRS) for logistic and technical support.

---

[1] http://www.zimnes.org

References

Banse, K. (1995). Zooplankton – pivotal role in the control of ocean production. *ICES Journal of Marine Science*, **52**: 265–277.

Bottger-Schnack, R., Lenz, J. and Weikert, H. (2004). Are taxonomic details of relevance to ecologists? An example from oncaeid microcopepods of the Red Sea. *Marine Biology*, **144**: 11270–114.

Brander, K. M., Dickson, R. R. and Edwards, M. (2003). Use of Continuous Plankton Recorder information in support of marine management applications in fisheries, environmental protection, and the study of ecosystem response to environmental change. *Progress in Oceanography*, **58**: 175–191.

Harris, R. P., Wiebe, P. H., Lenz, J., Skjoldal, H. R. and Huntley, M. (eds). (2000). *ICES zooplankton methodology manual*. London: Academic Press.

Lindley, J. A., Reid, P. C. and Brander, K. M. (2003). Inverse relationship between cod recruitment in the North Sea and young fish in the Continuous Plankton Recorder survey. *Scientia Marina*, **67**: 191–200.

Molinero, J. C., Ibanez, J. C., Nival, P., Chiffet, M. and Nival, P. (2005). North Atlantic and northwestern Mediterranean plankton variability. *Limnology and Oceanography*, **50**: 1213–1220.

Molinero, J. C., Ibanez, J.C., Souissi, S., Buecher, E., Dallot, S., and Nival, P. (2008). Climate control on the long-term anomalous changes of zooplankton communities in the northwestern Mediterranean. *Global Change Biology*, **14**: 11–26.

Reid, P. C., Colebrook, J. M., Mathews, J. B. L. and Aiken, J. (2003). The Continuous Plankton Recorder: concepts and history, from plankton indicator to undulating recorders. *Progress in Oceanography*, **58**: 117–173.

Russell-Hunter, W. D. (1970). *Aquatic productivity: an introduction to some basic aspects of biological oceanography and limnology*. New York: Macmillan Publishing Co.

Sommer, U. (1996). Plankton ecology: the past two decades of progress. *Naturwissenschaften*, **83**: 293–301.

Stevens, D., Richardson, A. J. and Reid, P. C. (2006). Continuous Plankton Recorder database: evolution, current uses and future directions. *Marine Ecology – Progress Series*, **316**: 247–255.

PART III

Outputs and impact: field guides and applications

10

A field guide to the dragonflies and damselflies of Britain and Ireland

S. J. Brooks

10.1 Introduction

In the mid 1990s interest in the British dragonflies amongst amateur naturalists had probably never been greater. The British Dragonfly Society had a membership of over 1500 and the Dragonfly Recording Network was receiving thousands of records each year. Several field guides to the British species had been published in the preceding decade but by 1997 most were out of print. The time was right for a new style field guide that, as well as featuring high-quality illustrations and descriptions of the British species, would include for the first time all the age- and sex-related colour forms, as well as detailed autecological information, which was recently becoming available from field observations. This new field guide would encourage dragonfly enthusiasts to take their interests beyond simple identifications and distributional recording and also draw in new recruits, especially from amongst bird-watchers, by presenting the guide in a modern, attractive and informative format.

10.2 Background

Dragonflies (Odonata) are captivating insects and consequently have featured in some of the earliest books describing the natural world (e.g. Mouffet, 1634; Ray,

Descriptive Taxonomy: The Foundation of Biodiversity Research, eds M. F. Watson, C. H. C. Lyal and C. A. Pendry. Published by Cambridge University Press.
© The Systematics Association 2015

1710; Harris, 1782; Curtis, 1823–1840). These early books sought to catalogue Nature and also inspire an interest in natural history by providing, in many cases, beautiful and lavish colour paintings of the animals and plants the authors described.

British dragonflies have appeared in many such books, but the first book to deal exclusively with the British species appeared just over 100 years ago. It was written by W. J. Lucas, a school teacher and enthusiastic amateur naturalist (Lucas, 1900). This scholarly work includes colour illustrations of the adults of all the species then known to occur in Britain as well as high-quality drawings of many of the larvae and eggs. In addition to species descriptions, there is also information on the biology, behaviour and distribution of each species. Thirty years later, the book was supplemented by an illustrated volume on the British dragonfly larvae (Lucas, 1930). These seminal books set a benchmark in quality, and inspired a new generation of entomologists to take up the study of dragonflies and pass their knowledge and enthusiasm on to others. And this surely is one of the most important functions of handbooks and field guides: to impart knowledge and to inspire the reader to take up their own study of the group.

One person to be inspired by Lucas's books was Cynthia Longfield, who worked in a voluntary capacity on dragonflies at the Natural History Museum, London, from 1927 to 1957. By the early 1930s Lucas's *British dragonflies* was out of print and the study of British dragonflies had become neglected (Longfield, 1949: 5). To address this situation Longfield (1937) published what can now be seen as the first true field guide to British dragonflies. The title appeared in the Wayside and Woodland series, published by Warne, and has all the hallmarks of a modern field guide: it is pocket-sized, provides illustrated accounts of each species in turn, and includes notes on biology, distribution (at the vice county level) and flying season. In fact, it is remarkable how little the format of most field guides has changed when this book is compared with the most recently published dragonfly field guides. Nevertheless, there is a taxonomic formality that pervades Longfield's book which is not apparent in today's guides. The book also features a lengthy chapter on collecting, setting and preserving dragonflies for the insect cabinet, something which is strongly de-emphasised in modern field guides. However, this was typical of the time. For example, sections on collecting dragonflies also feature in more generalist texts on studying pond life (Furneaux, 1932).

In the second edition of her book, Longfield (1949) included W. F. Evans's, by then 100-years old, colour paintings of several of the adult species. However, most species were illustrated in her book using black-and-white photographs of set specimens and line drawings of diagnostic morphological characters. These are not wholly adequate for accurate species identification in the field, and are somewhat inadequate as a source of inspiration for future dragonfly enthusiasts. In fact, it was not until the mid 1970s that the next field guide to British dragonflies appeared. During the intervening period a small cadre of dragonfly enthusiasts, taking inspiration from the wonderful New Naturalist book on dragonflies (Corbet et al., 1960), had continued to struggle with dragonfly field identification and begun to record these insects on a systematic basis. The nascent British Odonata Recording Scheme, the fruits of whose labours were manifest in the first atlas to British Odonata (Skelton, 1974), was really kick-started by the appearance of a new-look field guide, written by another school teacher, Cyril Hammond (1977).

This slim, large-format book, which had to be fitted into a rucksack when taken on fieldwork, provided huge (typically 14–15 cm in length) full-colour paintings of the males and females of each of the British species, as well as some of the colour forms. This meant that for the first time most adult dragonflies could be accurately identified in the field. The book also provided brief notes on diagnostic features, flight period, typical field habits and habitat, status and distribution. The distribution was also summarised in 10 km square dot-maps. The keys provided for larval identification were those originally published by Gardner (1954). The book was demonstrably inspirational since it provided an enormous boost to the Odonata Recording Scheme and, as a result, was instrumental in the formation of the British Dragonfly Society (Hammond and Merritt, 1983: 9). An examination of the distribution maps that appeared in the second edition (Hammond and Merrit, 1983) shows the impact of the thousands of additional records that had been generated, and meant that the actual distribution of the species, rather than the recorders, was now revealed.

The large increase in the number of people interested in dragonflies was made evident by the number of national (e.g. McGeeney, 1986; Gibbons, 1986) and local field guides (e.g. Benton, 1988; Mendel, 1992) that appeared in the decade following the publication of Hammond's book. Also, the shift in focus of dragonfly enthusiasts away from collecting towards field observation, recording and photography was apparent in these guides, which, for the first time, featured high-quality images of live dragonflies in natural settings and rather longer notes on behaviour.

By the mid 1990s most of these guides had gone out of print. The British Dragonfly Society by then had over 1500 members and there were an increasing number of new dragonfly recorders, especially amongst birdwatchers, who were eager to get to know the group. The time seemed right for a new field guide to the British Odonata.

10.3 Output drivers

The earlier field guides had generated a lot of interest in dragonflies but were now largely unavailable. They provided a means to identifying the British species in the field but nevertheless did have significant drawbacks. The adult British species include a bewildering number of age-related and sex-related colour forms, many of which were not illustrated in the existing guides, leading to obvious difficulties in accurate identification. Many dragonfly enthusiasts were keen photographers but were having difficulty identifying their images because the dragonflies were often captured in side view, whereas traditionally the species were illustrated in field guides showing the dorsal view. People who were developing a new interest in dragonflies wanted to know where they could go to see a good range of species. The guides had provided broad-scale distribution maps, but his was not enough to pinpoint individual sites. People's interest would also be fuelled if they could understand and interpret the fascinating and complex behaviour that dragonflies exhibit. However, explanations of this were largely available only in textbooks, although the excellent book by Peter Miller (1987, 1995) helped to bridge the gap between field guides and textbooks by providing an identification guide and an accessible guide to dragonfly biology and behaviour in one volume. An increasing number of birdwatchers were turning to dragonflies as a way of filling the relatively dull summer season and they were used to far more comprehensive field guides.

10.4 Audience

While I was thinking about the way these audience needs could be fulfilled, primarily by considering what I would have liked in a guide when I first became interested in dragonflies, I was contacted by Andrew Branson, of British Wildlife Publishing. He floated the idea of producing a new generation guide to British dragonflies, featuring the artwork of Richard Lewington. Our aim for this new field guide would be to provide amateur dragonfly enthusiasts, birdwatchers and other interested naturalists with the means to make accurate field identifications of any adult dragonfly that they encountered in Britain, to interpret much of the adult dragonfly behaviour they observed, and to tell them where some of the best dragonfly sites in Britain were to be found. In addition, new illustrated keys would enable them to identify larvae and larval exuviae, and an introductory section would provide an overview of dragonfly ecology to put their observations in context.

10.5 Format

The book, which was first published in 1997 (Brooks and Lewington, 1997), is pocket-sized for easy transport and reference in the field. In some ways it follows the format that has become familiar in field guides, so readers can easily find their way around the book. There is a general introduction to dragonfly ecology and there are species accounts, which include sections on diagnostic field identification characters, status and distribution, flying season and notes on the ecology and behaviour of each species. Larvae can be identified using a dichotomous key, illustrated with uncluttered line drawings, and a key to adult families, illustrated with colour photographs, helps novices find the right part of the book to make their species identifications.

A major feature of the book is the large, high-quality, accurate colour paintings by Richard Lewington. These illustrate all the commonly encountered adult colour forms. Paintings arguably provide the best means for accurate identification, since not all the diagnostic characteristics of a species may be clearly visible on a photograph. Nevertheless, the paintings are supplemented with high-quality photographs, the majority provided by Robert Thompson, one of the most outstanding insect photographers of the day. These colour images, together with the simple layout, make the book attractive in its own right, and display the vivid and beautiful appearance of dragonflies to great advantage.

There also are a number other features included in the book which at the time were novel in a dragonfly field guide. The book includes a regional guide, the first of its kind in a dragonfly field guide, which gives details and map references to 66 top dragonfly localities from around the country. Each regional account is written by a dragonfly specialist who knows the sites intimately and thus provides a unique insight into the importance of these localities. The species accounts are also contributed by specialist authors, who have studied in detail the species described, and are therefore highly authoritative. The ecological notes included under each species are more extensive than in previous guides and draw on the author's own expertise and observations, and also on the wealth of information being disseminated by the growing numbers of amateur enthusiasts and professional ecologists. The species paintings themselves are unobtrusively annotated to highlight diagnostic characters that confirm identification in the field.

10.6 Arrangement and layout

The book can be used and enjoyed equally well at home or in the field. The informative introduction provides a readable account of dragonfly ecology and helps to put what follows into context. Field trips can be planned in advance at home with reference to the regional guides. These accounts are especially useful when visiting sites for the first time or those that are situated far from home, when on holiday for example. Larvae and exuviae are particularly difficult to identify to species level in the field because the diagnostic features may be obscured by debris or they may be too small to be seen with the naked eye. Users of the book are recommended to confirm their identifications at home and a dichotomous key is provided as the most suitable means of securing an accurate identification.

However, a key to the adults is not the best approach for the British dragonflies. Once the correct family has been determined it is much simpler to flick through the illustrations and compare the specimen with the illustrations by checking the diagnostic features. Notes on how to distinguish similar species, another novel feature of the book, are provided in each species description.

Each section of the book is colour-coded for easy navigation. The page numbers appear on the mid outer margin of each page, so they are readily apparent when the pages are flicked through, and are enclosed in a particular coloured box together with the section title or, in the case of the species accounts, the family name. The text is concise and informative. The introduction covers the first 27 pages, 20 pages are devoted to the regional guides and the remaining 110 pages focus on identification. Each species account comprises about 1000 words and the illustrations and accompanying text mostly appear on facing pages. The book is highly illustrated throughout with colour paintings and photographs showing diagnostic characteristics for accurate adult and larval species identification, photographs demonstrating aspects of dragonfly behaviour and photographs of typical dragonfly habitats.

10.7 Contents of the book

The book is divided into three principal sections: an introduction, the regional guides and the identification section. The topics discussed in the introductory section have sometimes been covered in previous guides but those books often seem to present the information as bald facts. My intention in this guide was to prompt the reader to think further, to get behind the facts and so interpret dragonfly morphology, behaviour or distribution in terms of the ecological drivers. This approach would promote a deeper understanding of dragonflies in the reader and so enhance the hobby and perhaps result in the reader developing their own projects and insights.

The introduction begins with a discussion of the characteristic differences between the two suborders (the Zygoptera and Anisoptera). The fossil record is then summarised followed by an account of world dragonfly diversity in terms of species and habitats. These sections help to put the British fauna into a wider context. To further contextualise dragonflies, their vision and flight is then discussed. These are perhaps the most significant of their senses and abilities and an assessment here helps to provide background to a basic understanding of their behaviour.

There then follows a synopsis of the key features of the dragonfly life cycle covering the egg stage, the larva (including development, body form and its relationship to habitat, feeding, respiration, larval interactions, movement, diapause, and metamorphosis), emergence and adult behaviour (including migration and dispersal, finding a mate, mate recognition, keeping a mate, mating, oviposition and feeding). The intention of this general account is to help readers understand why dragonflies appear and behave the way they do, and to interpret some of the behaviour readers are likely to witness while they are observing dragonflies in the field.

The chapter on distribution is given some prominence because many of the users of the book are likely to be dragonfly recorders. The purpose of this chapter is to offer some suggestions about what might be driving dragonfly distribution in Britain by thinking about regional patterns of distribution. These distribution patterns suggest that climate is likely to be the most important driver, but that habitat type and quality have an underlying influence. The likely impacts of recent and future climate change are discussed and what makes some species rare is also considered. A broad classification of wetland habitats is then presented together with the typical species likely to be found in them and the conservation threats these habitats currently face. Taken together these two chapters will help the reader to predict which species are likely to be found in a particular habitat and to understand how conservation priorities can be set. This is followed by the final chapter in the introduction which outlines how legislation has been used to help conserve dragonflies but how this is likely to be inadequate by itself. Dragonfly enthusiasts cannot afford to be complacent!

10.8 Regional guides

The purpose of second major section of the book is to highlight some of the best dragonfly sites in Britain, describe them and the dragonflies they support, and encourage readers to visit them. The sites in each region are described by local experts who know the sites well. This section was innovative at the time and some people expressed disquiet that by promoting the sites they could be damaged. This fear has proved to be unfounded and in fact by increasing the number of people who value these sites, there is more likelihood of their successful long-term conservation. The sites were chosen carefully to ensure that only those that could withstand visitor pressure and which supported strong populations of any rare species were mentioned. I feel that this section provides a celebration of these key dragonfly sites. I had been frustrated at the vagueness to which sites had been referred in past guides and wanted to help readers, especially those new to the subject or who were visiting regions with which they were unfamiliar, find some of the best and most spectacular sites in the country and see the rare species.

The section opens with suggestions of how the reader can find good dragonfly sites for themselves by searching maps and considering the habitat requirements and distributions of the British species. Once at the site, readers are prompted to focus their studies by posing questions that they could research or answer themselves by careful observation. Field-craft and recommended items of equipment are also discussed and described. All this will enhance their enjoyment of the hobby, encourage them to get more deeply involved in studying dragonflies and continue this interest for many years, and to value these insects and the wetlands they inhabit.

A total of 66 sites from throughout Britain and Ireland appear in the regional guide. The habitats are described, and in some cases illustrated with photographs, together with the most significant species of dragonflies that occur at each site. Grid references are provided for each site to allow their easy location.

10.9 Identification

The identification section begins with a glossary and then provides a dichotomous species-level key to the larvae. This key combines characters used in the larval key of Gardner (1954) and in the works of other authors, in particular Heidemann and Seidenbusch (1993). The key was constructed to be as simple and practical as possible and is illustrated with clear line drawings, supplemented with photographs of live larvae from each of the families. A family key to adult dragonflies then follows, illustrated by photographs of live individuals. This is intended to help novices find the correct part of the book to identify a particular species and well as providing an opportunity to include some very attractive photographs.

10.10 Species accounts

The bulk of the book is devoted to the species accounts. The main aims of these accounts are to provide a means of easy and accurate identification of each species, and also to provide autecological information to further enhance the readers' appreciation and understanding of behaviours observed in the field. These extended species accounts were another innovative feature of the book and are intended to draw the reader further into the study of dragonflies. The species are arranged systematically by family and within each family. This means that similar species are placed close to one another and aids accurate identification. The description of each species and the accompanying illustrations usually appear on facing pages (Fig 10.1). The text of each species account is written by a specialist author. Here, and throughout the rest of the book, no references are cited in support of statements. This decision was taken to assist the readability of the book, although there are obvious drawbacks to this approach especially in the case of statements that are the result of the author's personal observations and do not appear elsewhere in the literature. The authors of the key papers to which reference was made are acknowledged at the beginning of the book.

Each species account is organised in the same way and includes descriptions under the headings: jizz; field characters; similar species; status and conservation;

ecology and behaviour. 'Jizz' is an innovative feature in a dragonfly field guide but is familiar to birdwatchers and describes the general flight behaviour and typical habits of the species. It can be a useful guide to initial identification. 'Field characters' describe the diagnostic features. Species with which the species under consideration could be confused are distinguished under the 'similar species' heading. This is another novel feature of the book, but one that is essential if accurate identifications are to be ensured. The status and threats to conservation are described, followed by relatively long autecological notes on the larva and adult. I had found the paucity of autecological information in previous guides frustrating. This information was often repeated from one guide to the next and gave no real flavour of the essence of the species. This lack of information did not reflect the wealth of data that was becoming available from professional ecologists and, more significantly, from amateur enthusiasts who were publishing in volumes such as the *Journal of the British Dragonfly Society*. By providing more detailed autecological information in the guide, not only would this help the reader to understand better the behaviour they were witnessing, but would also highlight any unusual behaviour that might be observed. It would also emphasise which species were still poorly known and would further encourage the reader to undertake studies of their own, and to emulate their peers by publishing their data in one of the appropriate journals.

The highly detailed, accurate and beautiful paintings of whole adult specimens are the focus of the book, and are unrivalled in any other guide to the British species. They provide dorsal and lateral views, and illustrate all the most frequently encountered age-related and sex-related colour forms. This was the first time that this level of comprehension had been achieved in a field guide, but is essential to avoid erroneous identifications. Where appropriate, paintings of enlarged critical morphological characters were also included. The paintings are complemented by high-quality colour photographs of some species, which further enhance the appearance of the book. Diagnostic characters are highlighted using brief annotations positioned next to the appropriate part of the painting. This innovative feature was included in order to draw the user's attention to these characters and minimise the chance of novices focussing on trivial characters. Also included with the species description is a map showing the distributional range of each species in Britain and a simple bar chart indicating the flying season. A two-tone colour code was used on the maps to distinguish the core area of a species from those areas where it was less common.

The book finishes with a list of recommended further reading and useful addresses, a checklist to the British species and an index.

Since 1997 four editions of the book have been published and this has enabled updates to be made. These updates principally reflect changes in the British dragonfly fauna, but the opportunity has also been taken to make a few minor corrections,

Migrant Hawker
Aeshna mixta Latrielle

Description

Jizz The Migrant Hawker is a medium-sized, late-summer and autumn dragonfly. The species is often seen flying in large numbers at treetop level in woodland glades or hedgerows. Mature males patrol low down along the edges of still and slow-moving waters, hawking and periodically hovering to look for ovipositing females.

Field characters Ab 43-49mm; hw 37-40mm. Males are predominantly blue; females appear brown and dull yellowy green. The immature Migrant Hawker has grey to pale lilac markings. On cool days the mature-male coloration may change to lilac-grey. The yellow triangle at the base of the abdomen in both sexes distinguishes the Migrant Hawker from the Common.

Similar species The Migrant Hawker is slightly smaller than the Southern and Common Hawkers. The male Southern Hawker is distinguished by the broad green antehumeral stripes and the predominantly green abdomen with the last three segments blue. The male Common Hawker has narrow, yellow antehumeral stripes; in the Migrant these stripes are much reduced in size. The male Hairy Hawker has similar sky-blue spots, but is slightly smaller, is downy, flies in early summer and has broad antehumeral stripes. The male Azure Hawker also has extensive blue markings but is confined to Scotland.

Both sexes of the Migrant Hawker have a brown costa; the Common Hawker's is diagnostically yellow. While the female Migrant Hawker is medium brown with dull yellowy green spots, the female Southern Hawker has extensive apple-green markings and the female Common Hawker has mainly lemon-coloured ones.

Status and conservation

In the 1940s this species was an uncommon migrant from southern Europe, but it has gradually extended its range from a pioneering breeding population in south-east England. Today, the majority of breeding sites are south and east of a line from Hull to south Wales, but it continues to expand north and west. The species has taken advantage of post-war gravel pits and reservoirs. In 2000, it was recorded for the first time in south-east Ireland. It is common in south-east England, with regular migrations from the Continent increasing the population in late summer. There are records of spectacular mass migrations across Europe in certain years. The species is widespread in central and southern Europe.

Ecology and behaviour

Habitat Larvae are found in ponds, lakes, gravel pits, canals and slow-moving rivers. They can also tolerate brackish water in coastal ditches, but are not found in the acidic heathland ponds in which the Common Hawker thrives.

The **larvae** hatch in early spring and grow rapidly under warm conditions throughout summer to emerge from late July to September. The rapid development of the larvae may restrict them to the warmer climate of the south, where the food supply may be more abundant earlier in the year. Larvae feed on invertebrates which they actively hunt among plants and detritus.

Emergence takes place at night in late summer and autumn. The larva crawls up a vertical plant stem of 10cm or more to emerge. The immature adult remains away from water for 7-10 days. The **flight season** lasts from late July to well into the autumn.

Large numbers of immatures can sometimes be seen feeding in open woodland, meadows, hedgerows or parks, flying high with crisscrossing flight paths and without obvious signs of aggression. They hawk back and forth along a beat, this broken occasionally by periodic soaring to a greater height after prey. Feeding occurs mainly in the afternoon and early evening. Migrant Hawkers that are seen flying high over open water are probably feeding, and not involved in territorial or sexual behaviour. Adults can be seen as late as November, hawking and sunning themselves on sheltered vegetation. Sunbathing most often occurs in the morning or after foraging. They prefer a site

Figure 10.1 Example of species description and illustrations from *Field Guide to the Dragonflies and Damselflies of Great Britain and Ireland.*

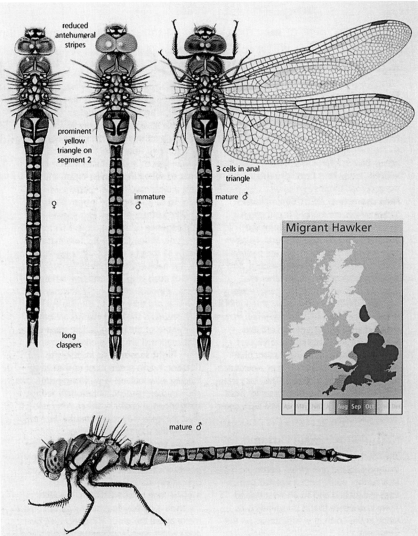

reduced antehumeral stripes

prominent yellow triangle on segment 2

♀

immature ♂

3 cells in anal triangle

mature ♂

long claspers

Migrant Hawker

Aug Sep Oct

mature ♂

low down, sheltered and facing the sun, with a clear escape flight path. When perched, the body hangs vertically, oriented to catch the most sunlight.

Mature males visit open water during the middle of the day and may remain into late afternoon. Each male will take up a shoreline territory which it patrols without showing a great deal of aggression towards other males. Flight is low over the water, with inquisitive hovering at any bays or breaks in marginal vegetation in search of females. A female will be chased vigorously and, if possible, the two insects will pair in flight before settling in a tree or among shoreline vegetation to copulate for a lengthy period of time. The female usually oviposits alone, although tandem oviposition has been recorded. Eggs are laid in stems of plants such as bulrush (*Typha*) and Yellow Flag (*Iris pseudacorus*) by the water's edge, quite often above the water-line in anticipation of rising water levels before the next spring. With this strategy the eggs are probably safer from predators. Females have been observed ovipositing in bare mud as well. The eggs diapause in winter.

Andrew McGeeney

Figure 10.1 (*cont.*)

to improve the tonal quality of the colour images, to make a few changes to the regional guide section, and to add a species checklist. A new paragraph has been added to the chapter on distribution to outline the recent changes in the British fauna in response to climate change. New text and paintings have been added to describe four additional species that have recently been added to the British list, including one (*Erythromma viridulum*) that is a recent colonist. In addition, new colour paintings have been added to show the females of *Hemianax ephippiger* and *Anax parthenope*, and the illustration of an immature male *Anax imperator* has been added. These changes have been achieved without adding any additional pages.

10.11 Trends in more recent guides

Since the publication of the first edition of the *Field guide to the dragonflies and damselflies of Great Britain and Ireland*, several new guides to British dragonflies have appeared. Some of these have adopted some of the innovative features first tried in Brooks and Lewington (1997) and some have introduced innovations of their own. One of the new features of the guide produced by Powell (1999) was to use colour paintings to illustrate dragonflies in natural poses in an attempt to capture the essence of dragonflies in the wild rather than producing taxonomic illustrations that owed more to pinned specimens. Hill and Twist (1998) produced a book devoted solely to descriptions of outstanding dragonfly sites. In the guide by Smallshire and Swash (2004) a photomontage of living dragonflies is used to illustrate and compare the species and their various colour forms. These authors also include an additional eight European species that currently have never been recorded from Britain but which they consider to be potential migrants. Perhaps the most spectacular recent publication is the guide to Ireland's dragonflies by Nelson and Thompson (2004), which combines a large format with superb photographs and a detailed text to produce the first 'coffee-table' dragonfly book. The first publication covering solely the larval stages since Lucas's (1930) work, appeared in 2007. Volume one covers the Anisoptera (Cham, 2007) and volume two, covering the Zygoptera, was published more recently (Cham, 2009). The most recent field guide to the British species (Dudley et al., 2007) has a similar layout and format to Brooks and Lewington (1997) with the addition of a detailed site guide highlighting 94 of the best Odonata sites in Britain (although Ireland is not included). From the same publishing house as Brooks and Lewington (1997), there is a field guide to European dragonflies by Dijkstra (2006). In many ways this is a natural extension to the British guide because both books have a similar approach and general appearance. Once more it features the artwork of Richard Lewington and draws on the expertise of European Odonata specialists to provide information on the species and the places to see them.

10.12 Conclusions

Seventeen years after its first publication the *Field guide to the dragonflies and damselflies of Great Britain and Ireland* is still in demand. It is in its fourth edition and is still selling consistently, despite other similar books being widely available. This, and the short-listing of the book for the Natural World Book Prize in 1998, suggests that the book is fulfilling its role successfully. The pocket-sized field guide format is still popular. To some extent the book broke the mould of previous field guides by attempting comprehensive coverage of all the adult colour forms, by providing more in the way of autecological information and by providing a guide to some of the top dragonfly sites in Britain. That this format and coverage is popular and successful is reinforced by the appearance in subsequent guides by other authors of similar features. I have tried to make the book more than just an identification guide. In addition it is a guide to dragonfly ecology and behaviour, and I have attempted to encourage readers to think more deeply about their observations, to carry out their own studies in order to enhance their long-term enjoyment of their hobby and to become more deeply involved in dragonfly conservation. By understanding dragonflies they are likely to be more valued. There is a lot more to dragonflies than identifying them!

Acknowledgements

I would like to take this opportunity to thank Andrew Branson, of British Wildlife Publishing, who commissioned the field guide, and Richard Lewington, who created the paintings and line drawings. The book was developed, and owes its contents and final appearance, to the collective thoughts of, and discussions between, the three of us.

References

Benton, E. (1988). *The dragonflies of Essex.* Essex Naturalist No. 9. London: Essex Field Club.

Brooks, S. J. and Lewington, R. (1997). *Field guide to the dragonflies and damselflies of Great Britain and Ireland.* Hook, UK: British Wildlife Publishing.

Cham, S. (2007). *Field guide to the larvae and exuviae of British dragonflies. Volume 1: dragonflies (Anisoptera).* British Dragonfly Society. Available from: http://www.british-dragonflies.org.uk/.

Cham, S. (2009). *Field guide to the larvae and exuviae of British dragonflies. Volume 2: damselflies (Zygoptera).* British Dragonfly Society. Available from: http://www.british-dragonflies.org.uk/.

Corbet, P. S., Longfield, C. and Moore, N. W. (1960). *Dragonflies.* The New Naturalist. London: Collins.

Curtis, J. (1823–1840). *British Entomology: being illustrations and descriptions of the genera of insects found in Great Britain and Ireland, etc.*, 8 volumes. Privately published.

Dijkstra, K.-D. B. (2006). *Field guide to the dragonflies of Britain and Europe: including Western Turkey and North-Western Africa.* Gillingham, Dorset: British Wildlife Publishing.

Dudley, S., Dudley, C. and Mackay, A. (2007). *Watching British dragonflies.* Shrewsbury: Subbuteo Natural History Books.

Furneaux, W. (1932). *Life in ponds and streams.* London: Longmans, Green and Co.

Gardner, A. E. (1954). A key to the larvae of the British Odonata. Introduction and Part I, Zygoptera; Part II, Anisoptera. *Entomologist's Gazette*, **5**: 157–171; 193–213.

Gibbons, B. (1986). *Dragonflies and damselflies of Britain and northern Europe.* Twickenham: Hamlyn.

Hammond, C. O. (1977). *The dragonflies of Great Britain and Ireland.* Colchester: Harley Books.

Hammond, C. O. and Merritt, R. (1983). *The dragonflies of Great Britain and Ireland*, Second Edition. Colchester: Harley Books.

Harris, M. (1782). *Exposition of English insects.* London: White.

Heidemann, H. and Seidenbusch, R. (1993). *Die Libellenlarven Deutschlands und Frankreichs.* Keltern: Verlag Erna Bauer.

Hill, P. and Twist, C. (1998). *Butterflies and dragonflies: a site guide.* Chelmsford: Arlequin Press.

Longfield, C. (1937). *The dragonflies of the British Isles.* London: Frederick Warne.

Longfield, C. (1949). *The dragonflies of the British Isles*, Second edition. London: Frederick Warne.

Lucas, W. J. (1900). *British dragonflies (Odonata).* London: Upcott Gill.

Lucas, W. J. (1930). *The aquatic (naiad) stage of the British dragonflies (Paraneuroptera).* London: Ray Society.

McGeeney, A. (1986). *A complete guide to British dragonflies.* London: Jonathan Cape.

Mendel, H. (1992). *Suffolk dragonflies.* Ipswich: Suffolk Naturalists' Society.

Miller, P. L. (1987). *Dragonflies.* Second Edition. Naturalists' Handbooks 7. Slough: Richmond Publishing.

Miller, P. L. (1995). *Dragonflies*, Second Edition, Revised 1995. Naturalists' Handbooks 7. Slough: Richmond Publishing.

Mouffet, T. (1634). *Insectorum sive Minimorum Animalium Theatrum.* London: Cotes.

Nelson, B. and Thompson, R. (2004). *The natural history of Ireland's dragonflies.* Belfast: National Museums and Galleries of Northern Ireland.

Powell, D. (1999). *Guide to the dragonflies of Great Britain.* Chelmsford: Arlequin Press.

Ray, J. (1710). *Historia Insectorum.* London: Churchill.

Skelton, M. J. L. (1974). *Insect distribution maps scheme: Orthoptera, Dictyoptera and Odonata preliminary distribution maps.* Huntingdon: Biological Records Centre.

Smallshire, D. and Swash, A. (2004). *Britain's dragonflies.* Old Basing: WildGuides.

11

Sangha trees: an identification
and training guide to the trees
of the northern Republic of Congo

A. H. Wᴏʀᴛʟᴇʏ ᴀɴᴅ D. J. Hᴀʀʀɪs

11.1 Introduction

A flurry of recent taxonomic initiatives, such as the Encyclopedia of Life[1] project
and the Global Biodiversity Information Facility[2], have exemplified one of the most
crucial issues facing systematists today: the question of how best to supply basic
taxonomic information to those who need it most. This issue is of growing concern
because the worldwide biodiversity crisis demands immediate conservation action
based upon scientific evidence, which in turn relies upon accurate species-level
identifications. This chapter describes a UK Darwin Initiative-funded project,
Building capacity for forest inventory in the Republic of Congo, which aims to supply
such information to stakeholders in the Republic of Congo (Congo-Brazzaville).

The tropical forests of the Congo Basin require urgent protection from encroach-
ment and exploitation, yet there is little scientific information available on which
to base conservation strategies. Few people can identify more than a handful of
forest tree species in this area and the most appropriate existing identification guide
is out of print. In Congo, forest managers have recognised the need for plant

[1] http://www.eol.org   [2] http://www.gbif.org

1111
Descriptive Taxonomy: The Foundation of Biodiversity Research, eds M. F. Watson,
C. H. C. Lyal and C. A. Pendry. Published by Cambridge University Press.
© The Systematics Association 2015

identification tools suitable for local users. In response, a project was initiated to provide training and tools within Congo so that accurate species identifications can be made without the need to 'parachute in' experienced botanists from distant parts of the world. Working with local partners, including the Wildlife Conservation Society (WCS)–Congo and Université Marien Ngouabi, Brazzaville, this capability is being transferred both by training Congolese individuals in the techniques of plant identification and by providing permanent resources to support long-term training and identification activities.

The project focuses on the Sangha Trinational Landscape, a network of protected areas situated in a zone of contiguous forest covering parts of Cameroon, the Central African Republic and the Republic of Congo (Fig 11.1). The Landscape, named for the Sangha River which flows through the area, was officially designated in 2000 in a coordinated agreement between the governments of the three countries. One of the main challenges faced by conservation managers in the Sangha Trinational Landscape is timber extraction. Much of Central Africa is under logging

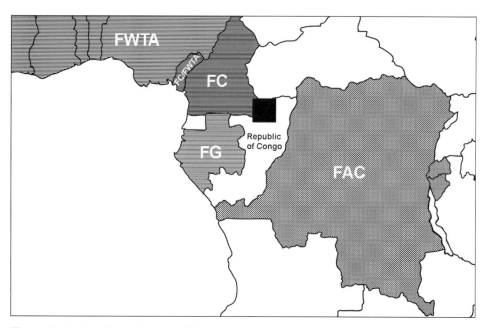

Figure 11.1 Map of sub-Saharan Africa showing the Republic of Congo and regions covered by the nearest recent Floras. The black square shows the approximate extent of the Sangha Trinational Landscape, the area covered by *Sangha trees* (Harris and Wortley, 2008). FWTA, *Flora of west tropical Africa* (Hutchinson and Dalziel, 1954); FAC, *Flore d'Afrique Centrale (Congo-Kinshasa, Rwanda and Burundi)* (Bamps, 1972 and subsequent volumes); FC, *Flore du Cameroun* (Aubréville, 1963, and subsequent volumes); FG, *Flore du Gabon* (Aubréville, 1961, and subsequent volumes).

concessions, making areas such as the Landscape crucially important for the conservation of old-growth forests. Conservation of forests depends upon accurate identification of forest trees; therefore one of the key resources provided by the project is an identification manual for over 500 species of trees in the Sangha Trinational Area (Harris and Wortley, 2008). The terms 'field guide' and 'identification manual' are used interchangeably in this chapter.

11.2 Review of existing literature

At present, there is very little taxonomic information on Central African plants. For instance there is no Flora or field guide for the Republic of Congo. The nearest Floras (Fig 11.1) are the *Flora of west tropical Africa* (Hutchinson and Dalziel, 1954–1972), whose coverage extends only as far east as Southwest Cameroon and is rather out of date, although still widely used, the ongoing *Flore d'Afrique Centrale (Congo-Kinshasa, Rwanda and Burundi)* (Bamps, 1972 and subsequent volumes), formerly *Flore du Congo, du Rwanda et du Burundi* and *Flore d'Afrique Centrale (Zaïre, Rwanda and Burundi)*, which covers the Democratic Republic of Congo plus Rwanda and Burundi, and the *Flore du Cameroun* and *Flore du Gabon* (Aubréville, 1961, 1963 and subsequent volumes), both of which are so far incomplete. The only Flora to cover the Sangha Trinational Landscape area is the *Flora of tropical Africa*, of which the first volume was published in 1868; this has also never been completed. All of the above are monolingual (*Flora of tropical Africa* and *Flora of west tropical Africa* in English, the others French), and therefore useful only to a subset of those working in this area.

In our experience, each of these references can be to some extent useful, in different taxonomic groups. However, Floras are not easy to use for botanical inventory work. Many are prohibitively expensive, multi-volume works, far too large and heavy to take into the field, while others, such as *Flora of west tropical Africa*, contain only brief species descriptions and few illustrations, making quick identifications, particularly by non-specialists, extremely difficult (see Chapter 7, Kirkup et al., in this volume).

In addition to Floras, plant taxonomic literature for the Republic of Congo is limited to a few geographically-broad, taxon-specific works, such as those for rattans (Sunderland, 2007), *Impatiens* (Grey-Wilson, 1980), *Crotalaria* (Polhill, 1982) and *Celosia* in tropical Africa (Townsend, 1975). Although very useful for the particular groups covered, the number of genera thus covered remains very low. Even if such publications were available for a majority of taxa, the total cost and lack of portability, due to the inclusion of many species not relevant to any particular area, limits their practical usefulness for inventory work. Checklists are also available to some parts of Central Africa (e.g. Moutsamboté et al., 1994; Cable and Cheek, 1998; Cheek et al.,

2000; Harris, 2002), but these usually provide little information for species identification and are of limited usefulness outside each specific area covered.

In the absence of an identification guide of broad taxonomic scope covering the Sangha Trinational Landscape, and with the most relevant title, *La forêt dense d'Afrique Centrale* (Tailfer, 1989) out of print, the two books that have been found most useful for day-to-day identifications are *Les arbres de la Guinée Équatoriale, Région Continentale* (Wilks and Issembé, 2000) and *Woody plants of Western African forests* (Hawthorne and Jongkind, 2006), both centred on areas a long distance from the Sangha Trinational Landscape. Both guides are notably rich in images (primarily line drawings) and relatively low in text.

In sum, there is a marked absence in the botanical literature of any kind of useful, portable, illustrated identification guide to the trees (or indeed, any plants) of the Sangha Trinational Area. The available literature tends to be either too detailed and specialised for those unfamiliar with botanical jargon, or inappropriate for species-level identification in the area of interest. Part cause, and part effect, of this is an associated lack of botanical expertise among local researchers in identifying native tree species. These two factors – the lack of trained personnel and the lack of taxonomic resources – combine to result in a dearth of reliable plant identifications upon which to base research and conservation.

11.3 Aims of the present project

At the request of local researchers and forest managers the current project was instigated to provide a partial solution to the problem outlined above. The project recognises that while at present training by UK staff is an integral part of developing local botanical skills, this is not a long-term solution. In addition to trained taxonomists or para-taxonomists, there is also a need for trained trainers, identification resources and training materials. Thus, the project aims to provide two main components: training itself, and the resources needed for training and identification.

The training component has comprised dedicated courses for graduate-level biologists covering collecting techniques, plant identification and data management; focussed working sessions with high-level trainers, such as herbarium and university staff; development of undergraduate courses for Marien Ngouabi University; and the completion by one trainee of a UK-based Master of Science degree in the biodiversity and taxonomy of plants at the Royal Botanic Garden Edinburgh.

The training resources developed by the project include a checklist to the tree species of northern Congo[3], specific checklists for protected areas in the Sangha

---

[3] Harris, D. J. and Wortley, A. H. (2007). Draft checklist of the trees of the Northern Republic of Congo. Unpublished: available from authors.

Trinational Landscape and elsewhere, a field manual to the trees of the area, *Sangha trees* (Harris and Wortley, 2008; on which this chapter focuses) and a complementary database of digital images, available both on CD-ROM and on the World Wide Web.

11.4 Aims of *Sangha trees*

The specific purpose of the field manual, *Sangha trees* (Harris and Wortley, 2008), is to provide a permanent resource for plant identification now and a handbook for training botanists in the future, thus enabling long-term, accurate scientific research and conservation. The manual provides comprehensive coverage of over 500 species of forest trees found in the Sangha Trinational Landscape. In order to suit practical *in situ* species identification and training by local conservationists, researchers, foresters and students, it was designed with the following criteria in mind:

- **Exhaustive coverage:** *Sangha trees* aims to cover all native tree species within a specified geographical distribution, habitat and size range. One reason this guide is unusual is that no species are excluded on the basis of rarity. This is important because frequency is a criterion that cannot immediately be known in the field, so the users of a guide in which rarity is used as a criterion for exclusion will be unable to tell if a given tree is likely to be covered or not. In an area where the flora is relatively unknown, the inclusion of all known species means that if a tree is found to fit the criteria of distribution, habitat and size yet cannot be matched to any in the guide, the user can be relatively confident that the species is a new record for the area.

- **Specimen-based:** each species included in the manual is represented by at least one herbarium collection taken within the Sangha Trinational Landscape.

- **Minimal text content:** for usability and portability, the text is limited to facts that are immediately useful for species identification: morphological characters and names. Thus, details such as literature references, distribution details and conservation status are omitted from the manual and documented elsewhere.

- **Minimal information:** brevity also extends to the choice of characters covered, such that only those useful for identification are included. For forest trees the availability of fertile material is very low (less than 1% of specimens collected from forest plots having flower or fruit, in our experience), so descriptions focus on ubiquitous characters such as bark slashes, smells and fallen leaves. Duplication of characters between text and images is also minimised.

- **Image rich:** high-quality, informative images are provided for every species, enabling the maximum possible number of characters to be compared without reference to the text; we term this the 'image rich, text poor' model.

- **Fully bilingual:** text in both French and English.
- **Inexpensive:** the finished manual is economical to print from a PDF file and to reproduce by photocopying, thereby widening its availability.
- **Portable and durable:** enabling the manual to be carried into the forest and to withstand daily use in forest conditions. Furthermore, by being easily and cheaply reproduced, copies can be replaced as soon as they wear out.

The next section addresses how these characteristics were achieved, discussing some of the questions and issues that arose during the production of *Sangha trees*.

11.5 Field guide production

11.5.1 Species to include

Often, the first issue to be considered when producing a field guide is which species to include. Having already discussed the criteria of distribution, habitat and rarity, the main question to be considered in *Sangha trees* was one of size: 'which species in the area are large enough to be considered trees?', or 'how does one define a tree?' Clearly, single-stemmed, self-supporting, woody, forest species with a girth much larger than that of a man (e.g. the *Zanthoxylum*, Rutaceae, in Fig 11.2A) should be included. But the plant shown intermingled with *Megaphrynium macrostachys* (Marantaceae) in Fig 11.2B (*Duvigneaudia inopinata* (Prain) J.Léonard, Euphorbiaceae) is less than 5 cm in diameter at breast height (dbh), and situated at the forest edge, so is this also a forest tree? Could it be a sapling of a larger species or is this its maximum size? The crucial question is, 'would it be useful to the user to include this species in the field manual?' Different field guides, designed for different audiences, have answered these questions differently; some (e.g. Hawthorne and Jongkind, 2006) include every woody species; others concentrate on only the largest species (e.g. Wilks and Issembé, 2000). For *Sangha trees* a pragmatic approach was taken, with slightly different sizes of tree being included depending on the group. As a baseline every species that can attain a height of at least 3 m or a girth of at least 5 cm was included. Species that do not achieve such sizes were included where special reasons exist, for instance where there are other, larger species in the group whose saplings might be confused with members of this species (e.g. *Drypetes molunduana* Pax and K.Hoffm., Putranjivaceae, the smallest species in a genus containing many larger tree species).

11.5.2 Species arrangement

Having generated a list of species, the next question that arose was how to arrange them in the field manual. Many solutions to this question have been adopted, ranging from purely alphabetical, to strictly taxonomic, to character-based, with

Figure 11.2 Example species covered by *Sangha trees*. (A) *Zanthoxylum tessmannii*;
(B) *Duvigneaudia inopinata*. A black and white version of this figure will appear in some
formats. For the colour version, please refer to the plate section.

almost every possible variation in between. For *Sangha trees* it was decided to organise the species within families, generating the subsidiary question of which family concepts to use. The family circumscriptions chosen were based upon those of the Angiosperm Phylogeny Group (APG, 1998; APG II, 2003), because this molecular phylogenetic approach was considered to represent the likely future of botanical taxonomy. APG families not only match what the majority of the next generation of botanists is being taught, but are increasingly being used in both scientific literature and herbaria (Haston et al., 2007, 2009).

From a more practical point of view, the APG classification is perhaps the best system yet established for identification, with the families often being more coherent and having a greater number of diagnostic characters than those in previous classification systems. For example, Malvaceae *sensu* APG comprises elements of the long-standing families Bombacaceae, Malvaceae, Sterculiaceae and Tiliaceae. Previously, for some members of this complex, it was very difficult to tell to which family a sterile specimen belonged, making further identification at genus and species level extremely hard. For instance, *Pterygota bequaertii* De Wild. (previously Sterculiaceae) and *Duboscia macrocarpa* Bocq. (previously Tiliaceae), along with other species, both share fibrous bark, stipules, trinerved leaf bases, swollen petioles and stellate hairs. Starting from a family concept based on Malvaceae *sensu lato*, it is easier to move straight to the characters that distinguish the species (such as differing leaf shape and indumentum), rather than struggling to determine to which of several families, lacking distinct diagnostic characters, they belong.

A phylogenetic approach was also adopted for ordering families, based on the 'linear APG' system developed at the Royal Botanic Garden Edinburgh for herbarium arrangement, and also directly transferable to field guides and floras (Haston et al., 2007). A phylogenetic arrangement enables users to access the field manual by a widely used but little documented method – browsing (Hawthorne and Jongkind, 2006). This intuitive approach to searching for a name, based upon flicking through a book to an image that looks approximately right and then homing in on nearby species, is particularly suited to those with some botanical training but lacking a complete knowledge of the flora: exactly the audience at which *Sangha trees* is targeted. The linear APG system (Haston et al., 2007), is based upon the best current estimate of the phylogeny of flowering plants. It is one of many possible linear arrangements that could be derived from the same phylogenetic tree (branching pattern), and is not necessarily the best, but was considered the most likely system to provide consistency and commonality across the botanical community.

Within families, genera were circumscribed based upon the most recent available revisions but arranged alphabetically. This is because, unlike at interfamilial level, within many families there is as yet no good phylogenetic tree, so no 'linear' arrangement based upon a phylogeny is possible. In addition, many existing genera are potentially non-monophyletic, so trying to organise them in a phylogenetic pattern is illogical.

11.5.3 Field guide design

The third and, perhaps, most obvious, decision to be made regarding a new field guide is the broad issue of design. There are a huge number of questions to be answered (discussed in much more detail in Lawrence and Hawthorne, 2006), but a few of those that were considered for *Sangha trees* are listed below:

- Page size, e.g. A4, which is easy to photocopy, versus A5, which is more portable in a small bag or pocket.
- Whether to have a fixed allocation of space to each species (and, therefore, a fixed number of species per page) or to allow the text to flow.
- Whether identification characters are presented as a list, a continuous paragraph, or annotations to the illustrations.
- Whether (in a bilingual text), the French and English text is presented as separate paragraphs or intermixed character by character.

Each of these questions may be answered differently depending on the target audience. For *Sangha trees* the final layout comprises A4 pages bearing two species, one above the other, each with text and illustration adjacent to one another, French text following the English text, a running header showing the family name and each family starting on a new page (Fig 11.3).

Considering in more detail the species descriptions in Fig 11.3, these were designed to be as brief as possible, and to focus upon sterile diagnostic characters, particularly those not visible in the illustration, such as colour, slash, smell and bole diameter. Certain key characters – bole diameter, habitat, leaf arrangement (alternate or opposite) and leaf structure (simple or compound) – are shown for every species. The remainder of the characters comprise those that are useful for distinguishing the species, which therefore differ between groups.

Figure 11.4A,B shows example illustrations from the manual. Line drawings were chosen for several reasons. Aside from their aesthetic quality, good drawings can be highly accurate and easy to interpret, drawing attention to the most important diagnostic characteristics without losing the appearance of the whole. More pragmatically, they are simple and economical to print and photocopy, always well-focused and require no time-consuming editing (such as removing unwelcome backgrounds or adjusting colour densities). For ease of comparison and identification, a common format was used for the illustration of every species. If possible, all were drawn to the same scale (×0.7), but much larger leaves or leaflets were by

Dialium polyanthum

Maximum diameter: >60 cm
- Slash with red latex.
- Leaves alternate, compound.
- Leaflets alternate, c. 5.
- Leaflets ovate to obovate, with base often rounded, especially on young leaves.
- Leaflet tip tapering and often emarginate.
- Secondary veins c. 4–8 pairs, looping c. 5 mm inside the margin.
- Tertiary venation forming a clear squarely reticulate pattern below when dry.
- Leaflets thick, glabrous.
- Leaflets drying discolorous, pale pinkish-brown.
Habitat: Terra firma.

Diamètre maximum: >60 cm
- Tranche à latex rouge.
- Feuilles alternes, composées.
- Folioles alternes, env. 5.
- Folioles ovées à obovées, à base souvent arrondie, surtout sur les jeunes feuilles.
- Folioles effilées et souvent émarginées au sommet.
- Nervures secondaires env. 4–8 paires, en boucle env. 5 mm en dedans de la marge.
- Nervation tertiaire formant un réseau bien visible carré-réticulé en dessous sur le sec.
- Folioles épaisses, glabres.
- Folioles discolores, rosâtre-brun pâle en séchant.
Habitat: Terre ferme.

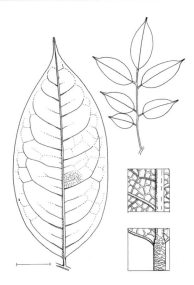

Dialium tessmannii

Maximum diameter: c. 50 cm
- Slash sometimes with red latex.
- Leaves alternate, compound.
- Rachis, petiolules and midrib below with long reddish hairs.
- Leaflets sub-opposite, 8–10 pairs.
- Leaflets with long, fine, pointed extension to midrib at tip, sometimes lost.
- Secondary veins slightly impressed above when dry.
Habitat: Terra firma.

Diamètre maximum: env. 50 cm
- Tranche parfois à latex rouge.
- Feuilles alternes, composées.
- Rachis, pétiolules et nervure médiane dessous avec poils longs rougeâtres.
- Folioles subopposées, 8–10 paires.
- Folioles avec extension longue, fine, pointue de la nervure médiane à l'apex, parfois fêlée.
- Nervures secondaires un peu imprimées dessus sur le sec.
Habitat: Terre ferme.

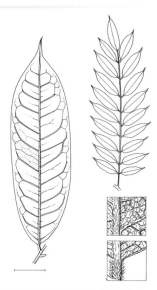

Figure 11.3 Layout of *Sangha trees*, example pages from Leguminosae. Reproduced with permission from Harris and Wortley (2008).

LEGUMINOSAE-CAESALPINIOIDEAE (FABACEAE-CAESALPINIOIDEAE)

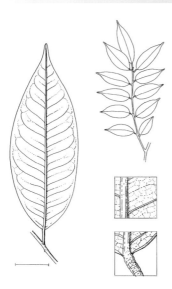

Dialium zenkeri

Maximum diameter: c. 50 cm
- Slash with red latex.
- Leaves alternate, compound.
- Leaflets alternate or sub-opposite, 6–8 pairs.
- Leaflets parallel-sided.
- Leaflets glaucous below when fresh.
- Leaflets discolorous, matt below when dry.
- Margin often revolute at base when dry.
Habitat: Terra firma.

Diamètre maximum: env. 50 cm
- Tranche à latex rouge.
- Feuilles alternes, composées.
- Folioles alternes ou subopposées, 6–8 paires.
- Folioles aux bords parallèles.
- Folioles glauques dessous sur le frais.
- Folioles discolores, mates dessous sur le sec.
- Marge souvent révolutée à la base sur le sec.
Habitat: Terre ferme.

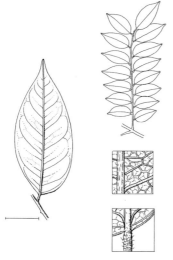

Erythrophleum suaveolens

Maximum diameter: >60 cm
- Bark rough.
- Slash dark red.
- Leaves alternate, compound, bipinnate.
- Leaflets alternate, c. 10–18 per pinna.
- Petiolules distinct, sometimes with sparse short hairs.
- Leaflets asymmetric, more or less ovate.
- Secondary venation drying a similar colour to lamina, not obvious.
- Secondary, tertiary and quaternary venation similarly prominent above and below.
- Leaflets shiny above and slightly shiny below.
Habitat: Terra firma.

Diamètre maximum: >60 cm
- Écorce rugueuse.
- Tranche rouge foncé.
- Feuilles alternes, composées, bipennées.
- Folioles alternes, env. 10–18 par penne.
- Pétiolules distincts, parfois avec poils épars courts.
- Folioles asymétriques, ± ovées.
- Nervation secondaire de même couleur que le limbe en séchant, pas clairement visible.
- Nervures secondaires, tertiaires et quaternaires de même proéminence, saillantes sur les deux faces.
- Folioles brillantes au-dessus, et un peu brillantes au-dessous.
Habitat: Terre ferme.

Figure 11.3 (*cont.*)

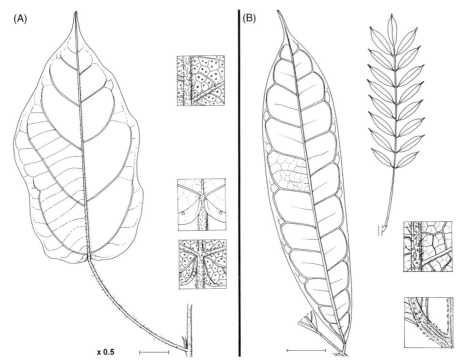

(A)   (B)

x 0.5

Figure 11.4 Illustrations from *Sangha trees*. (A) *Macaranga spinosa* (Euphorbiaceae); (B) *Dacryodes edulis* (Burseraceae). Reproduced with permission from Harris and Wortley (2008).

necessity drawn to a smaller scale and the new scale indicated on the plate. The temptation to draw particularly small leaves at a larger scale simply to fill the page was resisted. Most of the drawings are restricted to sterile characters, shown on a single leaf or leaflet, with enlargements of the leaf undersurface and base shown at a scale of ×10, to correspond with the view seen through an ordinary hand lens. Cartoons were added for additional features that are particularly useful and readily available, such as a distinctive bole shape or fruits that lie on the ground beneath the tree for a large part of the year, and also to show the shape of an entire compound leaf (e.g. Fig 11.4B).

The final important aspects of field guide design, often neglected but crucial to enable users easily to navigate the text, are the access-routes to the species. Rather than traditional keys, *Sangha trees* uses 'cross-cutting lists of species', a technique employed by Hawthorne and Jongkind (2006), among others, to enable easy searching for species with one or more distinctive characters, or to provide a starting point based on common character combinations. Finally, there is an introduction explaining the design to the reader, a glossary to potentially unfamiliar botanical terms, an index to species names including authors and synonyms (these are not shown on the species pages where they are likely to confuse non-taxonomists) and a list of selected references.

11.5.4 How *Sangha trees* was assembled

For simplicity this chapter makes an artificially clear-cut distinction between design and process. In practice the design of a field guide develops as the process goes on, and the process simultaneously evolves to suit the changing end-product. For *Sangha trees*, the production process was broadly as follows.

A preliminary species list, roughly corresponding to the criteria outlined above, was generated from a combination of sources. Fifteen years of research in the region, crystallised in the publication *Vascular plants of the Dzanga-Sangha Reserve* (Harris, 2002), provided the obvious starting point to developing a species list of the whole Trinational Landscape. This was extended through collections made from every tree over 10 cm dbh located in 30 permanent 1-hectare forest plots within Nouabalé-Ndoki National Park, Congo, and adjacent forestry concessions. These were supplemented by opportunistic collection in habitats other than *terra firma* forest: roadsides, riversides, seasonally inundated forest and forest dominated by *Gilbertiodendron dewevrei* (De Wild.) J.Léonard. All the specimens collected were examined in Congo by the authors, in order that particularly interesting trees (and particularly poor specimens) could be recollected as necessary.

Having generated a set of 18 000 specimens, and thus a species list for the Sangha Trinational Landscape, the manual was written through the traditional process of 'shuffling specimens'. Working within a taxonomic group (usually a genus or group of related genera), specimens were sorted into morphospecies based on shared characters and fixed character differences with other such groups. The morphospecies were then named using the most recent available monographical revisions or Flora accounts. Describing new species was considered beyond the scope of *Sangha trees*, so unnamed species were simply labelled '*sp. A,*' although names of new species submitted or in press at the time were included.

The completed species list for *Sangha trees* contains 522 species in 264 genera and 61 families. As is typical of biological communities (Scotland and Sanderson, 2004), these statistics imply that most families contain relatively few genera and most genera relatively few species, while a few disproportionately large genera and families dominate the assemblage. In the Sangha Trinational Landscape, the largest tree families are Rubiaceae, with 79 species and Leguminosae, with 56. The largest genera are not in these families, being *Ficus* (Moraceae), with 19 species and *Drypetes* (Putranjivaceae), with 16.

Species names and specimen identifications were stored in a BRAHMS[4] database. The taxon database contained different fields for tree size, habitat and description, designed to make data entry as consistent as possible. It should be noted, however, that it remained very difficult to ensure the same terminology was used in the description of each species, necessitating careful checking.

At this stage a representative, mature, preferably sterile specimen of each species was selected and sent to a professional botanical illustrator, with instructions regarding any particular characters which were to be emphasised in the drawing, such as stipules, hollow twigs or fruit characters. Photocopied versions of the illustrations were returned to the authors for comparison with the specimens and to ensure that all the important characters were clear; modifications were requested and the photocopies returned, in a process that continued backwards and forwards (thanks to the patience of the illustrator) until the drawings were considered ready for publication. The originals were then scanned at 720 dpi to produce electronic copies for inclusion in the manual.

An automated reporting process was used to generate the English text for each species, from the BRAHMS database, in the following format:

> Family name [given only once at the start of the family]
>   Genus species
>   *Maximum diameter*: [one of the categories: <15 cm, c. 30 cm, c. 50 cm, >60 cm]
> ■ Character 1.
> ■ Character 2.
> ■ Etc.
> *Habitat*: [*terra firma* or wet places, with the predominant habitat listed first].

The text was then checked against the specimens to ensure it was correct and included all necessary diagnostic characters. The final English version was then translated into French. The French translation was also checked and then copied into the database so that a full report of the text, including English and French, could be generated from the database in a single move.

11.5.6 Testing

Once the text for all species had been generated, with keys, cross-cutting lists, introduction and glossary written, it is important to test that the field guide works, using independent testers. This is usually achieved (Lawrence and Hawthorne, 2006) by observing the testers using it, in the field and in the herbarium, in order to answer two important questions:

---

[4] http://herbaria.plants.ox.ac.uk/BOL/home

1. Does the field guide contain the right information? That is, the species people need to identify and the characters most useful to identify them?

2. Is the guide usable by the target user-group? That is, can they identify plants quickly and easily (using the keys and otherwise) and can they ascertain whether or not a specimen belongs to one of the species covered by the guide?

For a detailed account of testing protocols see Lawrence and Hawthorne (2006).

11.5.7 Planning and budgeting

The costs and workload of producing a field guide vary enormously depending on the scope and design of the guide itself, the state of existing knowledge of the flora, where it is to be produced and printed and how it is to be distributed. One thing that cannot be over-emphasised is the importance of calculating an approximate budget from the start. With this in mind, a checklist of the main costs (and approximate percentage of the overall cost) encountered in the production of *Sangha trees* is provided, to give an idea of the kind of things that need to be considered. Obviously, not all of these will be applicable to every field guide project, and some projects may encounter additional costs that are not listed here.

1. Specimen collection, including the cost of field trips, collecting materials and equipment, staff and shipping specimens (c. 60%).
2. Staff time for specimen curation, data entry and taxonomic work (c. 10%).
3. Staff time for writing text (c. 10%).
4. Illustration, plus equipment and staff time for scanning illustrations (c. 10%). Those using digital photographical images should consider instead the costs of hardware, software and staff time for managing images.
5. Translation (c. 2%).
6. Testing (<1%).
7. Proofreading, by native speakers of all languages used (<1%).
8. Design and typesetting (often out-sourced; c. 2%).
9. Printing and paper costs (c. 3%).
10. Distribution, including hard-copy distribution (postage) or the costs of making the publication available online (<1%).
11. Publicity (<1%).

The total cost of producing *Sangha trees* is estimated at c. £150 000. One essential factor in estimating costs is a realistic assessment of the number of species to be covered, which will proportionately affect each of these costs in turn. One of the main obstacles in writing *Sangha trees* was an initial underestimation of the number of species involved, which affected both the budget and amount of staff time needed to complete the project.

11.5.8 Related products

A field guide can only reach its full potential when used by a trained user-group. As such, *Sangha trees* comprises one part of a broader project including structured training and the production of other resources including checklists and teaching materials. One output which is particularly closely related to the manual and forms an important complement to it, is a database of digital images. As discussed above, colour digital photographs were not chosen to illustrate the manual, being expensive to print, difficult to reproduce, and often harder to interpret than line drawings of the same species. However, digital images (of fresh material or herbarium specimens) have a vital role to play in the provision of modern taxonomic resources, as evidenced by the large number of online image databases and 'digital herbaria', that have sprung up in recent years (see also Chapter 1, A. G. Miller et al., in this volume). Examples include the Tropical Plant Guides Page at the Chicago Field Museum[5], the Australian Virtual Herbarium[6] and the Virtual Field Herbarium at Oxford University[7], UK.

Thousands of digital images of *Sangha trees* collected during this project will be made available online in conjunction with the Oxford University Virtual Field Herbarium, which already contains over 3000 images of African plant species, mostly from West Africa. It is hoped that the images from the Sangha Trinational Area will provide a valuable contribution and range extension to the database. In addition, the images have been supplied on CD to complement the field manual (Harris et al., 2009), which will be particularly useful for confirming identifications in areas with no, or an unreliable, internet connection. By including images of not just leaves, but fruits, flowers, crowns, boles, bark and bark slashes, the images complement and add to the information available in the text and line-drawings of *Sangha trees.*

The ultimate aim of making digital images available, as in similar projects is to democratise the process of field guide production such that individuals throughout the world can download images and generate identification guides specific to their particular needs and situation. Thus, foresters can download images of the bark slashes of economically important trees; ecologists can print a guide to the fruits and seedlings of a specific area; or researchers interested in a limited range of habitats can search for images of species collected in just those situations.

---

[5] http://fm2.fieldmuseum.org/plantguides   [6] http://avh.chah.org.au/
[7] http://herbaria.plants.ox.ac.uk/VFH

11.6 Conclusions

Field guides are crucial to the sustainable exploitation, management and protection of tropical forests. They provide a resource for identification and a tool for training future botanists. Used in conjunction with suitable training, and provided alongside checklists and other, novel resources such as digital image databases, they provide invaluable support for conservation and research.

The design and process of production of any field guide tend to develop as the project proceeds. However, as *Sangha trees* reached publication, it became clear that the development of appropriate and efficient working protocols is crucial to completing such a project on time and on budget. It is hoped that this chapter will help other authors to develop such protocols, by raising awareness of some of the issues that need to be considered, and providing examples of the ways in which they might be approached. In particular, the issue of species number needs to be considered carefully, especially in areas such as the Sangha Trinational Landscape, with a poorly known flora and a paucity of existing literature from which to start.

One of the crucial factors in writing a successful field guide is putting together a team of people competent to achieve each of the many different tasks involved, and a budget sufficient to cover them. This includes a collecting team with logistical support, taxonomists, illustrators, translators, typesetters and printers. The importance of a carefully designed, well-managed and regularly backed-up database for storing the species information should also not be underestimated, and should be designed to enable, as far as possible, consistent input and extraction of both specimen and taxon data.

The stages to be considered in the production of a field guide include planning a budget, generating a species list, ordering the species and higher taxa and designing the format and layout of illustrations and text. Additional important features that render a guide navigable and user-friendly include keys or other means to identification, glossaries and indices. Finally, and preferably during all stages of production, the field guide and its various components should be tested and the results of such testing implemented in producing a final, usable guide.

Acknowledgements

This chapter is based on a paper presented at the Systematics Association Biennial Meeting at the Royal Botanic Garden Edinburgh, August 2007. The authors would like to thank the organisers of the symposium *Floras and Faunas Serving Biodiversity Research*, Mark Watson and Chris Lyal, for inviting us to contribute to the proceedings volume. This project was funded by the UK Darwin Initiative. We are grateful to WCS-Congo, the Centre d'Etudes sur les Ressources Végétales and Jean-Marie Moutsamboté at the Institut Développement Rural, Université Marien Ngouabi for their support. We are also particularly grateful to the collection teams at Nouabalé-Ndoki National Park and John Poulsen and Connie Clark at the Projet de Gestion Ecologique Dans la Zone Périphérique du Parc Nouabalé-Ndoki for their invaluable efforts towards providing the raw data for *Sangha trees*. We would also like to thank Rosemary Wise for her illustrations, William Hawthorne for advice and discussions on field guide production and the Virtual Field Herbarium and Denis Filer for database support. AHW would like to thank the EU Synthesys programme and the staff of the Nationale Plantentuin van België, including Piet Stoffelen and Elmar Robbrecht, for their help with the Rubiaceae section of the manual.

References

APG (1998). An ordinal classification for the families of flowering plants. *Annals of the Missouri Botanical Garden*, **85**: 531–553.

APG II (2003). An update of the Angiosperm Phylogeny Group classification for the orders and families of flowering plants: APG II. *Botanical Journal of the Linnean Society*, **141**: 399–436.

Aubréville, A. (ed.) (1961). *Flore du Gabon*. Paris: Muséum National d'Histoire Naturelle.

Aubréville, A. (ed.) (1963). *Flore du Cameroun*. Paris: Muséum National d'Histoire Naturelle.

Bamps, P. (1972). *Flore d'Afrique Centrale*. Brussels: Jardin botanique national de Belgique.

Cable, S. and Cheek, M. (1998). *The plants of Mount Cameroon, a conservation checklist*. Richmond: Royal Botanic Gardens, Kew.

Cheek, M., Onana, J.-M. and Pollard, J. (2000). *The plants of Mount Oku and the Ijim Ridge, Cameroon, a conservation checklist*. Richmond: Royal Botanic Gardens, Kew.

Grey-Wilson, C. (1980). *Impatiens of Africa*. Rotterdam: Balkema.

Harris, D. J. (2002). *The vascular plants of the Dzanga-Sangha Reserve. Scripta Botanica Belgica* 23. Meise: National Botanic Garden (Belgium).

Harris, D. J. and Wortley, A. H. (2008). *Sangha trees: an illustrated identification manual*. Edinburgh: Royal Botanic Garden Edinburgh.

Harris, D. J., Moutsamboté, J.-M., Armstrong, K., Kami, E., Mouandza, J.-C., Niangadouma, R., Walters, G. and Wortley, A. H. (2009). *Plantes d'Afrique Centrale: la collection de référence en images* (double CD-ROM). Edinburgh: Royal Botanic Garden Edinburgh.

Haston, E., Richardson, J. E., Stevens, P. F., Chase, M. W. and Harris, D. J. (2007). A linear sequence of Angiosperm Phylogeny Group II families. *Taxon*, **56**: 7–12.

Haston, E., Richardson, J. E., Stevens, P. F., Chase, M. W. and Harris, D. J. (2009). The Linear Angiosperm Phylogeny (LAPG) III: a linear sequence of the families in APG III. *Botanical Journal of the Linnean Society*, **161**: 128–131.

Hawthorne, W. D. and Jongkind, C. (2006). *Woody plants of Western African forests: a guide to the forest trees, shrubs and lianes from Senegal to Ghana*. Richmond: Royal Botanic Gardens, Kew.

Hutchinson, J. and Dalziel, J. M. (1954–1972). *Flora of west tropical Africa*. London: Crown Agents for Overseas Governments and Administrations.

Lawrence, A. and Hawthorne, W. D. (2006). *Plant identification: user friendly guides for biodiversity management*. London: Earthscan.

Moutsamboté, J.-M. et al. (1994). Vegetation and list of plant species identified in the Nouabalé-Ndoki forest, Congo. *Tropics*, **3**: 277–293.

Polhill, R. M. (1982). *Crotalaria in Africa and Madagascar*. Rotterdam: Balkema.

Scotland, R. W. and Sanderson, M. J. (2004). The significance of few versus many in the tree of life. *Science*, **303**: 643.

Sunderland, T. C. H. (2007). *Field guide to the rattans of Africa*. Richmond: Royal Botanic Gardens, Kew.

Szlachetko et al. (1961–onwards). *Flore du Gabon*. Paris: Association de Botanique Tropicale.

Tailfer, Y. (1989). *La forêt dense d'Afrique Centrale. Tome 1 et 2*. Paris: Agence de Coopération Culturelle et Technique.

Townsend, C. C. (1975). *The genus Celosia (subgenus Celosia) in tropical Africa*. Richmond: Bentham-Moxon Trust.

Various authors (1972-onwards). *Flore d'Afrique Centrale. Spermatophytes*. Brussels: Jardin Botanique National de Belgique.

Wilks, C. and Issembé, Y. (2000). *Les arbres de la Guinée Équatoriale, Région Continentale*. Bata: CUREF.

12

Millennium Seed Bank collector guides

D. Hopkins

12.1 Introduction

The Millennium Seed Bank Project (MSBP) is a long-term global conservation initiative, based in the Seed Conservation Department (SCD) of Royal Botanic Gardens, Kew, at Wakehurst Place. The initial aim of this project, which commenced in 1999, was to collect and conserve the entire seed-bearing flora of the UK, and to build suitable storage facilities for these collections. Phase Two, the International Programme, was introduced in 2000, with the new purpose of collecting 10% of the entire global seed-bearing flora, principally from dry lands, by 2010. This incorporated a second specific aim, which focuses on developing bilateral research, training and capacity-building relationships worldwide. This aim means that the knowledge gained in Phase 1 is shared, so the other institutions worldwide have the capacity to collect and store seeds independently throughout the current partner countries. Therefore, the majority of collecting in the participating countries is done by the partner institutions, with support and training from teams at SCD where necessary. There are more than 50 partner institutions working with the MSBP, and the majority of these partnerships have proved very successful, with countries such as the USA, China and Australia working almost independently.

However, it became apparent that some countries needed extra support in meeting their targets, despite the best efforts of in-country experts and

Descriptive Taxonomy: The Foundation of Biodiversity Research, eds M. F. Watson, C. H. C. Lyal and C. A. Pendry. Published by Cambridge University Press.

'International Coordinators' from the MSBP. The ability to plan what and where to collect has proved to be much more difficult in some areas, due principally to two limitations. The first problem, encountered by several countries, concerned the targets set by the project. As in any funded project, specific deliverables are given in order to satisfy funding requirements. In the case of the Phase Two project, it was decided that a seed collection would only be counted as new if it was a completely new species for the MSBP, regardless of whether it was newly collected for a country. This has caused difficulties in some countries with low levels of endemism, or few habitat types. For example, the flora of Botswana has much in common with neighbours Namibia and South Africa, resulting in many potential new species for Botswana having already been added to the MSBP by partners in those countries. The second limitation applies to some areas where there is simply a lack of published information, especially the information held within traditional Floras. This includes keys to genera and species, illustrations, species descriptions and ecological information such as distribution, habitat and phenology. It is often the case that areas lacking a Flora will also be limited in related sources such as checklists, Red Data lists and field guides. It follows that in these areas there is also limited botanical research carried out, resulting in a general deficiency of up-to-date literature and reference material (including herbarium specimens which are sources of locality and habitat information).

In order for a country to achieve its target number of new species to add to the MSBP, it is important that each collection is made in the most cost-effective way. An obvious way to do this is to plan collection trips over several days (or weeks), collecting as many species as possible, with minimum duplication of precollected species. In other words, each institution should aim for the lowest average 'cost' for every species collected. In the most extreme case, a team could, in theory, spend day after day searching different areas to find a previously uncollected species, which happen not to be in fruit when found. Therefore, in order to implement a successful trip, it is important to know *what* species to collect, *where* to find them and *when* to attempt to find these species to ensure they are fruiting at the time. Success can therefore be increased with the use of a list of target species, the distribution and locality information for each of these, and knowledge of the phenology.

12.2 End-product development

12.2.1 Addressing the problem: team development

With these factors in mind, and with the aid of an Enhancement grant from the Millennium Commission, in January 2004 a Species Targeting Team was established at the Herbarium of the Royal Botanic Gardens, Kew. The purpose was to help MSBP partner countries target specific areas and species for seed collection, and to aid in the planning of collection trips to help make them as successful and efficient as possible. Ten countries in the Middle East and Africa were chosen to receive direct help in their species targeting: Lebanon, Jordan, South Africa, Botswana, Malawi, Kenya, Tanzania and the Francophone countries of Madagascar, Burkina Faso and Mali. In addition, training and project development was also provided to partner institutions in Namibia and Chile.

In order to address the problems of collection duplication and a paucity of available literature, it was decided that a series of collection guides would be produced to aid in targeting species, planning collection trips and providing diagnostic information whilst in the field. The Species Targeting Team compiled as much information as possible from the specimens available at Kew, and analysed and manipulated these data to incorporate them in the guides. The team comprised four specimen digitisers, along with four specialists (covering botanical literature research, conservation assessments, geographical information systems (GIS) work and data compilation), and a project manager who liaised with in-country partners and the International Coordinators at Wakehurst. As three of these partners were in Francophone countries, it was decided to also employ two further digitisers to database specimens located at the Muséum National d'Histoire Naturelle, Paris, as this has more specimens from Madagascar, Burkina Faso and Mali than Kew. It was also important to produce these guides in collaboration, to ensure the techniques were appropriate and could be applied by the partners in the future.

12.2.2 Species targeting: what should be collected?

Targeting was aimed initially towards species falling into the three 'Es': *Endemic* – with a limited distribution; *Endangered* – threatened or vulnerable species at the local, regional or international scale; and *Economically important* plants of these countries. It is estimated that a total of 20% of all species collected by 2010 by the MSBP fell into one of these categories. These three Es are important when prioritising species for collection and seed banking, but the number of species fulfilling these criteria is obviously limited. Therefore, we also target based on another series of categories, trying to ensure that all species fulfil at least one of the following: *ecological importance*, such as pioneer or dominant plants within a certain habitat; *phylogenetic uniqueness*, such as a monospecific genera; *orthodox seeds*, which are able to retain their viability during the drying process, and are therefore easily bankable; *material for research*, such as important crop or medicinal plants, or species on which introduction research is being carried out; *rare seeds*, those where it is difficult to find high levels of quality or quantity; and lastly any other *new species* not already in the seed bank.

The species lists, based on the above criteria, also take into consideration national and institutional priorities. In many cases, the partners have suggested specific areas of importance to focus on, for example, Mount Mulanje and the Nyika Plateau in Malawi, or the Wolkberg and Cape areas of high endemism in South Africa. Some partners have an interest in certain families, and request additional information concerning these; this has resulted in the compilation of lists of endemic and near-endemic species of Rubiaceae, Euphorbiaceae and Orchidaceae for both Kenya and Tanzania, and endemic families in Madagascar. In countries with lower levels of endemism, more general lists are produced based on species distribution and threat levels for habitats and species. Once a provisional list has been compiled, each species is checked to ensure that the correct current nomenclature has been used, and that all possible synonyms have been included. They are then compared with the Seed Bank Database (SBD), which holds information on all collections stored in the MSBP, to avoid duplication.

12.2.3 Guide content: what information should be included?

Once it has been decided which species should be targeted, it is imperative to determine where and when attempts should be made to collect them. Much of this information can be found on herbarium specimens, specifically the locality infor-mation, describing where the plant was collected and when. Sometimes, an accu-rate measurement of latitude and longitude is given on the label, recorded from a global positioning system (GPS) at the time of collection, but older specimens need to be retrospectively geo-referenced using gazetteers, maps and itineraries of the collectors. The date a specimen was collected, and the phenological condition of the specimen, is used to compile phenological information for each species. The availability of specimen information varies between species, dependent on the range and rarity of each taxon. Species poorly represented at Kew were supple-mented with specimen information from the Paris herbarium and from collections held in partner countries, e.g. records in Pretoria's Precis database were included in the guides for South Africa, and the National Museums of Kenya and the National Herbarium of Tanzania (Tropical Pesticides Research Institute) provided informa-tion for Kenya and Tanzania. Literature research provided additional locality and phenological information and also a check on the validity of all the listed species names. A short, 100-word plant description was written to aid identification, emphasising characteristics which distinguish the species from similar species.

The next stage of guide preparation involved using the databased specimen information to calculate provisional conservation assessments. A GIS programme, ArcMap, was used to create distribution maps for each species, with individual localities represented as points. These data were used to calculate two measures of range size, the Extent of Occurrence and the Area of Occupancy, used to determine threat rating thresholds in International Union for the Conservation of Nature

(IUCN)'s criteria guidelines (IUCN, 2001). In the case of South Africa, where many of the endemic species are currently being researched in-country, interim conservation assessments have been produced. In these cases, or indeed when a species has already been fully assessed and submitted to IUCN, these more detailed criteria results are presented in the guide. If the known distribution of the species covers many countries, it is sometimes preferable to calculate the preliminary conservation threat ratings at a country or regional level, rather than making a global assessment. It is simply not time-effective to database specimens from all countries, when so many different species need to be analysed. Furthermore, this additional external information is not used in the collector guides, as maps and locality tables only cover the country in question. However, if a species is later thought to be of particular interest, and a full assessment required, data from all countries is then added to the database to be included in this assessment.

Finally, each species is checked in the Seed Information Database (SID). This provides any known information on seed behaviour, morphology and germination research. The seed behaviour, whether the seeds are orthodox or recalcitrant, is included in the guide at the species level or, if appropriate, at the genus or family level.

12.3 The BRAHMS database

Following a series of trials, it was decided to use the BRAHMS (*B*otanical *R*esearch *A*nd *H*erbarium *M*anagement *S*ystem) database for the duration of the project. This database has been specifically designed for the digitisation of species and collection data, as well as a method of curating herbaria and facilitating the publication of Floras, species checklists and monographical accounts.[1] BRAHMS is comprised of a series of linked database files, covering collections information, taxon-level information, geographical localities, bibliographical records and linked images. A separate BRAHMS dataset is created for each different country. For each species up to 30 herbarium specimens were digitised. Each specimen is given a unique barcode, which is included in the database along with all the label information. Additional information can be included, e.g. images can be linked to the relevant species name, as can conservation assessments, distribution maps and seed behaviour information. Synonyms are linked to the accepted name, to ensure all records are available for query irrespective of what name is used on the specimen. Bibliographical reference records are linked to the species names, allowing reference lists to be created for each species or for the whole project.

All the required information from the collections and taxon databases is exported from BRAHMS into a Microsoft Word template document, which includes the

---

[1] http://www.brahmsonline.com

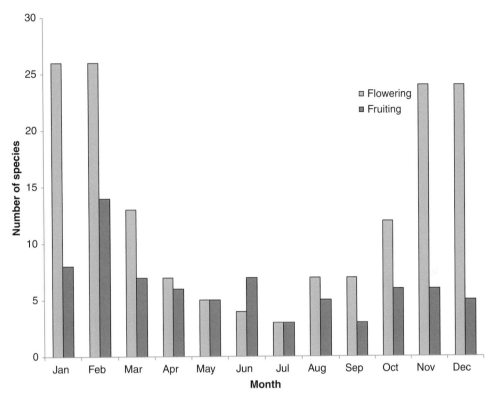

Figure 12.1 Phenology graph for endemic Rubiaceae of Tanzania, illustrating the fruiting and flowering times of all species in the guide as an indication of when collection trips should be planned.

macros, mark-up, formatting and layout needed to generate pages for the collector guide. The development of this system enables the transfer of data from BRAHMS into a recognisable guide format in minutes, which is an important time-saving device, considering each guide covers approximately 100 separate taxa. This document is then checked for punctuation or spelling errors, and manually edited so that it fits on the two standard pages per species.

In this way, information from multiple sources is combined and manipulated to produce a number of user-friendly products to aid in the planning of collection trips. A distribution map is provided for each species, along with a table of geo-referenced localities. Phenology data are presented as a series of maps, showing the density of fruiting and flowering species across the target area for each month of the year. The months in which flowers and fruits have been observed for each species is shown in a table, and summarised graphically (Fig 12.1).

Herbarium specimens are scanned to illustrate each species. Where possible, a fruiting specimen is used, but if this is not available or is unsuitable, a flowering or sterile specimen is shown. Additional images are included in an appendix at the end of each guide.

The presentation of data in the guides was specifically designed with the end users in mind, and to address the needs of planning and conducting successful seed collecting trips. One obvious omission from the guides is the presence of diagnostic keys, especially in the family-based guides, or even where several species of the same genus are included. However, one key feature of the guides is the time in which they take to produce. Turnover time is extremely quick, with a guide taking approximately 3 months to complete, from the initial digitisation stage to the guide being distributed to the partners: average guide production time over 4 years was actually less than 1.5 months per guide, due to projects overlapping. The production of keys, and more detailed taxonomic research, would slow this process considerably, with no great benefit for their main purpose.

12.4 The end result

The main section of each collection guide consists of the information for every species, presented as a series of double-sided pages (Fig 12.2). The first page includes the scientific name with its place of publication, along with an image of a specimen, and a series of boxes containing symbols summarising the conservation assessment criteria, the level of endemism if relevant, the seed behaviour (at the species, genus or family level), and the habit of the plant. The second page provides a short description of the plant with any additional notes for identification, along with the habitat, range and uses. A distribution map shows points for all the specimens databased, and a table provides detailed locality data, including the geo-referenced coordinates, altitude, habitat and associated species, for a selection of the localities. Phenology information is included as a single-row table, and any references used are cited.

Introduction pages at the front of the guide explain the abbreviations and symbols used, along with a country map, the monthly fruiting and flowering phenology maps, and the phenology summary graphs and tables. In addition there are complete species lists, ordered both alphabetically, and according to the level of threat determined by the conservation assessments. At the end of the guide an appendix of additional images is added, showing flowering or sterile specimens of species. An English–French translation of common descriptive words, both botanical and habitat-based, is included in the guides for Madagascar, Burkina Faso and Mali. In order to prevent damage during fieldwork, each page is laminated in plastic and the guide produced in a plastic ring binder. This enables people to just take into the field the relevant pages for the target species, whilst the other pages could be left behind to save weight and save wear and tear. Before the guides are distributed, a confidentiality agreement is added. This is to be signed by the receiving institutes, and legally prevents the guides being passed on to third parties, or the data being used for any other purposes. This is due to the perceived high sensitivity of information as there are detailed geo-referenced locality data, which in some cases pinpoints populations of rare species to within metres.

12.5 Improvements and development

Towards the end of the project a questionnaire was sent to project partners to request feedback to address any problems with using the guides and to investigate potential improvements. Responses were received from institutions in 8 of the 10 partner countries, as well as other interested parties and team members in the UK. In general, feedback was very positive with the guides reported as being easy to use and understand. The phenology maps and tables, which assist in planning the timing of trips, were reported to be the most useful feature. These not only show information for individual species, but also provide a good estimate to the number of species likely to be fruiting in an area at any one time. This is becoming more important with the increasing unpredictability in weather patterns for many countries. However, rainfall times for previous years can be compared with current patterns in order to attempt a kind of calibration to predict fruiting times. Locality information was also highly appreciated which, along with habitat details, enabled previously recorded populations to be relocated. Improvements were mainly suggested for the botanical information, as partner institutions in some countries employ non-botanists on collection trips. The plant descriptions provided in the guides were already short and simplified, but it was felt that these were still quite complicated, especially for families such as Poaceae and Cyperaceae.

One major limitation of the guides is that they cannot be freely distributed. The majority of species in the first series of guides focussed on 'sensitive' plants, such as endangered and endemic species, and provided specific latitude and longitude information for the known populations of these plants. Also, many of the guides focus on 'popular' species groups, such as succulents in Botswana, endemics of South Africa and endangered orchids in Kenya and Tanzania. Therefore, if these guides were widely available, it is possible that populations of rare species could face an increased risk of population decline from over-collection.

A series of modifications were therefore made to the format of the guides, in order to increase their usability. Diagnostic features have been improved, with the original single paragraph plant description now being split into separate headings of Habit, Leaves, Inflorescence, Flowers and Fruits. It was felt that the plant descriptions should not be simplified, as they provide a good level of information for those with botanical knowledge. However, a glossary of terms has been designed and included to aid

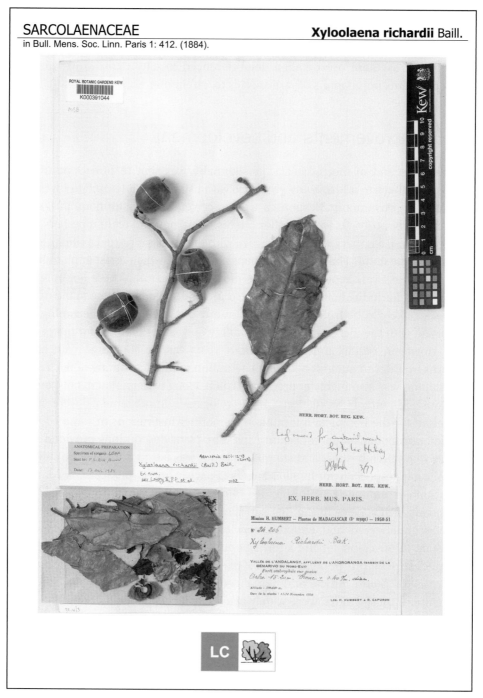

Figure 12.2 An example of the two pages produced for each species in the guides.
A black and white version of this figure will appear in some formats. For the colour version, please refer to the plate section.

SARCOLAENACEAE   ***Xyloolaena richardii*** Baill.

Description: Shrub to 5 m; branches slack, scattered; bark rough. Leaves large, glabrous, entire, alternate, persistent, elliptic-ovate, usually less than twice as long as broad, apex lacks a mucron; petiole to 12 9mm long. Floral receptacle 1-flowered. Flowers yellow; involucre large, woody; sepals 5, rolled up in bud, with short hairs; petals 5, ovate, alternating with the sepals; stamens numerous, inserted into disc; ovary 3-locular, locules with 15-20-ovules; style long, hollow; stigma slightly dilated. Fruit subsessile, globulose, brownish.

Notes: Can be distinguished by its elliptic to ovate leaves, yellow flowers & large woody involucre in fruit.

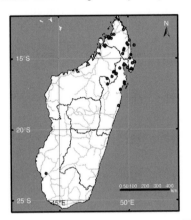

Local distribution: Widespread.

Habitat: Littoral forests on sand and quartzite.

Vernacular: Fakody, Fombaotoafo, Pesoala, Takodibe, Tamboro, Tsikody zahana, Vahitoambody, Voakoropetaka, Voantiambody, Voantsatroka.

Date	Locality	Habitat	Phen.	Alt.	Lat-Long	Err.	Src.	C.
12/03/1951	Antsiranana, Ambilobe, Matsoborilava, Levika, environs de Matsoborilava.	Base des collines greseuses.	fl.		13°17' S, 49°01' E	2	GAZ-i	
04/1974	Mahajanga, Mandritsara, Seuil de Mandritsara, ca. 8-10 km E du village d'Antsiasiaka.	Forêt dense sempervirente.	fl.	850	16°04' S, 49°10' E	2	c	P.
23/03/1991	Mahajanga, Analalava, Manongarivo, 30 km SE of Ankaramy, western slopes of Antsatrotro.	Along river bank.	fl.	200-1200	14°08' S, 48°21' E	2	GPSb	
07/1994	Toamasina, Antalaha, Andranobe, Andranobe Nord, Sud Ambanizana, Masoala.		fr.	200	15°40' S, 49°58' E	2	e	P.
24/01/1999	Antsiranana, Antalaha, Antsiranana, Cap Est, open fields just W of hotel.		fl.	5	15°15'37" S, 50°28'46" E	2	e	P.
25/10/2002	Antsiranana, Vohimarina (Iharana), Tsarabaria, Antsiranana, 35 km S of Vohémar, Manakana.	Littoral forest, on sand.	fr.	5	13°42'56" S, 50°06'11" E	2	e	P.
31/01/2003	Toamasina, Soanierana-Ivongo, Antanambao, Ambodimanga, forêt d'Antanambao.	Forêt littorale, sable.	fr.	5	16°46'27" S, 49°43'22" E	2	e	P.

J	F	M	A	M	J	J	A	S	O	N	D

Ref: Lowry II, P.P. et al (2002).

Figure 12.2 *(cont.)*

non-botanists. A translation of this glossary has also been made, for inclusion in the guides for the francophone countries. The original design of using one herbarium sheet as the illustration has been modified, and now consists of a series of pictures. Ideally, a series of photographs accompany the different plant description headings, but often these are not available. In these instances, close-up images of herbarium specimens are used, and in some cases line drawings are incorporated.

The other major design change is that the information has been divided into two parts that complement each other, but which can also be used separately. These will be printed in book form, rather than the current folder style, due to changes in the number of pages and the design layout. The first part consists of a list of geo-referenced localities for each species. Whereas previously only around 10 localities could be listed for each species, now all localities will be included. Therefore, species will take up varying numbers of pages depending on the amount of specimen data. Distribution maps and phenology information are also included for each species. The second part will contain the remainder of the information from the previous guides, and the diagnostic features listed above. A distribution map is again included, but if the range is limited to one area of the country, a larger-scale map will be used. A notepad feature has also been added for each species, allowing notes to be made in the guides whilst in the field. For example, it has been reported that phenology information, especially from the older specimens, has been inaccurate. Therefore, it is useful to be able to confirm the locality of a species, and note that it does not yet have mature fruits directly in the guide, rather than on separate sheets.

12.6 Project achievements

Within the 4-year project, a total of 36 guides were compiled; a production rate averaging 3 guides every 4 months. Each guide incorporated, on average, over 100 separate taxa, which generated a large amount of data. For example, in order to target the most threatened species it was necessary to research many more taxa than were actually used in the final guides (Table 12.1).

Table 12.1 Final output figures for the Millennium Seed Bank Project Enhancement Team

Outputs	Numbers achieved
Collection guides	36
Taxa in the guides	2888
Specimen data digitised	88 600
Taxa researched	9200
Preliminary conservation assessments	5000
Full conservation assessments	180

Of the 10 partner countries involved, not all requested the same level of information. Three guides were produced for Botswana at the beginning of the project, the first covering rare and endemic species, the second threatened species and the third information on the trees of Botswana. One guide each was compiled for Lebanon and Jordan, although each contained close to 200 species. The two guides for Malawi focussed on the specific areas of Mount Mulanje and the Nyika Plateau, whilst guides for South Africa have been produced regularly throughout the four years, covering nine different regions of high endemism and importance. Nine guides have been sent to Kenya and Tanzania, each covering a different family. Two general guides each for Burkina Faso and Mali have been completed, focussing on species with limited distributions, and two additional guides covering useful plants and the Poaceae were completed for these two countries combined. Finally, Madagascar has had one guide covering the important species from specific habitats, chosen by the partners, and has received another four covering endemic families and genera, and threatened species.

12.7 Reusability and longevity of the data

The guides were designed specifically to help locate target species for the MSBP, and therefore it is not anticipated that they will be used as long-term field guides. Indeed, the information provided may change with use in the field. It has already been seen that some localities presented from the herbarium sheets are no longer areas of viable habitat, due to habitat destruction and changes in land use. However, the guides will provide a good basis for additional research. Additionally, they can provide a starting point for the development of area and country checklists, especially for those countries which currently lack this information.

The preliminary conservation assessments also provide the basis for future work on full IUCN-standard conservation assessments. Species with a high-threat level rating were analysed in more detail, and assessment submitted to the IUCN for inclusion in the Red List database. This is important since the availability of Red Lists for plant species is severely limited in tropical countries (Pitman and Jørgensen, 2002). It is anticipated that this work will continue in-country, following a series of workshops involving training in both BRAHMS and in the production of full IUCN conservation assessments. The guides indicate which species should be investigated in more detail, and the collection trips provide the opportunity to ground truth the information.

In addition to the obvious benefits provided to the partners, there are further advantages of these methods and procedures. All Kew specimens added to the country datasets in BRAHMS are assigned a unique barcode, enabling the digitised label information to be transferred into the main Kew Herbarium database:

HerbCat. A similar scenario is in place in Paris, where all specimen data were entered into their Sonnerat database, and extracted for transfer into BRAHMS for use in the guides. Therefore, the project has contributed greatly to the legacy information available in both herbaria. All images scanned at Kew are also copied to the Kew Image database, which is available online.

Data repatriation is an important part of the project, as correct taxonomy and geo-referenced locality information can be provided for all duplicates at each partner institution. Funding for the targeting team terminated in June 2008, and it is important that the targeting of species can continue in-country. The availability of the datasets containing locality information will enable the collecting teams to plan trips based on previously uncollected species. For example, during a recent trip to Mali and Burkina Faso, a database extract was made for all uncollected species fruiting at the required time, and the locality information for these species mapped using GIS. From the accumulation of these points, target areas could be established, and routes could be planned in order to maximise the collection potential. These methods are becoming increasingly important as more species are collected, as it becomes more challenging to find new, previously uncollected plants.

12.8 Moving forward

In general, the guides have proved a success, and are now regularly used for planning and conducting seed collection trips. Since the guides have been distributed to partners, species from the guides have steadily been collected and added to the SBD, as a direct result of the locality and phenology information provided. For example, after receiving their guides, Lebanon, Jordan, Botswana and Malawi had collected over half of the listed species in the guides within two years. Burkina Faso and Mali received their first guides in January 2007, and have been using them for planning subsequent trips. By the end of 2007 they had already collected 10% of the species in the guides. This included a trip planned during the rainy season, which is typically a time when no collections are attempted. However, phenological information suggested many species should be fruiting at this time, and the trip across southern Mali and western Burkina Faso proved extremely successful, with 25 species collected in 6 days.

Many of the partners are now using BRAHMS to input data accumulated on collection trips, and intend to add their own herbarium specimens to the database. With the addition of the information from Paris and Kew, it is anticipated that the training received will enable the institutions to manipulate these large datasets independently. Many outputs can be produced using these data, and the partners will be left with the capacity to create a number of these, including species list compilation and route planning for collection trips, and the creation

Figure 11.2 Example species covered by *Sangha trees*. (A) *Zanthoxylum tessmannii*; (B) *Duvigneaudia inopinata*. A black and white version of this figure will appear in some formats.

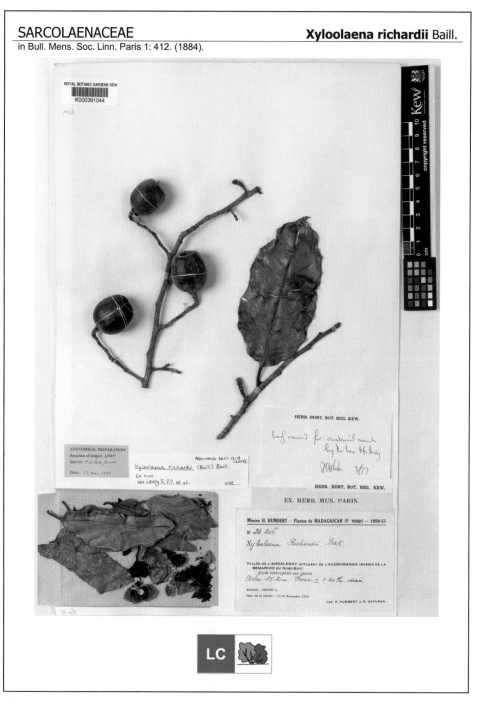

SARCOLAENACEAE
in Bull. Mens. Soc. Linn. Paris 1: 412. (1884).

Xyloolaena richardii Baill.

Figure 12.2 An example of the two pages produced for each species in the guides.
A black and white version of this figure will appear in some formats.

SARCOLAENACEAE
Xyloolaena richardii Baill.

Description: Shrub to 5 m; branches slack, scattered; bark rough. Leaves large, glabrous, entire, alternate, persistent, elliptic-ovate, usually less than twice as long as broad, apex lacks a mucron; petiole to 12 9mm long. Floral receptacle 1-flowered. Flowers yellow; involucre large, woody; sepals 5, rolled up in bud, with short hairs; petals 5, ovate, alternating with the sepals; stamens numerous, inserted into disc; ovary 3-locular, locules with 15-20-ovules; style long, hollow; stigma slightly dilated. Fruit subsessile, globulose,brownish.

Notes: Can be distinguished by its elliptic to ovate leaves, yellow flowers & large woody involucre in fruit.

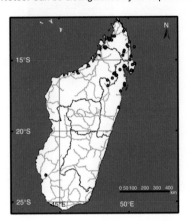

Local distribution: Widespread.

Habitat: Littoral forests on sand and quartzite.

Vernacular: Fakody, Fombaotoafo, Pesoala, Takodibe, Tamboro, Tsikody zahana, Vahitoambody, Voakoropetaka, Voantiambody, Voantsatroka.

Date	Locality	Habitat	Phen.	Alt.	Lat-Long	Err.	Src.	C.
12/03/1951	Antsiranana, Ambilobe, Matsoborilava, Levika, environs de Matsoborilava.	Base des collines greseuses.	fl.		13°17' S, 49°01' E	2	GAZ-i	
04/1974	Mahajanga, Mandritsara, Seuil de Mandritsara, ca. 8-10 km E du village d'Antsiasiaka.	Forêt dense sempervirente.	fl.	850	16°04' S, 49°10' E	2	c	P.
23/03/1991	Mahajanga, Analalava, Manongarivo, 30 km SE of Ankaramy, western slopes of Antsatrotro.	Along river bank.	fl.	200-1200	14°08' S, 48°21' E	2	GPSb	
07/1994	Toamasina, Antalaha, Andranobe, Andranobe Nord, Sud Ambanizana, Masoala.		fr.	200	15°40' S, 49°58' E	2	e	P.
24/01/1999	Antsiranana, Antalaha, Antsiranana, Cap Est, open fields just W of hotel.		fl.	5	15°15'37" S, 50°28'46" E	2	e	P.
25/10/2002	Antsiranana, Vohimarina (Iharana), Tsarabaria, Antsiranana, 35 km S of Vohémar, Manakana.	Littoral forest, on sand.	fr.	5	13°42'56" S, 50°06'11" E	2	e	P.
31/01/2003	Toamasina, Soanierana-Ivongo, Antanambao, Ambodimanga, forêt d'Antanambao.	Forêt littorale, sable.	fr.	5	16°46'27" S, 49°43'22" E	2	e	P.

J	F	M	A	M	J	J	A	S	O	N	D

Ref: Lowry II, P.P. et al (2002).

Figure 12.2 *(cont.)*

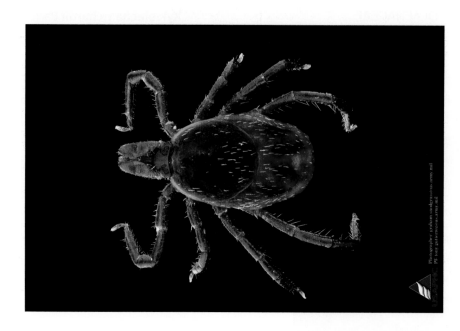

Figure 14.2 Arthropod vector of disease: *Ixodes scapularis* carries Lyme disease. A black and white version of this figure will appear in some formats.

Figure 14.1 Arthropod vector of disease: sand flies carry Lieshmaniasis. A black and white version of this figure will appear in some formats.

Figure 14.3 This image of *Ips paraconfusus* is a vertical compilation of over 100 stacked images with only the 'in focus' portions extracted and compiled. A black and white version of this figure will appear in some formats.

Figure 14.4 Stereo pair of *Ips paraconfusus*. A black and white version of this figure will appear in some formats.

Figure 16.1 Fogging at Kakamega forest, Kenya (courtesy: W. Freund). A black and white version of this figure will appear in some formats.

Current status: *Papilio abderus* Hopffer, 1856, a synonym of *Papilio garamas* Geyer, 1829

Text and fig. of the original description: Type specimen (Lectotype):

Figure 16.4 Types and museum specimens. Original description, illustration and type specimen photograph of the papilionid *Papilio abderus* Hopffer, 1856 (= Papilio garamas Geyer, 1829). Lectotype from Museum für Naturkunde – Leibniz Institute for Research on Evolution and Biodiversity, picture available at http://globis.insects-online.de/ species&tree_h=.Papilionidae.Papilioninae.Papilionini.Papilio.Pterourus.339.8547. A black and white version of this figure will appear in some formats.

Figure 17.1 Digital photos taken by ROV Holland I during NUI Galway cruise CE13008 aboard *RV Celtic Explorer*. Clockwise from top left: giant hydroid at approximately 1500 m depth, *Acesta excavata* (~600 m), crinoid (1200 m), black coral (1200 m). Laser dots (where shown) 10 cm apart. All photos copyright Marine Institute. A black and white version of this figure will appear in some formats.

Figure 18.1 A composite plate of *Arisaema intermedia*, DNEP1 327, as taken in the field in Solu Khumbu, Nepal (A. G. Miller). A black and white version of this figure will appear in some formats.

of specimen labels following the trips. Discussion is also under way for the use of these data in the production of new guides and checklists, produced in-country by the partners, with background support provided by the MSBP if required. In this way, products can be designed in a way to meet the specific needs of each partner at any given time.

References

IUCN (2001). *IUCN Red List categories and criteria: version 3.1.* IUCN Species Survival Commission. Gland and Cambridge: IUCN.

Pitman, N. C. A. and Jørgensen, P. M. (2002). Estimating the size of the world's threatened flora. *Ecology*, **298**: 989–999.

13

Training in tropical plant identification

D. J. Harris, S. Bridgewater and J.-M. Moutsamboté

13.1 Background

In the past, most large herbaria had at least one member of staff who could be counted on to put an unnamed specimen to family, if not to genus, wherever it came from in the world. Some individuals had legendary abilities to identify plants in the field around the globe. Not all, however, were great teachers and equally adept at passing on their knowledge. When asked why a specimen was in the Icacinaceae, for example, they would develop an enigmatic smile and say 'because it looks like one'. Amongst experienced field botanists there is much talk about the 'gestalt' and 'overall impression' of a plant. There can often be a sense of awe and mystery about these people and their skill, and in coffee-room discussions you can hear that someone 'had a very good eye'. Although it takes many years to become an excellent field botanist in biodiverse regions, we believe that there is, in fact, little mystery involved, and that an essential framework for the identification of most tropical plant groups can be developed quickly.

Although some of the great generalists pass on their knowledge to acolytes, often it seems that the skills they have built up over their careers are lost when they retire or die. Associated with the loss of the present skilled generation, there has been a change in working practices of those that are replacing them, which is resulting in a reduction in the number of competent generalists. In part this is due to changing

Descriptive Taxonomy: The Foundation of Biodiversity Research, eds M. F. Watson, C. H. C. Lyal and C. A. Pendry. Published by Cambridge University Press.
© The Systematics Association 2015

career structures and different methods being used in plant taxonomy. Young botanists no longer spend long periods with older colleagues, or extended periods working either in the field, or with herbarium specimens from a wide range of families. Molecular sequence alignment and the bureaucratic demands of fund-raising, project management and fulfilling publication expectations are time consuming. We predict that due to these changes there will soon be a sharp drop in the number of botanists in the 40–70-year-old age bracket who are capable of identifying plants from many different groups quickly and accurately.

Where formal teaching of identification skills does exist, in the overwhelming majority of cases it focuses on flowering and fruiting material. Although students may have a great ability to dissect flowers, be able to discuss the nuances of placentation type, construct floral formulae and draw elegant half-sections of flowers, such knowledge is of limited value to the field botanist who needs to identify plants. This is because in the tropics, most of the time, the majority of plants are neither in fruit nor flower. Inventory work, therefore, has to be based on sterile characters. Although an understanding of floral morphology is important, and we acknowledge that fertile characters are required for species delimitation in certain problematic groups, for the day-to-day business of plant identification floral morphology is frequently irrelevant. A change in teaching emphasis is required.

A few exceptional botanists have recognised this fact and a number of books now exist that attempt to teach how to identify tropical plants without flowers or fruits. These include Letouzey (1969), Gentry (1993), Ribeirio et al. (1999) and Hawthorne and Jongkind (2006). In addition, for a number of years courses around the world have been running that teach these identification skills, offered by institutions such as the Royal Botanic Garden Edinburgh; the National Herbarium of the Netherlands, Leiden; the Royal Botanic Gardens, Kew; and the Organisation of Tropical Studies and Tropical Science Centre, Costa Rica.

In summary, there are a small number of botanists who are highly skilled at identification of tropical plants, and the skills required to identify plants without flowers or fruits is held by an even smaller subset of people. A system for fast-tracking the transfer of these skills is required.

There is a view that one cannot train people to reach a high level of identification skills over a short period. Instead it is believed that botanists build up their ability and knowledge over decades. We fundamentally disagree with this view. We advocate that, with the growing need for accurate and rapid identifications, it is vital for taxonomic generalists to think about how to effectively and quickly transmit the skills and knowledge that they have acquired to the next generation of botanists. In this chapter we discuss our experiences of teaching tropical plant identification based on experiences in Belize and the Congo, with examples of techniques that we have found useful.

13.2 What needs to be taught?

Before we can discus the specifics of what needs to be taught, the process of identification needs to be examined. Identification is a multi-step process eventually leading to matching an unknown plant to a named description in a book, an illustration, or a herbarium specimen. The steps include: collecting; examining and describing an unknown plant; noting of local names; providing a preliminary taxonomic identification at family, genus or species level; making a herbarium specimen; consulting the academic literature and with colleagues; the use of keys and descriptions; and matching of specimens in a herbarium. Each of these steps is not always necessary, practical, nor done in the order outlined above. However, together they comprise the essential elements of the identification process.

We think that the most important single step in the identification of an unknown tropical angiosperm is assigning it to a family (see also Chapter 11, Wortley and Harris, in this volume). This first level of identification is crucial. If it is correct, then the subsequent steps are possible. Conversely, if the wrong family is chosen any further identification effort is unlikely to succeed. Of course, identification to a generic or species level would be better. However, the plant diversity in tropical systems at these levels is often too high to allow beginners to make significant progress in the field. In contrast, family diversity is manageable, with only a few hundred commonly occurring. Furthermore, it is usually possible to communicate sterile family characters to beginners fairly easily and for them to understand and remember them.

For other groups of organisms (birds, insects, etc.), family level identification may not be the appropriate level at which to teach, but for tropical flowering plants this is the rank at which most skilled taxonomists ask the question 'what is this?' when presented with an unknown plant. It is invariably the rank which most taxonomists use as the entry point for an unknown specimen, and hence, we believe it should be the focus for the teaching of sterile specimen identification.

As the multi-step approach described above suggests, although initial identification of an unknown plant to family is an essential part of identification, it is only one part of the process. Students have to be taught all the other parts of the complex procedure. The resources available to aid this vary greatly depending on the region, the vegetation type and the taxonomic group. Some areas of the tropics have good coverage by Floras, with certain regions even being covered by local Floristic publications. Checklists and local herbaria may be available. However, many areas are poorly covered, or with out-dated literature – if any exists at all. Where illustrated field or photographical guides occur, these often only focus on the '100 most important trees' and, thus, can be of limited value to the generalist conducting inventories who need to name everything they find. Thus, when training students it is important to make sure that they are aware of the range and shortcomings of the resources that are available for the focus area, if they are to translate their preliminary family-level field determinations to generic and species level.

In addition to the above, it is important to empower trainees to make some sort of qualitative judgement of their identification. This can be problematic. Experienced botanists know how confident they are about a determination and have ways of communicating any uncertainty by indications such as '?', 'cf.', 'sp. aff.' or 'vel sp. aff.'. Beginners also need to be taught to assess their confidence in each identification and to be able to qualify those for which they have some doubt. The assessment of levels of confidence needs to be done at each step in the identification process and in context. For example, trainees should learn that with opposite, simple leaves, and an intrapetiolar stipule, they are very probably looking at a member of the Rubiaceae. Whereas a plant with stipules, stellate hairs and basal venation could be a Euphorbiaceae, but they should also consider Malvaceae, and so they need to look for extra characters. At the family level they need to be able to judge which combinations of characters will lead to a precise identification and which combination will give rise to a shortlist of families, all of which should be considered. At the genus and species level botanists need to be able to assess their confidence and communicate it to others.

13.3 Who needs to be taught?

We have aimed our training in identification at post-graduate level professional biologists. This does not mean to say that we are against the training of para-taxonomists. In countries such as Costa Rica para-taxonomists have been trained to a superb level and are essential personnel of most diversity surveys. However, they usually work with academic taxonomists. It is our fear that in future, there will be far fewer of these botanists with the ability to discuss and assess the quality of survey work with professional para-taxonomists, and translate the knowledge of the para-taxonomists into reports and publications. We suggest that academic biologists need the identification skills of para-taxonomists. We have found that motivated biologists can be taught sterile family-level angiosperm identification skills in a diverse tropical environment to a professional level during an intensive two-week field course. After this time the participants can often reach the same level of generalist identification skills as many practising taxonomists. In our experience, about 1 in 10 of the people taught have sufficient aptitude and interest for us to encourage them to become professional taxonomists. However, the remainder still have a high level of identification skills and are competent at the end of a two-week field course to conduct field-based plant diversity surveys. Although many of the trainees we have taught do not continue in taxonomy, this experience is highly valuable for managers and decision-makers in the conservation and environmental fields. They may not need to identify plants on a daily basis, but they have a much greater understanding of the practicalities and value of field studies, the need for training and the collection of herbarium specimens, and the importance of supporting herbaria. Just exposing decision-makers to the processes of identification will increase the understanding of the pivotal role that taxonomy has in resolving the global biodiversity crisis.

We make a case here for the practical vocational training of university-educated scientists who have the potential to become taxonomists, and people from disciplines which will require them to make identifications of tropical plants, as well as those in management positions.

13.4 How can identification skills be taught?

Below are outlined some of the techniques and methods we have found useful in two courses in plant identification. One course has taken place in Belize in Central America and the other in the Republic of Congo in Central Africa.

13.4.1 Field courses

We think it is important to teach identification in the field. This is because it is the practical skills of field botany which are required to be added to more theoretical classroom training. It is also more interesting and inspiring for students, and many related subjects (e.g. ecology, inventory and quantitative survey techniques) can be brought into the teaching. Fresh material is always in abundant supply in the field, and is easier to identify to family than preserved material. Making herbarium specimens allows the trainees to understand all the processes involved in the production of these specimens, and to see the differences and the similarities between dried and fresh material, and to appreciate the value of the specimens in herbarium collections and the data they contain. The transformation of fresh material to dried and pressed specimens is often difficult for novices to grasp; the best way for them to learn is for them to be responsible for that process.

13.4.2 Course location

We recommend using sites with suitable accommodation including: staff to provide meals; some electric power; classroom facilities; and a range of vegetation types with high biodiversity close to the accommodation. We were fortunate to be able to work in areas which had not been fully inventoried. This meant that during the training we were able to make significant contributions to the knowledge of the flora, which both the trainees and the trainers found rewarding. We have taught from one site or from two, but not more. We suggest that any daily travel time should be kept to an absolute minimum, and if more than one site is chosen that care should be taken to balance the opportunity to see different plants with the disadvantage of travelling between sites.

13.4.3 Course duration

We have run identification courses from 10 to 15 days long. We found that 14–15 days is about the optimum. However, even after a 10-day course we found that trainees had made enough progress to continue by themselves.

13.4.4 Classroom facilities

We have found that a ratio of field time to classroom time of 1:2 was best for learning identification. We found it useful to leave as early as possible in the morning and look at plants *in situ*, and then collect specimens in field presses and in plastic bags for examination back at the classroom. We left all the literature behind when going into the field. We used field stations with concrete floors, insect-proof buildings and electric lights: the educational experience is far greater in comfortable conditions.

   Although it is tempting to spend the majority of time in the field, we have found that this can be counterproductive. Trainees tend to become quickly confused and despondent if they are not allowed an opportunity to make sense of the diversity they collect. We have found that a few hours of collecting can be processed in an afternoon or evening. If more material than this is brought back it cannot be examined on the same day. It is important that the students feel in control and begin by only processing small amounts of material.

13.4.5 Materials

Each trainee was provided with their own notebook, hand lens and secateurs. General collecting and processing equipment and literature was provided for use by the group. Although a variety of books and Floras were available to trainees (e.g. *Flora of Guatemala* and *Flora Mesoamericana* for Belize, *Flore du Cameroun* and *Flora of west tropical Africa* for Congo, the majority of teaching is based around a key text. In Belize that was Gentry (1993) and in Congo that was Letouzey (1969). A botanical glossary was particularly useful.

13.4.6 How to look at a plant

The most important thing to teach trainees is how to look at and describe a plant. A student who volunteers to describe a plant without guidance very rarely does this systematically. We showed them how to describe a plant logically, in a manner similar to most plant descriptions, i.e. starting with the whole plant, then describing its base up through the parts. We paid particular attention to any characters that are useful for identification at the family level. Family identification can usually be done by an analysis of the type of leaf (simple, compound etc.), its insertion (opposite, alternate, etc.), with other important characters being the presence of stipules, latex, glands and smells. We explicitly instruct students how to hold a hand lens, how to examine a leaf with reflected and transmitted light, and instruct them to always look for all the characters described above for each plant examined.

13.4.7 No names please, only characters

In the first few days we asked the students not to propose family names when they find a new plant. Instead they were asked to tell us the characters that they could observe. This allows those students who do not know a plant to be able to say something about it. This builds their confidence and provides a means of ascertaining if students are really looking at a plant in a systematic fashion as they have been taught. By concentrating on a suite of essential characters they learn the characters and identification process. Family names then usually follow quickly, with the students better able to understand the character differences between them. Telling people names first followed by characters does not seem to work nearly as well.

It seems that there are two ways of recognising plants. Without doubt there is the 'gestalt' – overall look and feel of a plant – which can then be reinforced by looking for a few key characters known to be possessed by the plant. This is how many experienced herbarium botanists work when they 'shoot from the hip' with a name. This process involves pattern recognition and image-based thinking. The second way is for a list of characters to be created, and then the family named deduced from a short list of families known to possess those characters. This latter process is the one best suited to beginners. The first method, that of pattern recognition, seems only to work after multiple images of a taxon have been built up in somebody's head over time. Although useful, it is not possible for beginners who are often seeing a family for the first time.

By asking students to give characters instead of names they are:

1. being forced to look at a plant carefully;
2. starting to associate characters with families; and
3. articulating the characters they see, enabling them to communicate with other botanists about the plant in question.

13.4.8 Assessment

Trainees were assessed on a logbook in which they recorded their notes and observations from the course, the specimens and label data, which they collected for approximately 5 herbarium specimens, and a practical exam in which they were asked to identify to family 25 plants without flowers or fruits.

13.4.9 Terminology

Technical botanical terms can be confusing and frustrating for beginners. Many students are frightened and intimidated by them. Thus, it is important to introduce such terms slowly, and reassure them that an in-depth knowledge of technical terms is not essential for identification. However, although we try to keep technical terms to the minimum, a basic understanding of some concepts of plant morphology is important. On the first day, basic terms such as petiole, stipule, compound leaf, petiolule, glands and pellucid punctations are described and illustrated with examples. It is possible to identify many plants to family based solely on knowledge of the presence or absence of these few easily understood characters. More technical terms, and characters specific to a few families are introduced later as and when they are encountered.

13.4.10 Teaching identification in context of inventory work

We find that once students begin to realise that identification of tropical plants is not a 'dark art' and is well within the capability of anyone with an interest to learn, it is hard to stop them from keying out things they find, such is their enthusiasm. However, during the two-week course different exercises are undertaken each day that provide novel vehicles for plant collecting and identification. This helps to keep everyone engaged, and is also important in developing other essential skills, in addition to identification, needed for inventory work. Such skills include: the collection and processing of herbarium specimens; the keeping of field collecting books; the collection of global positioning system (GPS) data; plotless and plot-based inventory techniques; ethnobotanical methods; digital photography; writing vegetation descriptions; and ground truthing of satellite and radar images. All of these skills involve identification so it is very easy to keep the theme of identification consistent through a varied programme.

13.4.11 Making herbarium specimens

We have found that making high-quality herbarium specimens is a very useful part of training for identification. This is mainly because in many poorly known tropical areas it is an essential part of making accurate species-level identification. In addition, we have found that it is another way to reinforce characters for the trainees and allows the whole group to see the specimens collected by their colleagues. Some extra characters only become visible after the careful preparation of herbarium specimens.

We found that the making of herbarium specimens was best managed by clear guidance from the trainers. We told which trainees to collect which plants. This allowed us, as a group, to make a significant contributions to our understanding of several botanically poorly known areas. As all the specimens collected by the trainees where destined for national and international herbaria, we made it clear to students that their specimens and associated data where to be of the highest calibre. It allowed us to control how much time and effort was being put into collecting. We always made sure that the main aim of the course, identification, was not overtaken by an enthusiasm to collect lots and lots of specimens. All trainees were able to make top-quality herbarium specimens, some of which included new country records.

13.4.12 Repetition, constant revision

We found that continually repeating the main characters for each family encountered was necessary for the whole group to keep learning. We varied the method of repetition as much as possible, for example with short quizzes, revision sessions, hand movements, play-acting and a continual discussion of families which might be confused.

13.4.13 Ratio of trainers to trainees

We found that a ratio of one trainer to five trainees is ideal to keep the trainees engaged with sufficient supervision without exhausting the trainers. With higher ratios trainers tend to suffer from burn-out and trainees learn more slowly.

13.4.14 Level of trainers

Trainers with a high degree of field experience are essential. However, it is not always necessary for the training courses to be done in regions the trainers know well. Indeed, we have found that it can be easier and more rewarding to teach in areas where the trainers do not know the flora completely. The repeated teaching of the same taxa as representative examples of families can become tedious to the trainers. Teaching is more enjoyable and stimulating for the trainers if they are encountering new taxa, and the students are able to witness the process they are being taught being used by the trainers when they encounter unknown plants.

13.4.15 Daily routine

A strict daily routine provides the teaching with structure. Typically, the daily rhythm consists of going into the field early in the morning (c. 7 am) to conduct a preplanned exercise (e.g. establish an ecological transect) and to look at and collect plants. The group returns to the field station by the late morning, has a wash and a change of clothes. After a midday meal and drink the trainees are then usually sufficiently refreshed, and in an appropriate frame of mind, to sit down with the plants collected and key them out on sterile characters using the key texts. As the trainees work with plants in the afternoon the trainers are available to answer questions and provide encouragement. We have found it counterproductive for the trainers to provide family names. A series of names told to a student will quickly be forgotten unless the characters defining those families are understood. Thus, trainees are asked to suggest names and to list those characters which have resulted in their choice. The trainers respond to those characters first and then to the name. The trainees are asked to give a level of confidence in that name. If they are right, they are told so. If they are wrong, the characters of the incorrect family are discussed so that the student understands why the plant in hand is unlikely to belong to it. They are then given guidance to key out the plant again until the right family is arrived at.

After an evening meal we found it helpful to have a clear starting time for the evening session with a short presentation to summarise important families/characters learnt that day (e.g. those families with sap, and how to distinguish them; the Sapindales and how to tell them apart, etc.). This also enables the students to gauge their progress. We have found it a useful exercise towards the end of the two-week course for the students to compile their own matrix listing the characters they have learnt and the families which have them.

13.5 Difficulties

We believe that knowledge of relatively few characters, and the application of a logical process in describing a plant, is all that is required to confidently identify many plants to the family level. However, we do admit that there are many exceptions to the rules. In the first few days of the course an attempt is made to repeatedly steer the students towards plants that the trainers know are typical for a particular family. This builds up confidence in the system being taught and stimulates enthusiasm. However, as the course progresses students are encouraged to roam and collect whatever they find. Thus, exceptions to the rules are found – the rare Leguminosae with opposite leaves, or a Sapotaceae with no apparent sap. As the students realise the scale of the exceptions there is generally a crisis in confidence as they come to terms with their system not being foolproof. However, this 'big dip' is usually short lived. Although many exceptions to the family rules exist, and a number of families lack a defining suite of characters, nevertheless, the students realise that by applying the rules they have been taught, they are able to make sense of much of the diversity they find. A foundation for building future knowledge levels has been established

13.6 End product

At the end of 15 days we have introduced students to tropical plants and to a range of collecting, inventory and ecological techniques. The majority of students have seen a whole suite of families, genera and species they have not seen before. At the end of the course we have a practical exam where the students are asked to identify to family level sterile plants they have not seen before on the course. All the students can identify accurately to family level more than half of what they are given, with a significant proportion (10–25%) able to identify over 75%. For the majority of trainees, it is the first time they have attempted to identify plants in a diverse tropical environment by themselves, and we think it is a significant achievement for them to be succeeding at family-level identification without flowers and fruits after only two weeks.

As trainers, each time we have taught a course we have learnt new characters ourselves, found plants we had never seen before and made herbarium specimens that represent new country records. Although this is satisfying, what has been most rewarding, however, is producing significant numbers of young botanists who at the end of this training period have had the tropical flora demystified, and who feel they have the skills and confidence to go out and start making inventories of tropical habitats, identify plants in the field and make high-quality herbarium specimens. They may not be able to identify everything they find, but the basics are in place. Becoming a great field botanist only comes by honing identification skills over time. If younger generations are to rival those of the past they must take the same route: continual practice.

References

Gentry A. H. (1993). *A field guide to the families and genera of woody plants of northwest South America.* Chicago: University of Chicago.

Hawthorne, W. and Jongkind, C. (2006). *Woody plants of Western African forests.* Richmond: Royal Botanic Gardens, Kew.

Letouzey R. (1969). *Manuel de botanique forestiere, Afrique tropicale.* Nogent-Sur-Marne (Val-de-Marne): Centre Technique Forestier Tropical.

Ribeiro, J. E. L., Hopkins, M. J. G., Vincentini, A., Sothers, C. A., da S. Costa, M.A., de Brito, J. M., de Souza, M. A.D., Martins, L. H. P., Lohmann, L. G., Assunção, P. A. C. L., da C. Pereira, E., da Silva, C. F., et al. (1999). *Flora da Reserva Ducke. Guia de identificação das plantas vasculares de uma floresta de terra-firme na Amazônia Central.* Manaus, Brasil: INPA.

14

Field identification of vectors and pathogens of military significance

A. G. Gutierrez

14.1 The problem: field identifications by non-specialists

Military personnel deployed in the field often suffer more casualties due to endemic vector-borne disease than to engagement with enemy combatants. The most dangerous of these are carried (vectored) by biting arthropod vectors mostly of the bloodsucking variety. Among the diseases encountered by soldiers are malaria, dengue fever and yellow fever, carried by certain mosquito species; encephalitis and Lyme disease, carried by certain ticks; and leishmaniasis, carried by some species of sand flies (Fig 14.1).

The pathogens may be protozoan, bacterial or viral in nature. These debilitating, and sometimes deadly, diseases are rarely detected in the environment before significant casualties mount up. In fact it is usually the diagnosis of the casualties that provide the detection.

In my laboratory at the US Army Center for Health Promotion and Preventive Medicine at Aberdeen Proving Ground, Maryland, I have been working on mechanisms that would allow minimally trained personnel to perform surveillance on the vectors and the diseases prior to the advent of human casualties. There are two problems to overcome. One involves the accurate identification of the vector species of arthropods. This is best done visually by examining all the species caught,

Descriptive Taxonomy: The Foundation of Biodiversity Research, eds M. F. Watson, C. H. C. Lyal and C. A. Pendry. Published by Cambridge University Press.

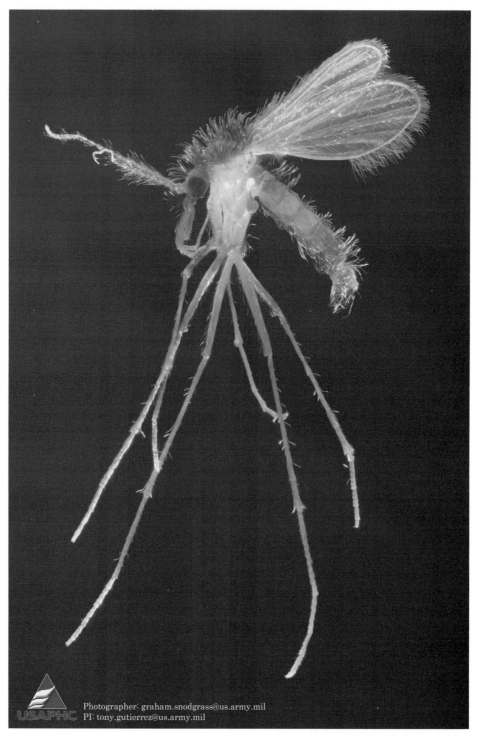

Photographer: graham.snodgrass@us.army.mil
PI: tony.gutierrez@us.army.mil

Figure 14.1 Arthropod vector of disease: sand flies carry Lieshmaniasis. A black and white version of this figure will appear in some formats. For the colour version, please refer to the plate section.

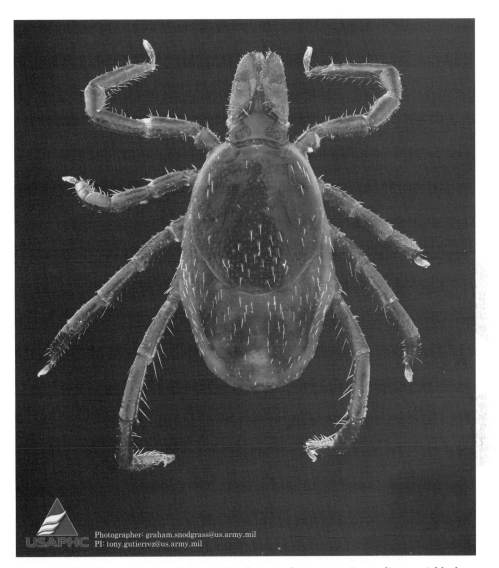

Photographer: graham.snodgrass@us.army.mil
PI: tony.gutierrez@us.army.mil

Figure 14.2 Arthropod vector of disease: *Ixodes scapularis* carries Lyme disease. A black
and white version of this figure will appear in some formats. For the colour version,
please refer to the plate section.

either in special traps designed to attract and collect biting insects, or by dragging
flannel cloths through brush in the case of ticks (Fig 14.2).

Although the collection is easily done by soldiers with preventive medicine
training there are rarely entomologists present to identify and pick out the true
vector species. In the case of mosquitoes there may be dozens of species caught of
similar appearance, while only one or a few might be the actual vector species.

Species identification mistakes made here can further confound the second problem of determining if the potential vectors are carrying the suspected pathogens. Obviously if non-vectors are included in the testing, the many false negative results would invalidate the survey.

This second problem involves a method of detecting DNA sequences unique to the pathogen in all DNA extracted from the vector. This is the test for the disease in the vector. The technique used is polymerase chain reaction (PCR), which is a form of sequence-specific DNA amplification involving an enzyme-mediated reaction that must be repeatedly cycled through 3 elevated temperatures, 95, 55 and 72°C, 20–30 times. This is normally performed in a well-equipped molecular biology laboratory at fixed installations. It is not possible to ship collected specimens to these laboratories, which are sometimes in different countries, test them for pathogens and arrive at useful information before the resident vectors have transmitted their pathogens to the soldiers at the deployment site. Therefore, the gist of the second problem is how to perform PCR on site. The first attempts used a mobile kit assembled and sold by MJ Research, a company that manufactured a small 25-sample desktop PCR thermal cycler. The kit consisted of the smallest marketed versions of all the equipment necessary for PCR packaged in a rugged impact-resistant suitcase. It was first used by the author during hantavirus surveys on collected deer mice in 1996. M. J. Research's 'Mobile PCR Lab.' required considerable laboratory skill and so could only be effectively used by an experienced molecular biologist. It also required at least four electrical outlets to power equipment. It has since been discontinued. In 1998, Idaho Technologies, Inc. developed an improved mobile PCR device called the RAPID (*R*uggedised *A*dvanced *P*athogen *I*dentification *D*evice), which integrated both the PCR and detection into a suitcase-type format that used hot air to cycle the sample reactions and a laser/optical detection module to detect amplified pathogen DNA. Unfortunately it also required laboratory skills in DNA extraction, reagent prep and electrical outlets.

14.2 The solutions

14.2.1 Vector identification in the field

To solve the first problem of accurate and expert identification of vectors, I created photographically realistic computer-generated three-dimensional (3D) models of the vectors, which could be viewed via a head-mounted display connected to a wearable computer. The models were interactive and so could be manipulated by the viewer via a mouse or toggle input device. The manipulation included rotation in all three axes as well as zooming to any magnification supported by the resolution of the model's surface. The model itself was embedded in an internet-ready HTML web page which could be accessed offline from the computer's hard drive, a flash card or from the internet itself. The models were created in 3ds Max, a high-end 3D modelling, texturing and animation software commonly used in the gaming industry for character creation. The display software is Viewpoint Media Player (VMP), available free online[1], an Internet Explorer plug-in that displays the model on a web page and allows user interactivity. The wearable computer with heads-up display was manufactured by Xybernaut, Corp. Although soldiers liked the hardware and had no problem viewing and using the images for identification, the hardware proved problematic for field use. The head-mounted display, the many cables running from it and the belt-worn computer proved nearly impossible to wear while negotiating some of the thick brush in the field. The light plastic display was not rugged enough for the normal wear and tear of field use. In any case, the company has since gone out of business and mobile computing has definitely migrated to the handheld device. The final destination of this segment of personnel computing seems to be the video-enabled, internet-capable mobile phone. The leading example of this technology in 2007 appears to be the Apple iPhone. The fact that the iPhone and its many emerging clones aren't compatible with VMP or other interactive 3D applets but are very good at displaying video has led me to devise another type of high-resolution 3D imaging scheme.

In this case I've used actual photographs of the arthropods to create the 3D image. The inherent shallow depth of field (DOF) encountered in macrophotography of these subjects has been overcome by employing an AutoMontage system from Syncroscopy, a division of SynOptics, Inc. This system employs a computer numerically controlled photomicroscope with Z (focus up and down) and X and Y (stage movement) limits set by the operator to fully encompass the 3D subject. The operator then sets the number of photos to be taken from the top focal point to the bottom. As many as 250 separate images are then compiled by the attached computer to yield a single image with all points of the image in perfect focus. An example image of a bark beetle about 3 mm in length is shown in Fig 14.3.

The animation portion of the image is created by mounting the specimen on a pin with superglue or a similar compound, the axis of which is in line with the central axis of the specimen. The pin itself is mounted on a rotary chuck with a stepper motor, which is computer controlled. This can either be rotated manually or via the computer to take an automontage set every 5° of a complete 360° rotation (resulting in 72 images or frames). The frames are then named to start with their appropriate position in the rotation from 1 to 72 and placed in a single folder on the computer's hard drive. These high-resolution, extended DOF images can then be imported as a folder into Adobe Photoshop's 'Image ready' and instantly be converted to an animated GIF (graphics interchange format). This would result in a

---

[1] http://www.viewpoint.com

Ips paraconfusus

Figure 14.3 This image of *Ips paraconfusus* is a vertical compilation of over 100 stacked images with only the 'in focus' portions extracted and compiled. A black and white version of this figure will appear in some formats. For the colour version, please refer to the plate section.

two-dimensional (2D) animation of a repeating 360° rotation, which could be viewed as an inserted animation on any website and most electronic documents.

To create a 3D animation with extended DOF each numbered frame is opened in Photoshop. 'Canvas size' is then selected under the 'Image' menu for that frame. The image position on the canvas grid is moved to the upper right. The canvas dimensions are then doubled in width. In the resulting blank space to the left place a copy of the next higher frame in number. This produces a stereo pair for cross-eyed stereo viewing. Do this for each frame until you have 72 stereo pairs in the folder. Import this folder into 'Image ready'. This will produce an animated GIF, which when viewed with suitably crossed eyes such that the right eye is viewing the left image and the left eye is viewing the right, a stunning 3D rotating image will appear flanked by two 2D images. The overwhelming advantage to this type of imagery is that the entire surface of the specimen can be viewed, the entire surface is in sharp focus, and all 3D relationships are revealed. Unlike other forms of 3D viewing this method retains high resolution and completely accurate coloration. These animated images can be viewed in electronic forms of web browsers, Word documents, PDF files and PowerPoint presentations, as well as on devices such as mobile phones. The rotary chuck and sample can be seen below in close-up and in the AutoMontage setup. A portion of a frames folder with 72 5°-offset rotations is also shown. A resulting single-frame stereo pair is shown in Fig 14.4, and an animated

Figure 14.4 Stereo pair of *Ips paraconfusus*. A black and white version of this figure will appear in some formats. For the colour version, please refer to the plate section.

version of this can be viewed online[2] and a marked-up version used for species identification is in the same gallery.

14.3 Pathogen identification using DNA in the field

The second problem of creating a truly portable PCR device required a change in the paradigm of the design of PCR thermal cyclers. Most commercial thermal cyclers change the temperature of the entire space occupied by the sample vessels. This is true even though the volume of the samples is miniscule compared to the volume of the sample space. Additionally, in most designs the 'space' is a massive metal block. This requires an enormous amount of energy to change temperatures and considerable time to reach the elevated temperatures in the entire mass of the metal block. This situation occurs because thermal-cyclers 'evolved' from laboratory heating blocks which were originally designed to hold one temperature for extended periods of time. To create a field expedient thermal-cycler, I designed a rotary mechanism that moves sample cassettes of glass capillary tubes (for rapid

---

[2] http://www.elenagt19.smugmug.com/gallery/3269372#185653683

heat transfer) to three small stationary blocks of fixed temperature. The time required to transfer the temperature to the samples is under five seconds. The movement from one block to the next takes one second. When organised in a hexagonal array with hexagonally shaped blocks, six faces can be used on each block simultaneously.

Each tri-lobed rotor fits on a spindle, which rotates it over a cam, causing the sample cassettes to be thrust against one heated block-face after another in the correct sequence. Six rotors fit in the hexagonal array. Adjacent rotors rotate in opposite directions. The adjacent rotors alternate clockwise and counterclockwise rotation to match the correct sequence of temperatures in the cycle. This is accomplished by enmeshed gears below each spindle. The entire gear set can be run by one stepper motor with a single worm screw driving any one of the gears and the whole assembly is carried in a rugged aluminum case. The top of the case has pictograph controls and LED outputs per sample for positive (LED on), negative (LED off) results for pathogen DNA. This design processes 108 samples simultaneously (8 controls, 100 experimental) in 5–10 minutes. The mechanical design is protected by US Patent 6 875 602 with international patents pending. The amplified DNA is detected optically using fluorescent dye chemistry such as TAqMan or similar reagent sets. The use of freeze-dried reaction mixes pack-aged in the capillary tubes to include PCR primer sets and dyes has already been demonstrated by several laboratories and is anticipated for use in this system.

14.4 Conclusion

I believe that this system of accurate vector identification with a video-capable handheld device and DNA analysis in a simple ruggedised field portal PCR device will allow relatively untrained personnel to detect pathogens by percentage infec-tivity of 100 vectors sampled per test site. This will give medical workers in deployed areas valuable information toward preventing the transmission of vector-borne diseases before the first casualty occurs. The PCR device also has potential for species identification and monitoring of endangered, invasive and emerging groups in field biological research.

PART IV

The influence of technology on data gathering in the field

15

The changing role of collections and field research

S. KNAPP

15.1 Introduction

Every herbarium or museum I have ever worked in has suffered from lack of space for ever-increasing collections. Constraints on funding for large institutions, coupled with the historic lack of support for taxonomy as a discipline, has sometimes meant that institutions have felt the need to get rid of specimens – something most systematists would say they abhor on principle. Here I will explore alternative ways of thinking about specimens and the documentation of the diversity of life on Earth for the twenty-first century, which might involve us casting aside preconceived notions of what the best or only way to collect could be. Perhaps we ought to only collect specimens for DNA analysis – a leaf in silica gel or an insect in alcohol? What should be collected as a matter of routine? How difficult might it be to obtain permission to do a new sort of collecting? None of these questions has an easy answer, and I will explore some possible alternative approaches to the traditional insect on a pin or herbarium specimen. Collecting itself has also changed radically. Systematists collect for a variety of reasons – floristic, faunistic and monographical research all have different goals, and perhaps require different collecting strategies. I will suggest that the future need not be exactly the same as the past, and that we can tailor our collecting to purpose much more effectively than we have done. New collecting techniques will also open up biodiversity inventory and study in some

Descriptive Taxonomy: The Foundation of Biodiversity Research, eds M. F. Watson, C. H. C. Lyal and C. A. Pendry. Published by Cambridge University Press.
© The Systematics Association 2015

parts of the world beyond the systematic community – something that should not frighten us, but that we should welcome as the diversity of life comes under ever greater threat.

15.2 Why collect specimens?

Taxonomists collect specimens as the evidence with which they construct hypotheses of identity or relationships. As such, specimens are an integral and essential part of taxonomic practice and are part of what makes taxonomy (defined here as phylogeny, identification and description, see Godfray and Knapp, 2004) a scientific discipline. A specimen is a preserved organism, or part of an organism, that is a data point recording that organism's occurrence at a particular place in a particular time. Specimens have remained essentially the same since the beginning of taxonomy as a science, and it is thanks to them that we have the records of what plants and animals were found when European explorers first reached new lands. In this chapter I will focus primarily on herbarium specimens, partly because I am a botanist and therein lies my experience, but also because vascular plants are a taxonomic group on the margin between the small, very well-described groups like birds or mammals, and the large, species-rich taxa like insects or fungi. What botanists may experience with plant collections may resonate with scientists working in other groups at different times in the history of those disciplines, not all groups will be the same.

Vascular plants encompass some 250 000–400 000 known species and have traditionally been preserved for study with flattened, dried plants or portions of plants mounted on paper. A good specimen has all the parts needed for identification – flowers, fruits, leaves, etc. Linnaeus himself gave instructions for how to prepare 'good' herbarium specimens (Linnaeus, 1751), and within the botanical community, generally accepted protocols for collecting have been in use for decades, varying slightly between individuals or institutions. Regardless of how they are collected, all herbarium specimens differ considerably from the live plant from which they were taken, being flat and dry; interpreting this material takes special skill. Herbarium specimens collected in the eighteenth, nineteenth or twentieth centuries are all very similar, although those more modern collections tend to have better locality and plant description data than earlier material. A locality label that states 'New Granada' (present day Colombia) or 'India' is of little or no use in assessing range or habitat specificity. We are astonished today at Joseph Hooker's refusal to allow local collectors in India to put specific localities on specimens sent to Kew (Enderby, 2008); his argument was they were not on maps – but his insistence means that these specimens are less useful today than they might have been. Because of their size, herbarium specimen labels now contain detailed information about location, habitat and the plant itself – botanists are truly lucky to have this wealth of data attached to each collection (ideally!). The labels on zoological specimens tend to be less data-rich, although this is changing as specimens are linked to databases of further information. As herbarium specimens age, they often lose colour and older specimens without descriptive labels can be as difficult to interpret as a black and white photograph. Not all specimens are equal.

Specimens are also not the end product of the science of taxonomy; a nineteenth-century obsession with the number of specimens collected by a given botanist created a sort of 'cult of numbers' – the more specimens you had collected, the better botanist you were. This is peculiar to botany, where each collection is numbered in sequence, associated with the collector's name. This system is fantastic for identifying particular collections as unique, thus *Knapp 8394* (*Solanum uleanum* Bitter, collected in Peru in 1986) is a unique identifier for this event, a sort of 'barcode' for the collection – but not for the individual specimens, which consist of duplicates in different institutions. Numbering is great for this purpose, but can create a mania for numbers over information or utility.

Specimens are properly collected for three principal reasons:

1.   to sample diversity in unexplored areas;
2.   to collect samples for particular analyses; and
3.   to document the diversity of particular areas of interest.

The kinds of specimens resulting from these three types of collecting are somewhat different, and exploring that difference is important to an analysis of what sorts of collections we might need in the future. This short chapter is not a comprehensive review of different collecting methods or futures in all groups, but a personal exploration of some ideas I feel we as a taxonomic community need to consider in the future.

15.3 Types of collecting: general versus targeted

When the rest of the world was relatively unknown to European botanists, collections were made of everything; a record of what people found in new lands. Today's scientific collecting, some 300 years later, has quite naturally evolved. Collection of specimens can be caricatured as being bimodal, but of course there are all variations of these two extremes. On the one hand, collecting is still done in regions where little exploration has been done, often in association with floristic projects (Knapp et al., 2001). These sorts of collections, which could be characterised as general collecting, are like those of the early explorers and tend to add considerable knowledge about distribution of species in regions or add new records to country distributions. On the other extreme are collections made for specific research projects, which can be characterised as targeted collecting, where specific plants are sought for specific purposes such as molecular studies. This sort of collecting tends to be focused on areas where the plants are already known – if one wants to get a sample of species X it is of course logical to go to somewhere where species X has been found before. Collections, therefore, are of different value, although once in a museum or herbarium, they are all assumed to have been collected for the same purpose.

Herbarium managers bemoan collections of common tropical weeds – bans on accessions of some species, like *Asclepias curassavica* L., are sometimes mooted. But this can carry risks; recent work on the widespread weedy tree genus *Trema* (Yesson et al., 2004) revealed that hidden in what everyone had assumed was a single 'trash' weed, were two quite different taxa with different life histories and biology. Assumptions can be dangerous!

Like common weeds collected again and again, a species targeted for molecular studies and collected over and over again in the same locality adds no new distribution knowledge to our global dataset. Vouchering of collections used in molecular studies is of course important (e.g. Peterson et al., 2007), but perhaps we ought to be thinking of other ways to record the occurrence of something in the same place where it has been recorded before. These targeted collections are useful for those doing the analysis using new data, but unless carefully done, often add little to the overall sum of knowledge about the distribution of the species. Distribution of course is not the only goal of collecting, but since specimens occupy considerable space in museums and herbaria (see below) the more purposes they can serve the better.

15.4 Non-traditional specimens

In the nineteenth century collectors like Alfred Russel Wallace shot and collected birds in quantities that today seem rather shocking (Knapp, 2008c). In the modern context, specimens of birds and mammals are no longer routinely collected as evidence of occurrence in a particular region; observational records are accorded high status. Birds and mammals are relatively species-poor groups compared to other sectors of biodiversity, and the state of knowledge about their taxonomy and distribution is very complete (whatever that may mean!). Rapid biodiversity inventories in remote tropical regions (e.g. Vreisendorp et al., 2006) do not make collections of these groups, but instead record them with various kinds of observational methods. Birds are recorded using photographs and recordings of songs, bats by sound alone (see iBats[1]) and new mammals sometimes even described

---

[1] http://www.ibats.org

with photographical collections alone (Jones et al., 2005). These sorts of records can sometimes be controversial, as has been shown with the debate over the 'rediscovery' of the ivory-billed woodpecker in the southern USA (Fitzpatrick et al. 2005; Hill et al. 2006), but if a species thought to be extinct is sighted again, is it really ethical to shoot it in order to document its existence? Although plants (and many other more species-rich groups) are still largely collected using the traditional museum methods, it is worth, I think, examining how observational records could be used to augment our knowledge of these groups, thus moving much of the rest of biodiversity from being space-hungry and physical-object based to being more digitally and observationally based.

A few examples will suffice to show what I mean. Perhaps for surveys of relatively well-known floras, like that of Britain or some parts of the USA, photographs of flowers (taken to a standard, see below) could be used as distributional records, rather than yet more herbarium samples being taken of something that is already represented in local and national herbaria (see also Chapter 1, A. G. Miller et al., in this volume). For particular types of studies, for example those involving surveys of the genetic structure of populations of known species over large (or small) geographical ranges, a more appropriate type of collection for vouchering these data could be photographs of individual plants or populations of plants, coupled with a permanently archived sample of the tissue used to assess the genetic variability, say a leaf in silica gel. For some organisms video is proving to be a useful new collection technique (De Ley and Bert, 2004; see NemATOL[2]); these data can be archived and serve as vouchers when an entire individual is needed for DNA extraction for molecular studies. Perhaps when a specimen is recollected for molecular analysis from known populations (or even individuals! – I have done this myself in Bolivia) a new herbarium specimen is not necessary; it will not add anything to an overall dataset other than another date record. A photograph plus the DNA-extractable sample can do that just as well. When germplasm bank samples are used in molecular phylogenetics work perhaps it is not necessary to make a new voucher every time, although sometimes seeds can be mixed up and identities confused! If vouchers for germplasm bank accessions are digitised and made available then a plant grown can be compared easily; here too a photographical voucher would be better than yet another herbarium specimen of the same individual or population.

Taxonomists are few, taxa are many and no single scientist can afford to travel to sample his or her taxon throughout its range. If a species can be identified from a photographical record then anyone can contribute to a global dataset of occurrences. In order to test if this was possible we have asked biological colleagues to photograph *Solanum* species wherever they go, with a view to adding these

---

[2] http://nematol.unh.edu

collections to distributional records on a website dedicated to *Solanum* (Solanaceae Source[3]). These people knew what solanums looked like, so sent back photographs that by and large were identifiable to species or at least to species group. We requested a global positioning system (GPS) reading attached to the photograph, thus providing a data point that could be reverified by field observation if necessary. Of the photographs received, only a few were not identifiable or were of unrecognised taxa; these new records have increased our knowledge base by adding new data to a global dataset.

The Solanaceae Source website, established as part of the Planetary Biodiversity Inventory project called PBI Solanum (see Knapp et al., 2004; Knapp, 2008a), has made the taxonomy and diversity of *Solanum* highly visible in a new environment. We regularly receive emails from a wide range of users asking if we would like photographs of particular taxa. To us, this is an exciting indication of an interest in participating in the process of taxonomic investigation by non-scientists or by those not already involved in taxonomy itself. The acceptance of observational records as 'specimens' would mean that anyone who could provide an observation with the necessary associated data could contribute to increasing our understanding of biodiversity, truly opening up and expanding the data we can use. Citizen science and public participation are both of interest to not only the scientific community but also to those funding science; if we are to accelerate the documentation of life on earth we need more than the diminishing community of taxonomists to be contributing. Websites such as Flickr[4] can be models for the exchange of data, and the Encyclopedia of Life[5] project (see Knapp, 2008b) will certainly also be a forum for such amplification of contribution. The development of this sort of participation will necessarily be patchy; there are many amateurs interested in groups such as Araceae (the arum lilies, see International Aroid Society[6]) who might want to contribute, while groups of tiny, but important, invertebrates may receive less input. The taxonomic community needs to engage with this idea, however, if we are to really ramp up our input to meet the growing need for taxonomic and distributional information – we need to really address the taxonomic impediment in new and creative ways.

Permission to collect specimens can also be problematic; new emphasis on sharing the benefits of biodiversity has meant that the old model of collect and take back to the home institute has, fortunately, gone forever. However, fears about lack of cooperation, or even worse biopiracy, can hamper real efforts to understand biodiversity. Collecting permits are essential, but the bureaucracy associated with them can be daunting. The fact that scientists engaged in scientific collecting do obtain permits for their work does not mean that others collect with permits;

[3] http://www.solanaceaesource.org   [4] http://www.flickr.com   [5] http://www.eol.org
[6] http://www.aroid.org

institutions must be careful about where and how specimens are collected and what they accept – most now have policies for accessions that exclude material not collected with the correct permits and documentation. Sometimes traditional specimens are impossible to obtain.

Observational records ('collections'), whether associated with DNA-extractable material or not, are not new for some taxonomic groups. For those groups where they will be new, however, it is important that we establish standards so that they will be maximally useful. I would suggest that there are several elements that *must* be part of the data associated with these new types of collection; firstly, a georeference point that will allow reobservation or collection if necessary, and secondly, a date of 'collection'. For plant groups, ideally different views of diagnostic or important characteristics would be taken, and photographs of the whole plant and its habitat. For DNA-extractable material, it would be best, in my view, if it were archived in a DNA bank (such as those at the American Museum of Natural History or the Royal Botanic Gardens, Kew), rather than just as a sequence on GenBank[7] (Harris, 2003). As we establish new web-available taxonomies (see Godfray et al., 2007), it is imperative that we post standards for new types of collections for particular groups. These must, however, not be so difficult to attain as to discourage people from contributing, as scientists we know science is great fun, let's let others participate and find that out as well!

15.5 Why go in the field at all?

Herbaria and museums are full of plant collections, many of these institutions suffer from severe overcrowding and even when new buildings are constructed, growth often outstrips capacity thought to be ample at the time. So perhaps we might save space and time by not going in the field at all, and by investing more time in studying and documenting the collections we already have. New species are often found in the herbarium (see Granados-Tochoy et al., 2007) as well as in the field! Fieldwork, however, is critical at this time in the study of plant diversity, especially fieldwork undertaken in previously unexplored or under collected regions. In general, biologists working on relatively well-known groups are now discovering rare taxa; they are usually not discovering species of wide distribution. This of course is not the case for species-rich groups of small organisms, where even the widespread are relatively unknown.

Collecting is still important to the study of biodiversity; it provides the baseline of evidence upon which we make hypotheses about the natural world. Collecting, however, does not need to always be the same. Different taxa require different collecting strategies, and the different uses to which collections are put should be

---

[7] http://www.ncbi.nlm.nih.gov/genbank

carefully considered as those collections are made. Observations as 'collections' have the potential to greatly enhance our knowledge base, just as they have done in more well-studied, less species-rich groups such as birds. Expanding our concept of what a collection is also has the potential to broaden the range of people who feel empowered to contribute to the study of biodiversity, something that can only increase stewardship for natural resources and the data resource used to monitor and measure diversity in a changing world.

Uses of new types of collections, be they images, DNA-extractable samples or combinations of these two, are limited only by our imaginations. In addition to traditional uses like monographical or phylogenetics studies, these new collections can be used for vouchered genetic studies on populations, in detailed studies of biogeography, in order to study the effects of climate change through phenological monitoring, involving the public in scientific research through personal contribution, or you name it. If the observation, be it a traditional specimen or an image or another type of record, is geo-referenced and well-documented it will have multiple uses far into the future. Flexible standards need to be set for various taxonomic groups in order that new sorts of collections contributed by others are maximally useful, and that this new way of thinking encourages others to be involved rather than creating a mystique around taxonomy that limits involvement. Taxonomists are too few and stretched too thinly over the surface of diversity to not be flexible in seeing how new sorts of collections can be used, not only to ease the space pressure on our institutions, but to greatly enhance our impact and efficiency in the study of the diversity of life on earth.

Acknowledgments

I thank Mark Watson and Colin Pendry for inviting me to present these ideas at the Biennial Meeting of the Systematics Association in Edinburgh in 2007, and for having patience with the writing of this highly personal set of ideas; discussions with my colleagues have influenced my thinking, but any errors are of course my own.

References

Bebber, D. P., Carine, M. A., Wood, J. R. I., Wortley, A. H., Harris, D. J., Prance, G. T., Davidse, G., Paige, J., Pennington, T. D., Robson, N. K. B., and Scotland, R. W. (2010). Herbaria are a major frontier for species discovery. *Proceedings of the National Academy of Sciences*, USA **107**(51): 22169–22172.

De Ley, P. and Bert, W. (2004). Video capture and editing as a tool for the storage, distribution and illustration of morphological characters of nematodes. *Journal of Nematology*, **34**: 296–302.

Enderby, J. (2008). *Imperial nature: Joseph Hooker and the practices of Victorian science*. Chicago: University of Chicago Press.

Fitzpatrick, J. W., Lammertink, M., Luneau Jr., M. D., Gallagher, T. W., Harrison, B. R.

and Sparling, G. M., Rosenberg, K. V., Rohrbaugh, R. W., Swarthout, E. C. H., Wrege, P. H., Swarthout, S. B., Dantzker, M. et al. (2005). Ivory-billed Woodpecker (*Campephilus principalis*) persists in continental North America. *Science*, **308**: 1460–1462.

Godfray, H. C. J. and Knapp, S. (2004). Introduction: taxonomy for the twenty-first century. *Philosophical Transactions of the Royal Society, series B*, **359**: 559–569.

Godfray H. C. J., Clark, B. R., Kitching, I. J., Mayo, S. J. and Scoble, M. J. (2007). The Web and the structure of taxonomy. *Systematic Biology*, **56**: 943–955.

Granados-Tochoy, J. C., Knapp, S. and Orozco, C. I. (2007). *Solanum humboldtianum* (Solanaceae): an endangered new species from Colombia rediscovered 200 years after its first collection. *Systematic Botany*, **32**: 200–207.

Harris, J. D. (2003). Can you bank on GenBank? *Trends in Ecology and Evolution*, **18**: 317–319.

Hill, G. E., Mennill, D. J., Rolek, B. W., Hicks, T. L. and Swiston, K. A. (2006). Evidence suggesting that Ivory-billed Woodpeckers (*Campephilus principalis*) exist in Florida. *Avian Conservation and Ecology – Écologie et conservation des oiseaux*, **1**(3): 2. Available online: http://www.aceeco.org/vol1/iss3/art2.

Jones, T., Ehardt, C. L., Butynski, T. M., Davenport, T. R. B., Mpunga, N. E., Machaga, S. J. and De Luca, D. W. (2005). The Highland Mangabey *Lophocebus kipunji*: a new species of African monkey. *Science*, **308**: 1161–1164.

Knapp, S. (2005). *Footsteps in the forest: Alfred Russel Wallace in the Amazon*. London: Natural History Museum.

Knapp, S. (2008a). Taxonomy as a team sport. In *The new taxonomy*, Q. Wheeler (ed.) Systematics Association Special Volume 76. London: CRC Press, pp. 33–53.

Knapp, S. (2008b). Naming nature: the future of the Linnaean system. *The Linnean*, Special Issue **8**: 161–167.

Knapp, S. (2008c). Alfred Russel Wallace, conservation and sustainable development. In *Natural selection and beyond: the intellectual influence of Alfred Russel Wallace*, C. Smith and G. Beccaloni (eds.). Oxford University Press, pp. 201–220.

Knapp, S., Davidse, G. and Sousa S., M. (2001). Proyectos floristicos hoy y mañana: su importancia en la sistemática y la conservación. In *Enfoques contemporaneos para el estudio de la biodiversidad*, H. M. Hernandez, A. N. Garcia Aldrete, F. Alvarez and M. Ulloa (eds). Mexico: Instituto de Biología, UNAM, pp. 331–358.

Knapp, S., Bohs, L., Nee, M. and Spooner, D. M. (2004). Solanaceae: a model for linking genomics and biodiversity. *Comparative and Functional Genomics*, **5**: 285–291.

Linnaeus, C. (1751). *Philosophia botanica*. Leiden.

Peterson, A. T., Brumfield, R. T., Moyle, R. G., Nyári, A. S., Remsen Jr., J. V. and Robbins, M. B. (2007). The need for proper vouchering in phylogenetic studies of birds. *Molecular Phylogenetics and Evolution*, **45**: 1042–1044.

Vriesendorp, C., Pitman, N., Rojas Moscoso, J. I., Pawlak, B. A., Rivera Chávez, L., Calixto Méndez, L., Vela Collantes, M. and Fasabi Rimachi, P. (eds.) (2006). *Perú: Matsés. Rapid biological inventories report 16*. Chicago: Field Museum of Natural History.

Yesson, C., Russell, S. J., Parrish, T., Dalling, J. W. and Garwood, N. C. (2004). Phylogenetic framework for *Trema* (Celtidaceae). *Plant Systematics and Evolution*, **248**: 85–109.

16

Field methods for inventorying insects

C. L. Häuser and K. Riede

16.1 Introduction

Insects are 'the little things that run the world' (Wilson, 1987a). They form an important component of functional biodiversity as herbivores, detritivores, predators, pollinators or vectors of diseases. In spite of small individual body size, insects in tropical forests contribute several tons of biomass for every hectare of forest, compared to a few kilograms per hectare for birds and mammals (Fittkau and Klinge, 1973), and insect herbivores have been identified as important mediators in forest processes (reviewed by Rinker and Lowman, 2004). Social insects in particular make up more than one-third of animal biomass in Amazonian *terra firme* rainforest (Davidson et al, 2003). On a single tree in the Peruvian rainforest, Wilson (1987b) found 43 species of ants, and the total number of individuals is estimated as 8 million ants and 1 million termites per hectare (Hölldobler and Wilson, 1990). In fact, the ongoing debate about how many species live on earth was triggered by fogging tropical rainforest canopies, where Erwin (1983) collected more than 1000 kinds of beetles from one Panamanian tree species (*Luehea seemannii*). Most of the insects were hitherto undescribed, 'new' species. From this dataset, Erwin (1983) extrapolated a total of 30 million extant arthropod species on Earth.

Due to this overwhelming diversity, comprehensive inventories of insects are among the most challenging frontiers for global biodiversity assessment, particularly

Descriptive Taxonomy: The Foundation of Biodiversity Research, eds M. F. Watson, C. H. C. Lyal and C. A. Pendry. Published by Cambridge University Press.

because most insect species are 'rare' (many species have been described from and are represented in collections by singletons – i.e. one specimen, hence, only of one sex!). However, the rarity of insects might simply be due to the fact that their habitat and hence the appropriate sampling method are not known. For example, the fauna of tropical canopy grasshoppers was only known from singletons until the 1970s. A systematic search for grasshoppers inhabiting the Peruvian rainforest canopy initiated by Descamps (1976) revealed an entire, hitherto unknown, fauna rich in species and individuals (Amédégnato, 1997).

An interesting case is provided by sound-producing insects, such as crickets or cicadas, which reveal their presence reliably by species-specific songs (Riede, 1998). They probably have a lower biomass than vertebrates, but contribute considerably (and at dusk or night even predominantly) to the characteristic soundscape of a tropical forest, which can be deafening in the case of South East Asian cicada dusk choruses (Gogala and Riede, 1995).

These few examples indicate that the study of insects is of interest both for the ecologist and for the taxonomist (see also New, 1996). While the former might be interested in community ecology or the role of insects in the food web, the latter is mainly interested in species discovery, which seems to be particularly rewarding in tropical forests. Both need sampling techniques, which are crucial for inventories and are the main theme of our review. Matching the huge diversity, there is a great variety of qualitative and quantitative collecting techniques for insects, only briefly sketched below. The actual techniques employed will depend on the scope and emphasis of the study, be it targeting specific taxa or surveying an entire ecosystem. In addition, the habitat(s), available time and resources strongly determine the method(s) of choice. Mass-collection techniques produce huge numbers of insect specimens, which have to be sorted into groups, counted, assigned to morphospecies and eventually be sent to specialists for exact determination or description (for further challenges applying a morphospecies concept, see Krell, 2004). These costly procedures are often avoided by discarding insects other than the target group, which could be a certain subfamily or larger group. Alternatively, massive sampling endeavours lead to accumulation of huge and space-consuming repositories of more or less sorted insect material stored in alcohol. We present below a short synoptic overview of insect inventorying techniques, review the present state of knowledge resulting from mass-collecting techniques, present examples for non-invasive bioacoustic inventorying and outline the needs for more efficient and coordinated inventorying efforts. These include application of standard protocols to ensure both efficiency and sustainability of records and data generated. In addition, we will focus on data processing and dissemination techniques, which is another bottleneck for inventorying the huge number of insect species inhabiting our planet.

16.2 Pursuit of the smallest game: individual collecting and observing techniques

For almost any insect group, targeted search and collecting efforts by the individual, experienced specialist are an important, if not the most effective way, towards a comprehensive inventory of any given insect fauna. For active search numerous specialist approaches and techniques exist depending on target taxa and specific environment, which cannot be reviewed here to any extent. Whether they involve active chasing and netting of individual specimens, sweeping vegetation with an insect net, the use of an aspirator for obtaining smaller-sized specimens, sieving through leaf litter or soil samples, or rearing adults from early stages collected in substrate or hosts, the results of all these techniques are largely determined by the individual researcher's experience, a factor which is difficult to standardise. Targetted searching techniques for individual specimens become even more indispensable for any inventory when including or focusing on groups with an endophytic, (endo-) parasitic, subterranean or otherwise hidden life style; such groups consequently present the most challenges for use as model organisms for biodiversity estimates or standardised ecological studies. Standardised sampling protocols for special groups such as termites relying on repeated time-based efforts may partly overcome these problems (e.g. Jones and Eggleton, 2000), but differences remain between comprehensive inventories undertaken by individual 'experienced' researchers and standardised approaches.

   For more information on individual collecting techniques and gear, standard equipment and tools, and special techniques for targeting individual taxa or habitats, general manuals and texts should be consulted, such as Gibb and Oseto (2005) and Martin (1977).

16.3 Mass collecting and recording techniques

We present a brief sketch below of common sampling techniques, but suggest the reader use the cited references for more detailed information. A comprehensive textbook compilation is given in Southwood and Henderson (2000).

16.3.1 Fogging (insecticide knockdown)

Applying insecticides through fogging is widely used in pest control, and a wide range of commercial fogging machines is available. The scientific use for sampling canopy insects by insecticide fogging goes back to Roberts (1973) in Costa Rica. Since then, the technique has been further tested and modified by several research groups and projects, employing fumigation, mist and smoking techniques for entire tree crowns (Fig 16.1). Fumigated insects falling down from tree crowns are

Figure 16.1 Fogging at Kakamega forest, Kenya (courtesy: W. Freund). A black and white version of this figure will appear in some formats. For the colour version, please refer to the plate section.

collected on plastic sheets laid out on the ground, by plastic trays or aluminium funnels (for a short review, see Adis et al., 1998). Insecticide fogging has become established as a standard technique for assessing arthropod diversity, especially in tropical forest canopies, since the early 1980s (Erwin, 1983; Paarmann and Stork, 1987; Basset et al., 1997; Adis et al., 1998). A variety of 'knockdown' insecticides have been tested, but natural pyrethrum is now established as a standard, because it permits collection of live specimens, and its biodegradability facilitates application in ecologically sensitive habitats. Apart from using pyrethrum as an active agent, all other intents and recommendations to standardise fogging procedures, such as suggested by Adis et al. (1998), have not been followed, each research group establishing their own preferences with respect to tree selection, equipment and setup, fogging procedures, collecting trays, etc.

For comparing results from canopy fogging, variables such as tree height, surrounding canopy structure, weather and especially wind conditions, as well as seasonal and other effects of the local environment, will influence the results. Wind drift of insecticide fog and falling insects strongly affect what is collected, but in all studies huge numbers of insects as well as other arthropod specimens can be collected from just single trees. Due to the considerable costs of even single fogging events and the possible adverse ecological impact, it is not used or recommended for regular sampling or monitoring. Although first developed and applied in tropical forests, fogging techniques have also been used successfully to study canopy faunas of temperate forests (Stork and Hammond, 1997; Floren and Schmidl 2008). With the recently increased possibilities of canopy access (Basset et al., 2003), the fogging of entire tree crowns from the ground is also becoming less needed and giving way towards more restricted or focussed application of the technique, e.g. to certain parts of a tree such as individual branches or parts of the bark or trunk (Floren and Schmidl, 2003).

16.3.2 Extraction techniques

Leaf litter, soil and the mesocavernous superficial stratum (MSS) harbour a high, underestimated richness of insect and other invertebrate fauna that play an important role in ecosystems. A special set of traps and extraction techniques allows capture of arthropods living in the surface of soil up to a depth of 50–60 cm. Common techniques use Berlese funnels and Winkler extraction devices, which, however, have shown only limited success rates for termites in tropical forests (Jones and Eggleton, 2000). Further applications using Winkler extraction techniques for ecological studies and biodiversity assessments are reviewed by Krell et al. (2005). MSS traps are more difficult to install, but can remain in the MSS for a long time, revealing a hitherto little known fauna (Ducarme et al., 2005).

16.3.3 Passive, non-attractant traps

Pitfall traps

For collecting and inventorying ground-dwelling insects and other arthropods, pitfall traps together with Barber traps (Barber 1931) are the most effective and long-established methods, for which a considerable body of literature exists (e.g. Houseweart et al., 1979; Borges and Brown, 2003;Woodcock, 2005). They consist of cans, jars or other containers sunk into the ground, usually equipped with a funnel on top, and partly filled with a killing and preserving liquid like ethylene glycol. For targeting individual taxa or guilds, pitfall traps can also be supplied with specific attractants or baits (see below: 'Baited traps, pheromone traps').

Flight interception traps, Malaise traps

Apart from active pursuit, flying insects are best recorded by setting up invisible obstacles in their flight paths. In its simplest form, a glass pane or transparent panel is put up vertically and connected with a pan or collecting container at the bottom. These window traps work well for many Coleoptera and other groups, which react by dropping to the ground when hitting a screen or baffle in flight. Based on this principle, several adapted trap designs have been developed for special applications (e.g. Wilkening et al., 1981).

The Malaise trap is one of the most widely used methods, and has developed as the standard technique for recording insects in flight over more than 50 years (Malaise, 1937; Townes, 1972; Steyskal, 1981). The basic design consists of a sideways open tent or a converging arrangement of vertical screens or baffles, with a collecting bottle or container mounted at the highest point of the sloping roof (Fig 16.2). Flying insects intercepted by the screens generally attempt to escape by

Figure 16.2 Malaise trap at El Ventorillo, Spain (courtesy: J. Nieves-Aldrey).

moving upwards and are channelled through a funnel into the apical collecting vial, usually containing alcohol or another suitable preservation fluid.

Malaise trapping has become an established survey method, particularly for Diptera and Hymenoptera (Roberts, 1972; Darling and Packer, 1988), but has also been successfully applied to other groups (Walker, T. J., 1978; Hosking, 1979). It has been used in several large-scale regional sampling and inventory programmes, both in temperate regions and the tropics (Schneider and Duelli, 1997; Nieves-Aldrey et al., 2003; Brown, 2005), and has even been adapted as a combined windowpane interception trap for use in the forest canopy (Basset, 1988). Several further modifications and specific designs have been developed and tested, and Malaise traps have frequently also been used in combination with baits and/or pans or other interception traps, particularly when targeting specific taxa such as biting flies or aphids (Darling and Packer, 1988; Muirhead-Thomson, 1991).

Malaise traps are among the most effective means for collecting large numbers of specimens, and under favourable conditions yield enormous numbers of specimens within a few hours, although traps can be operated for longer periods, even covering an entire season. Apart from technical and design factors such as size, screen colour and mesh size, killing agent, etc., the main factors influencing the catch are the placement and orientation of the trap, particularly taking into account prevailing wind directions, and other circumstances of the habitat. The number of specimens accumulating during Malaise trapping projects often exceeds that collected by fogging, simply due to the fact that Malaise traps can be placed cost-efficiently for months. Protocols proposed for insect inventories and surveys always include Malaise trapping, particularly for Hymenoptera and Diptera, but successful implementation is highly dependent on available resources and work force, especially for sorting the collected materials which represent the most cost- and labour-intensive aspects of any such project.

16.3.4 Attraction traps

Light traps

Light trapping has become a generalised term referring to all methods of attracting nocturnal insects with lamps or artificial light sources, whether they are actually connected to a trap or just being operated in front of screens, walls or other reflective surfaces where incoming insects are then recorded or collected manually (Fig 16.3). The attraction of nocturnal insects to light has been common knowledge from early periods of human civilisation (Lödl, 1987; Steiner and Nikusch, 1994), and has been used systematically for scientific purposes since the times of Alfred Russel Wallace, who regularly employed a lantern to collect moths and other nocturnal insects on Borneo and during his travels throughout

Figure 16.3 Light trapping with manual collecting (Borjomi National Park, Georgia).

the Malay Archipelago in the mid 1850s (Wallace 1869). With the spread of electricity and the availability of high emission lamps and portable power sources, light trapping has become the standard technique for inventorying nocturnal insects, especially moths (Lepidoptera), but also for many nocturnal groups of Blattodea, Coleoptera, Dermaptera, Diptera, Mantodea, Neuroptera, Orthoptera and other orders, which are rarely if ever recorded otherwise. A considerable body of literature exists devoted to light trapping, which cannot be considered here comprehensively (for reviews, see Lödl, 1984; Muirhead-Thomson, 1991; Steiner and Nikusch, 1994; Fry and Waring, 2001; Nowinsky, 2003; Wirooks, 2005; Steiner and Häuser, 2011).

A variety of different lights and lamp types have been employed, but most lamps in use for light trapping today have a strong emission in the ultraviolet (UV) range of the spectrum, such as high pressure mercury vapour lamps, and black light or actinic tubes. Whereas the overall attraction and results for insects are generally highest with UV-emitting lamps, other lamp types tested produce significantly different results regarding species composition and abundance, and thus might be more applicable targeting specific taxa (Walker, A. K. and Galbreath, 1979). In addition to the different types of lamps and light bulbs employed, light traps also come in a large variety of designs and makes, ranging from makeshift constructions with free hanging light bulbs to commercially available, fully automated traps used for pest control and monitoring (Muirhead-Thomson, 1991; Leinonen et al. 1998; Fry and Waring, 2001). For any analysis of results actual light traps, where lamps are fitted to a box or other container with a funnel to automatically collect incoming insects, should be distinguished from individual, manual collecting at light. Whereas automated traps, sometimes combined with suction traps and a series of rotating containers, are convenient for larger scale and/or longer term monitoring, especially of individual pests, vectors or other limited target taxa, manual light trapping remains the preferred technique for more comprehensive, qualitative inventorying of a local fauna or community. For certain groups, particularly Lepidoptera, manually operated lights are also to be preferred over actual light traps, as specimens need to be handled individually to ensure a sufficient state of preservation for subsequent preparation and easy determination.

For any kind of setting or equipment used, major factors influencing light trapping results are other light sources, particularly moonlight, and weather, mostly temperature and wind (Bowden, 1982; Taylor, 1986; Yela and Holyoak, 1997; Butler et al., 1999). Another important factor influencing the results is the exact placement of the light trap at the site, such as the height above ground, especially so in a highly structured landscape, such as mountain environments or in forests or other habitats with dense vegetation (Steiner and Nikusch, 1994; Wirooks, 2005; Beck and Linsenmair, 2006).

Under suitable conditions, light trapping results in large numbers of records, and a weak light in the tropics can easily attract several thousand specimens during a single evening or night. Light trapping is one of the most cost-efficient mass collecting technique for many insect taxa, and like Malaise traps and fogging techniques, requires the processing of enormous numbers of specimens and records. Although several short- and long-term regional and local light trapping monitoring programmes have been established, most use different equipment and protocols adapted for the specific conditions and purposes, and general light trapping protocols have not yet been established at an international level.

Water panels, yellow pans

Water panels and yellow or differently coloured pans attract many flying insects and, if filled with detergent or a mix of water and preservative fluids, trap individuals attracted by the colour directly inside the pan. They are sometimes used in combination with flight interception traps. Yellow water pan traps are used in applied entomology for monitoring aphids (e.g. in Mexico: Peña Martinez and Bujanos,

1990), while Campbell and Hanula (2007) found blue the most effective colour to attract pollinators.

Baited traps, pheromone traps

For specific groups or individual taxa, traps supplied with bait or specific attractant are employed. Carrion- or dung-feeding insects can often be best surveyed and obtained by either collecting around naturally occurring carcasses or faeces or by placing them in a controlled setting or a specific trapping device, such as baited pitfall traps. Many developments and experiments have been carried out in applied entomology, especially for attracting blood-sucking insect vectors, parasites of livestock and agricultural pests (e.g. Underhill et al., 1978). For capturing fruit-feeding butterflies (widespread in many tropical habitats), butterfly traps consisting of a gauze cylinder with an opening at the bottom, where some fermenting fruit is placed as bait, are used (Austin and Riley, 1995). Attracted butterflies are trapped in the upper, closed part of the trap when trying to escape (Rydon, 1964; Hughes et al., 1999).

Insect taxa from several orders such as some Lepidoptera groups have been collected almost exclusively by pheromone baits. Male clearwing moths (Lepidoptera: Sesiidae) are reliably attracted by synthetic sex attractants (isomers of 3,13-octadien-1-ol (ODDA) and 3,13-ODDOH acetates: Voerman et al., 1978). (As an aside, the sesiid *Carmeta odda* (Duckworth and Eichlin, 1977) was named for the pheromone abbreviated 'ODDA'.) Arrays of sticky traps baited with different isomeric combinations were employed to inventory sesiid communities in Panama and Wisconsin (Greenfield, 1983). The Pherobase[1] is a comprehensive database of pheromones and semiochemicals, listing a wide variety of substances and insect species. Pheromone traps can be highly efficient to search for or verify the occurrence of a certain species or group, but are very specific; hence, they are of limited use for comprehensive inventories.

16.3.5 Acoustic monitoring

Non-invasive acoustic registration of singing insects is particularly useful in habitats where visual observation or collection of specimens is difficult or even impossible. Up to now, most researchers have concentrated on the small fraction of insects producing loud songs perceived by humans, mainly cicadas (Cicadidae) and Orthoptera, using comparatively cheap audio equipment (e.g. Riede, 1997). An extensive acoustic sampling protocol is suggested by the Tropical Ecology Assessment and Monitoring Network (TEAM) Initiative, using digital recording at programmable time intervals with a handheld computer (Brandes, 2005). Meanwhile, a wide variety of semi-automatic monitoring

---

[1] http://www.pherobase.com

schemes and techniques are available (reviewed by Obrist et al., 2010) Many insect groups, however, produce ultrasound or vibrational signals not perceptible to man. Using appropriate microphones and amplifiers, acoustic inventorying and monitoring could easily be extended to novel target groups communicating by vibration (e.g. treehoppers: Hemiptera: Membracidae: Cocroft and McNett, 2006) or underwater stridulation as documented for water bugs (Corixidae: Jansson, 1973). Drosopoulos and Claridge (2006) provide an excellent compilation of studies demonstrating the high diversity of vibratory and acoustic communication in insects.

16.4 From sampling methods to protocols

Basset et al. (1997: 45) provide a key to assist in the selection of methods for sampling insects in tropical forests, particularly in tree canopies. The authors differentiate 18 techniques, including some highly specialised procedures such as rearing (emphasis on concealed fauna) or extraction from epiphytes. Comparing results from surveys of leaf-feeding beetles in Papua New Guinea, they conclude that 'none of the methods examined can be considered as the panacea for investigating a wide range of ecological topics' (Basset et al., 1997: 44), and suggest a combination of techniques to get more comprehensive samples.

An even greater challenge is to make results comparable across studies. This requires standardisation of protocols (New, 1996), defining not only technical details of the trap or sampling apparatus, but ideally also sampling intervals, placement and data processing (for a study of distinct light traps, see Blomberg et al., 1978). A number of protocols have been published, using standardised equipment and procedures (e.g. Jones and Eggleton, 2000; Rohr et al., 2007). However, only a few have become more widely accepted. Examples are the Ants of the Leaf Litter (ALL) protocol, surveying ants using mini-Winkler extractor and pitfall traps (Agosti and Alonso, 2000), or the TEAM acoustics protocol, targeted at registration of frog and cricket songs (Brandes, 2005). The Rothamsted light trap programme provided valuable insights into seasonality and abundance fluctuations of British insects, but only for one locality (Southwood et al., 2003). In contrast, pheromone traps are commercially available and applied worldwide, but targeting mainly a few 'pest' species. In summary, entomologists surveying under-explored habitats such as tropical rainforests are either using highly specialised sampling techniques for their target group, or apply the above-mentioned collecting techniques such as fogging, soil extraction, pitfall, malaise and light trapping with modifications according to their experience and regional requirements.

16.5 Results from mass collection and recording techniques

What are the results from all these sampling efforts? How many new species have been described, how did they contribute to insect conservation or control, and how can users access these results? In the following section, we present some results from mass collection methods, taking them as a starting point for a discussion on how to improve entomological inventories in the future. All techniques generated huge datasets, which in most cases could only be assessed at a morphospecies level without much taxonomic depth (e.g. New, 1996; Krell, 2004). In the few cases of more detailed taxonomic analysis, a high percentage of undescribed, 'new' species has been confirmed for most tropical sites (Desutter-Grandcolas and Nischk, 2000; Floren et al. 2001; Lampe et al., 2007 based on Wagner, 2001). However, due to the taxonomic impediment, up-to-date revisions are pending even for many groups in temperate regions. From the 1 000 000 insect specimens from Malaise traps collected by Nieves-Aldrey et al. (2003), the authors sorted 13 000 insect specimens and identified 2700 Hymenoptera species. This dataset is impressive not only because of the huge number of specimens collected, but also because of the high number of 10 Hymenoptera species new to science (Platygastridae: Buhl, 2001), and 170 new for Spain. However, a similarly thorough analysis of Diptera collected during this survey could not be accomplished.

16.5.1 Fogging

The application of insecticides to whole tree communities is among the most innovative techniques applied within recent decades, facilitating the study of hitherto inaccessible, unknown and species-rich insect communities inhabiting the rainforest canopy. The analysis of entire insect communities living on one or few tropical tree species provided valuable insights for community ecologists. However, due to the high number of hitherto undescribed species, evaluation of collections from fogging samples has had to be based on morphospecies (i.e. 'species' sorted and classified by morphological similarity, often lacking taxonomic names below genus or even family level). Extrapolations of total insect numbers were based on such morphospecies datasets. The stages of Erwin's extrapolation start from his fogging exercise in Panama, which yielded 1000 morphospecies of canopy beetles, with an estimated 160 being host-specific. From these 160 species, he reports:

1. Beetles represent 40% of known arthropods: 400.
2. Canopy 2× rich as forest floor: 600.

That is, a rough estimate of 600 host-specific tropical arthropod species. Assuming monophagy, and a comparatively conservative and reliable number of

50 000 tropical tree species worldwide, there might be $600 \times 50\ 000 = 30$ million arthropod species on earth. The majority would be insects, particularly beetles (12 million, i.e. 40%).

This estimate is now considered as a 'guesstimate' because it is based on highly debatable assumptions of the proportion of host-specific insect species and the degree of endemicity/regional variability. Because total numbers depend heavily on these assumptions (i.e. if there are 10 or 100 monophagous insects for a single tree species), there is an ongoing debate discussing species guesstimates. Numbers range from 5 and 80 million, the latter based on 'tweaking Erwin's formula' (Stork, 1988, and table in Erwin, 2004: 261). Another approach was to interpret and extrapolate the ratio of described versus undescribed taxa, mostly based on taxonomic descriptions from the megadiverse group of insects. These studies resulted in somewhat lower, but still high, numbers of between 1.8 and 6.6 million (Hodkinson and Casson, 1991). Meanwhile, there is a general consensus that there is at least a total number of 5 million species on earth, by far exceeding the 1.7 million species for which taxonomic descriptions are available. Hence, there is an approximate ratio of one scientifically described to three undescribed species. Because these estimates were made two decades ago, it might be interesting to have a look at some of the actual species descriptions based on morphospecies from these collections. However, and in spite of tremendous progress in collection data federation through the Global Biodiversity Information Facility[2], species descriptions based on collections made by fogging are difficult to find. Advanced search tools, such as the EDIT (European Distributed Institute of Taxonomy) Specimen and Observation Explorer for Taxonomists[3] tool, are based on the TOQE (Thesaurus Optimised Query Expander) system (Güntsch et al., 2009), but still do not provide search options for type material or methods. In particular, collection databases and search tools should be adapted to monitor the status of taxonomic analysis for hitherto undescribed species (the 'types of tomorrow': Riede et al., 2006).

16.5.2 Acoustic surveys

The analysis of insect sounds started with simple, descriptive musical annotation. It progressed considerably during the mid twentieth century, using tape recorders and the recently introduced spectrographs and oscilloscopes. Oscilloscope tracks for European grasshopper songs were compiled by Ragge and Reynolds (1997). Their book contains graphical representations of song structure, revealing the species-specific temporal features for most of the European species, and is still the most comprehensive and authoritative source. The advance of computer technologies has allowed digital recording and analysis, facilitating temporal and spectral analysis.

---

[2] http://www.gbif.org   [3] http://search.biocase.org/edit/index

The striking differences in song structure of morphologically similar species helped taxonomists to diagnose and describe 'cryptic species', many of which cannot be determined without a sound recording. In a seminal paper, T. J. Walker (1964) reviewed studies on songs and taxonomy of North American Orthoptera. These studies revealed that many of the hitherto morphologically defined species are complexes of cryptic species, and estimates that 'approximately one-fourth of the species of gryllids and tettigoniids of the eastern USA had never been recognised or had been wrongly synonymised' (Walker, T. J., 1964: 346). The recent discovery and description of 'virtuoso katydids' (at least five species of katydids belonging to the *uhleri* group of the genus *Amblycorypha*: Walker, T. J., 2004) suggest that his prediction is probably true, and that new species are described even from well-studied regions (in this case, Gainesville, Florida, USA). The bioacoustic studies of Nischk and Riede (2001) in the Ecuadorian rainforest led to the description of 11 new species (Desutter-Grandcolas and Nischk, 2000; Nischk and Otte, 2000), and an even higher number of additional 'types of tomorrow' (specimens waiting to be described, see Riede et al., 2006).

Even in Europe, acoustic analysis of cicada species has led to the discovery of new and important information about the biogeography of the *Cicadetta* species (Sueur and Puissant, 2007)

16.5.3 From inventories to monitoring

It is evident that entomological surveys in tropical habitats are still in the phase of species discovery, i.e. dealing with inventories. Monitoring requires targeted surveys at selected sites and in regular intervals. For insects, monitoring is often limited to few well-studied groups such as the Lepidoptera (Thomas, 2005), or selected species, such as the migratory monarch butterfly (Walker, T. J., 1978).

For temperate forest habitat – mixed hardwood and hemlock forests in Virginia, USA – Rohr et al. (2007) identified the beating-sheet method as most efficient for sampling Coleoptera and Hymenoptera. However, the aim of this study was to find surrogate insect groups for monitoring biodiversity. To calibrate the usefulness of their surrogate, the authors applied 11 different collection methods, covering soil, understorey and canopy, and sampling 8636 specimens from 167 families. It is evident that these programmes are cost-intensive, so that budget constraints determine and limit the methodology, even in temperate habitats.

16.6 Discussion: progress and challenges

There are an increasing number of datasets from comprehensive sampling of tropical insect faunas, including rainforest canopies. However, we are still far from a standardised, well-designed sampling scheme which would allow the highly needed step from guesstimates to estimates. Most species are still represented by singletons, waiting to be described by a dwindling number of specialists. The examples presented here illustrate that the 'taxonomic impediment' (i.e. lack of sufficient taxonomic resources and expertise) has not been overcome, especially for species-rich, tropical regions (Miller and Rogo, 2002). While logistical problems of sampling in the tropics are decreasing, new problems emerge, from difficulties in obtaining permits (e.g. Prathapan et al., 2008) to the mere rapid disappearance of entire forest areas due to logging, burning or flooding by dams.

To date, the selection of sites for major inventory or collection endeavours has been mostly opportunistic, even within sites. For fogging, the selection of trees is extremely important, but has usually been made according to criteria depending on the focus of the investigation. Most sites have been within biodiversity 'hotspots' (e.g. Borneo, Amazonia), but there are many tropical hotspot regions without any major fogging site (e.g. Madagascar). For the time being, one must conclude that 'opportunistic' site selection and focussed participation of specialists has probably been more decisive for the advancement of our knowledge of individual insect biota and also to the discovery of insect species than any innovative or spectacular methodology.

Digital data capture during such expeditions is of great help for timely publication of expedition results, at least in preliminary format. Digital photography in entomology, however, is still focussing mainly on museum and particularly type specimens (Fig 16.4, Ingrisch et al., 2003; Häuser et al., 2005; Riedel, 2005), but there are initial promising intents to post and identify insect pictures from the field, using Web 2.0 tools.

Acoustic recording of insect sounds seems a potentially efficient tool for species discovery and description. However, bioacoustic identification is time-consuming and requires expert knowledge. The potential for regular monitoring of insect population densities and phenology has not yet been exploited. However, digital data capture of insect sounds lowers the cost of registration and publication of songs. The DORSA[4] (Digital Orthoptera Specimen Access) sound repository provides online access to a collection of approximately 5000 digitised Orthoptera songs with reference to voucher specimens. A small subset was used to programme and train neural networks for species identification, and feature extraction tools were used to label all DORSA cricket songs (Grylloidea) with their species-specific carrier frequency and pulse distance (Riede et al., 2006). In spite of these promising results, an efficient connection and data flow

---

[4] http://www.dorsa.de

Current status: ***Papilio abderus* Hopffer, 1856**, a synonym of ***Papilio garamas* Geyer, 1829**

Text and fig. of the original description: Type specimen (Lectotype):

Figure 16.4 Types and museum specimens. Original description, illustration and type specimen photograph of the papilionid *Papilio abderus* Hopffer, 1856 (= Papilio garamas Geyer, 1829). Lectotype from Museum für Naturkunde – Leibniz Institute for Research on Evolution and Biodiversity, picture available at http://globis.insects-online.de/ species&tree_h=.Papilionidae.Papilioninae.Papilionini.Papilio.Pterourus.339.8547. A black and white version of this figure will appear in some formats. For the colour version, please refer to the plate section.

between sound repositories, neural network tools and users has not yet been established. This would require distinct tools, such as web-based user interfaces and applications running on portable computers, to allow classification and identification in the field.

Both digital imaging as well as digital sound recordings should ideally be linked to a voucher specimen (Huber, 1998) and, whenever possible, associated to other materials such as tissues or gene sequences, to ensure subsequent taxonomic identification and eventual species description.

16.7 Conclusions and recommendations

Most of the techniques discussed here are definitely necessary for comprehensive insect inventories at any site. But are they sufficient? As we have learnt from history, any new technique reveals hitherto undescribed species, often in high numbers, and the emergence of new techniques in the future certainly cannot be excluded. While these developments cannot be predicted, it might be worthwhile reconsidering site selection and sampling intervals. Only few protocols include these aspects. However, the few studies comparing sites or covering distinct seasons or even years have revealed a huge influence on species accumulation curves. Colwell and Coddington (1994) quantified the comparison of species richness among sites, summarised by a simple complementarity index. It is evident that site coverage is not at all sufficient to assess insect species richness on a global level. Some sampling programmes for the Neotropics are heading in that direction (Erwin, 2004), but other areas remain almost completely uncovered for insects, even in highly endangered rainforest biota with high endemism (e.g. the Congo Basin, Madagascar).

The taxonomic impediment (i.e. the waning number of entomologists observed by, e.g. Holden (1989)) remains among the major bottlenecks for the generation of more comprehensive insect inventories (Miller and Rogo, 2002). DNA barcoding will certainly facilitate progress and reliability, particularly by rapid identification of cryptic species and larval stages (see Janzen et al., 2005, for an enlightening case study on Neotropical caterpillars). However, even DNA barcoding alone will neither solve the taxonomic impediment nor the basic flaws in sampling programmes outlined above.

As a possible response, the European Union-supported EDIT launched an ATBI+M[5] (All Taxa Biodiversity and Inventorying + Monitoring) initiative for selected European, and subsequent non-European pilot sites. This project involves taxonomists from the start. Workflow models and database standards are being developed and new field-recording tools tested, with the overall goal to minimise efforts for primary data capture and subsequent data management (Häuser et al., 2009). Models and standards include all steps from field records to deposition of specimens in collections, data capture and integration of records within federated databases. Individual records should be based on voucher specimens and determined by taxonomists, using standard classifications wherever possible (e.g. Fauna Europaea for European sites[6]). All localities have to be geo-referenced, preferably by global positioning system (GPS), using decimal degrees and WGS84 as a standard (see Chapman and Wieczorek, 2006). Specimens will be labelled and referenced using a system of unique identifiers that allows efficient linking with gene-sequence and/or multimedia data. Validated datasets will be connected to the Global

---

[5] http://www.atbi.eu/wp7/   [6] http://www.faunaeur.org

Biodiversity Information Facility, from where they can be accessed through the new, user-friendly search and mapping portal. The data model covers observations documented by digital images, sound recordings, literature and other sources, and is intended to provide baseline data both for taxonomic research purposes as well as conservation assessment and management needs.

Acknowledgements

We gratefully acknowledge financial support within EDIT by the European Commission (FP 6, contract no. 018340). For help with valuable information and literature, many thanks to Daniel Bartsch, Joachim Holstein, Axel Steiner, Hans Peter Tschorsnig and Karin Wolf-Schwenninger (all SMNS, Stuttgart); for permission to reproduce photographs, thanks to Joséluis Nieves-Aldrey (MNCN, Madrid) and Wolfram Freund (ZFMK, Bonn). Chris Lyal (NHM, London) and an anonymous reviewer provided much appreciated advice and recommendations.

References

Adis, J., Basset, Y., Floren, A., Hammond, P. M. and Linsenmair, K. E. (1998). Canopy fogging of an overstorey tree – recommendations for standardization. *Ecotropica*, **4**: 93–97.

Agosti, D. and Alonso, E. (2000). The ALL protocol: a standard protocol for the collection of ground-dwelling ants. In *Ants: standard methods for measuring and monitoring biodiversity*, D. Agosti, J. Majer, E. Alonso and T. R. Schultz (eds). Washington D.C.: Smithsonian Institution Press, pp. 204–206.

Amédégnato, C. (1997). Diversity of an amazonian canopy grasshopper community in relation to resource partitioning and phylogeny. In *Canopy arthropods*, N. E. Stork, J. Adis and R. K. Didham (eds). London: Chapman and Hall, pp. 281–319.

Austin, G. T. and Riley, T. J. (1995). Portable bait traps for the study of butterflies. *Tropical Lepidoptera*, **6**: 5–9.

Barber, H. S. (1931). Traps for cave-inhabiting insects. *Journal of the Elisha Mitchell Scientific Society*, **46**: 259–266.

Basset, Y. (1988). A composite interception trap for sampling arthropods in tree canopies. *Journal of the Australian Entomological Society*, **27**: 213–219.

Basset, Y., Springate, N. D., Aberlenc, H. P. and Delvare, G. (1997). A review of methods for sampling arthropods in tree canopies. In *Canopy arthropods*, N. E. Stork, J. Adis and R. K. Didham (eds). London: Chapman and Hall, pp. 27–52.

Basset, Y., Novotny, V., Miller, S. E. and Kitching, R. L. (2003). Methodological advances and limitations in canopy entomology. In *Arthropods of tropical forests: spatio-temporal dynamics and resource use in the canopy*, Y. Basset, V. Novotny, S. E. Miller and R. L. Kitching (eds). Cambridge: Cambridge University Press, pp. 7–16.

Beck, J. and Linsenmair, K. E. (2006).
Feasibility of light-trapping in
community research on moths:
attraction radius of light, completeness
of samples, nightly flight times and
seasonality of Southeast-Asian
hawkmoths (Lepidoptera: Sphingidae).
*The Journal of Research on the
Lepidoptera*, **39**: 18–36.

Blomberg, O., Itämies, J. and Kuusela, K.
(1978). The influence of weather factors
on insect catches in traps equipped with
different lamps in northern Finland.
Annales Entomologici Fennici, **44**: 56–62.

Borges, P. A. and Brown, V. K. 2003.
Estimating species richness of
arthropods in Azorean pastures: the
adequacy of suction sampling and pitfall
trapping. *Graellsia*, **59**: 7–24.

Bowden, J. (1982). An analysis of factors
affecting catches of insects in light traps.
Bulletin of Entomological Research, **72**:
535–556.

Brandes, T. S. (2005). *Tropical ecology,
assessment, and monitoring (team)
initiative: acoustic monitoring
protocol*. Version 2.1. Available at:
http://www.teamnetwork.org/files/
protocols/amphibian/TEAMAcoustic-
PT-EN-2.1.pdf.

Brown, B. V. (2005). Malaise trap catches
and the crisis in Neotropical dipterology.
American Entomologist, **51**:180–183.

Buhl, P. N. (2001). Ten new species of
platygastrid wasps from central Spain.
Graellsia, **57**: 141–153.

Butler, L., Kondo, V., Barrows, E. M. and
Townsend, E. C. (1999). Effects of
weather conditions and trap types on
sampling for richness and abundance of
forest Macrolepidoptera. *Environmental
Entomology*, **28**: 795–811.

Campbell, J. W. and Hanula, J. L. (2007).
Efficiency of malaise traps and colored
pan traps for collecting flower visiting
insects from three forested ecosystems.

Journal of Insect Conservation,
11: 399–408.

Chapman, A. D. and Wieczorek, J. (eds)
(2006). *Guide to best practices for
georeferencing*. Copenhagen: Global
Biodiversity Information Facility.

Cocroft, R. B. and McNett, G. D. (2006).
Vibratory communication in
treehoppers (Hemiptera:
Membracidae). In *Insect sound and
communication*, S. Drosopoulos and
M. F. Claridge (eds). Boca Raton, FL:
CRC Press, pp. 305–317.

Colwell, R. K. and Coddington, J. A. (1994).
Estimating terrestrial biodiversity
through extrapolation. *Philosophical
Transactions of the Royal Society of
London B*, **345**: 101–118.

Darling, D. C. and Packer, L. (1988).
Effectiveness of Malaise traps in
collecting Hymenoptera: the influence
of trap design, mesh size, and location.
The Canadian Entomologist,
120: 787–790.

Davidson, D. W., Cook, S. C., Snelling, R. R.
and Chua, T. H. (2003). Explaining the
abundance of ants in lowland tropical
rainforest canopies. *Science*,
300: 969–972.

Descamps, M. (1976). La faune dendrophile
néotropicale. I. Revue des
Proctolabinae. *Acrida*, **5**: 63–167.

Desutter-Grandcolas, L. and Nischk, O.
(2000). Chant et appareil stridulatoire de
deux Trigonidiinae originaires
d'Equateur (Orthoptera: Grylloidea:
Trigonidiidae). *Annales de la Société
entomologique de France (N.S.)*,
36: 95–105.

Drosopoulos, S. and Claridge, M. F. (eds)
(2006). *Insect sound and
communication*. Boca Raton, FL: CRC
Press.

Ducarme, X., André, H. M., Wauthy, G. and
Lebrun, P. (2005). Comparison of
endogeic and cave communities:

microarthropod density and mite species richness. *European Journal of Soil Biology*, **40**: 129–138.

Duckworth, W. D. and Eichlin, T. D. (1977). Two new species of clearwing moths (Sesiidae) from eastern North America clarified by sex pheromones. *Journal of the Lepidopterists' Society*, **31**: 191–196.

Erwin, T. L. (1983). Beetles and other insects of tropical forest canopies at Manaus, Brazil, sampled by insecticidal fogging. In *Tropical rain forest: ecology and management*, S. L. Sutton, T. C. Whitmore and A. C. Chadwick (eds). Oxford: Blackwell, pp. 59–76.

Erwin, T. L. (2004). The biodiversity question: how many species of terrestrial arthropods are there? In *Forest canopies*, Second Edition, M. D. Lowman and H. Rinker (eds). Amsterdam: Elsevier Academic Press, pp. 259–269.

Fittkau, E. J. and Klinge, H. (1973). On biomass and trophic structure of the central Amazonian rain forest ecosystem. *Biotropica*, **5**: 2–14.

Floren, A. and Schmidl, J. (2003). Die baumkronenbenebelung – eine methode zur erfassung arborikoler lebensgemeinschaften. *Natur und Landschaft*, **35**: 69–73.

Floren, A. and Schmidl, J. (eds) (2008). *Canopy arthropod research in Europe – basic and applied studies from the high frontier*. Nuremberg: Bioform Entomology.

Floren, A., Riede, K. and Ingrisch, S. (2001). Diversity of Orthoptera from Bornean lowland rain forest trees. *Ecotropica*, **7**: 33–42.

Fry, R. and Waring, P. (2001). *A Guide to moth traps and their use*. Orpington, UK: The Amateur Entomologists' Society.

Gibb, T. and Oseto, C. (2005). *Arthropod collection and identification: laboratory and field techniques*. Boston: Academic Press.

Gogala, M. and Riede, K. (1995). Time sharing of song activity by cicadas in Temengor Forest Reserve, Hulu Perak, and in Sabah, Malaysia. *Malayan Nature Journal*, **48**: 297–305.

Greenfield, M. D. (1983). Reproductive isolation in clearwing moths (Lepidoptera: Sesiidae): a tropical-temperate comparison. *Ecology*, **64**: 362–375.

Güntsch, A., Hoffmann, N., Kelbert, P. and Berendsohn, W. (2009). Effectively searching specimen and observation data with TOQE, the thesaurus optimized query expander. *Biodiversity Informatics*, **6**: 53–58.

Häuser, C. L., Steiner, A. and Holstein, J. (2005). Digital imaging of butterflies and other Lepidoptera: more or less 'flat' objects? In *Digital imaging of biological type specimens. A manual of best practice*, C. L. Häuser, A. Steiner, J. Holstein and M. J. Scoble (eds). Stuttgart: Staatliches Museum für Naturkunde, pp. 251–264.

Häuser, C. L., Kroupa, A., Monje, J. C. and Eymann, J. (2009). Taxonomic expertise and new tools for biodiversity inventory and monitoring of conservation areas: The EDIT ATBI+M approach. *Mitteilungen der Deutschen Gesellschaft für allgemeine und angewandte Entomologie*, **17**: 343–346.

Hodkinson, I. D. and Casson, D. (1991). A lesser predilection for bugs, Hemiptera (Insecta) diversity in tropical forests. *Biological Journal of the Linnean Society*, **43**: 101–109.

Holden, C. (1989). Entomologists wane as insects wax. *Science*, **246**: 754–756.

Hölldobler, B. and Wilson E. O. (1990). *The ants*. Cambridge, MA: Belknap Press of Harvard University Press.

Hosking, G. P. (1979). Trap comparison in the capture of flying Coleoptera. *New Zealand Entomologist*, **7**: 87–92.

Houseweart, M. W., Jennings, D. T. and Rea, J. C. (1979). Large capacity pitfall trap. *Entomological News*, **90**: 51–54.

Huber, J. T. (1998). The importance of voucher specimens, with practical guidelines for preserving specimens of the major invertebrate phyla for identification. *Journal of Natural History*, **32**: 367–385.

Hughes, J. B., Daily, G. C. and Ehrlich, P. R. (1999). Use of fruit bait traps for monitoring of butterflies (Lepidoptera: Nymphalidae). *Revista de Biología tropical*, **46**: 697–704.

Ingrisch, S., Riede, K., Lampe, K. H. and Dietrich, C. (2003). DORSA – a 'virtual museum' of German Orthoptera collections. *Memorie della Societa Entomologica Italiana*, **82**: 347–354.

Jansson, A. (1973). Stridulation and its significance in the genus Cenocorixa (Hemiptera, Corixidae). *Behaviour*, **46**: 1–36.

Janzen, D. H., Hajibabaei, M., Burns, J. M., Hallwachs, W., Remigio, E. and Hebert, P. D. N. (2005). Wedding biodiversity inventory of a large and complex Lepidoptera fauna with DNA barcoding. *Philosophical Transactions of the Royal Society of London B*, **360**: 1835–1845.

Jones, D. T. and Eggleton, P. (2000). Sampling termite assemblages in tropical forests: testing a rapid biodiversity assessment protocol. *Journal of Applied Ecology*, **37**: 191–203.

Krell, F. T. (2004). Parataxonomy vs. taxonomy in biodiversity studies – pitfalls and applicability of 'morphospecies' sorting. *Biodiversity and Conservation*, **13**: 795–812.

Krell, F. T., Ching, A. Y. C., DeBoise, E., Eggleton, P., Giusti, A., Inward, K. and Krell-Westerwalbesloh, S. (2005). Quantitative extraction of macro-invertebrates from temperate and tropical leaf litter and soil: efficiency and time-dependent taxonomic biases of the Winkler extraction. *Pedobiologica*, **49**: 175–186.

Lampe, K. H., Rohwedder, D. and Schmidt, C. (2007). African Coleoptera type specimens collected by Thomas Wagner in the collection of the ZFMK. *Bonner zoologische Beiträge*, **55**: 163–178.

Leinonen, R., Söderman, G., Itämis, J., Rytkönen, S. and Rutanen, I. (1998). Intercalibration of different light-traps and bulbs used in moth monitoring in northern Europe. *Entomologica Fennica*, **9**: 37–51.

Lödl, M. (1984). *Kritische Darstellung des Lichtfanges, seiner Methoden und seine Bedeutung für die ökologisch-faunistische Entomologie*, 2 volumes. Dissertation, Formal-Naturwissenschaftliche Fakultät, Universität Wien.

Lödl, M. (1987). Die Bedeutung des Lichtfanges in der zoologischen Forschung. *Beiträge zur Entomologie*, **37**: 29–33.

Malaise, R. (1937). A new insect trap. *Entomologisk Tidskrift*, **58**: 148–160.

Martin, J. E. H. (1977). *The insects and arachnids of Canada. Part 1. Collecting, preparing, and preserving insects, mites, and spiders*. Ottawa: Canada Communication Group.

Miller, S. E. and Rogo, L. M. (2002). Challenges and opportunities in understanding and utilisation of African insect diversity. *Cimebasia*, **17**: 197–218.

Muirhead-Thomson, R. C. (1991). *Trap responses of flying insects*. London: Academic Press.

New, T. R. (1996). Taxonomic focus and quality control in insect surveys for biodiversity conservation. *Australian Journal of Entomology*, **35**: 97–106.

Nieves-Aldrey, J. L., Fontal-Cazalla, F., Garrido-Torres, A. M. and Rey del Castillo, C. (2003). Inventario de Hymenoptera (Hexapoda) en El Ventorillo: un rico enclave de biodiversidad en la Sierra de Guadarrama (Espana central). *Graellsia*, **59**: 25–43.

Nischk, F. and Otte, D. (2000). Bioacoustics, ecology and systematics of Ecuadorian rainforest crickets (Orthoptera: Gryllidae: Phalangopsinae), with a description of four new genera and ten new species. *Journal of Orthoptera Research*, **9**: 229–254.

Nischk, F. and Riede, K. (2001). Bioacoustics of two cloud forest ecosystems in Ecuador compared to lowland rainforest with special emphasis on singing cricket species. In *Epiphytes and canopy fauna of the Otongan rain forest (Ecuador). Results of the Bonn–Quito epiphyte project, funded by the Volkswagen Foundation*, volume 2, J. Nieder and W. Barthlott (eds). Books on Demand: GmBH, pp. 217–242.

Nowinsky, L. (ed) (2003). *The handbook of light trapping*. Szombathely, Hungary: Savaria University Press.

Obrist, M. K., Pavan, G., Sueur, J., Riede, K., Llusia, D., Marquez, R. (2010). Bioacoustic approaches in biodiversity inventories. In *Manual on field recording techniques and protocols for all taxa biodiversity inventories*, J. Eymann, J. Degreef, C. L. Häuser, J. C. Monje, Y. Samyn and D. Vandan Spiegel (eds). ABC Taxa, **8**(1): 68–99.

Paarmann, W. and Stork, N. E. (1987). Canopy fogging, a method of collecting living insects for investigations of life history strategies. *Journal of Natural History*, **21**: 536–566.

Peña Martinez, R. and Bujanos, R. (1990). *Monitoring aphids in Mexico. Aphid-plant interactions*. Columbus, OH: Ohio State University.

Prathapan, K. D., Rajan, P. D., Narendran, T. C., Viraktamath, C. A., Aravind, N. A. and Poorani, J. (2008). Death sentence on taxonomy in India. *Current Science*, **94**: 170–171.

Ragge, D. R. and Reynolds, W. J. (1997). *The songs of the grasshoppers and crickets of Western Europe*. London: Harley.

Riede, K. (1997). Bioacoustic monitoring of insect communities in a Bornean rainforest canopy. In *Canopy arthropods*, N. E. Stork, J. Adis and R. K. Didham (eds). London: Chapman and Hall, pp. 442–452.

Riede, K. (1998). Acoustic monitoring of Orthoptera and its potential for conservation. *Journal of Insect Conservation*, **2**: 217–223.

Riede, K., Nischk, F., Thiel, C. and Schwenker, F. (2006). Automated annotation of Orthoptera songs: first results from analysing the DORSA sound repository. *Journal of Orthoptera Research*, **15**: 105–113.

Riedel, A. (2005). Digital imaging of beetles and other three-dimensional insects. In *Digital imaging of biological type specimens. A manual of best practice*, C. L. Häuser, A. Steiner, J. Holstein and M. J. Scoble (eds). Stuttgart: Staatliches Museum für Naturkunde, pp 251–264.

Rinker, H. B. and Lowman, M. D. (2004). Insect herbivory in tropical forests. In *Forest canopies*, Second Edition, M. D. Lowman and H. Rinker (eds). Amsterdam: Elsevier Academic Press, pp. 359–386.

Roberts, R. H. (1972). The effectiveness of several types of Malaise traps for the collection of Tabanidae and Culicidae. *Mosquito News*, **32**: 542–547.

Roberts, R. H. (1973). Arboreal Orthoptera in the rain forest of Costa Rica collected with insecticide: a report on the grasshoppers (Acrididae) including new species. *Proceedings of the Academy of Natural Sciences Philadelphia*, **125**: 46–66.

Rohr, J. R., Mahan, C. G. and Kim, K. C. (2007). Developing a monitoring program for invertebrates: guidelines and a case study. *Conservation Biology*, **21**: 422–433.

Rydon, A. H. B. (1964). Notes on the use of butterfly traps in East Africa. *Journal of the Lepidopterists' Society*, **18**: 51–58.

Schneider, K. and Duelli, P. (1997). Fangeffizienz von Fenster- und Malaisefallen im Vergleich. *Mitteilungen der Deutschen Gesellschaft für allgemeine und angewandte Entomologie*, **11**: 843–846.

Southwood, T. R. E. and Henderson, P. A. (2000). *Ecological methods*, Third Edition. Chichester: Wiley-Blackwell.

Southwood, T. R. E., Henderson, P. A. and Woiwod, I. P. (2003). Heteroptera as caught in a light-trap at Rothamsted, UK. *European Journal of Entomology*, **100**: 557–561.

Steiner, A. and Häuser, C. L. (2011). Recording insects by light-traps. In *Manual on field recording techniques and protocols for all taxa biodiversity inventories and monitoring*, J. Eymann, J. Degreef, C. L. Häuser, J. C. Monje, Y. Samyn and D. Vandan Spiegel (eds). *ABC Taxa*, **8**(2): 400–422.

Steiner, A. and Nikusch, I. (1994). Beobachtungsmethoden bei Nachtfaltern. In *Die Schmetterlinge Baden-Württembergs. Band 3: Nachtfalter I*, G. Ebert (ed). Stuttgart: Eugen Ulmer Verlag, pp. 28–50.

Steyskal, G. C. (1981). A bibliography of the Malaise trap. *Proceedings of the Entomological Society of Washington*, **83**: 225–229.

Stork, N. E. (1988). Insect diversity: facts, fiction and speculation. *Biological Journal of the Linnean Society*, **35**: 321–337.

Stork, N. E. and Hammond, P. M. (1997). Sampling arthropods from tree-crowns by fogging with knockdown insecticides: lessons from studies of oak tree beetle assemblages in Richmond Park (UK). In *Canopy arthropods*, N. E. Stork, J. Adis and R. K. Didham (eds). London: Chapman and Hall, pp. 3–26.

Sueur, J. and Puissant, S. (2007). Similar look but different song: a new *Cicadetta* species in the *Montana* complex (Insecta, Hemiptera, Cicadidae). *Zootaxa*, **1442**: 55–68.

Taylor, R. A. J. (1986). Time series analysis of numbers of Lepidoptera caught at light traps in East Africa, and the effect of moonlight on trap efficiency. *Bulletin of Entomological Research*, **76**: 593–606.

Thomas, J. A. (2005). Monitoring change in the abundance and distribution of insects using butterflies and other indicator groups. *Philosophical Transactions of the Royal Society of London B*, **360**: 339–357.

Townes, A. (1972). A light-weight Malaise trap. *Entomological News*, **83**: 239–247.

Underhill, E. W., Steck, W., Chisholm, M. D., Worden, H. A. and Howe, J. A. G. (1978). A sex attractant for the cottonwood brown borer, *Aegeria tibialis* (Lepidoptera: Sesiidae). *The Canadian Entomologist*, **110**: 495–498.

Voerman, S. A., Minks, A. K., Vanwetswinkel, G. and Tumlinson, J. H. (1978). Attractivity of 3,13-octadien-1-ol acetates to the male clearwing moth *Synanthedon myopaeformis* (Lepidoptera: Sesiidae). *Entomologia Experimentalis et Applicata*, **23**: 301–304.

Wagner, T. (2001). Seasonal changes in the canopy arthropod fauna in *Rinorea beniensis* in Budongo Forest, Uganda. *Plant Ecology*, **153**: 169–178.

Walker, A. K. and Galbreath, R. A. (1979). Collecting insects at lights: a test of four types of lamp. *New Zealand Entomologist*, **7**: 83–85.

Walker, T. J. (1964). Cryptic species among sound-producing ensiferan Orthoptera (Gryllidae and Tettigoniidae). *Quarterly Review of Biology*, **39**: 345–355.

Walker, T. J. (1978). Migration and re-migration of butterflies through north peninsular Florida: quantification with Malaise traps. *Journal of the Lepidopterists' Society*, **32**: 178–190.

Walker, T. J. (2004). The *Uhleri* group of the genus Amblycorypha (Orthoptera: Tettigoniidae): extraordinarily complex songs and new species. *Journal of Orthoptera Research*, **13**: 169–183.

Wallace, A. R. (1869). *The Malay Archipelago: the land of the Orang-utan, and the Bird of Paradise*. London: Macmillan.

Wilkening, A. J., Foltz, J. L., Atkinso, T. H. and Connor, M. D. (1981). An omnidirectional flight trap for ascending and descending insects. *The Canadian Entomologist*, **113**: 453–455.

Wilson, E. O. (1987a). The little things that run the world: the importance and conservation of invertebrates. *Conservation Biology*, **1**: 344–346.

Wilson, E. O. (1987b). The earliest known ants. *Paleobiology*, **13**: 44–53.

Wirooks, L. (2005). *Die ökologische Aussagekraft des Lichtfangs – Eine Studie zur Habitatbindung und kleinräumigen Verteilung von Nachtfaltern und ihren Raupen*. Havixbeck-Hohenlohe: Wolf and Kreuels.

Woodcock, B. A. (2005). Pitfall trapping in ecological studies. In *Insect sampling in forest ecosystems*, S. Leather (ed). Oxford: Blackwell, pp. 37–57.

Yela, J. L. and Holyoak, M. (1997). Effects of moonlight and meteorological factors on light and bait trap catches of noctuid moths (Lepidoptera: Noctuidae). *Environmental Entomology*, **26**: 1283–1290.

17

From seabed to World Wide Web: an overview of marine zoological sampling, data processing and potential production of digital marine Faunas

A. L. ALLCOCK

17.1 Introduction

Marine environments cover approximately 70% of the earth's surface and are extremely diverse. They are three-dimensional, interconnected and undergo constant water movement, hence sampling the same area twice can yield radically different results. Many marine habitats are often extremely inaccessible and may, in extreme cases, be more than 6 km below the sea surface. Only in a few cases are researchers actually able to see the area being sampled. Sampling methods are, therefore, quite different from those used in terrestrial biology.

Our knowledge of marine fauna has undoubtedly been enhanced by the Census of Marine Life[1] (CoML). CoML was a 10-year programme from 2000 to 2010 whose mission was to 'to assess and explain the diversity, distribution, and abundance of life in the world's oceans' (Ausubel, 2001). CoML comprised 17 individual programmes, all but four of which had a fieldwork element. Although perhaps there was a bias toward

[1] http://www.coml.org

Descriptive Taxonomy: The Foundation of Biodiversity Research, eds M. F. Watson, C. H. C. Lyal and C. A. Pendry. Published by Cambridge University Press.
© The Systematics Association 2015

benthic sampling of the oceans, all habitats were explored by at least one of the component programmes. All of these programmes but one had dedicated cruises, reflecting that it is not possible to sample marine fauna without a ship, with the exception of near-shore habitats. It could be argued that one reason that a large part of marine research takes place in nearshore habitats is because of their accessibility. It follows, however, that the least documented habitats and therefore those in greatest need of taxonomic treatment are the more remote, less accessible, offshore habitats. Only a tiny proportion of the seafloor and the open ocean has ever been sampled.

17.2 Selection of sampling locations

17.2.1 Nearshore and littoral habitats

Because of their accessibility, the fauna of littoral habitats is usually well known. However, its composition is affected by three major physical factors: height on the shore, exposure to wave action and substrate type. Much has been written on each of these topics (see, for example, Ballantine, 1961; Lewis, 1964; Kaiser et al., 2005). Other physical factors such as shore topography (e.g. angle of decline) and fresh-water input will also have an effect. For production of a marine Fauna, it is, therefore, essential to sample as many varied habitats as possible. Although ecologists tend towards more quantitative methods such as stratified random sampling (e.g. Thompson, 2002), systematic sampling, which is often used in marine environments when the primary objective is to map distributions, may be more appropriate when the objective is to include rare species (McDonald, 2004). Simple transect searches (e.g. from the top of the shore to the bottom) are highly effective on hard substrates, especially when individuals are sought from a particular taxon (e.g. molluscs). The problem with this technique is that small organisms are usually secreted in cryptic habitats and may only be found if entire areas of shore flora and fauna are removed, bagged and subsequently sorted in the laboratory. On soft shores, most of the fauna is infauna so continuous transect searches are inappropriate. Substrate has to be removed, bagged, sieved and sorted to extract the fauna. The factors discussed above should be considered when selecting areas of substrate to remove.

Subtidally, it is much harder for divers to remove and bag epifauna for subsequent laboratory sorting. Hand corers may be used on soft substrates, with the sediment bagged whilst still underwater (e.g. Mudroch and MacKnight, 1994), and coral heads, etc., may be bagged prior to their removal but, generally, line-search techniques are used by divers.

17.2.2 Offshore habitats

In sampling offshore habitats, the requirement for ship time introduces an element of sample planning that is perhaps not seen in other environments. Cruise programmes are generally planned several years in advance. The planning stages involved will depend greatly on the ship and will be affected by the ship's size, the nation to which she belongs and the funding mechanism for that ship. Some ships are dedicated to working for a single institute. Institutes with dedicated ships tend to be fisheries institutes or large well-funded institutes, although they may be smaller institutes with a small vessel capable of sampling local coastal environments. But many ships are run as national resources and sea-time is allocated through competitive research proposals.

On small ships, the scientific crew may be restricted to those who wrote the original research proposal. In this case, all researchers are likely to have had significant input into the selection of sampling sites. With larger ships, especially those which traditionally invite foreign nationals to participate in cruises, a small steering group has usually proposed the general scientific objectives of the cruise, and additional researchers subsequently submit proposals to join the cruise. Although the precise cruise track and sampling locations may not have been finalised at this point, it is inconceivable that every cruise participant will have a major input to these decisions. However, since participants submit research proposals because the general objectives of the cruise are consistent with their research, input to cruise planning by every individual is rarely necessary. Furthermore, this mechanism is an excellent way to provided added value to cruise programmes, and for individual researchers from smaller institutes to gain access to the sampling opportunities provided by bigger programmes.

17.3 How technologies have changed working practices

The wide range of habitats encountered in the marine environment necessitates a wide range of sampling equipment. Many of these are extremely simple and have not altered in decades. For example, the primary 'equipment' of littoral sampling on hard substrates tends to be the quadrat, whilst that of soft sediments tends to be the corer. In offshore habitats, although traditional equipment such as pelagic and bottom trawls, Agassiz trawls and rectangular midwater trawls (RMTs) are still widely used, innovative sampling equipment is constantly being developed and this process is undoubtedly aided by technological advances. An overview of some of the most common sampling techniques/equipment, the habitats to which they are applied and the type of fauna they collect, is provided in Table 17.1. The range of marine sampling equipment available is extremely extensive, since big laboratories tend to have technical teams that build their own equipment, and even small laboratories will modify nets and grabs to meet their own particular needs. The list given, therefore, covers general types of equipment and in no way attempts

Table 17.1 Sampling equipment commonly used in the marine environment

Equipment	Brief description	Appropriate habitat	Target fauna
Quadrat	Wooden or metal square of known size marking a set area of benthos	Used intertidally and subtidally by divers	Sessile benthic fauna
Hand corer	Plastic or metal tube driven into the sediment to remove known volume	Used intertidally and subtidally by divers on soft sediment	Benthic infauna
Sediment vacuum	Plastic tube with suction point used to vacuum up soft sediments from the seafloor	Used subtidally by divers	Benthic infauna
Pushnet	Small nets that are pushed along the shallows usually by hand	Sensitive shallow water habitats such as seagrass beds and fish nursery grounds	Shallow-water nekton
Plankton net	Fine-mesh nets usually towed from a vessel	Photic zone	Small zooplankton
Bongo net	Fine-mesh nets usually towed from a vessel	Photic zone	Small zooplankton
Rectangular midwater trawl	Medium-sized trawls (usually 8–25 m^2) of varying mesh size, often with opening/ closing mechanism to allow fishing at set depths	Pelagic waters	Zooplankton
Neuston net	Tapering net attached to a rectangular metal frame	Air/water interface	Nekton
Benthopelagic trawl	Large trawl designed to fish close to the bottom but with a high-floating headline	Demersal	Demersal nekton
Bottom trawl	Large weighted trawl designed to drag along the seafloor	Benthic shelf and slope	Benthic macrofauna
Epibenthic sled	Metal sled that drags along the bottom with net (or nets) set above the seafloor	Demersal	Demersal macrofauna, particularly amphipods
Agassiz trawl	Net attached to small rectangular metal frame which drags along the seafloor	Benthic shelf, slope and deep sea	Benthic macrofauna

Table 17.1 (*cont.*)

Equipment	Brief description	Appropriate habitat	Target fauna
Box corer	Large metal corers usually with a rectangular base that cut into soft sediment triggering a closing mechanism	Benthic soft sediments on shelf, slope and in deep sea	Benthic macro- and microfauna
Multicorer	An array of plastic tubes that core into the sediment. A closing mechanism operates to contain the sediment while corer is hauled to the surface	Benthic soft sediments on shelf, slope and in deep sea	Benthic micro- and meiofauna
Trap	Mesh boxes of varying mesh sizes that are easy to enter and hard to leave. May or may not be baited. Can be set in deep areas and released using acoustic devices	Almost any	Particularly fish and amphipods
ROV	Remotely operated vehicles usually carrying camera systems. Connect to vessel by cable. May carry other equipment such as CTD, multibeam	Restricted only by cable length	Photography of macrofauna plus collecting of macro/ microfauna/ meiofauna by robotic arm or slurp sampler and deployment of cores depending on set up
AUV	Autonomous underwater vehicle, powered by batteries, often with cameras but other equipment e.g. multibeam, CTD	To about 6000 m depth	Photography of macrofauna
Submersible	Manned underwater vehicle with an array of cameras, robotic arms and collecting boxes	Deep sea, particularly sensitive environments such as vents which can't be sampled with benthic trawls	Photography of macrofauna plus collecting of macro/ microfauna/ meiofauna by robotic arm or slurp sampler

Table 17.1 (*cont.*)

Equipment	Brief description	Appropriate habitat	Target fauna
			and deployment of cores depending on set up
Lander	Any device which is deployed on the seafloor and subsequently released, usually via acoustic devices	To several thousand metres depth	Mainly photographs but can be modified to collect organisms
Unmanned aerial vehicle	Unmanned aerial vehicle	Surface waters	Photography of marine megafauna

to be exhaustive. Technological advances have probably had the greatest impact on sampling of deep, sensitive habitats such as submarine canyons and hydrothermal vents. Trawls are inherently unsuitable for these environments as they would snag on the uneven terrain destroying both the equipment and the habitat. However, the development of remotely operated underwater vehicles (ROVs), which are considerably cheaper than manned submersibles, has had an impact on the potential production of marine Faunas in that it is increasingly possible to obtain *in situ* digital photographs of live organisms (e.g. Fig 17.1), particularly macrofauna, from inaccessible habitats, and then collect those organisms. Autonomous underwater vehicles (AUVs) have also extended the efficiency with which the sea floor can be mapped for macrofauna (e.g. Thresher et al., 2014). AUVs can be deployed and left to operate while the vessel conducts other operations, substantially enhancing the amount of data that can be collected during a research expedition. Recent developments in unmanned aerial vehicles may transform the way marine megafauna are surveyed (e.g. Hodgson et al., 2013), but are likely to focus on well-known fauna and so play less of a transformative role in terms of marine Faunas.

Technological advances have also affected the efficiency of sampling. Advances in acoustic methods e.g. multibeam, swath bathymetry, etc., have enabled researchers to target aggregations of zooplankton and fishes more accurately and to ensure that an area of sea floor is suitable for equipment deployment. This technology can also be deployed on ROVs, AUVs and deep-towed vehicles, providing resolution sufficient to identify coral abundance (e.g. Huvenne et al., 2011).

Technological advances in other fields, such as satellite imagery, also mean that many more associated data are available with samples. Although this may not affect

Figure 17.1 Digital photos taken by ROV Holland I during NUI Galway cruise CE13008 aboard *RV Celtic Explorer*. Clockwise from top left: giant hydroid at approximately 1500 m depth, *Acesta excavata* (~600 m), crinoid (1200 m), black coral (1200 m). Laser dots (where shown) 10 cm apart. All photos copyright Marine Institute. A black and white version of this figure will appear in some formats. For the colour version, please refer to the plate section.

systematists, these data may prove useful to researchers in other fields, e.g. ecology, where data need to be integrated into larger studies (see below).

17.4 The value of specimens

Because of the difficulties in sampling the seafloor outlined above, it is not possible to locate rare fauna, note the position, and return at a later date, as it might be, perhaps, in terrestrial botany. In addition, because many of the organisms are small and motile, it is very difficult to obtain photographs of sufficient quality to identify fauna to species level. Additionally, voucher specimens are essential for the description of new species; hence, photography alone is rarely sufficient, although in some cases it plays a very important role. Some taxa, especially benthic sessile taxa, do not survive the collecting process in good condition. For example, sponges are often destroyed as they are scraped off rocks and subsequent examination of their spicules is not sufficient to provide an accurate identification. In these cases, photography may be as important as collection of the specimen itself. The Sponge Barcode Initiative[2] requests that researchers submitting sequences not only provide photographs of tissue sections and spicule preparations but also an *in situ* photograph of the sponge. Other barcoding initiatives (e.g. the Barcode of Life project) also request photographs where possible, but more importantly, request that voucher specimens are deposited.

The submission and databasing of voucher material is an important component of barcoding initiatives as it ties each genetic sequence to its source specimen (Ratnasingham and Hebert, 2007) and ensures that the barcoding system is rooted on known taxon concepts.

17.5 Have working practices changed to increase the generalised scope of the data collecting (e.g. for reuse by others)?

Having access to details of all equipment operated at all stations almost certainly increases the scope for data reuse by researchers in other fields. In fact, such data have often been available and are detailed in early cruise reports, which often had a separate volume for station data. However, because of developments in equipment, including those associated with water chemistry (e.g. CTD instruments, etc.), there are often now many more data associated with specimens that might be of interest to other researchers.

The increase in digital imaging has certainly increased the scope for data reuse by others and has been responsible for driving web-based biodiversity projects such as those within Wikipedia and the Tree of Life. The ability to process large numbers of specimens and hold data pertaining to these specimens electronically is also particularly beneficial to the production of online Faunas. Data can easily be imported to geographical information systems (GISs), many of which now publish dynamically to the web, allowing rapid and easy specimen mapping.

17.6 How are data integrated into data management systems when back at base?

The provision of collection data in electronic formats has increased the ease with which data can be integrated into data management systems. These systems may be personal (e.g. an Access or MySQL database on a researcher's personal computer),

---

[2] http://www.spongebarcoding.org

institutional (e.g. a museum's collection database) or multinational (e.g. the CCAMLR data centre, OBIS).

Multinational data management systems are the most use to the wider community as both personal and institutional systems are rarely widely known about or accessible (although some institutionally held datasets are made available via the World Wide Web). Although standards for the exchange of biodiversity data have been developed by Biodiversity Information Standards[3] (a not-for-profit scientific and educational association formerly known as the Taxonomic Database Working Group), conditions of data submission and data retrieval from multinational systems vary.

CCAMLR[4], the Convention on the Conservation of Antarctic Marine Living Resources, is part of the Antarctic Treaty legislation and came into force in 1982. CCAMLR is responsible for the acquisition, compilation, analysis and dissemination of data on all harvested species within the area governed by the Antarctic Treaty. Because the CCAMLR data centre was set up in response to a major piece of international legislation, data collection is thorough and all Treaty Member States contribute to data submission. The data are, therefore, extensive and accurate, and submission forms are used to ensure completeness and comparability. Although the data are not publicly available, the CCAMLR data centre does respond positively to requests for data from individual scientists and protocols exist for the release of data (CCAMLR, 2006).

OBIS[5], the Ocean Biogeographic Information System, is a Census of Marine Life Project and is an associated member of GBIF, the Global Biodiversity Information Facility[6]. OBIS collects and provides, through the World Wide Web on an open access basis, 'taxonomically and geographically resolved data on marine life and the ocean environment' (Costello et al., 2007). OBIS uses the World Register of Marine Species[7] (WoRMS) as its official taxonomic reference list, ensuring taxonomic consistency throughout its dataset. The WoRMS database is maintained by taxonomic experts and is, therefore, an authoritative nomenclatural database.

First conceived at a conference sponsored by the CoML, in its first 10 years, the achievements of OBIS were remarkable: it amassed nearly 20 million records within 600 separate databases. Currently, it is home to nearly 40 million records. To ensure its continuing success and expansion, OBIS has simplified the submission process, and now provides a simple Microsoft Excel template on which data can be submitted.

Searches on various taxa suggest, however, that data may be slow to reach OBIS. Faunal identification is undoubtedly a time-consuming process, and it is likely that complete faunal lists are not available for some groups many years after cruises. However, the two greatest pressures of modern academia are to maximise grant

---

[3] http://www.tdwg.org   [4] http://www.ccamlr.org   [5] http://www.iobis.org
[6] http://www.gbif.org   [7] http://www.marinespecies.org

income and publication outputs. Submission of partial, or even complete, datasets to digital archives is rarely a priority with funders or employers, although funders are increasingly focusing on the importance of long-term data management. Compared, for example, to GenBank[8], there is limited incentive to submit data. The number of nucleotide sequences on GenBank has grown exponentially, doubling every 10 months (Mizrachi, 2007). This was achieved by an agreement with the major journal publishers that they will not accept manuscripts involving nucleotide sequences unless those sequences have been submitted to GenBank and the accession number cited with the article. If a similar agreement could be reached on faunal records, then the coverage of OBIS would undoubtedly increase, with many records linked directly to the primary scientific literature.

17.7 The future

Marine Faunas are much rarer than terrestrial Floras. This is true of Faunas generally, because of the very large numbers of animal species. Where marine Faunas have been produced, they tend to encompass a restricted geographical area, for example, the Isle of Man (Bruce et al., 1963). Marine Faunas that encompass wider areas, for example, the British Isles and north-west Europe (Hayward and Ryland, 1990) are necessarily incomplete. Marine species are spread across widely divergent taxa, each of which is known in detail only by subject specialists. Putting together a team that can cover all the marine taxa and who have the time to commit to the production of a Fauna is an exceedingly difficult task. Hayward and Ryland (1990) took approximately 25 years from its inception to publication. Pragmatic decisions were taken about coverage: all vertebrates other than fish were excluded; coverage extended mainly to only about 30 m depth, although some faunal groups such as fish and decapods were relatively comprehensively covered; meiofauna were excluded; and nematodes, flatworms and most other parasites were also excluded because a specialist could not be found to participate in the project (P. J. Hayward, pers. comm.).

Polhill (1990) estimated the rates of production for some of the major regional Floras. These ranged from 110 to 770 species completed per year, which illustrates the difficulties of producing paper publications even with a team of dedicated specialists. In the modern era, with pressure on rapid output, even monographs (worldwide coverage of a specific faunal group) are rare, and descriptive works tend to focus on a single faunal group with local, national or, more rarely, regional (e.g. Mediterranean) coverage. The available literature is, therefore, generally fragmented (Bisby and Coddington, 1995).

---

[8] http://www.ncbi.nlm.nih.gov/genbank

The World Wide Web is the natural place to concatenate fragmented information into a comprehensive Fauna. Several projects have been pursuing this idea for a number of years. For example, the Tree of Life[9] (ToL; e.g. Maddison et al., 2007) was developed in the mid 1990s and was one of the earliest projects to gain support from a wide range of taxon experts.

The fourfold goals of the ToL, as stated on the ToL website, are: (1) to present information about every species and significant group of organisms on Earth, living and extinct, authored by experts in each group; (2) to present a modern scientific view of the evolutionary tree that unites all organisms on Earth; (3) to aid learning about and appreciation of biological diversity and the evolutionary ToL; (4) to share information with other databases and analytical tools, and to phylogenetically link information from other databases.

The last goal is crucial, in that it provides the mechanism by which ToL shares data with the Encyclopedia of Life[10] (EoL), envisaged for several years (Wilson, 2003), announced in May 2007 and greatly developed since then. EoL has very similar ambitions to ToL, but EoL has major financial backing, and draws information from hundreds of different sources. These sources include small regional and taxon-specific databases as well as global facilities, such as OBIS.

The ambition of EoL is essentially to draw together all of the world's knowledge on all the taxa in all of the kingdoms on earth. If its ambitions are realised, it will become the ultimate Flora and Fauna of life on earth.

References

Ausubel, J. H. (2001). The Census of Marine Life: progress and prospects. *Fisheries*, **26**(7): 33–36.

Ballantine, W. J. (1961). A biologically-defined exposure scale for the comparative description of rocky shores. *Field Studies*, **1**(3): 1–19.

Bisby, F. A. and Coddington, J. (1995). Biodiversity from a taxonomic and evolutionary perspective. In *Global biodiversity assessment*, V. H. Heywood (ed). Cambridge: Cambridge University Press, pp. 27–57.

Bruce, J. R., Coleman, J. S. and Jones, N. S. (eds). (1963). *Marine fauna of the Isle of Man*, Second Edition.

Liverpool: Liverpool University Press.

CCAMLR (2006). *Basic documents*. Available at: www.ccamlr.org/pu/E/e_pubs/bd/all.pdf.

Costello, M. J., Stocks, K., Zhang, Y., Grassle, J. F. and Fautin, D. G. (2007). *About the Ocean Biogeographic Information System*. Available at: www.iobis.org.

Hayward, P. J. and Ryland, J. S. (1990). *The marine Fauna of the British Isles and Western Europe*. Oxford: Oxford University Press.

Hodgson, A., Kelly, N. and Peel, D. (2013). Unmanned aerial vehicles (UAVs) for

---

[9] http://www.tolweb.org   [10] http://www.eol.org

surveying marine fauna: a dugong case study. *PLoS ONE*, **8**(11): e79556.

Huvenne, V. A. I., Tyler, P. A., Masson, D. G., Fisher, E. H., Hauton, C., Hühnerbach, V., Le Bas, T. P. and Wolff, G. A. (2011) A picture on the wall: innovative mapping reveals cold-water coral refuge in submarine canyon. *PLoS ONE*, **6**(12): e28755.

Kaiser, M. J., Attrill, M. J., Jennings, S., Thomas, D. N., Barnes, D. K. A., Brierley, A. S., Polunin, N. V. C., Raffaelli, D. G. and Williams, P. J. le B. (2005). *Marine ecology. Processes, systems, and impacts*. Oxford: Oxford University Press.

Lewis, J. R. (1964). *The ecology of rocky shores*. London: English University Press.

Maddison, D. R., Schulz, K.-S. and Maddison W. P. (2007). The Tree of Life web project. *Zootaxa*, **1668**: 19–40.

McDonald, L. L. (2004). Sampling rare populations. In *Sampling rare or elusive species*, W. L. Thomson (ed). Washington, D.C.: Island Press, pp. 11–48.

Mizrachi, I. (2007). GenBank: The nucleotide sequence database. In *The databases. The NCBI handbook.*

Bethesda: National Library of Medicine. Available at: www.ncbi.nlm.nih.gov/entrez/query.fcgi?db=Books.

Mudroch, A. and MacKnight, S. D. (1994). *CRC handbook of techniques for aquatic sediments sampling*. Boca Raton, FL: CRC Press.

Polhill, R. M. (1990). Production rates of major regional floras. In *The future of Flora Malesiana*, A. S. George, C. Kalkman and R. Geesink (eds). The Hague: Nijhoff, pp. 11–20.

Ratnasingham, S. and Hebert, P. D. N. (2007). BOLD: the barcode of life data system (www.barcodinglife.org). *Molecular Ecology Notes*, **7**: 355–364.

Thompson, S. K. (2002). *Sampling*. New York: John Wiley and Sons.

Thresher, R., Althaus, F., Adkins, J., Gowlett-Holmes, K., Alderslade, P., Dowdney, J., Cho, W., Gagnon, A., Staples, D., McEnnulty, F. and Williams, A. (2014) Strong depth-related zonation of Megabenthos on a rocky continental margin (700–4000 m) off Southern Tasmania, Australia. *PLoS ONE*, **9**(1): e85872.

Wilson, E. O. (2003). The Encyclopedia of Life. *Trends in Ecology and Evolution*, **18**: 77–80.

18

Advancements in electronic data capture for botanical field research in temperate regions

M. F. Watson, A. G. Miller, M. R. Pullan,
C. A. Pendry and S. G. Knees

18.1 Introduction

A casual observer might quip that little has changed in botanical exploratory field research in the last century. Herbarium specimens are still routinely collected today, pressed and dried, using well-tried and tested techniques (see Bridson and Forman, 1989) that would not be unfamiliar to Charles Darwin and Joseph Hooker. George Engelmann's manuscript instructions for the collection and preservation of botanical specimens, written in the mid nineteenth century, eloquently describe these processes and could almost have been written for students of today (Englemann, 1986 – posthumously published). That's not to say that progress has stood still in the methods used to collect, prepare and preserve specimens. In wet tropical conditions several chemical methods have been used to preserve plant material in the field before later drying, for example using formaldehyde (Schultes, 1947) or more commonly alcohol (the 'Schweinfurth' method, e.g. Hodge, 1947 or Bridson and Forman, 1998: 223), and glycerine can be used to help conifers retain their leaves (Page, 1979). There have also been developments in heat drying of

Descriptive Taxonomy: The Foundation of Biodiversity Research, eds M. F. Watson,
C. H. C. Lyal and C. A. Pendry. Published by Cambridge University Press.

specimens in the field, notably in using novel heat sources such as electric heating coils, arrays of light bulbs (Hildreth et al., 2007), electric hairdryers (Eggli and Leuenberger, 1996), bottled (propane) gas burners (Croat, 1979) or even hot air vents from air-cooled car engines (Tillett, 1977). Sometimes this also involves elaborate drying frames (Tillett, 1977; Croat, 1979) and modern fire-retardant fabrics. Additional plant material may be collected for specialist analysis, such as root tips or flower buds fixed in for karyological studies (Bridson and Forman, 1989), and more recently leaf material for DNA analysis is now routinely collected by rapid dehydration methods using silica gel (Chase and Hills, 1991) or chemical fixation using NaCl/CTAB solution (Štorchová et al., 2000) or Whatman FTA[*] paper (Smith and Burgoyne, 2004; Tsukaya et al., 2005).

Considering logistical arrangements for field research, nineteenth-century explorers would certainly have welcomed the use of plastic bags and modern fabrics for field presses to better preserve the precious material prior to final pressing. They would perhaps appreciate even more the technological advancement in camping equipment and outdoor clothing that make fieldwork today a lot more comfortable than in their day. However, these advances are gradual improvements rather than step changes to the way that botanical material is collected and recorded. More amazing to them would be the ability to readily pinpoint exactly where you are on Earth, vertically and horizontally, the ability to take virtually unlimited photographical images, and the ability to readily record, copy, search and manipulate collection and habitat data whilst in the field.

Publications that document fieldwork techniques are surprisingly few, and in practice people acquire their fieldwork methodologies largely as taught by their seniors. These methodologies are then developed and enhanced by sharing experiences during collaborative field research and experimentation with alternative ideas. During the last decade at Royal Botanic Garden Edinburgh (RBGE) we have seen major changes to the way that we undertake field research in the Himalaya and Arabia, especially in the integration of electronic data recording and data capture. This has been fuelled through the 'cross pollination' of ideas resulting from international collaborative expeditions with American and Chinese scientists during 10 multidisciplinary expeditions on the Biotic Survey of the Gaoligong Shan project (Yunnan, China), joint expeditions to Nepal with Japanese botanists of the Society of Himalayan Botany and participation of RBGE's Arabian specialist Anthony Miller and informatics expert Martin Pullan on expeditions to Nepal as part of a training programme funded by the UK Darwin Initiative. The following pages document the adoption and integration of global positioning system (GPS) technology, digital photography and portable computers into our fieldwork methodologies. We highlight their advantages in enhancing data capture and outputs of field research whilst bearing in mind their limitations in practical field conditions.

18.2 Latitude, longitude and altitude

Herbarium specimens and observational field data that have accurate geo-locations are considerably more useful than those which are poorly geo-referenced (Rhoads and Thompson, 1992; Schaffer et al., 1998). Mapping species occurrence is fundamental to describing and analysing organism distributions, and records that are referenced with latitude or longitude, or to a known grid system (such as UTM or the British Ordnance Survey grid), can be readily incorporated into mapping programmes or other analyses needing geospatial data. Just by including an accurate latitude and longitude immediately enables plant record data to be used by a wider audience of bioscientists, including ecologists, climate modellers and conservation scientists (Margules and Pressey, 2000; Ponder et al., 2001; Williams et al., 2002).

Historically, recording latitude and longitude data involved time-consuming processes of interpretation, estimation and calculation from printed maps. Depending on the quality of maps available, this was easier in some countries than others. The problems associated with this task are well-illustrated by the general lack of latitude and longitude on many older herbarium specimens which, even when they are given, are usually accurate only to the nearest minute. Furthermore, for general collections of herbarium specimens the time needed to calculate a latitude and longitude from maps meant that at best these were undertaken for general collecting areas rather than individual collections, and sometimes just at major landmarks such as the start and end of a day's hike. Since the mid 1990s, the development and continued improvement of GPS technologies have revolutionised the recording of geo-location data so that today it is quick and easy to record the latitude and longitude of every specimen collected, photographical image taken or field observation record made (Letham, 2008).

Over the last 15 years portable global positioning system receivers (GPSr) have been refined from expensive, bulky, power-hungry systems to battery efficient, tiny handheld or camera-mountable units at moderate cost – they are even incorporated within some models of digital cameras. Today it is possible to quickly record and store very accurate location data as a latitude and longitude, or in a local grid system of your choice, almost anywhere on Earth. Improvements in battery life and equipment capability are such that a modern GPSr can be left switched on all day recording the route taken (usually termed 'track') as well as specific locations when specifically instructed ('waypoints'). Accuracy of the calculated location continues to improve following the removal of 'Selective Availability' by the US military in 2000, and advancements in GPSr technology, particularly improved antennae sensitivity and data processing power. Today a regular civilian GPSr with good satellite reception, equipped with a modern high-sensitivity antenna and efficient averaging algorithms, is capable of locating sites to an accuracy of just a few meters anywhere on Earth (Letham, 2008).

The recording of altitude, or elevation above sea level, is the other important spatial measurement that has benefited from advancements in technology. Prior to the availability of aneroid barometers in the late nineteenth century, field botanists had to rely on laborious methods of calculating altitude, such as the measurement of the boiling point of water. The barometric altimeter was a revelation, and facilitated the frequent, easy measurement of altitude. Technological developments in barometric altimeters since then have improved reliability, accuracy and reduced size so that sophisticated units can now fit into a wristwatch. The main drawback of barometric altimeters is their inherent reaction to changes in air pressure. This may have resulted from a change in altitude, but equally from a change in weather pattern causing an increase or decrease in atmospheric pressure. Barometric altimeters thus need regular, often daily, calibration against a known height, or at least a careful monitoring of overnight changes.

GPS technology offers an independent way to measure altitude as calculated from the position angle of satellites in the sky. Early GPSr units were, however, notoriously inaccurate in the altitudes they calculated, and fieldworkers have since been sceptical of relying on altitude readings based solely on GPS. The inaccuracy of the early GPSr readings was mainly due to the technical limitations of how many satellites these first units could simultaneously lock onto and the low sensitivity of the antennae they were using. These have both been radically improved, and a modern GPSr has a high sensitivity antenna and can simultaneously lock onto 12 or more satellites. Even so, the accuracy of the altitude reading is highly dependent on the vertical angle of the satellites available and their distribution across the sky: satellites clustered together directly overhead give strong signals, but poor angles from which to calculate altitude. Given a good view of the sky, a modern GPSr should be able to lock onto signals from six or more satellites well spaced across the sky and so give a very reliable measure of altitude to within just a few meters. We have found that the best GPSr units for use on fieldwork are those that include an integrated barometric altimeter, which by default is used to calculate the displayed altitude, but is automatically calibrated when reliable satellite measurements are available.

A GPSr is now an indispensable fieldwork tool: for scientific recording and for safety in the field. It can record and store accurate location and altitude data quickly and easily, both for specific localities (waypoints) and for routes taken (tracks). The navigation features can be used to navigate back to a known locality (e.g. collection site or base camp) or to follow a predefined route. Some GPSr units are also able to display maps, but generally these are only available for countries in Europe and North America. Accuracy of the location reading is primarily affected by the number and position of satellites visible to the GPSr, and an indication of the accuracy is either given by the number of satellites to which the unit is 'locked on' or more commonly by a distance measure of dissolution of position placing you within a circle of known radius. This is a significant advance on using map-based recording of location data and enables fieldworkers to record a detailed location of every specimen they collect. Indeed, one could argue that the latitude, longitude and altitude is all the location data one needs, but for practical purposes it is still advisable to record a text description of the collection location, if only to later sort out 'boggles' in the data.

Although having accurate collection data for all your samples is clearly best practice, increasing the number of collection localities geo-referenced increases the volume of data that need to be recorded and managed. Localities displayed on early GPSr units were invariable copied into field collection books and then transcribed when back home either directly onto specimen labels or into database systems. This is a time consuming process and prone to human error at each stage the data are transcribed. Today it is easy to connect a GPSr to a computer so that waypoints and route files can be rapidly downloaded (or uploaded), and the data available immediately in electronic format. This saves time in the field and back home when working-up field notes, and avoids transcription errors, but you need to organise how you are going to do this and how to integrate this with your other working practices. This is discussed further below when considering the use of portable computers in the field.

Although there are many advantages to using a GPSr to record locality data, there are some important issues that must be born in mind. Although it is easy to get a location reading using a modern GPSr, it should not be relied upon as a 'black box' solution without some basic understanding of the underlying principles. The first issue is the understanding of the accuracy of the reading that is given. A GPSr uses line-of-sight radio communication with navigation satellites and so it does not work well when this is obstructed by mountains, buildings or even people – cloud cover has no effect. These obstacles will reduce the number of available satellites, increase the time needed to get a reading and probably reduce the accuracy of the resultant position fix. Technology advancements in recent years have improved performance under dense forest cover, and although tree cover is less of a problem than it used to be with high-end GPSr units, it still can be a limiting factor. All GPSrs will give an indication of the accuracy of the reading, and accuracy measurements, such as dilation of position, should ideally be recorded alongside the position fix as without this it is impossible to later differentiate low accuracy readings from high. The second main issue relates to the display settings set by the user. From our experience, the two major mistakes are the incorrect setting of the *display units* and improper setting of the *map datum*. Both of these can have significant effects on the location data the GPSr displays on its screen and so on what data are copied into a field notebook. The latitude/longitude display can be set by the user to present the position in one of three formats: 'Decimal Degrees' (DD.DDDD); 'Degrees, Decimal Minutes' (DD MM.MM); and 'Degrees, Minutes, Seconds' (DD MM SS.S). The most common problem we encounter is when the display is set to 'Degrees, Decimal Minutes' and the reading is misread and transcribed as if it were 'Degrees, Minutes, Seconds'. Most, if not all, GPSr units default to the world standard map datum 'WGS84'; however, the user can opt to change this to one of numerous local map datums (e.g. the 'Ordnance Datum' used for the Ordnance Survey National Grid). As the Earth is not a regular shape, a local datum is used to produce maps better suited to a country's topology and position on Earth, and this datum used for the calculation of the latitude and longitude or local grid for use with those maps. When you change the datum in the display setting this will change the displayed latitude and longitude; for example, changing from WGS84 to UK Ordnance Datum will displace the longitude about 100 m to the west. Thus, when manually transcribing position data it is vital to understand and also record what datum has been used. These kinds of mistakes can often go unnoticed whilst in the field, but if you are using a portable computer equipped with mapping software (GIS systems or even Google Earth[1]) then you can check the reliability of your records close to source. If you are using a computer in the field then using the data download facility offers another way of reducing these errors. A GPSr internally stores location data using the WGS84 datum and in decimal degree format, and so downloading position information from a GPSr to a computer has the benefit of not only eliminating human errors in transcribing, but also ensuring the reliability of recording the datum and units used.

In summary, the advantages of using a GPSr are:

- quick and easy recording of geo-location data: latitude, longitude and altitude;
- recording of accuracy levels;
- persistent electronic data storage (of waypoints and routes);
- data download/upload capabilities linking with a computer; and
- additional uses in navigation and fieldwork safety.

The disadvantages are:

- problematic when in high-sided valleys and sometimes under dense canopy; and
- errors caused by inappropriate setting of display units and map datum.

18.3 Digital photography

Digital photographical equipment has seen significant developments over the last decade, first with integrated 'all-in-one' compact cameras, and now with high-end

---

[1] http://www.earth.google.com

digital single-lens reflex (dSLR) cameras becoming widely available, offering the versatility of interchangeable lenses and increasingly higher image resolutions. The reducing costs and improved capabilities of semi-professional dSLRs now make them excellent fieldwork tools for recording plant characteristics, the habitats in which they grow and documenting the fieldwork event itself. In addition, some compact digital cameras have high-quality optics with good macro capabilities that are ideal for taking close-up images (down to 1 cm distance) of small parts of plants in field conditions. We now routinely use compact cameras with macro lenses (e.g. Canon Cybershot G12) to record details of the plants we collect, especially for dissections of flowers and other important small characters (Fig 18.1; and see Chapter 1, A. G. Miller et al., in this volume). This is undertaken at the time of collection, usually using a matt-black background to improve the clarity of the image and facilitate later image processing. Pieces of black velvet are an ideal background, but black microfleece clothing or matt black notebook covers are also effective. Getting the white balance right makes a big difference to the images (especially if storing images in camera-processed formats, e.g. JPG, rather than RAW files), so camera calibration against a white background is very important. We also add LED ring lights and a small pop-up light tent to our equipment list as this diffuses glare at bright times of the day and reduces problems of movement in the wind.

After an initial investment in equipment a great many images can be taken at almost no extra cost. This enables the routine taking of images to enrich and thoroughly document field research and the collections. As the quality and ease of capture of images increases, so does the myriad of uses to which these images are put, both using electronic media and in print. It is now possible to easily prepare popular well-illustrated publications such as comprehensive photographical field guides, and images taken in the field can readily be used in composite plates providing illustrations for the description of new species (Knees et al., 2007; and see Chapter 1, A. G. Miller et al., in this volume).

The immediacy of digital images is now taken for granted. Whilst standing in the field we can review our work using the camera screen, delete obvious rejects and check that we have captured our subject matter with images of suitable quality. No longer will we return home and later find that problems with the camera or film have left us with an incomplete or missing photographical record. Problems can be spotted and corrected in the field. Digital images are also immediately available for use, duplication and distribution. Simply this could be the copying of unprocessed image data cards and distribution to collaborators or saved as backups, but it is more useful to download onto a computer device and carry out some processing of the images before dissemination. If this is undertaken in the field then it is possible to more thoroughly check the quality using the larger computer screen than is possible on the camera display.

Figure 18.1 A composite plate of *Arisaema intermedia*, DNEP1 327, as taken in the field in Solu Khumbu, Nepal (A. G. Miller). A black and white version of this figure will appear in some formats. For the colour version, please refer to the plate section.

Digital camera technology is developing at a rapid pace with higher resolution and more fully featured cameras at reducing costs. This is not the place to expand on these, but it is appropriate to cover one recent technological advancement – the use of GPSr in digital photography. Part of the image file generated by a digital camera records the details (or 'metadata') about the image, such as date, time, equipment used, camera settings, etc. These data are stored in the Exif[2] component of the image file and read by image processing software. Some compact cameras and professional digital SLR cameras are now equipped with an integrated GPSr and many semi-professional SLR cameras can be linked to a more capable external GPSr. If the GPSr has a location fix at the time a photograph is taken then the latitude, longitude and altitude is written into the Exif. In this way the image is permanently stamped with a geo-location. This technology has been used very successfully on fieldwork in Nepal where a Nikon D300 was linked to a small, dedicated GPSr unit (Dawn Technologies di-GPS[3]). Images taken with cameras that cannot geo-tag images at the time of capture can be geocoded later using stored data recorded on a stand alone GPSr and software which compares the time stamp in the image file and GPSr data to deduce the location of each image. This can only be done if all devices have a synchronised time – so it is important to check time zone settings and time calibrations for all your electronic devices when travelling long distances.

Switching to digital photography comes at a price, and not just the initial investment in camera equipment. Electronic equipment is more sensitive to damage than its mechanical counterparts, especially in high humidity and wet climates, and the more technologically complex the equipment the more there is to go wrong. So its use in more extreme environments could be problematic. There is also the reliance on electrical power – in this case alkaline or rechargeable batteries. Modern digital cameras are surprisingly battery efficient, especially dSLRs, but provision needs to be made for either recharging batteries in the field or taking an adequate supply of spares. Storage and backup of digital images is also a serious issue, especially for large numbers of high-resolution image files (e.g. a 10 megapixel camera saving in both unprocessed and uncompressed RAW and high-quality JPEG uses about 20 Mb per image taken). High capacity and high-speed flash memory cards (such as Compact Flash, Secure Digital, Sony Memory Sticks, etc.) are now moderately inexpensive, but relying on these alone is risky as they are vulnerable to corruption and data loss. Images must be backed-up in the field to guard against loss. If you have a computer with you then downloading to the hard drive is the simplest option, either by directly connecting the camera or by using the memory card and card reader. Image files can then be recopied onto optical media (such as recordable DVDs) or onto an external portable hard drive. Another option is to use a

[2] http://en.wikipedia.org/wiki/Exchangeable_image_file_format
[3] http://www.di-GPS.com

dedicated multimedia storage device that can read your camera memory cards and also copy to external devices. This has the added benefit of a larger LCD screen to review images and the ability for basic sorting of images. To cover all eventualities we routinely use a combination of these: a laptop computer, an Epson P-5000 Multimedia Storage Viewer and several USB external hard drives.

Again, these technologies rely on electricity, and although the multimedia storage device can be powered from a stock of rechargeable batteries, these are specific to the unit and genuine products are expensive. Spare batteries are not really an option for laptop computers on a long expedition, and so we have found that the most efficient way of providing all the electrical power needed for the wide range of equipment used by expedition members is to use a small portable generator. We find that running a small 0.9 kW Honda EU10i generator for 3 hours uses only 1 litre of petrol and is sufficient to provide enough electricity to power our laptops, recharge all the batteries and equipment used by the expedition team and also to provide light in the evening. The Honda EU10i is only 13 kg and about the same size as regular in-flight carry on luggage, so it is readily portable even on a trek-based expedition. Recent fieldwork in Arabia has successfully used portable solar panels to recharge batteries, especially when a base camp is established for long periods during the day.

If you are capturing large numbers of digital images then at some point you will need to have a mechanism to organise and most likely rename them, and also record extra information about them. Similar to 35-mm slide transparencies you can arrange images in folder systems, but unlike slide film you do not have a slide mount that you can write extra information on, so you will need an alternative solution for this. This could involve: renaming the image with a long file name including the extra information; using image handling software to write metadata into the Exif field tags; or storing metadata in an external application (such as a spreadsheet or database) with a link to the image file name and location. Although file renaming and arrangement into folders can be done using a multimedia storage device, this soon becomes impractical, and a capable computer is really the only viable option. Software utilities can help bulk renaming of image files, but this is still a time-consuming process. After experimenting with alternative systems we have opted for managing images and their metadata using a database and integrated into the data recording process whilst in the field (discussed below). Whichever option you choose the closer to the time of collection that you can record these image data the better the quality will be. Leaving image management until you return home will be a daunting task for a large number of images, and problems of missing data and ambiguities will be difficult to rectify.

In summary, the advantages of digital photography for fieldwork are:

- large number of images captured with little additional cost;
- more complete documentation of the collections and collection areas;

- image quality can be checked at the time;
- images can be backed-up;
- images are immediately available for use;
- images are easily distributed.

The disadvantages are:

- high initial setup costs (but reducing);
- equipment sensitive to damage and breakdowns;
- reliance on batteries for electrical supply;
- need to provide for backups and storage of images;
- need to arrange and index large numbers of images;
- problems in associating metadata with images.

18.4 Data recording using portable computers in the field

Pen and paper has long been the mainstay of data recording in the field. Collecting locality, plant description and habitat details have traditionally been written in notebooks at the time of collection and either transcribed into a main collection book or the field notebooks themselves kept as the permanent record. On returning home, field data would have then been transcribed either onto handwritten or typed specimen labels, or more recently reproduced on printed labels generated from a word processor or a computer database. This is a time-consuming process, which invariably leads to a reduction in the quantity and scope of the data recorded. Furthermore, it is inherently prone to error at each stage which the data are transcribed until the step when data are entered in electronic form. With reducing costs, increased reliability and enhanced functionality, portable computers such as laptops, netbooks, tablets and smart phones now offer great potential for use in the field and in moving the point of electronic data capture as close as possible to the time of collection. This reduces the transcribing of data and so improves the accuracy, efficiency and quantity in which data are recorded. As Gosline (2004) reported of fieldwork in western Cameroon, 'there is no doubt that the use of portable computers in the field and supervised data entry have made possible the impressive numbers of specimens collected and processed . . .'. Taking portable computers on fieldwork for data recording then opens up possibilities for their use for other purposes such as processing digital images, downloading of collection event location data stored on a GPSr, and access to digital data on publications and past collections. With the appropriate connectivity (mobile broadband or satellite data links) it is also possible for remote access to the internet, to transfer files or even have live connections to database systems held elsewhere.

At RGBE we have experimented in the use of laptops in the field on many expeditions to remote locations in Nepal and Arabia and found them to be a reliable and efficient means of recording and storing field collection data. At present, we still use field notebooks during the day and assigning unique collection numbers to the specimens and supplementary materials (e.g. DNA samples) at the time of collection. Data are then entered onto our floristic database later in the day when back at camp. On the first of these expeditions we used the laptop computer to mimic our main field collecting book and simply recorded specimen label data into a spreadsheet, which on return was used to populate our main floristic database. This was a major improvement on the handwritten collecting book, but was prone to error largely due to problems with inconsistencies in spellings and cells auto-filling incorrectly. We found that the main step-change in data capture was when we started using our floristic database system in the field as this dramatically increased the accuracy and volume of data that we can record (discussed further below).

Our ultimate goal is to push the time of electronic data capture back to the time that the plant material is captured. This will require the use of handheld computers in the field. The UK Overseas Territories (OTS) team, based at the Royal Botanic Gardens, Kew, is now doing this and routinely uses GPS-enabled PDAs (Portable Data Assistants) in the field in Cameroon to record collection data (M. Cheek, pers. comm.). Data are downloaded from the PDAs onto a laptop and then merged into their main project database in the evening. During the day small solar chargers (PowerTraveller SolarMonkey[4]) are used to power the PDAs.

The use of pen and paper for data recording certainly has the benefit of being low technology, inexpensive and easy to understand, but, as discussed above, using computers has many advantages over pen and paper. People may question the wisdom of relying on computers for data recording in the field, particularly in that electronic data can be lost or become corrupted. But the same could be said of paper-based records, which also can become unreadable through damage or the hard copy lost. It can also be argued that electronic records are actually far safer than pen and paper as they are easy to copy and so readily backed-up on to optical discs (CD-ROM, DVD), external hard drives, flash media or the hard drives of other portable computer devices. Not so for the traditional field collection book, which can only be replicated in hard copy through time-consuming and error-prone transcribing or by photocopying – a luxury rarely possible in remote fieldwork locations. The ability to easily copy data also enables the easy distribution of data to collaborators during fieldwork, making it immediately available for people to use.

---

[4] http://www.powermonkey.com

In summary, the use of portable computers in the field offers many exciting opportunities. The advantages for use during fieldwork are:

- improved efficiency in data recording, especially in later data transfers;
- improved accuracy in data stored;
- improved volume of data stored;
- ease of backup, improved data security;
- ease of data-sharing amongst colleagues (e.g. collection lists); and
- the ability to process and sort digital images in the field.

The disadvantages are:

- potentially high setup costs;
- not easily understood by untrained people;
- some kind of data management system is needed;
- difficult to use in extreme climates (e.g. wet and high humidity);
- security of equipment (more prone to theft and damage); and
- reliance on electricity for running and/or recharging batteries.

18.5 Data management systems: collection data

Data management whilst in the field is here focussed on recording information about the location, the plant collections themselves, the environments in which they grow and the species that occur with them. Although examples are herein drawn from botanical fieldwork, primarily aimed at the collecting of herbarium specimens and observational occurrence records, the main principles should be applicable to other kinds of data.

When recording field data using a pen and paper it is usual to break down the recorded information into categories, partly to ensure that complete information is recorded for each collection, and partly with a mind towards producing the final specimen label (Bridson and Forman, 1989). This categorisation, or atomisation, of data is even more important when managing in electronic format as this enables a computer to understand these data, to query across the dataset and to generate outputs in a variety of formats from the same dataset, e.g. specimen labels and lists of collections. Although word-processing packages can be used to store information in categorised form (e.g. using tables), it is more likely that a field researcher will choose to use either a spreadsheet or database system.

When we first started using laptop computers in the field we opted to use a spreadsheet to store the collection data. Spreadsheets have an immediate appeal, as they are readily available, easy to set up and intuitive to use. We set up our spreadsheet in a similar format to past hard-copy collection books, with columns for the categories of data (collection number, field determination, latitude, longitude, altitude, etc.) and rows for the collections themselves. This proved very easy to use by us and our collaborators, and at the end of the expedition we were able to hand out copies to the participants and generate collection lists for the permit-issuing authorities. The problems came when we returned home and tried to import the data into our institutional database. It soon became apparent that the data were not as 'clean' as we expected, mostly due to misspellings, cut and paste errors and errors caused by inadvertent acceptance of auto-fill and auto-format suggestions that introduced errors. Although a lot of time was saved by entering data in this way, the lack of data-integrity checks at time of input created quite a few problems that needed correcting later. Furthermore, we soon found that simple spreadsheets were limiting when linking with other electronic data sources, such as downloaded GPSr waypoints and digital images. Although using a spreadsheet was a nice, simple way to start electronic data capture, we soon reached their limits of what was practical and needed a structured database system to take things forward.

Using a well-structured relational database has many advantages over a flat-format spreadsheet, the major being that data are stored once and reused by forming links. In practical terms this means that select lists are used for recording common data such as the names of plants, people and places, ensuring that they are accurately recorded. This and other data integrity checks can be built into database systems resulting in a data-entry tool that, although often more difficult to use than a spreadsheet, has extra benefits in maximising the quality of the data being recorded and speeding up data entry through quick lookups on select lists. Using a database system has added advantages in that it can be developed or customised to suit different working practices, draw on other electronic resources such as downloaded GPSr waypoints and include links to digital images. Once entered in the database data can be queried in more sophisticated ways than possible in a simple spreadsheet, and bespoke reports generated (e.g. temporary specimen labels). The main difficulty of using a database system is that finding one that suits your requirements is not straightforward and you will inevitably need access to a database developer or someone who can troubleshoot problems. It will also inevitably be more complicated to use than a simple spreadsheet and so expedition participants will need some training to use it properly.

18.6 Data management systems: digital images

Digital photography is increasing exponentially the number of photographs that we capture in the field and has greatly facilitated their subsequent use in scientific and popular publications – in both print and electronic media. Using digital images has become routine in the complete documentation of plants in the field, not only to record features *in vivo* before specimens are made, but also to document habitats and fieldwork methods and as photographical vouchers for plant occurrence records (see Chapter 15, Knapp, in this volume). It is not uncommon to take literally thousands of digital images in just a few weeks in the field. This presents a major challenge to order, categorise and name the images so that they can be used by others. The management of digital images can be undertaken after returning home, relying on notes taken in the field to pair up images to collections and localities. But, as discussed above, this is prone to error, and it is much better to undertake at least some categorising of images in the field.

We started digital image management in the field on the first expeditions where we took laptop computers. Initially we tried renaming each file to include information on the collection number for photographs of plants actually collected, or location, plant names, etc., for other images. This proved time-consuming, especially as the number of images grew, and this method soon became unworkable, even using software to help with batch renaming. In later expeditions images of plant collections were not renamed, but rather put in folders bearing the collection number. Other images were treated in a similar way, usually within subfolders of those taken on a single day. This proved a useful system and facilitated copying and manual incremental backups on optical media with limited data capacity. Having now moved over to using our floristic database in the field, we are now able to link images to records in the database and use the database system to rename, manage and search our store of digital images. In practice we have found that it is still useful to retain use of the low-technology manual arrangement in a folder system combined with database management as this speeds up the process of linking images with database records and aids incremental backups. This has the added advantage of providing some independence in workflows, allowing the parallel sorting of images whilst the database system is used for other tasks.

18.7 Towards an integrated approach to data recording during fieldwork

Technological developments in handheld GPSr units, digital cameras and portable computers have all had significant impact on botanical fieldwork, especially in temperate regions where environmental conditions are more amenable to electronic equipment. It is now possible to capture field data in electronic format on a huge scale, and the challenge now is to maximise the benefits whilst avoiding being swamped with data, and risking spending too much field time working with computers rather than studying plants. Our solution is to take an integrated approach to data recording, interweaving the capture and management of electronic data as part of our fieldwork processes, not regarding this as an extra task to do after the event. Fieldwork workflow processes need to be streamlined so that they optimise the concurrent capture of digital data and reap the benefits of having data available to aid later processes, such as specimen sorting at the end of an expedition.

Our aim is to move the point of electronic data capture as close as possible to the time of initial collection. This is now routine for geo-location data where a GPSr is used to store the route taken during the day, and the waypoint information for each collection event. Images are now beginning to be geo-tagged at the time they are taken using linked or integrated GPSr units, and this will soon become routine as the equipment becomes cheaper, less 'battery-hungry' and more readily available. Currently other field data are recorded in field notebooks and entered into our floristic database when back at camp. Geo-location and image data are downloaded at the same time and integrated with the other field data. This has proved a very efficient way of working on several expeditions, but the ultimate goal would be to use handheld computer devices during the day and negate the need for field notebooks. This is already being used to good effect by Martin Cheek and colleagues in the UKOTS team at Royal Botanic Gardens, Kew (discussed above), and we are experimenting with portable devices that will fit into our fieldwork methodologies. Current developments in mobile computing relating to increased processor power, improved screen technology and, particularly, longer battery life and weight reduction, look set to significantly enhance the functionality of handheld mobile devices in the near future and offer exciting possibilities for extending data capture at the time of collection. The utility of globally unique identifiers (GUIDs) to unambiguously link data is gaining momentum (Speers and Edwards, 2008; and see Chapter 20, Hyam, in this volume), and this could be very usefully applied to fieldwork. GUIDs in the form of linear or more likely two-dimensional barcodes offer the potential for linking replicate herbarium specimens, ancillary collections and images to database records and also representing generic information – such as expedition or contact details. Soon fieldworkers will be equipped with preprinted barcodes to use on their collections: somewhat reminiscent of the tear-off duplicated numbers on past preprinted field collection books!

Capturing electronic data in the field has had some important spin-off advantages that we had not initially appreciated. The most significant of these is the large volume of observational records that we are now able to document. Common species, especially dominant trees, are often under-collected and so poorly represented in herbaria. Distribution maps produced from herbarium specimens are, thus, incomplete and do not represent the true picture (Fig 18.2A). Occurrence data can be inferred from the list of 'associated species' sometimes listed on specimen labels, but they will be scattered throughout the collections in a herbarium. Unless a herbarium has a complete dataset of digitised label data it would be very laborious

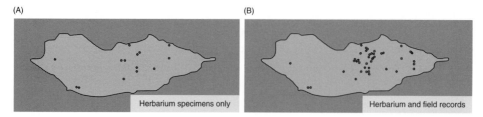

Figure 18.2 The known distribution of Dragon's Blood Tree (*Dracaena cinnabari*) on Soqotra. (A) Distribution using only extant herbarium specimens. (B) Distribution enhanced with field observation records databased during recent field research.

to extract these records as an associated species even from a medium-sized herbarium. When entering data on a collecting locality in the field we also list the common species encountered but not collected. These observational field records are treated within the database as full plant records in their own right, can be given unique field numbers, and incorporated into outputs, such as distribution maps (Fig 18.2B). Digital images can be linked to the field records, providing some vouchering of the record and enabling later verification. Using these methods we can provide enriched habitat data for the specimens we collect, and also document a great deal of additional observation records with full collection details that can be used by other bioscientists.

18.8 Concluding remarks

We have found that taking computers, handheld GPSr units and digital cameras into the field and directly recording field data into a database system has greatly improved the quality and quantity of the data collected. Each of these has drawbacks and implications on fieldwork logistics and research processes, but we believe that the benefits far outweigh these. Technological developments are fast moving, with new equipment presenting exciting opportunities for biological field recording. For example, new generation internet- and GPS-enabled mobile phones can now provide live connections to online mapping systems, such as Google Earth, pinpointing your location on aerial photographs and topographical maps. The challenge is to integrate the best of these developments into our field research practices. No one technology or software solution will suit everyone, and this article has deliberately concentrated on documenting the principles, as we see them, rather than recommending specific solutions. Accurately geo-tagged biodiversity occurrence data in electronic format are needed as a foundation to many areas of taxonomy, ecology, ecosystem function and conservation. These techniques offer exciting opportunities to increase our output of high-quality data to meet these needs and maximise the impact of time spent in the field.

References

Bridson, D. and Forman, L. (eds) (1989). *The herbarium handbook*, Third Edition. Richmond: Royal Botanic Gardens, Kew.

Chase, M. W. and Hills, H. H. (1991). Silica gel: an ideal material for field preservation of leaf samples for DNA studies. *Taxon*, **40**: 215–220.

Croat, T. B. (1979). Use of a portable propane gas oven for field drying plants. *Taxon*, **28**: 573–580.

Eggli, U. and Leuenberger, B. E. (1996). A quick and easy method of drying plant specimens, including succulents, for the herbarium. *Taxon*, **45**: 259–261.

Englemann, G. (1986). Instructions for the collection and preservation of botanical specimens. *Annals of the Missouri Botanical Garden*, **73**: 504–507.

Gosline, G. (2004). The Royal Botanical Garden, Kew Western Cameroon specimen database. In *The plants of Kupe, Mwanenguba and the Bakossi Mountains, Cameroon*, M. Cheek, B. J. Pollard, I. Darbyshire, J.-M. Onana and C. Wild (eds). Richmond: Royal Botanic Gardens, Kew.

Hildreth, J., Hrabeta-Robinson, E., Applequist, W., Betz, J. and Miller, J. (2007). Standard operating procedure for the collection and preparation of voucher plant specimens for use in the nutraceutical industry. *Analytical and Bioanalytical Chemistry*, **389**: 13–17.

Hodge, W. H. (1947). The use of alcohol in plant collecting. *Rhodora*, **49**: 207–210.

Knees, S. G., Laser, S., Miller, A. G. and Patzelt, A. (2007). A new species of *Barleria* (*Acanthaceae*) from Oman. *Edinburgh Journal of Botany*, **64**: 107–112.

Letham, L. (2008). *GPS made easy: using global positioning systems in the outdoors*, Fifth Edition. Seattle, WA: The Mountaineers Books.

Margules, C. R. and Pressey, R. L. (2000). Systematic conservation planning. *Nature*, **405**: 243–253.

Page, C. N. (1979). The herbarium preservation of conifer specimens. *Taxon*, **28**: 375–379.

Ponder, W. F., Carter, G. A., Flemons, P. and Chapman, R. R. (2001). Evaluation of museum collection data for the use in biodiversity assessment. *Conservation Biology*, **15**: 648–657.

Rhoads, A. F and Thompson, L. (1992). Integrating herbarium data into a geographic information system: requirements for spatial analysis. *Taxon*, **41**: 43–49.

Schaffer, H. B., Fisher, R. N. and Davidson, C. (1998). The role of natural history collections in documenting species declines. *Trends in Ecology and Evolution*, **13**: 27–30.

Schultes, R. E. (1947). The use of formaldehyde in plant collecting. *Rhodora*, **49**: 54–60.

Smith, L. M. and Burgoyne, L. A. (2004). Collecting, archiving and processing DNA from wildlife samples using FTA* databasing paper. *BioMed Central Ecology*, **4**: 4. Available at: http://www.biomedcentral.com/1472-6785/4/4.

Speers, L. and Edwards, J. L. (2008). International infrastructure for enabling the new taxonomy: the role of the Global Biodiversity Information Facility (GBIF). In *The new taxonomy*. The Systematics Association Special Volume Series 76, Q. D. Wheeler (ed). London: CRC Press, pp. 87–94.

Štorchová, H., Hrdličková, R., Chrtek, J., Tetera, M., Fitze, D. and Fehrer, J. (2000). An improved method of DNA isolation from plants collected in the field and conserved in saturated NaCl/CTAB Solution. *Taxon*, **49**: 79–84.

Tillett, S. S. (1977). Technical aids for systematic botany: new models of plant-press drier. *Taxon*, **26**: 553–556.

Tsukaya, H., Iokawa, Y., Kondo, M. and Ohba, H. (2005). Large-scale general collection of wild-plant DNA in Mustang, Nepal. *Journal of Plant Research*, **118**: 57–60.

Williams, P. H., Margules, C. R. and Hilbert, D. W. (2002). Data requirements and data. Sources for biodiversity priority area selection. *Journal of Bioscience*, **27**: 327–338.

PART V

New technologies: their current use and future potential

19

Extending Floras and Faunas to include users' views

A. L. Weitzman and C. H. C. Lyal

19.1 Introduction

We are in a time of change between 'traditional' Faunas and Floras and a new way of working. To date, publication has taken the form of ink on paper, and users have had access to a range of information sources of broad compatibility: 'formal' Floras and Faunas, identification handbooks, field guides and other resources. There is perhaps a weak distinction between Faunas and Floras and checklists on one hand and field guides and other handbooks on the other. Generally, field guides tend to be more image-rich, morphology-poor and (non-specialist) user-friendly, whilst Floras and Faunas are often the reverse, and are assumed to be more authoritative – at least by taxonomists (see Chapter 4, Connor, in this volume). In the absence of the Faunas and Floras some technical users will attempt to use field guides, with greater or lesser success; the reverse also happens, though perhaps less frequently.

The time taken in the production of such resources, and particularly of the 'weightier' texts, has perforce limited the number that are produced, their coverage and the degree to which the included information and data are relevant to non-target users, but there has been little alternative to their employment. There is anything but a complete coverage of the biota either geographically or taxonomically anywhere in the world. However, in the past few years the development of biodiversity informatics has provided new prospects for floral and faunal works.

Descriptive Taxonomy: The Foundation of Biodiversity Research, eds M. F. Watson, C. H. C. Lyal and C. A. Pendry. Published by Cambridge University Press. © The Systematics Association 2015

There is increasing availability of both formal text and more disparate items of information and data about taxa through the internet. Taxonomic monographs have been turned into PDF files, websites hold species pages or lists and descriptions of subsets of regional biota, and there is a wealth of information and data about some individual species or assemblages. These resources are of course packaged in a variety of ways, and more or less directed at particular user types. There is clear potential for developing applications and resources to access these resources and 'short-cut' the traditional means of compiling Floras and Faunas, thus meeting the needs of many kinds of users more rapidly. However, whilst building novel systems we need to keep in mind that such changes need directing – what do we need? What should the future of Floras and Faunas be?

19.2 Traditional resources: problems with the present

All the printed resources referred to above, from the 'heavyweight' Floras and Faunas to checklists and field guides, are subject to similar limitations, constraints and issues, which impact on the users' ability to find and extract their required information.

One overarching problem is, as already noted, that a Fauna or Flora can take a considerable amount of time to compile and publish – some approach monographs in their content, thus taking tremendous effort. In the context of a shrinking taxonomic workforce with the appropriate degree of expertise (and interest) and, in some areas, a greater priority on taxonomic products other than Floras and Faunas, there is a major set of bottlenecks on production. Because of these limitations, floral and faunal treatments are not available for all groups and regions.

Paper products, of course, are available in limited print runs, and ultimately will go out of print; key works simply may not be available outside of major libraries for this reason. Even while a work is in print it may be poorly disseminated and, hence, inaccessible to many people who might otherwise use it. Although it may have been found by one of the abstracting services, such services may not be accessible (by cost or library size) or even known to all users. Library catalogues have limited metadata, because they tend to focus on being able to find a particular book or volume, while users of taxonomic information tend to focus on finding content within a book, volume or article. Taxonomists spend part of their educational time learning to navigate the library, frequently bypassing library catalogues altogether.

Where Floras and Faunas exist and can be obtained, the content may not be as accessible as required by users. For a start, the work may not be indexed or, if it is, the index may not be inclusive of all desired content. Given the variety of information and data that may be contained within a work, and the potentially different priorities of the various users, it would be a very difficult task to compile a 'complete' index. Instead, indexes typically include such elements as scientific and common names and their synonyms (and sometimes any known associations of the 'target' species such as hosts or pests); less frequently geography, colour or morphology are already indexed or made accessible. Some users, at least, will require considerable expertise or a long time to locate what they require.

Traditional products are, of course, fixed in time, having been compiled and published only once (or several times with revisions). This inevitably means that they are potentially incomplete. In a world in which plant and animal species are changing their distributions and sometimes morphology rapidly due to climate change, environmental modification or other factors, a Fauna or Flora may well not accommodate, for example, novel invasive species or changes in distribution. A published Flora or Fauna may also be incomplete or inaccurate because of taxonomic changes, including newly described taxa, transfer of species between genera, genera between tribes, etc., or synonymy or replacement of names. Some of these changes may have been made in publications outside the geographical region covered by the Fauna or Flora, and will, therefore, not necessarily be found easily by the user.

Floras and Faunas are also, axiomatically, fixed in space, i.e. the region covered by their contents. Any diagnostic characters or keys within them, therefore, will compare a given taxon only with other taxa found within that area. Unfortunately, because of the limited number of keys available to many higher taxa, keys found in Floras and Faunas are frequently employed to identify organisms outside the region covered by users who have no other resource. However, the applicability of such keys to these extra-regional taxa often cannot be assessed, but may be low.

The content and format of traditional products is, of course, selected by the provider not the user. This may seem a trivial point, until one considers the many possible searches for information that users undertake, and the types of information that may be required. Thus 'niche' information, such as for example 'Red List' status, pest status, size data or ethology may not be included; this may not affect many users (especially those whom the author was targeting) but could be critical for others. The geographical or environmental granularity or classification may differ from that required by a user, and the fixed format does not permit an easy translation to other views. The taxonomic view presented by the author is likely not to include alternatives. In the past this has been unquestioned, but with the growth of information access through the internet the existence of competing classifications and taxonomic opinions has become clear. Moreover, a variety of names may be used for the 'same' entity in different publications, websites and in other resources, even those covering the same or contiguous geographical areas. Thus, the inability to compare different taxonomic views in a traditional publication may obscure the presence of a taxon from a non-specialist user, or may take considerable time to sort out (Brehm et al., 2007). A final and perhaps often unconsidered point is that a traditional paper publication lacks analytical tools, and the data are presented in such a manner that reuse in a different situation can only be accomplished through manual copying, the need for which is either taken for granted or seen as a factor precluding such reuse.

19.3 Responses in the computer age

The limitations of traditional floristic and faunistic publications as outlined above have led to several means of addressing them being developed for access via the internet.

Perhaps the simplest solution, and a response to the simplest need – availability of an original resource – are digital images of pages made available on the World Wide Web. Examples of these include the Electronic Biologia Centrali-Americana[1], which is a very extensive floristic and faunistic treatment of Meso-America captured as JPEG and image-based PDF files and navigated either by a high-level page-contents list or through use of the volume index. The initial problem was not only that the work was long out of print, but that full copies were very rare and very expensive. They were also physically very large, and an early use found for the World Wide Web version was as a download into handheld computers and employment as field guides. While improving accessibility for those who do not have a good library nearby, page images are otherwise not a great improvement over traditional publications. Searching for digitised items or content within those items can be very challenging: metadata for these projects tends to exist at the series or volume level (similar to a library catalogue). It can still be hard to find specific published items, such as an article or find content related to a particular taxon; it is difficult to find something if you don't know it's there.

A more refined solution is text generated by Optical Character Recognition (OCR) software, such as is available through initiatives including Biodiversity Heritage Library[2] (BHL), AnimalBase[3], InternetArchive[4] and Google Books[5]. OCRed text improves searchability to the extent that the OCR is accurate and full text search is available over multiple works. Accuracy of OCR is a major problem for taxonomic literature because much of it is old and includes multiple languages or archaic forms of language. Scientific Latin is a problem as are place names in various

[1] http://www.sil.si.edu/DigitalCollections/bca   [2] http://www.biodiversitylibrary.org
[3] http://www.animalbase.org   [4] http://archive.org   [5] http://books.google.com

countries. Italics and older typefaces are also difficult for OCR to interpret correctly. Thus, searches can be compromised by failure of the software to reproduce the correct spelling. For example, in a 2008 sample of nearly 400 pages text OCRed as part of the BHL project, only 14% of the scientific names recognised by the authors were correctly identified using purpose-built name finding software, using uBio[6] as a dictionary.

Full text searches also introduce problems for accurate searching across the internet, as pointed out by Majumdar (2007):

- 'High recall, low precision. Even if the main relevant pages are retrieved, they are of little use if another 28 758 mildly relevant or irrelevant documents were also retrieved. Too much can easily become as bad as too little.

- Low or no recall. Often it happens that we don't get any answer for our request, or that important and relevant pages are not retrieved. Although low recall is a less frequent problem with current search engines, it does occur.

- Results are highly sensitive to vocabulary. Often our initial keywords do not get the results we want; in these cases the relevant documents use different terminology from the original query. This is unsatisfactory because semantically similar queries should return similar results.

- Results are single web pages. If we need information that is spread over various documents, we must initiate several queries to collect the relevant documents, and then we must manually extract the partial information and put it together.'

Thus, there may be problems in locating relevant documents if unstructured key terms are used. Moreover, the result of searches may be retrieval of required information embedded in the context of unrequired text. The internet now allows far more focused and productive access to and extraction of information and data; the important point to take here is that to enable users to access this power one must be sure what the users want.

19.4 Meeting user needs

Users of Floras and Faunas include taxonomists, conservationists, ecologists, policy advisors, students and non-specialists. Each of these may have different interests in the content of the literature, and wish to use specific search terms and see results in particular ways. Some of the major uses of taxonomic literature and their relevance to different user groups are shown in Table 19.1.

---

[6] http://www.ubio.org

Table 19.1 Main users of Floras and Faunas and the major ways that they use them

Use\User	Taxonomists	Conservationists	Ecologists	Policy advisors	Students	Non-specialists
Restrict geographical or taxonomic range of taxa to examine for identification	++					
Identify specimens (both from within and outside region covered) using descriptions, keys and images	++	+	+		+	+
Locate information (taxonomic, morphological, distributional, associated taxa, ecological, etc.) about known biota	++	+	+		+	(+)
Find out if a species is present in a region	+	+	+	(+)	+	(+)
Review taxonomic acts by author	+					
Create lists of biota within region (e.g. for legal reasons, quarantine, conservation)	+	++	+	++	(+)	(+)
Check scientific name in use	+	+	+	+	+	(+)
Check common name in use	(+)	+	+	+	+	++

The challenge is to develop a new model for Floras and Faunas that meets those needs in the most effective manner, as well as capitalising on the work already done. Requirements of a novel system – the system we need now to create – include:

- accessing single publications accurately;
- accessing multiple data and information sources and types simultaneously (digitised literature; specimen/observation data; names/concept data; images; other datasets using names, etc.);
- dynamic access, that is allowing constant access to new information and data;
- access to information using wide variety of search term types (i.e. not just scientific or vernacular names);
- access to the most up-to-date possible Flora/Fauna of a user-defined area, given the internet resources available;
- the ability to produce local copy with user-defined-focus – e.g. taxonomic and/or geographical;
- the ability to allow the user to select the information set that best matches his or her needs;
- presentation only of data and information of direct relevance, not embedded in other material;
- access to the use of web services to analyse data extracted from multiple sources; and
- allowing annotation and addition to information presented.

One interesting requirement is that the user should be able to, in effect, compile a virtual Flora or Fauna from text and data compiled for other purposes. While the core of future content will be digitised legacy literature as well as new Faunas and Floras published electronically, this content will be accessible with and complemented by other data and information.

Another novelty in the requirements is for the content of digitised literature – of 'legacy' Faunas and Floras – to be searched in such a manner that the data contained can be extracted automatically and displayed in any context. For example, many texts contain specimen data, detailing where and when specimens were collected. If these data can be extracted they can be used in analyses of distributions in the same manner as can specimen data extracted from collections. This capacity for data-mining legacy literature holds the prospect of access to a vast quantity of data that are currently effectively inaccessible.

The requirements indicate the need for some quite complex components. The first of these is that the content be digitised. 'Digitised' in this context means that the information/data have been put into digital format using a means which carries its meaning, or to which meaning can be applied, and thus allows access to the meaning of the content. This might mean a 'perfect' OCR, or a rekeying of content as a starting point, and then, typically, put into a database or other medium that allows for data atomisation and complex searching. This process itself can be challenging (Willis et al., 2010, 2011). The atomisation is important for the possible repurposing of content and the extraction of data. From the database or equivalent, 'meaning' can be assigned using a means such as an XML schema. There are a number of 'standard' schemas that have been developed or are in the process of development for biodiversity and biological content, spearheaded by Taxonomic Databases Working Group (TDWG)[7]. These schemas are intended, at least in part, to allow access not only to the data held in a tailored standard but also to be examined with data held in another. To this end they are being designed to facilitate 'interoperability'. This interoperability between digitised resources, especially between different literature datasets and between literature and other datasets (specimens, names, etc.), is a further implication from the requirements listed above. Thus, any schema used for Faunas and Floras or their components should be interoperable with others designed for relevant other biodiversity or taxonomic resources. This interoperability will enable multiple resources containing different data types to be searched simultaneously, and the outputs of the search to be seen together.

A further implication of the requirements concerns the limitations of current literature. Authors regularly include information that is 'implicit', the simplest perhaps being the use of an initial letter only when a complete genus name that has been used 'recently' is meant. A review of taxonomic literature has revealed almost every component can be implicit, up to and including taxon descriptions, in that references are given to elements of a paper that need to be united in order to see the taxon treatment. In such cases any retrieval of information would be of greater assistance to the user if the implicit content was displayed, especially if it is displayed 'out of context', although ideally this should be done in a manner that allows clarity on what is original text and what is constructed implicit content.

In many cases implicit content as discussed above can be easily seen during the process of marking up text into XML; in others, however, the meaning of the author is not clear, and requires specialist interpretation. Moreover, given that content can be reinterpreted with new knowledge or changes in terminology or political boundaries there is a need to allow annotation or interpretation of published content in such a way that it is visible to a user/search system, attributed to the annotator and if appropriate can be fed back automatically to the data provider or author. This 'interpretation layer' will be of increasing importance as more and more literature is digitised and used by specialists.

---

[7] http://www.tdwg.org

19.5 From paper to XML

There are currently two broad models for extracting information from digitised literature, and the choice of methodology will depend on uses and a cost/benefit analysis. The first model is for limited (or no) parsing of the text into XML and a reliance on general text searching to locate elements of interest. An example of this approach is iSpecies[8]. The other model is of more detailed parsing. At one end of the spectrum is a fairly basic level of parsing as shown by Plazi.org[9], based on the schema 'taxonX', which permits extraction of some data free of context and some content within the original content, and is directed particularly at the retrieval of taxonomic treatments. At the other end of this spectrum is a much more detailed markup and an interface that permits detailed searches on terms in specific context(s) is the approach of INOTAXA[10], based on content marked up in the schema 'taXMLit'. Even this last interface does not use a schema that fully atomises all text, since taxonomic character information is not addressed deeply (although taxonomic characters can be found through the INOTAXA interface); however, this is covered in another schema, SDD[11], although this is not yet well-suited for legacy literature. These and other schemas for taxonomic literature are compared by Penev et al. (2011).

The difference in complexity of schemas means that currently the mark-up of text into taxonX is quicker and easier than markup into taXMLit. Depending on how the data are to be used a simple markup may be more effective. If the requirements as outlined above are to be met, however, the maximum benefit and minimum downstream work on the data extracted are to be found with the latter schema.

19.6 Interfaces to the content

The potential to repurpose digitised content and facilitate search and retrieval of different components according to user requirements means that interfaces to the same information and data can be specifically designed for different user groups and their needs. For example, taxonomists will be enabled to work more quickly by gaining faster access to entire works and particularly to relevant portions of works, especially by contextual searching. Thus, they may require the 'units' of retrieval to be taxon treatments and identification keys, with additional access to a range of information including specimen data, associated species, collector information, etc. They may wish to constrain a search by

---

[8] http://ispecies.org   [9] http://plazi.org   [10] http://www.inotaxa.org
[11] http://www.tdwg.org/standards/116

limiting it to the contents of a particular publication, a country or other region, to taxa described by a given author. As the body of interpretation and commentary on works grows, each subsequent taxonomist working on a group will not have to reverify publications, match specimen data from literature to collections, etc.

Conservationists may have different requirements from taxonomists, or at least requirements that overlap but have additional specific elements. They may be most concerned about accessing data rapidly, to meet external time constraints, and will require access to both the most recent data (names, distributions, etc.), and may be more concerned than taxonomists with determining the full range of taxa within a given region (e.g. a protected area). They may not require such direct access to descriptions, or need to see collector information. Overall, the range of tools and priorities for data-mining may be built specifically for their use, and in consultation. Similar specialised access formats to the same data are possible for other kinds of users, including for classroom curricula, and for non-specialists and policy advisors.

To investigate the potential for access we have built an interface with the primary target of taxonomists. A prototype, available on the INOTAXA website, demonstrates functionality. It allows simple, constrained, image and advanced (Boolean) searches, as well as a browse on three key subjects: taxa, geography and people. For simple and advanced searches the results returned from a search (on any search term, not just taxon names) are categorised as 'Treatments' (i.e. all discussions, descriptions or synonymies, etc., provided under a taxon name heading), 'Keys' (identification keys), 'Other' (i.e. all other mentions of the search term, such as in introductory text, indexes, bibliographies, etc.) and 'All' (i.e. all of the above in a single list). Taxon treatments are returned as full treatments, and it is possible to move from the result to the next treatment in the original source. For an advanced search there is a fifth category, 'Specimen records', which, in a different manner from the other categories, returns specimen records 'mined' from the text and available for download. The results (other than specimen records) are initially displayed in a list, each item of which is linked to an individual search result. The heading given to each result on the list indicates what it is. For example, a search on genus 'Aus' might return 'Treatment of Aus', 'Treatment of Aus bus', 'Key to species of Aus', 'Synonym in treatment of Aus bus', etc. From each full result it is possible to link back to an image of the original page (subject to copyright agreements).

One of several possible restricted simple searches allows the results to be restricted to 'region'. This will return what is in effect the contents of a Fauna or Flora culled from the information accessible within INOTAXA. Treatments will only be found, however, if they include the term (as entered); for geographical, taxonomic and people (and later others) some improvement will be made to this when synonyms are automatically included as part of the search via a separate lookup table (e.g. 'British Honduras' = 'Belize').

In the browse the hierarchy of localities can be accessed, so that a browse to 'Central America' will retrieve taxa found within the region. Again, this provides a virtual Fauna or Flora, with the added benefit that many of the data (names, specimen data, collectors, authors, etc.) can be extracted very rapidly and easily.

19.7 Other issues

As noted above, in order for such a system to work seamlessly, different forms of the same name (people, geographical locations, taxa and publications) must be linked together. In other words, a vocabulary for synonyms must be built for searching the taxonomic and related realms. A start to this exists, especially for botanical works, for taxonomic authors (Brummitt and Powell 1992), collectors (Lanjouw and Stafleu, 1954–1957; Chaudhri et al., 1972; Vegter 1976–1988), taxonomic works (Stafleu, 1967; Stafleu and Cowan, 1976–1988; Stafleu and Mennega, 1992–2000; Dorr and Nicolson, 2008–2009; TL-2 online[12]), and journals (Lawrence et al., 1968, Bridson and Smith, 1991; Bridson, 2004). Partial lists also exist for some of these data in some areas of zoology, but these are yet to be brought together. TDWG's Literature Interest Group[13] is working on compiling these into fully interoperable forms that will be available to any system.

19.8 Summary

The development of a successful novel system of presenting taxonomic information depends on understanding user needs, development of tools to meet those needs, development of standards to allow interoperability between different sources and types of information and the data upon which that information is based, and suitable digitisation of resources. Given the very fluid nature of user needs over time, the greater the flexibility and scalability of any novel system built the more likely it is to be able to meet developing and novel user needs. At a time when taxonomic expertise is decreasing, the more we can build persistent and repurposable tools the better.

---

[12] http://www.sil.si.edu/digitalcollections/tl-2/index.cfm
[13] http://www.tdwg.org/activities/literature

References

Brehm, J. M., Maxted, N., Ford-Lloyd, B. V. and Martins-Loução, M. A. (2007). National inventories of crop wild relatives and wild harvested plants: case-study for Portugal. *Crop resources and crop evolution*. Available at: http://www.springerlink.com/content/a56v59k4q5632324.

Bridson, G. D. R. (2004). *BPH-2: periodicals with botanical content*, 2 volumes. Pittsburgh, PA: Hunt Institute for Botanical Documentation.

Bridson, G. D. R. and Smith, E. R. (1991). *B-P-H/S. Botanico-periodicum-huntianum/supplementum*. Pittsburgh, PA: Hunt Institute for Botanical Documentation.

Brummitt, R. K. and Powell, J. M. (1992). *Authors of plant names*. Richmond: Royal Botanical Gardens, Kew. Available at: http://www.ipni.org/ipni/authorsearchpage.do.

Chaudhri, M. N, Vegter, I. H. and Wal, C. M. de (1972). *Index herbariorum: a guide to the location and contents of the world's public herbaria. Part 2 (3).Collectors I-L.* Utrecht: International Bureau of Plant Taxonomy.

Dorr, L. J. and Nicolson, D. H. A. (2008–2009). *Taxonomic literature. A selective guide to botanical publications and collections, with dates, commentaries and types.* Second Edition. Suppl. 7–8. Utrecht: International Bureau for Plant Taxonomy and Nomenclature.

Lanjouw, J. and Stafleu, F. A. (1954–1957). *Index herbariorum: a guide to the location and contents of the world's public herbaria. Part 2(1–2). Collectors A-H.* Utrecht: International Bureau of Plant Taxonomy and Nomenclature.

Lawrence, G. H. M., et al. (eds) (1968). *B-P-H. Botanico-periodicum-huntianum*. Pittsburgh: Hunt Botanical Library.

Majumdar, P. (2007). *Semantic web: the future of WWW*. Available at: http://hdl.handle.net/1944/584.

Penev. L., Lyal, C., Weitzman, A., Morse, D., King, D., Sautter, G., Georgiev, T., Morris, R., Catapano, T. and Agosti, D. (2011). XML schemas and mark-up practices of taxonomic literature. *ZooKeys*, **150** (Special issue): 89–116.

Stafleu, F. A. (1967). *Taxonomic literature. A selective guide to botanical publications with dates, commentaries and types.* Utrecht: International Bureau for Plant Taxonomy and Nomenclature.

Stafleu, F. A. and Cowan, R. S. (1976–1988). *Taxonomic literature. A selective guide to botanical publications and collections with dates, commentaries and types,* Second Edition. Utrecht: International Bureau for Plant Taxonomy and Nomenclature.

Stafleu, F. A. and Mennega, E. A. (1992–2000). *Taxonomic literature. A selective guide to botanical publications and collections with dates, commentaries and types,* Second Edition, Suppls 1–6. Utrecht: International Bureau for Plant Taxonomy and Nomenclature.

Vegter, I. H. (1976–1988). *Index herbariorum: a guide to the location and contents of the world's public herbaria. Part 2(4)-2(7). Collectors M–Z.* Utrecht: International Bureau for Plant Taxonomy and Nomenclature.

Willis, A., King, D., Morse, D., Dil, A., Lyal, C. and Roberts, D. (2010). From XML to XML: the why and how of making the biodiversity literature accessible to researchers. *Proceedings of the Seventh International Conference on Language Resources and Evaluation (LREC)*. Available at: http://www.lrec-conf.org/proceedings/lrec2010/index.html.

Willis, A., Morse, D., Dil, A., King, D., Roberts, D and Lyal, C. (2011).

Improving search in scanned documents: looking for OCR mismatches. In *Workshop on advanced technologies for digital libraries, Trento, Italy, September 8, 2009*, R. Bernardi, S. Chambers and B. Gottfried (eds). Heidelberg, New York: Springer, pp. 58–61.

20

Taxa, taxon names and globally unique identifiers in perspective

R. Hyam

20.1 Nomenclatural codes

The nomenclatural codes arose as a codification of the accepted best practice in the application of scientific names for organisms. Major advances were made around the turn of the twentieth century when the International Commission on Zoological Nomenclature was founded (1895) and the International Botanical Congress published the *International rules of botanical nomenclature* (1905). Today there are a number of nomenclatural codes and proposed replacement codes including the ICN[1] (McNeill et al., 2012), the ICZN[2] (Ride et al., 1999), the ICNCP[3] (Brickell et al., 2009), the ICNB[4] (Lapage et al., 1992), and the PhyloCode[5] (Queiroz, 2006; Cantino and Queiroz, 2010). Of these by far the most significant

---

[1] International code of nomenclature for algae, fungi and plants: http://www.iapt-taxon.org/nomen/main.php

[2] International code of zoological nomenclature: http://www.nhm.ac.uk/hosted-sites/iczn/code

[3] International code of nomenclature for cultivated plants: http://www.actahort.org/chronica/pdf/sh_10.pdf

[4] International code of nomenclature of bacteria: http://www.ncbi.nlm.nih.gov/books/NBK8817

[5] http://www.ohio.edu/phylocode

Descriptive Taxonomy: The Foundation of Biodiversity Research, eds M. F. Watson, C. H. C. Lyal and C. A. Pendry. Published by Cambridge University Press.

for the majority of scientists are ICN and ICZN. Discussion here is restricted to these two codes because of their pertinence to biological information available electronically, but it should be noted that these codes probably govern the names of a minority of organisms. The majority of the organisms on earth are bacteria whose names would be governed by the ICNB (May, 1988).

Every scientific name that is validly published (available) at the rank of species and below is directly bound to a preserved type specimen that is stored in a reference collection. Names above the rank of species are indirectly bound to type specimens via nominated type species. The type specimens bind the names used in the literature into the biological reality found in the reference collections. The correct name for any circumscribed taxon is calculated from the first published name of which its type specimen is included within the circumscription of that taxon, taking into account the placement of the taxon within a particular classification and the names in use for other taxa in that classification (the nomenclatural rule of priority ICZN Article 23; ICN Article 11, 12). If there are no suitable name-bearing type specimens within the circumscription then a new name needs to be published and a type specimen assigned to it.

There are many complex rules concerning matters such as binomial names (ICZN Article 5; ICN Article 23), missing type specimens (ICZN Article 74; ICN Article 9) and publication of duplicate names (ICZN Article 52; ICN Article 53), but these are not relevant to the discussion presented here. Only the fact that names are determined via an algorithm based on name-bearing types is important to this discussion (ICZN Article 61; ICN Article 7).

20.2 The taxon concept model

For over 100 years the nomenclatural codes have been used to determine the names of taxa and scientists have cited names when they wanted to reference the taxa used in their experiments. Unfortunately this system is flawed. It is possible for radically different taxa to have the same name: two taxa need only share a single specimen – the type (Fig 20.1). The converse is also possible – two taxa could share all specimens except the name-bearing types, and so be almost the same but have two different names. Minor changes in taxon circumscription between classifications can lead to disproportionate changes in nomenclature (Fig 20.2). It is also possible for a taxon to change its name without changing its circumscription – if it is discovered to include an older name's type for example. Scientists who only cite names in their work, therefore, do not precisely cite the taxa to which their observations pertain. To precisely cite taxa they should also include details of the taxonomic treatment (circumscription) they are employing.

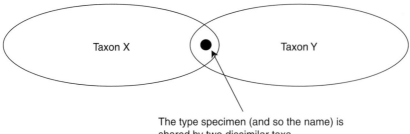

The type specimen (and so the name) is shared by two dissimilar taxa.

Figure 20.1 Dissimilar taxa (from different taxonomic treatments) can share a single unqualified name. Adapted from Kennedy et al. (2006).

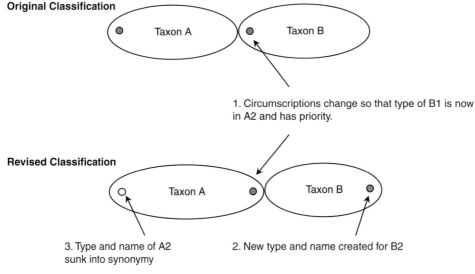

Figure 20.2 A slight change in circumscription moves the type of Taxon B into Taxon A. In the revised classification A has B's name and B has a new name. Adapted from Kennedy et al. (2006).

This separation between the notions of a name and the taxon to which that name refers is now widely accepted (Berendsohn, 1995; Pullan et al., 2000; Franz et al,. 2004; Kennedy et al., 2006; and works cited therein). The problems that can arise can be illustrated with a simple example. Take a hypothetical case where an ecologist wishes to combine two studies S1 and S2 in a meta-analysis. The studies include taxon names that occur in two taxonomic treatments, T1 and T2. T1 recognises two taxa called A and B whilst T2 recognises only one taxon called A and places the name B as a synonym of it. The ecologist has to make a decision as to whether it is safe to combine data from S1 and S2. If S1 uses the name A and S2 the name B then it probably is not safe without further investigation. The authors of S2 may have deliberately excluded material that the authors of S1 would have included. If both studies use the name A, then it is still potentially dangerous to combine the data because if either study were based on a different treatment one would have specifically excluded material that the other included. The only safe case is where both studies use the name B as this indicates they were both using taxonomic treatment T1 and therefore the same concept of B. It is therefore difficult to automatically combine data on the basis of names alone without a taxonomic judgement being made – probably by a human. This example only considers two possible taxonomic treatments. If there are other treatments that recognise B as the accepted name for different taxa then either S1 or S2 could have used one of those other treatments. In such a case it would not be safe to combine the studies even if they had used the same name. Indeed as it is impossible to know that all possible treatments have been found and accounted for (proving a negative) it is never totally safe to combine studies on the basis of taxon names even if those studies use the same name! This would appear to be a *reductio ad absurdum* and we should therefore examine what happens in real world data.

Names that are synonyms indicate that taxon concepts have changed – they once represented an accepted taxon that is no longer recognised. It may have been split into several parts and the type specimen now resides in another taxon with an older name that takes priority. Names that have synonyms also indicate changes in concepts. They were derived from combining multiple other taxa, or at least the parts of those taxa containing type specimens. Names that are of accepted taxa that do not have synonyms can be considered 'pure' as they represent a single taxon concept for the purposes of estimation (although even here it is possible to have multiple nested concepts that do not affect the names as mentioned above).

The Catalogue of Life[6] *2008 Annual Checklist* (Bisby et al., 2008) contains 1 192 015 accepted names and 720 040 synonyms, a total of 1 912 055 names. Of the accepted names, 262 293 have synonyms whilst 929 722 (48.6% of the accepted taxa) lack synonyms and could be considered to represent single taxon concepts. This is a crude estimate as the Catalogue of Life is a synoptic work and may provide a simplified view of the global nomenclature. Many groups are only partially studied and need further work. Those that are included may not have full synonyms. Geoffroy and Berendsohn (2003) carried out a more detailed analysis on a smaller group, *Reference list of German mosses* (Koperski et al., 2000), in which detailed examination of the relationships between 12 different classifications is presented. Geoffroy and Berendsohn (2003) conclude: 'In terms of databasing this means that only for 13% of the taxa the name can serve as a direct index to other data (and this

---

[6] http://www.catalogueoflife.org

can only be said for the set of treatments scrutinised by the authors)'. These two observations point towards the effect of taxon concepts being large and probably involving the majority of taxa. Despite this the use of a taxon concept-based approach remains very rare. Researchers continue to report their results using taxon names alone, not indicating the taxonomic treatment which they were following. It appears that the taxon concept effect, although real, has little detectable effect on the way the results of research are used.

In relatively recently surveyed areas of high endemism, for example New Zealand, where many taxa have only been described once and there have not been multiple rounds of taxonomic revision, the issues associated with taxon concepts as described above are likely to be be less significant. Unfortunately these areas are frequently prone to large numbers of misapplied names. This occurs when specimens are consistently identified to the wrong taxon, typically a similar looking European species. When this situation is detected the name of the European species effectively has two taxa associated with it, the 'right' one and the 'wrong' one. An analogy is a word with two meanings in two geographical locations.

20.3 Names as tags and 'taxonomic intelligence'

The taxon concept conundrum (that fact that the world gets by happily using names alone and not qualified taxon concepts) would remain an interesting sideline if it were not for the impact of the internet and the possibility of automatically, or semi-automatically, combining data from multiple sources. Large amounts of information are being tagged with taxon names and published on the internet. At the time of writing GBIF[7] contains 140-million occurrence records linked to names, GenBank[8] contains around 100-million sequences on over 260 000 named organisms. Searching for a commonly occurring scientific name using generic search engines such as Google[9] typically results in thousands of hits and hundreds of images. The iSpecies.org[10] website carries out this kind of federated search over multiple data suppliers automatically.

Some of the resources returned when searching for a name may provide synonymic names that can be fed back into the search process (query expansion) to retrieve more resources tagged with other related and presumably substitutable names. Projects such as uBio[11] offer query expansion services to support this process. uBio also exploits published taxonomies, such as Catalogue of Life, to expand queries up or down a taxonomic hierarchy. The combined process has been termed 'Taxonomic Intelligence' (Patterson et al., 2006).

---

[7] http://www.gbif.org   [8] http://www.ncbi.nlm.nih.gov/genbank
[9] http://www.google.org   [10] http://www.ispecies.org   [11] http://www.ubio.org

Progress has been both rapid and remarkable. The extant systems are proving useful in discovery of research materials. Unfortunately these methods can only lead to query expansion. Using the example above a search for A will return all resources tagged with either A or B. Likewise searching for B will return all resources tagged with B or A. The fact that one of the studies involved may have deliberately excluded measurements of B is not detected. The process results in the broadest possible interpretation of any taxon. It takes the *sensu lato* approach for everything – the ultimate 'lumpers' approach to taxonomy. This would occur even if the query expansion process permitted selection of a preferred classification over which the query were expanded because each synonym relationship has to be treated as a wholesale movement of a taxon not the movement of a type specimen alone. Splitting of taxa is by and large invisible.

The process of expanding from one tagged resource to other resources that bear the same or related names can be conceptualised as creating a 'graph' of resources where each resource is a node and the edges are formed by matching the name strings in the resources (the graph-based approach). For some names this graph of linked resources may be small. For others it could be enormous. These graphs are effectively a new form of taxon circumscription. Through this mechanism the *de facto* species concept is becoming the 'Google Species Concept' where a species is defined as anything that is returned by a search for its name.

The two most used statistical measures in information retrieval are 'precision' and 'recall'. Precision is the proportion of the resources returned that are relevant to the search terms used. Recall is a measure of the number or resources returned as a proportion of the number that should have been returned. If a search has 100% recall and 100% precision it will find all the relevant and only the relevant resources. The trouble with taking a 'taxonomic intelligence' approach to query expansion is that relevance is not clearly defined. If study S1 has deliberately excluded taxon B, but another resource (T2) says B is a synonym of A there is no way of excluding S1 from the search results for search term 'B'. Without knowing the classifications used by S1 not even a human can know to exclude it. Query expansion increases the likelihood that such results will be inappropriately included before a human can intervene.

Through the use of information retrieval techniques scientific names are effectively being used to build a 'Folksonomy' – a bottom-up classification emerging from social tagging of data. An observation is tagged with a name and is published on the World Wide Web. There is no differentiation between whether this is defining the taxon or referencing a predefined taxon. The boundary between identification and classification is not explicit. The observation tagged with a name may be a DNA sequence that will subsequently be used to confirm the identity of another 'unknown' sequence. No taxonomist needs to be involved in the process. Counter-intuitively taxonomic revisions (whether monographical or floristic/faunistic) are likely to make query results less reliable, because they introduce new name to name relationships through synonymy and so increase the results returned but decrease the precision of information retrieval.

This 'names as tags' approach provides compelling results in a short time span. It supplies usable systems for finding research materials. Its weakness is that it is likely to create misleading results if automated analyses require anything other than a *sensu lato* view of every taxon. This includes even apparently simple analyses such as plotting distribution maps. The danger is that precisely because these systems work so well for information retrieval people will assume that they are also suitable for research and inclusion in analyses. An analogy is using a high-magnification but low-resolution microscope. It is adequate for many tasks, but may not reveal the details necessary for research. Unless individual taxa are tagged with globally unique identifiers, fine-grained taxonomy will never be accessible to detailed or automated analysis.

20.4 Globally unique identifiers

The importance of globally unique identifiers (GUIDs) can be best illustrated with a mapping example. Imagine a data supplier who publishes a million occurrence records. Each record contains a longitude, latitude and a taxon name. A consumer of the data is interested in a subset of records that form dots within a particular polygon on a map. When the supplier updates their data the consumer sees the dots on the map change. What has changed? If a dot has disappeared has it been removed from the dataset or has its location changed? If a new dot appears on a map has it actually been moved from elsewhere or is it new data? If the taxon name for a dot changes is it a new record or a redetermination of an old record? None of these questions can be answered unless the dots bear identifiers that are separate from their content. The data consumer is probably most interested in change – monitoring the effects of environmental impacts. Although information can be gleaned from the two maps it is only in the form of coarse measures and does not separate experimental noise from biological signal. An example might be 'Data supplier X reports fewer occurrences of species Y from area Z this year than last'. It is difficult to speculate as to why this effect has occurred without being able to 'drill down' into the data and see why the changes have arisen.

If every record in the dataset has an immutable identifier then it would be immediately apparent to the consumer which records had changed, which were additions and whether the changes may be for biological reasons. Furthermore if each record had an identifier that was unique within a global scope (was guaranteed not to clash with identifiers from any other source) then the consumer could mix records from different data sources and still be sure to pick out biological signal

TAXA, NAMES AND GUIDS IN PERSPECTIVE

from data noise. The consumer could also individually credit the suppliers for use of their data.

For these reasons tagging data with GUIDs is the single most important step in enabling the sharing and integration of biological data across the internet. From the point of view of the hypothetical ecological study introduced above, if the taxa (not the names) in T1 and T2 had been tagged with GUIDs (as well as names), and the studies S1 and S2 had used the GUIDs to refer to the taxa (rather than just names), none of the ensuing complexity would have occurred. The ecologist could easily tell whether it was appropriate to combine results from S1 and S2. It would be reasonable for a machine to make this decision automatically and only bring matters to the attention of the ecologist if there was a conflict.

20.5 GUID technologies

The term globally unique identifier is used in two slightly different ways. In computer science GUIDs are values that are complex strings of characters that are extremely likely to be unique in any context. In the biodiversity informatics community the term is used in a narrower sense where GUIDs have three related properties: they are *globally unique*; they are *resolvable* (or actionable); and they *identify* a typed object.

20.5.1 Uniqueness

There are two principal ways of achieving global uniqueness. One is to generate a long and complex number that is highly unlikely to be generated twice and so is functionally unique. This approach enables distributed systems to uniquely identify data without significant central coordination. The most common implementation of this approach is the universally unique identifier (UUID) standard[12]. UUIDs are widely used in low-level computing applications such as distributed file systems. Another way to establish uniqueness is the use of a central issuing authority. An example of this approach is the domain name system (DNS), a hierarchical naming system for resources on the internet including websites and email servers. The Internet Corporation for Assigned Names and Numbers[13] (ICANN) issues top-level domain names such as '.com' to lower-level issuing authorities who issue subdomain names (e.g. 'example.com') who then have authority over issuing subdomains of these domains. Theoretically this can carry on for up to 127 levels but practically rarely exceeds 5 or 6. The domain names are then used in protocols, such as the hypertext transfer protocol (HTTP), which enable the addition of values after the domain name (e.g. 'http://example.com/123'). DNS has been used to define what is

---

[12] http://tools.ietf.org/html/rfc4122   [13] http://www.icann.org

termed a 'namespace'. The locally unique identifier '123' is, thus, globally unique when it is combined with 'http://example.com/'.

20.5.2 Resolution

UUID-type GUIDs would help solve the problem of the changing dots on the map given above. Each dot would have its own identifier and so any changes in the data could be distinguished from additions and deletions of dots. What UUIDs would not help with is the provenance of the data behind the dots. If the application needs to know more than the information provided to plot the map (such as the licensing terms or whether the data has been modified since issue) then it must be able to do something with the GUID to access the original data source. The GUID needs to be resolvable to some meaningful information. The identifier contains information which refers to data stored elsewhere, as opposed to containing these data itself. Accessing the value referred to by a reference is called 'dereferencing'. An analogy of this process would be the citing of references in published works. The citations act as identifiers that can be 'dereferenced' to the original papers in the library. Resolution of identifiers is only possible with some form of centralised authority with which the identifiers have been registered. Simply searching for identifiers does not provide authoritative data about GUID tagged data as it may result in multiple hits which may contain different data.

20.5.3 Typing

When a researcher fetches a referenced work from a library they are usually certain how to handle it. It will be a paper or a book of some form, probably in a language they can read or recognise. Likewise, when a machine de-references an identifier the response it receives needs to be understandable both syntactically and semantically so that it can display the response in an appropriate way or carry out further calculations. The GUID resolution, therefore, needs to be linked to some form of 'typing' mechanism. If a machine is presented with a GUID it should, for example, be able to tell the users that the GUID represents a taxon from a particular taxonomic treatment.

20.5.4 Technologies

There is some debate over the use of GUID technologies in the biodiversity informatics community. This debate is ongoing and some of the technologies involved are summarised here. Unfortunately it is not possible to avoid an 'alphabet soup' of acronyms when discussing these technologies.

The most widely used identifiers on the internet are HTTP uniform resource identifiers (HTTP URIs); these include the HTTP uniform resource locators (HTTP URLs), now very familiar as addresses for web pages. HTTP URIs on their own provide uniqueness and resolution, but not response typing. However, following the set of best practices proposed under the banner 'Linked Data' does provide response typing.

Life science identifiers[14] (LSIDs) were first proposed by the Object Modelling Group[15] and IBM. After several workshops the Taxonomic Databases Working Group[16] (TDWG) adopted LSIDs as its preferred GUID technology. They provide uniqueness, resolution and response typing. The default resolution mechanism is based on DNS (as with HTTP URIs), but there are very few clients that exploit it. Most LSIDs are resolved by being appended to the HTTP URL of a proxy program that fetches the associated data and metadata.

The motivation for TDWG choosing LSIDs over HTTP URIs was principally social. HTTP URIs are considered inherently unreliable by many users because of their experience with broken web-page links and their ease of creation. It takes a conscious action on the part of administrators to implement LSIDs and this instils a sense of importance to their maintenance. A similar motivation is given for the adoption of digital object identifiers[17] (DOIs) by the publishing community. DOIs have a similar resolution mechanisms to LSIDs using either an HTTP URI proxy or the 'Handle System'[18].

20.6 Standards

Adoption of GUIDs for taxa has effectively stalled. The major providers of nomenclatural data (IPNI[19], Index Fungorum[20], ZooBank[21]) have issued LSIDs for names and return data using a version of the Taxon Concept Schema[22] (TCS) rendered in RDF[23] as an OWL[24] ontology. Work is currently under way to formalise this as a TDWG standard, but in the meanwhile GBIF is using a checklist format based on the Darwin Core[25] standard to exchange taxonomic data. There are proposals for a Global Names Architecture[26] that will also track GUIDs for taxa, but implementation of this has yet to start. Without standard ways of identifying taxa and standard ways of encoding taxonomic assertions there is little impetus for the development of client applications which could better exploit the homogenous environment. This leads to little impetus for further labelling of taxa and the continued use of names strings, ambiguous as they are.

[14] http://sourceforge.net/projects/lsids/   [15] http://www.omg.org

[16] http://www.tdwg.org   [17] http://www.doi.org   [18] http://www.handle.net

[19] http://www.ipni.org   [20] http://www.indexfungorum.org/Names/Names.asp

[21] http://www.zoobank.org   [22] http://www.tdwg.org/standards/117

[23] http://www.w3.org/TR/rdf-primer   [24] http://www.w3.org/TR/owl-features

[25] http://rs.tdwg.org/dwc   [26] http://www.globalnames.org/

20.7 Summary

Scientific, type-based names are not adequate identifiers of taxa. Because of this the majority of names are ambiguous to some extent, but there appears to be little movement to change working practice and refer to taxa by referencing specific treatments or using GUIDs. Names are widely used as if they were social tags or key words. This leads to effective information retrieval applications, but results in the adoption of a *sensu lato* view of all taxa. Machine interpretation of taxonomic data will be imprecise until taxa (not names) are labelled with GUIDs. There is still debate around the best GUID technologies and response formats for names and taxa. This creates a chicken-and-egg situation and it is difficult to see a way around.

A tacit assumption has been made here that taxa can be defined i.e. that there is some mechanism by which one could circumscribe a taxon so that another person could ascertain, beyond reasonable doubt, that a specimen was a member of that taxon. This mechanism is termed the description or circumscription of the taxon. It is a protocol to test the hypothesis 'Specimen X is a member of taxon Y'. Every taxon has a separate protocol. The protocols may use different morphological or molecular characteristics. Although we will be able to automate (through the use of taxon concepts and GUIDs) the tracking of taxa and specimens that have been identified to those taxa, it appears unlikely we will be able to automate comparison of taxa between classifications because they are defined in unrelated ways; i.e. it will be possible to automatically determine that problems exist, but there can be no automatic mechanism for resolving these problems.

References

Berendsohn, W. G. (1995). The concept of 'potential taxa' in databases. *Taxon*, **44**: 207–212.

Bisby, F. A., Roskov, Y. R., Orrell, T. M., Nicolson, D., Paglinawan, L. E., Bailly, N., Kirk, P. M., Bourgoin, T. and van Hertum, J. (eds) (2008). *Species 2000 and ITIS Catalogue of Life: 2008 Annual Checklist*. [CD-ROM], Reading: Species. Available at: http://www.catalogueoflife. org/annual-checklist/2008.

Brickell, C. D., Alexander, C., David, J. C., Hetterscheid, W. L. A., Leslie, A. C., Malecot, V., Jin, X. B. and Cubey, J. J. (2009). *International code of nomenclature for cultivated plants (ICNCP or cultivated plant code) incorporating the rules and recommendations for naming plants in cultivation*, Eighth Edition. Regnum Vegetabile, 151, Scripta Horticulturae, 10. Leuven: International Society for Horticultural Science.

Cantino, P. D. and Queiroz, K. de (2010). *International code of phylogenetic nomenclature, version 4c*. Available at: http://www.ohio.edu/phylocode/ PhyloCode4c.pdf.

Franz, N., Peet, M., Robert, K. and Weakley, A. S. (2004). On the use of taxonomic concepts in support of biodiversity research and taxonomy. In

The new taxonomy, Q. D. Wheeler (ed.). Boca Raton, FL: CRC Press, pp. 61–84.

Geoffroy, M. and Berendsohn, W. G. (2003). The concept problem in taxonomy: importance, components, approaches. *Schriftenreihe für Vegetationskunde*, **39**: 5–14.

Kennedy, J. B., Hyam, R., Kukla, R. and Paterson, T. (2006). Standard data model representation for taxonomic information. *OMICS: A Journal of Integrative Biology*, **10**: 220–230.

Koperski, M., Geoffroy, M., Braun, W. and Gradstein, S. R. (2000). Referenzliste der moose Deutschland. *Schriftenreihe Vegetationsk*, **34**: 1–519.

Lapage S. P., Sneath, P. H. A., Lessel, E. F., Skerman, V. B. D., Seelinger, H. P. R. and Clark, W. A. (1992). *International code of nomenclature of bacteria (1990 revision)*. Washington D.C.: American Society for Microbiology Press.

May, R. M. M. (1988). How many species are there on earth? *Science*, **241**(4872): 1441–1449. DOI: 10.1126/science.241.4872.1441.

McNeill, J., Barrie, F. R., Buck, W. R., Demoulin, V., Greuter, W., Hawksworth, D. L., Herendeen, P. S., Knapp, S., Marhold, K., Prado, J., Prud'Homme. W. F., Smith, G. F., Weirsema, J. H. and Turland, N. J. (2012). *International code of nomenclature for algae, fungi, and plants (Melbourne code)*. Regnum Vegetabile, 154. Koeningstein: Koeltz Scientific Books.

Patterson, D. J., Remsen, D., Marino, W. A. and Norton, C. (2006). Taxonomic indexing – extending the role of taxonomy. *Systematic Biology*, **55**: 367–373.

Pullan, M. R., Watson, M. F., Kennedy, J. B., Raguenaud, C. and Hyam, R. (2000). The Prometheus taxonomic model: a practical approach to representing multiple classifications. *Taxon*, **49**: 55–75.

Queiroz, K. (2006). The PhyloCode and the distinction between taxonomy and nomenclature. *Systematic Biology*, **55**: 160–2.

Ride, W. D. L., Cogger, H. G., Dupuis, C., Kraus, O., Minelli, A., Thompson, F. C. and Tubbs, P. K. (1999). *International code of zoological nomenclature*, Fourth Edition. London: International Trust for Zoological Nomenclature.

21

E-publishing descriptive taxonomy: the convergence of taxonomic journals and databases

V. S. Smith

21.1 Introduction

No one perceives a database entry of, say, a specimen in a museum collection or a DNA sequence, as being as valuable as the scientific paper that describes it. Accordingly researchers are not (usually) awarded promotion based on the number of deposits made to a biological database or the annotations made to database record. Rather, current measures of peer recognition focus on the number of papers published, the citations these papers attract and their resulting 'impact' as determined through various metrics. Yet ironically, to the consumer at least, the database entry may be more valuable than a paper (Bourne, 2005). Databases containing the products of the taxonomic community (e.g. taxonomic names and concepts, specimen geospatial and temporal data, collection records, images, phenotypic and genomic character states and descriptions), can be more easily transmitted, reused and repurposed than much of the knowledge locked up within traditional descriptive papers. Indeed, the audience for these databases is likely to be far higher given the specialist nature and limited availability of most traditional taxonomic works. This assertion is borne out by download statistics from potentially analogous biological databases such as

Descriptive Taxonomy: The Foundation of Biodiversity Research, eds M. F. Watson, C. H. C. Lyal and C. A. Pendry. Published by Cambridge University Press.

GenBank[1] and the Protein Data Bank[2], which have shown substantial, if not exponential, growth over the past decade (Pruitt et al., 2009).

Comparable databases for taxonomy on the scale of resources like GenBank do not currently exist. Instead descriptive taxonomy continues to be disseminated in dense treatises that are usually only physically and intellectually accessible to specialists that have material access to these works, and the knowledge required to interpret their content. In consequence, most taxonomy is effectively withheld from use for a wide range of scientific applications, even to the point that it often cannot be readily incorporated into further taxonomic study. Why should this be so? Why should the taxonomic community persist in publishing descriptive taxonomic data in ways that limit its use to all but a handful of specialists? In this chapter I explore this question and highlight some of the technical and social developments that are taking place within the research and scholarly publishing industry, which are bringing change to the practice and dissemination of descriptive taxonomy.

Dissemination of results is one of the critical steps in the practice of science, and taxonomists, like other scientists, do this in many forms, through conference presentations, invited lectures and most importantly through publication. Publication is simply the act of making something publicly known through the preparation and distribution of multiple identical copies. In a scholarly context, however, scientific publishing takes on a special meaning. In 1665 Henry Oldenburg established the principles of scientific publishing as founding editor of *Philosophical Transactions of the Royal Society*. This was the first English language scholarly journal and was set up to disseminate, register, certificate and archive content that we would today recognise as science (Hall, 2002). These tenets of scholarly publishing are still relevant today despite the fact that the World Wide Web has supplanted print on paper as the primary medium for disseminating scholarly works. Online versions of publications are typically presented either as HTML web pages or as static PDF documents, with the internet used primarily as a convenient distribution medium for the text. As the electronic embodiment of the static printed page, the PDF document is directly comparable to the first scholarly articles published by the Royal Society in 1665, but it is antithetical to the spirit of the Web, which can support the constant updating and improvement of the published information on a continual basis.

Compared to what many database developers have achieved in terms of data integration, comprehension through novel visualisation techniques and real-time collaboration of authors, most modern publishers have failed to embrace alternative forms of publishing afforded by new, and increasingly web-based, technologies (Brown, 2008). An often cited reason for this is that changing and updating content conflicts with one of the original tenets of publishing as a means of producing

---

[1] http://www.ncbi.nlm.nih.gov/genbank   [2] http://www.rcsb.org/pdb

multiple, identical copies. It also makes peer review difficult, since this usually relies on small communities of experts to review changes, and this cannot usually be delivered in real time. Yet, neither of these challenges is insurmountable. Snapshot versions of dynamic documents can be created to facilitate citation, while unvetted or edited content can be flagged for subsequent review. Tools like MediaWiki[3], for the most part, solved these technical challenges many years ago. Perhaps other more commercial interests drive mainstream publishers to preserve the status quo. Nevertheless, within the context of descriptive taxonomy there are genuine issues that need to be addressed if new forms of publishing are to be considered.

In the following sections I highlight what I consider to be the major thematic challenges for the taxonomic community if we are to embrace new forms of publishing, and then examine the first tentative steps made by taxonomists to tackle these problems through new information technology infrastructures. Many of these issues are relevant to the wider scientific community, and are not limited to the problems of taxonomic publishing.

21.2 Challenges for e-publishing taxonomy

These challenges can be broadly divided into technical issues associated with the development of technologies and interfaces that support the taxonomic process, and social issues that require consensus solutions amongst the taxonomic and wider community. Perhaps not surprisingly, the social issues are the dominant features on this list and the technical issues from a computer science perspective are not especially complex, with the notable challenge of data integration.

21.3 Technical issues

21.3.1 Supporting the taxonomic workflow

This refers to the services and tools that capture the life cycle of taxonomic research from inception to publication. Taxonomic research is built from two resources: samples of the organisms involved (either specimens or observations) and the legacy of taxonomic investigation found in the published literature. Supporting the taxonomic workflow requires repurposing these data in a digital environment that supports the scientific process of taxonomy. The core of this process is encapsulated in a feedback loop between hypotheses of characters and taxa (Johnson, 2010). Taxonomists group specimens into taxa on the basis of empirical observations about the characters they exhibit. The resulting taxonomic concepts and the degree to which specimens are congruent with them may suggest new characters

---

[3] http://www.mediawiki.org

and character states, leading to modifications in the proposed taxon concept. The process is iterative and open ended, until a stable equilibrium is reached, at which point the taxon concept is fixed in the mind of the author and data are published as part of a taxonomic revision. This revision may incorporate a summary of published literature, checklists, and identification keys, in addition to the formalised descriptions (diagnoses) of taxa and supporting data (e.g. images, distribution maps, materials examined).

Data supporting the taxonomic workflow are replete with structure and organisation, making them eminently suited to automated process that might dynamically compile revisionary publications in real time. Indeed many taxonomists draw on databases in the compilation of these publications, so the fact that this structure is lost on publication is a major lost opportunity. Since all of the data used to compile taxonomic revisions can be stored within a database (even natural language sections like the abstract), it is possible to retain all the data structure and provide dynamic views of these datasets. This concept is not new. The DELTA (DEscription Language for Taxonomy) data format developed between 1971 and 2000 has supported the automated compilation of taxonomic keys and revisionary publications for some time (Dallwitz, 1980). This has been used in the production of many hundreds of descriptive taxonomic publications. However, this is a one-way process geared toward print-based publication and is relatively complex to use, only attracting a small fraction of taxonomic community that have the computing skills required to make use of the software (Walter and Winterton, 2007). Despite these problems the relative success of DELTA illustrates that the primary challenge for software developers supporting taxonomists is not in the development of the data architectures (databases and standards) storing the taxonomic data. Rather, it is in the development of an integrated experience for the taxonomist supporting the entire taxonomic workflow from project inception to publication. Such systems need to be integrated with services that, where possible, supply the underlying taxonomic data. This enables taxonomists to reuse and repurpose information that has been captured elsewhere, and publish their new digital data back to these hubs to benefit others. Data infrastructures, like the Global Biodiversity Information Facility (GBIF)[4] for specimen observational data and the Biodiversity Heritage Library (BHL)[5] for taxonomic literature, are central to this effort, despite the fact that they are at present, woefully incomplete (see Section 21.3.3, Digitisation).

21.3.2 Data integration

Integrating diverse sources of digital information is a major technical challenge for the taxonomic community (Page, R. D. M., 2008). Not only are we faced with numerous, disparate data providers, each with their own specific-user communities, but

---

[4] http://www.gbif.org   [5] http://www.biodiversitylibrary.org

also the information we are interested in is extremely diverse. For example, the Taxonomic Databases Working Group (TDWG)[6] currently lists 654 different database projects (TDWG-Statistics, 2010). Similarly, currently the GBIF lists 10 556 datasets from 317 different data publishers (GBIF-Statistics, 2010). Combine these with mainstream bioinformatics databases like GenBank and PubMed[7], plus the taxonomic literature digitised by the BHL (currently 28 million pages), and the magnitude of the challenge becomes readily apparent. Efforts to integrate these data are central to maximising the efficiency of the taxonomic publishing.

Initial efforts at data integration have taken two distinct paths; one focusing on shared identifiers (principally taxonomic names) to link data together, the other focusing on shared use of data standards. Of course there is some overlap between these approaches, but they have come to represent different philosophies about the future of biodiversity informatics. Use of shared identifiers to determine whether two items of data refer to the same entity allow resources to be linked or mined for information without being specifically structured to support this activity. In contrast shared uses of data standards require detailed agreement amongst the data providers about what data are to be integrated, how they are structured and the protocols by which they are shared. When implemented properly, data standards can support a very high level of integration. For example the Access to Biological Collections Data (ABCD[8]) schema is a comprehensive standard supporting the integration of data about specimens and observations for about 700 data elements. However, the complexity of ABCD means that simpler and less granular standards (e.g. the Darwin Core[9] schema with about 40 elements)[10] receive much wider use (Constable et al., 2010).

Taxonomic names as identifiers have received a great deal of attention, notably underpinning efforts in the BHL to aggregate information within digitised taxonomic literature (Rinaldo, 2009). However, taxon names have a serious limitation as identifiers since they are neither stable nor unique. The name *Morus*, for example, might equally refer to the seabird genus of the Gannet, or the plant genus for the Mulberry tree. A 250-year legacy of taxonomic research means that taxonomy is replete with such examples, and consequently taxon names can only facilitate a soft level of data integration that will not meet the standards of accuracy and completeness required by most taxonomists. Other forms of identifiers, such as specimen codes and GenBank accession numbers, can be used to successfully link otherwise disconnected facts in different databases, and increasingly controlled vocabularies

---

[6] http://www.tdwg.org   [7] http://www.ncbi.nlm.nih.gov/pubmed

[8] http://www.tdwg.org/activities/abcd

[9] http://wiki.tdwg.org/twiki/bin/view/DarwinCore/DarwinCoreVersions

[10] http://rs.tdwg.org/dwc

are being constructed (e.g. GBIF-Vocabularies[11]) to facilitate the shared use of homologous terms for this purpose. Shared identifiers also have the advantage that the structure of these links can also be exploited. For example, the PageRank algorithm (Page, L., et al., 1999) as outlined by R. D. M. Page (2008) provides a means to rank search results. This addresses the problem of how to weight the many thousand of otherwise identical entries in taxonomic databases. For instance, more important specimen records (e.g. holotypes) are likely to receive more citations (links) and, thus, be ranked of greater importance than those with fewer citations.

In recognition of the importance of shared identifiers to consistently identify the same object, the biodiversity informatics community has recently invested significant effort into developing a scheme of globally unique identifiers (GUIDs) (Clark et al., 2004). Numerous methods for generating such identifiers are available with discussion primarily focussed on three alternatives (HTTP uniform resource identifiers (URIs), digital object identifiers (DOIs) and life science identifiers (LSIDs)); however, a clear consensus on the most appropriate for biodiversity data has yet to be reached (see Chapter 20, Hyam, this volume).

21.3.3 Digitisation

Specimens and literature are the raw materials that feed into the scientific process of taxonomy. Enhancing access to these resources is fundamental to improving the efficiency of descriptive taxonomy, and digitisation provides a universal means of achieving this through a one-off investment. The scale of the required investment makes complete digitisation a seemingly insurmountable task (IWGSC, 2008). New technical approaches need to be considered to make this task less formidable.

It is estimated that there are more than 2.5 billion specimens in natural history collections worldwide (Duckworth et al., 1993) and approximately 320 million pages of descriptive taxonomic literature (Hanken, 2010). For example, the Natural History Museum in London alone has an estimated 70 million specimens, more than 1 million books, 25 thousand periodical titles, 500 thousand natural history artworks with extensive map, manuscript and photographical collections and archives comprising over 1 million further items. Other natural history institutions have collections of a comparable size. Given the scale of these collections, complete digitisation at the unit (e.g. specimen) level is almost impossible to fund. However, compared with the time, effort and money associated with gathering information required by modern taxonomic monographs, item-level digitisation may be cost-effective if the processes used can ensure adequate reuse and accessibility of the digitised data. At the very least, not digitising the output from new taxonomic efforts might be seen as a missed opportunity (Krishtalka and Humphrey, 2000).

---

[11] http://vocabularies.gbif.org

Taxonomy is the driver for most natural history digitisation efforts, and typically natural history digitisation is approached in the same rigorous, comprehensive and, consequently, slow manner that has become a trademark of the profession. Unfortunately, the scale of the task and the complex nature of many natural history items (e.g. card-mounted insects held on pins) means that these approaches are manual and usually very slow. Such methods cannot even keep pace with the new material entering collections, let alone a legacy of 250 years of taxonomy research. Increased mechanisation, coupled with small and often temporary compromises in the initial output from digitisation projects can, however, address this problem of scale. Combined with social incentives that better acknowledge the value of digitally published data, the task of item-level natural history digitisation is possible on a manageable time frame.

A combination of increased and more affordable computing capacity, high-quality digital cameras and extended-focus software has made imagery of even small specimens very fast and relatively inexpensive. Crucially, when these are combined with workflows adapted to exploit the standard properties of many natural history collections, the process of digitisation can be made much faster. For example, new high-resolution photography makes it possible to image whole collection draws containing hundreds of specimens in under a minute. These images are devoid of the parallax and edge-effect distortion, previously associated with composite specimen images. Because collection drawers are usually of a standard size and considerably fewer than the specimens they hold (perhaps hundreds of thousands, instead of tens of millions), the complete digitisation of entire collections is possible on a reasonable time frame. Comparable approaches can be used for items not stored in drawers. For example, million of specimens are mounted on regular-sized glass microscope slides. Using technology developed for imaging histological samples, slide-mounted specimens can be preloaded into rack-feeding scanners that can auto-focus to produce high-resolution images. Similarly, taxonomic literature can be imaged through high-throughput scanners or with imaging technology of the kind used for the BHL project. Even then, these approaches are not appropriate for all natural history collections. Some are mounted or stored in such a way that their essential characteristics cannot be imaged without item-level handling (e.g. the undersides of pinned butterflies and moths, and most specimens stored in spirit). Likewise, conventional images of some specimens have little or no practical value (e.g. selected palaeontological material or mineral samples where sub-surface features or chemical properties are the important discriminating properties of collections). Nevertheless, in many cases, some level of digitisation is both possible and of value to a major portion of the world's natural history collections. This value is significantly enhanced if images of metadata about the objects being digitised (e.g. specimen labels) can be simulta-neously captured during the imaging process. Even in cases where this is not possible, a unique identifier can be assigned to each physical object and its digital image so that metadata subsequently extracted from the object can be jointly associated with both the specimen and its image.

21.4 Social issues

21.4.1 Sustainability

Long-term support of users, software and the underlying hardware is arguably the greatest social challenge to new methods of publishing descriptive taxonomy. Publication of taxonomic research on the World Wide Web risks being perceived as more ephemeral than that published through traditional publication practices. Such concerns are well-founded. Web-links break, software and browser technologies change, users are fickle and research projects with their software developers come and go. A taxonomist considering whether to engage with new publication practices must balance such risks and the natural inertia of working with familiar tools against potential gains in efficiency, impact and personal profile derived from using novel publication approaches. At present this risk is too great for many scholars. A recent UK study of web-publishing practices across all academic sectors showed participation greatest amongst older more established scholars and younger graduate and postgraduate students, but a significant decline in participation amongst post-doctoral researchers and junior lecturers (Procter et al., 2010). These junior researchers and lecturers are highly dependent upon a cycle of traditional publications in order to maintain research grant income and enhance their academic credibility. Without engaging this large and risk-adverse group of researchers, efforts to find more efficient ways of publishing are, at least in taxonomy, likely to fail.

As more taxonomists publish their data in an integrated way, these systems become increasingly valuable to other users through a growing pool of available data. These so-called 'network effects' only become visible when a critical mass of users adopt the system (Benkler, 2006). Given the relatively small pool of potential taxonomists compared to other academic sectors, it is especially critical to engage and sustain mainstream taxonomic researchers in new publication techniques. Users of these systems need confidence that their contributions will be maintained and are available beyond the short life cycle of a typical research grant. Achieving this kind of sustainability for novel forms of data publishing would traditionally have required substantial and ongoing investment in hardware, software and human capacity. However, technical advances over the past 10 years mean these costs are now substantially reduced. Hardware (the traditional capital investment) can be outsourced at relatively low cost with service-level agreements that guarantee levels of data access, backup and document archive activity. In contrast software development is becoming the primary capital investment (Atkins et al., 2010). The standard scientific practice of constantly reinventing and rebuilding existing tools is increasingly untenable, leading to the potential for development of shared infrastructures that are of a high-enough quality to be used across multiple disciplines. These need to be designed with modern software methodologies so that they are technically sustainable. Even then, maintained support for successful projects will need sustaining beyond the life cycle of standard research grants. Institutions that underpin taxonomic research, like our major natural history national museums, might eventually consider taking on these costs for the taxonomic sector. This will only be likely if the cost of these new publication practices is less than those of author fees and access charges to traditional publications. To make this transition, need-driven and user-led experimental projects (so called bottom-up initiatives) will need to be coupled with management (top-down) incentives to encourage use of these systems. Natural selection processes will ensure that only the fittest survive, helping to identify those projects that require sustained support outside the life cycle of typical research grants.

21.4.2 Quality control and peer review

Perceptions about the scholarly merit of published resources supporting taxonomic data are a key factor in the assessment and use of taxonomic research. Evidence suggests that scholars distrust novel publication processes and tools such as online databases, weblogs (blogs) and online encyclopaedias (e.g. the Encyclopedia of Life (EOL)[12] or Wikipedia[13]) because they fall outside the norms associated with traditional publication practices (Procter et al., 2010). In particular, ambiguity over whether a resource has been peer reviewed are central to concerns over its scholarly credibility (Nentwich, 2006). Contributors are reluctant to engage with novel publication approaches over fears that their work will be perceived as less credible and because these outputs do not (generally) count in any form of research assessment. Similarly, those using these digital resources do not have the normal cues of quality assurance (e.g. journal impact factors or peer-review guarantees) to help assess scholarly value. For novel forms of publication to become mainstream, either the traditional mechanism of peer review needs to be replicated in a digital environment or other measures need to be developed to maintain confidence in taxonomic research.

Despite the dogma that peer review is the scientific community's most objective means of identifying 'truth', there is surprisingly little empirical evidence for this, or even on peer review's effectiveness in raising standards (Grayson, 2002). Recent high-profile cases have highlighted flaws in the peer-review process relating to instances of fraud due to fabrication, falsification or other forms of scientific

---

[12] http://www.eol.org   [13] http://en.wikipedia.org

misconduct (Anonymous, 2006). These issues are particularly important to taxonomic research because descriptive taxonomy involves reporting facts that are largely impossible for a reviewer to substantiate without reference to the source taxonomic material, and because the majority of peer review is still conducted anonymously. Similarly, long-running concerns over the possibility of bias or suppression by editors and reviewers have also been raised. This has even been the subject of specific study within the systematics research community (Hull, 1991). Collectively this evidence suggests that peer review is perhaps better at identifying the *acceptable truth* amongst scientists, rather than *objective truth* in science.

In practice, peer review of taxonomy is mostly an effort to ensure normal taxonomic practices and standards have been observed, coupled with an assessment of the work's importance relative to the perceived audience of the publication. Since the majority of descriptive taxonomic work has minimal short-term impact outside narrow specialist audiences, a subjective assessment of importance is largely irrelevant when reviewing most taxonomy. Increasingly it is common for taxonomic work to be published in taxonomic mega-journals that cross-cut many taxonomic groups (e.g. *Zootaxa* for animals, *Mycotaxon* for fungi and the *International Journal of Systematic and Evolutionary Microbiology* for microbiology), leaving reviewers with the more critical task of ensuring that authors have complied with taxonomic and editorial norms. In the light of new forms of digitised publication, it is reasonable to ask whether even these processes could be mechanised to some degree.

Automated checks of descriptive taxonomic research are conceivable because the components of published taxonomy are representations of reported facts that can be readily atomised into their component parts (Penev et al., 2009). Subjecting these components to algorithmic validation has a number of possibilities. Examples include simple checks to confirm the presence of required text (e.g. material examined) and component data (e.g. bibliographical citations, figure and table numbers and legends); validation of common data standards (e.g. geolocative data for specimens); tests to ensure consistent and positive terminology is used in diagnoses and taxonomic keys; and even tests to detect misconduct such as those used to identify plagiarism.

Arguably some of these tests already exceed the likely capabilities of human reviewers and would dictate a consistent level of quality that could be defined by the taxonomic community in collaboration with those maintaining the software infrastructure. The initial impact would be to reduce the burden on reviewers, minimise the transaction costs associated with publication and speed up the dissemination of taxonomic work. There would also be a number of benefits for the authors. Parts of the publication could be assembled automatically (e.g. maps of specimens localities from the materials examined section) and removal of human peer review would allow real-time instant publication of descriptive research. The long-term effects could be even more profound. Facilitating the publication of small incremental advances in taxonomy (e.g. single-species redescriptions and revisions) would facilitate more prioritised taxonomic research driven by opportunity and immediate user need. This approach would, in some cases, remove the necessity to produce lengthy monographs and revisions that risk never being completed/published due to changing author and publisher priorities. More importantly, the greater use of automated peer review would enable manuscript corrections to be made in versioned documents without the lengthy processes and formal procedures currently needed to correct published errors. Such errors are commonplace, especially as many traditional taxonomic journals are no longer using copy-editors. Making the process of correcting errors as easy and accountable as editing a Wikipedia article would have a profound impact on the long-term quality of published taxonomic works.

Online experiments with new forms of peer review are not without precedent. Indeed, they are not even particularly new. The arXiv server[14], founded in 1991 by the physicist Paul Ginsparg, is an electronic archive and distribution server primarily for physics and mathematics articles. Highly regarded within the scientific community, arXiv receives roughly 5000 submissions each month, and in 2008 passed the half-a-million-article milestone (Ginsparg, 2008). Each article (called an e-print) is not peer reviewed but may be recategorised by moderators. More recent attempts to address the problem of quality control in science include *PLoS ONE*. This electronic journal covers primary research from any science and medicine discipline and employs a hybrid system in which submissions receive editorial peer review to ensure the work is rigorous but leave the wider scientific community to ascertain significance, post publication. This is achieved through user discussion and rating features that facilitate debate and comment. More explicit two-stage reviewing is employed by the editors of *Atmospheric Chemistry and Physics* and a growing number of sister journals published by the European Geosciences Union. Editorial peer review is accompanied by a fixed-term community review period during which interested parties are invited to comment. A final decision is taken at the end of this fixed term, resulting in rejection, revision or publication.

With the possible exception of arXiv, current attempts to revise scholarly peer review are evolutionary rather than revolutionary (Jefferson, 2006). So far as I am aware, nothing currently exists in scholarly circles along the lines of automated review that I have suggested for taxonomic descriptions. This is partly because the taxonomic data services needed to facilitate this process are insufficiently developed by the taxonomic community. In addition, most publishers lack the domain knowledge required to build such a specialised system. Even if they did, it is unlikely they would have sufficient commercial incentive since these systems would not

---

[14] http://arxiv.org

simply map to other larger and more lucrative descriptive sciences (e.g. chemistry and astronomy).

A bigger challenge to addressing the failings of peer review comes from perceptions within the broader scientific community. Peer review is widely portrayed as a quasi-sacred process that makes science our most objective truth teller. Any science that rejects peer review endangers their very classification as a science. For example, peer review is a precondition for indexing in biomedical databases such as PubMed. For taxonomy to reject traditional peer review, it will need an exceptionally convincing case that the alternative will substantially improve quality and drive-up standards.

The best case for reforms comes from the sheer volume and pace of taxonomic information enabled by the internet and publishing tools such as blogs (Akerman, 2006). A shortage of professional (paid) taxonomists to facilitate peer review coupled with rising amateur interest and new outlets for publishing information on the Web, has the potential to create a perfect storm unless novel approaches to review can be found. On the Web, review is not so much a method of quality control, but rather a filtering and distribution system. Almost anything published (e.g. blog posts, images, videos and short articles) is discoverable thanks to various search and discovery tools that are freely available. The challenge is in filtering and aggregating this content according to its relevance and merit for a particular audience. Online, plenty of websites let their readers decide what makes front-page news. For example, Slashdot[15] and Digg[16] are vibrant and useful news services where users submit stories and others vote them up or down. Readers can personalise 'their' front page according to their own interests, and comment on stories, providing a real-time counterpoint that is often as illuminating as the original article. These systems have a similar effect to peer review, but mostly act on content that has already been through some form of selection. Perhaps combining this form of human selection (crowdsourcing) with algorithmic checks and validation as part of an integrated publishing system offers an opportunity to genuinely challenge the primacy of traditional peer review, at least for the descriptive sciences like taxonomy.

21.4.3 Copyright and intellectual property

Technology has radically altered the way taxonomists and the wider scientific community generate, access and publish information. In consequence, scientists cannot help but come into contact with copyright law and intellectual property issues through everyday activities like browsing the Web, or publishing some text. Technology, heedless of copyright law, has developed modes that insert multiple acts of reproduction and transmission that are actionable events under copyright statutes (Boyle, 2009). Unchallenged, current copyright legislation is counterproductive for science, even in the parochial world of descriptive taxonomy.

---

[15] http://slashdot.org   [16] http://digg.com

Copyright law was developed to regulate the creation of copies. In an analogue world of books and other printed resources this meant that many uses of analogue works are unregulated and free. For example, the acts of reading, lending or selling a book are exempt from copyright law because these ordinary acts do not create a copy. In contrast, in the digital world almost every single use of a digital object creates copies that potentially trigger the reaction of copyright. This has occurred not because legislators or politicians changed the law; rather, it has occurred because the platform through which people gain access and create these works has changed. In short, copyright law was developed for a radically different objective and is being unthinkingly applied across a range of contexts that were never originally intended (Lessig, 2008).

The paradigm case in copyright law concerns certain professionals who depend upon an exclusive right to control copies of their work as part of their business model. Copyright is a means by which these professionals (e.g. musicians) exercise their claim to this exclusivity in order to secure profit. Copyright was not developed to address the needs of other communities that rely on different business models to sustain their activities. For example, most of the scholarly community secure funds as a condition of employment though publicly funded academic institutions and not (usually) through controlling access to the products of work. On the contrary, scholars usually seek the widest possible dissemination of their work, incentivised by the peer recognition they receive and (other things being equal) commensurate financial remuneration through their employer. This was recognised by the famous sociologist of science Robert Merton who wrote about the common ownership of scientific discoveries, through which scientists give up their intellectual property rights (including copyright) in exchange for peer recognition and esteem. Merton (1942) said that 'property rights in science are whittled down to a bare minimum by the rationale of the scientific ethic'. A similar argument can be made for amateur communities, e.g. amateur taxonomists, who incidentally significantly outnumber professional taxonomists, which by definition rely on a different business model to sustain their amateur interests.

Copyright, as the exclusive right to make copies, is harmful to the scientific ethic but is used successfully by publishers to incentivise their publishing efforts. This is achieved through the profit gained by publishers controlling access to their printed works. The tension created by this between publishers and scientists has led to the development of new business models for science publishing in which the author, and not the consumer, pays the publisher for disseminating works (Velterop, 2004). This model, termed 'Open Access', has been independently accompanied by the development of licences (notably the Creative Commons[17] licences). The combination of Open Access publishing and Creative Commons licences enables users to gain free access and reuse of content under the specific

---

[17] http://creativecommons.org

terms of the licence without having to refer back to the rights holder. To date, approximately 1000 scholarly journals have adopted Open Access (Electronic Publishing Services), although this is often withheld for a period so that recent journal content can be sold in the traditional way. In taxonomy just one publisher (Pensoft) has adopted wholesale Open Access by charging a modest fee to the author. Arguably this is because the economics of taxonomic research mean that most taxonomists (especially amateur taxonomists) do not have access to the funds required to pay the substantial fees of traditional commercial Open Access journals.

The problem of copyright is particularly profound for taxonomy, because taxonomic works are often multi-authored compilations that contain substantial elements drawn from other published work. For example, a taxonomic monograph may contain an identification key with illustrations sourced from many hundreds of different publications. Under current copyright law reproduction of these illustrations requires tracing the rights and securing permissions from hundreds (possibly thousands) of publishers who retain the image rights. This expensive and time-consuming process is often impossible because rights holders cannot be traced. In these cases the scholar must prove they have performed due diligence when attempting to trace the rights to these so-called 'Orphaned' works, before they can be used (DCMS-and-BIS, 2009). The situation is further compounded by the fact that property rights can extend beyond traditionally published works to facts held in databases. In the USA facts known in the public domain but retrieved from a database can retain copyright protection if the arrangement of the data is deemed to be 'sufficiently original'. In the European Union copyright protection only extends to databases if their contents are considered to be 'original literary works' (e.g. original work that is written, spoken or sung), but additional protection is automatically conferred to databases if 'there has been a substantial investment in obtaining, verifying or presenting the contents of the database' (further details in the UK *Copyright and Rights in Databases Regulations Act*, 1997). As such, databases of taxonomic facts, such as the Species 2000 checklist of taxonomic names[18] and the Thompson Reuters Index to Organism Names (ION[19]), assert these rights of protection (e.g. Harling and Bisby, 2004), hindering reuse of their factual contents and setting a precedent that encourages other taxonomic database creators to use the same restrictive practices. An unfortunate side effect of the rights problem in taxonomy is that some rights holders seek to aggressively brand derivative works containing elements of their products in an attempt to maintain the independent profile of their projects. For example, aggregation efforts like the Encyclopedia of Life are littered with logos of contributing projects, diminishing the incentive for fresh contributions.

[18] http://www.sp2000.org   [19] http://www.organismnames.com

The original copyright legislation was not conceived for future technical opportunities afforded by new technologies such as the internet and databases in scholarly research. Consequently our copyright legislation has grown into a patchwork of technical, inconsistent and complex rules that touch almost every act of the scholarly process (Lessig, 2008), even in parochial disciplines like taxonomy. This regime is blocking our legal access to mix and reuse scholarly research like taxonomic data. For taxonomy, our primary defence is that no one sufficiently cares to take action against our community. This is (usually) because there is little or no financial loss to the affected parties. Nevertheless, it would be dangerous to build a new paradigm for database-driven taxonomy on a foundation that is illegal. Therefore, we need to find ways to avoid these legal barriers for taxonomy to progress.

Wider use of Creative Commons licences is central to this process. These enable authors of content to legally define the freedoms they give in ways that can be read by ordinary people, lawyers (so they are legally enforceable) and computers through expressions written in computer code (specifically Resource Description Framework). This has been extended for science through the Science Commons[20] deeds that provide a legal framework for sharing science data, including physical objects through standardised material transfer agreements. As with the Creative Commons licences, these deeds have three layers of access providing versions that can be read and understood by scientists, lawyers and computers. The goals of this effort are to facilitate the scientific ethic of sharing through an efficient intellectual property framework. This addresses many of the unintended consequences of our outdated copyright legislation associated with changing technologies for the production and dissemination of scientific information.

21.5 Early solutions to e-publishing descriptive taxonomy

New technologies have created an opportunity to revolutionise how taxonomy is performed and shared. These lend themselves to new forms of publishing that transcend the traditional linear flow of information from author to reader. Taxonomists are beginning to experiment with virtual research environments (VREs) that enable real-time collaboration and dissemination of taxonomic information while simultaneously affording new opportunities for data stewardship, curation and data-mining. These environments, while highly experimental, offer an alternative vision for the practice of taxonomic research that challenges the purpose and definition of traditional taxonomic publishing.

---

[20] http://sciencecommons.org

The following review of VREs is not intended to be comprehensive. Rather it is intended to be illustrative of the diverse approaches taken to tackling these challenges. Most of these projects are experimental and suffer from problems of stability and sustainability inherent to new software development. Notably each has been developed within the taxonomic community, rather than via independent commercial publishers. This reflects the specialised needs and purposes of these environments as seen by the taxonomic community, rather than from a traditional publisher's perspective.

21.5.1 Scratchpads

Scratchpads[21] (Smith et al., 2009) were developed through European Union-funded European Distributed Institute of Taxonomy (EDIT)[22] project as a data-publishing framework for groups of people to create their own virtual research communities supporting natural history science. These cater to the particular needs of individual research communities through a common database and system architecture. This is based on the Drupal[23] content management system and provides a scalable, flexible resource that facilitates the collaboration of distributed communities of taxonomists. Sites are hosted, archived and backed-up by the Natural History Museum in London and are offered free to any scientist that completes an online registration form. Registrants assume responsibility for the contents of each site, which (on approval) are instantiated at web domains of their choice. The default Scratchpad template has workflows to support the upload and publication of bibliographies, image galleries, specimen records, character datasets, documents, maps and custom data defined by the contributor. These can be uploaded to the site *en masse* through spreadsheets or created *de novo* through editing interfaces that support entry for single and multiple data records. Data are classified and aggregated around a taxonomy supplied by the user or imported automatically from a service provided by the Encyclopedia of Life project. Authenticated users can optionally supplement these data with information drawn from high-quality web-accessible databases (e.g. GBIF and BHL). This facilitates the rapid construction, curation and publication of content-rich web pages about any taxon. Users can withhold public access to unregistered users or create private groups. However, all public content is published by default under a Creative Commons (by-nc-sa) licence, which is a condition of use for all site contributions except multimedia. In addition, selected data types (taxonomy, specimens and literature) can be accessed through web services using documented standards and protocols. High-level administrative functions, including the control of permissions, user roles and the development of new functionality, are centrally managed by the Scratchpad development team. However, site contents and access rights are owned and controlled by registered users with sufficient privileges as dictated by the site maintainers.

[21] http://scratchpads.eu [22] http://e-taxonomy.eu [23] http://drupal.org

The Scratchpad framework currently serves over 6600 active users across almost 550 sites, spanning scientific, amateur and citizen science audiences. Sites range in function from supporting the work of societies and conservation efforts to the production and dissemination of taxonomic checklists, peer-reviewed journal articles and electronic books. As a derivative of Drupal, the source code is covered by version 3 of the GNU General Public License and is available from a subversion repository (Scratchpad-SVN[24]).

21.5.2 MX (MatriX)

MX[25] is a web-based content management system that is conceptually analogous to the Scratchpad project. MX enables taxonomists working at multiple institutions to access the same, shared information and data to build and publish taxonomic and phylogenetic research. The system can be used for the collaborative coding, storage and manipulation of multiple data types (morphological, molecular, specimen, image, descriptive, bibliographical, label, collection and associated information) through a grid matrix-style editor. A series of tabs provides a simple workflow that allows the user to navigate these data types. These are connected to engines that dynamically publish content in various forms. These include multiple-entry and dichotomous online keys with taxonomic catalogues (e.g. MX-Keys[26]) associated host data (Diapriidae[27]); linked images from the MorphBank[28] image database and supports various data export formats. MX is also integrated with a simple ontology builder (Hymenoptera-Glossary[29]), such that controlled terms in blocks of descriptive text (e.g. anatomical characters) can automatically be linked to referenced and illustrated term definitions.

MX was developed by Matt Yoder and Krishna Dole as part of National Science Foundation-funded projects at Texas A&M University. It is an open source (MySQL[30], Apache[31], Ruby on Rails[32]) application that is principally used by researchers working on US-funded Hymenoptera systematics projects.

21.5.3 EDIT cyberplatform

The EDIT Platform for Cybertaxonomy (Cyberplatform[33]) is a collection of tools and services that integrate to cover various aspects of the taxonomic workflow. The workflow is grouped into various editing activities (taxonomic hierarchies, collection and specimen records, descriptions, documenting fieldwork, literature

---

[24] http://svn.scratchpads.eu/viewvc/scratchpads
[25] http://sourceforge.net/projects/mx-database
[26] http://hymenoptera.ucr.edu/mx-database
[27] http://www.diapriid.org/public/site/diapriid/home   [28] http://www.morphbank.net
[29] http://hymglossary.tamu.edu   [30] http://www.mysql.com
[31] http://www.apache.org   [32] http://rubyonrails.org   [33] http://wp5.e-taxonomy.eu

management and managing geographical information systems (GIS) data), culminating in tools to generate taxonomic manuscripts for publication. At the heart of the Cybertaxonomy platform is a database (the Common Data Model – CDM) that acts as a repository for data produced by individual or groups of taxonomists in the course of their work. The CDM also acts as a technical back-end for data services that can be accessed by developers through a software (Java[34]) library. The primary Cybertaxonomy platform components consist of a desktop taxonomic editor, software to build a data portal, the CDM Java Library, a specimen search portal plus various tools supporting GIS-related functions. This software is packaged in three forms to enable individuals, local research groups and distributed research groups to install respectively on a desktop computer, a local intranet or on the internet. At present the Cyberplatform is primarily used by three exemplar groups that are explicitly funded through EDIT to use this system, although selected components of the Cyberplatform are used more widely. Notably the CDM is used by several taxonomic communities, including the European Register of Marine Species (ERMS[35]) and the Euro+Med Plantbase project (Euro+Med[36], see Chapter 6, Jury, in this volume).

21.5.4 Cate

CATE (Creating A Taxonomic E-science) (CATE[37]; Godfray et al., 2007) is a web-based system developed to facilitate the construction of consensus or consolidated taxonomic hypotheses. These are presented and navigated through a taxonomic hierarchy containing data common to modern taxonomic monographs (e.g. nomenclatural information, descriptive data, specimen records, observations, images, molecular data). The taxonomic hierarchy and associated content is added through an online workflow that supports peer review, enabling authorities with editorial privileges to comment and amend contributions as required. CATE facilitates an incremental cycle of revision and publication, with the current consensus classification and alternative taxonomic hypotheses being presented to end users, but with earlier versions and withdrawn hypotheses preserved and archived. Contributions (referred to as 'proposals') are refereed and opinions sought from the taxonomic community before a committee decides whether they should be incorporated into the next edition of the consensus taxonomy. As such, CATE moves beyond the paradigm of a static publication, providing a means for taxonomists to revise and publish the latest taxonomy of a group with traditional peer review, while documenting and archiving previous incremental changes.

---

[34] http://www.java.com   [35] http://www.marbef.org/data/erms.php
[36] http://www.emplantbase.org
[37] http://www.tdwg.org/biodiv-projects/projects-database/view-project/521/

CATE was established for two model groups (plants belonging to the Arum[38] family and Sphingid hawkmoths[39]) in order to ensure that the system is compliant with the botanical and zoological codes of nomenclature. A significant component of the CATE project concerned the digitisation of specimens and literature relevant to the model taxa. Technically CATE is a Java web application based upon the Spring Web Flow[40] framework. Data are stored in a relational database (MySQL) that was developed in conjunction with the EDIT Common Data Model (see the EDIT Cyberplatform). The project is currently restricted to the two model organism groups. However, the principles developed within CATE are exploited as part of a larger initiative led by Royal Botanic Gardens, Kew, to develop a system supporting the construction of an online revision for all monocot plants. The eMonocot[41] project breaks the link between content management and presentation, allowing data from multiple systems to be displayed within a single portal. Content from CATE Araceae, contributing Scratchpads, PalmWeb (part of the EDIT Cyberplatform) and the World Checklist of Monocots[42] is aggregated and can be searched as a single dataset. This approach could serve as a model to other communities wanting to unify distributed resources. Researchers can contribute data to a consensus taxonomy, even if the source systems use different classifications. An innovative feature of this system is a two-way annotation tool that supports annotation and discussion of data across the portal and source systems.

21.5.5 Solanaceae Source

Solanaceae Source[43] is taxonomic database for members of the genus *Solanum* that has been published on the World Wide Web. The treatment is the result of the PBI Solanum project, a worldwide study funded by the National Science Foundation under the Planetary Biodiversity Inventory program. Nomenclatural data (e.g. type records, authors and publications) coupled with additional descriptive information, illustrations and keys have been sourced from existing modern monographs. These have been coupled with new work coordinated on the remaining groups to build a definitive web-based guide to Solanaceae. The information technology component of this project differs from others listed here in that the development of a generic information technology infrastructure capable of supporting other taxonomic projects was not the primary goal of

---

[38] http://www.cate-araceae.org (unavailable as of 22 July 2014)
[39] http://www.cate-sphingidae.org (unavailable as of 22 July 2014)
[40] http://www.springsource.org/webflow   [41] http://e-monocot.org
[42] http://www.kew.org/wcsp/monocots
[43] http://www.tdwg.org/biodiv-projects/projects-database/view-project/544/

Solanaceae Source. Instead, the project makes use of two botanical databases (BRAHMS at the Natural History Museum London and KeEmu at New York Botanical Gardens) to import and manage the information. These data are aggregated into a Solanaceae Scratchpad[44] and presented on the web in the form of taxonomic treatments. The goal is to use these tools to produce printed manuscripts of new taxonomic research in addition to a comprehensive web resource on *Solanum*.

21.5.6 Species File

Species File[45] is a collection of programs that provides access to, and manipulation of, taxonomic information stored in multiple databases. Each database provides detailed information about taxa contained within the scope of the 'apex taxon' and is coupled to a website that provides the means to interact with and modify information held within the database. Central to Species File functions is the means to store nomenclatural information in a way that is fully compliant with the codes of zoological nomenclature. The Species File development team has produced a template that contains the basic database table structure as well as the stored procedures, user-defined functions and views used by independent Species Files. The template is used as the starting point for new species file databases and is capable of a limited number of customisations.

Species File has been developed by David Eades and colleagues in conjunction with the Illinois Natural History Survey. It was conceived and developed to manage information on the insect order Orthoptera (Orthoptera-SpeciesFile[46]), but in recent years has been adopted by 10 other insect research communities. At the time of writing, Species File databases contain taxonomic information on almost 52 000 valid species (circa 85 000 names) of which roughly half come from Orthoptera Species File.

The Species File Group (SFG) has developed a template that contains the basic database table structure as well as the stored procedures, user-defined functions and views used by Species Files. The template is used as the starting point for new Species File databases (SpeciesFile-Databases[47]). Species File is a MS Visual Studio application. Programming for Species File is done with Visual Studio.NET. The Active Server Pages (ASP) use Visual Basic Script and client side programming is done using JavaScript.

---

[44] http://www.tdwg.org/biodiv-projects/projects-database/view-project/544/
[45] http://software.speciesfile.org
[46] http://orthoptera.speciesfile.org/HomePage/Orthoptera/HomePage.aspx
[47] http://software.speciesfile.org/HomePage/Software/SoftwareHomePage.aspx

21.6 The future of descriptive taxonomic publishing

We are drowning in information, while starving for wisdom. The world henceforth will be run by synthesizers, people able to put together the right information at the right time, think critically about it, and make important choices

E. O. Wilson, Harvard University

What is startling about many ongoing efforts within the practice of taxonomy is that they are not more effectively integrated. This generates redundancy as stakeholders both inside and outside the taxonomic community invest significant time discovering, reorganising, integrating and analysing these resources, usually at great expense. The examples of VREs highlighted here suggest a way forward that addresses many of these challenges. These offer a vision for not only automating aspects of publishing taxonomy, but also to apply new methods that have the potential to revolutionise how taxonomic research is practised. Such systems, with sufficient users, could enable the tackling of grand-challenge problems that are untenable by other means, because of the opportunities they create for large-scale stewardship, curation and mining of enormous collections of heterogeneous taxonomic data. Online observatories that engage new users for taxonomy are also conceivable, thanks to the ease with which taxonomic data can be repurposed and represented for different audiences from a database. Likewise, more rational development and use of research instrumentation could be planned, since this can be plugged into VREs to dramatically reduce barriers of time and distance (distance in the geographical, disciplinary and organisational sense) that would otherwise interfere with the construction and operation of these systems. In the near term, VREs for taxonomy might integrate with analytical tools that require enormous storage and computing capacity. For example, in the morphometric analysis of specimen images for automated identification, or the analysis of very large phylogenetic trees. In the longer term, VREs may be connected directly to research collections in major museums and herbaria, providing remote access to specimens for conducting taxonomic research.

Central to the transformation of descriptive taxonomy is the need to change our concept of publication. In a database the power of taxonomy is amplified by ingenuity through applications and uses unimagined by the original authors and distant from the original field. In a paper, taxonomy languishes in obscurity, inaccessible and unused by all but the most determined. At present publicly funded research requires 'classical' publications. These attract peer recognition that influences the authors' reputation, employment and research opportunities. Without expanding the concept and recognition of publications that embrace alternative forms of dissemination, the chances of transforming taxonomy are significantly diminished. Through tools like VREs the Web can be used as an instrument of scientific research, blending social and technical solutions to address challenges that are otherwise insurmountable. As these tools mature taxonomists, for their discipline to survive, must embrace them.

Acknowledgements

Thanks to Chris Lyal for inviting me to write this chapter and Dave Roberts for providing valuable comments and corrections.

References

Akerman, R. (2006). Evolving peer review for the internet. *Nature (online edition)*. DOI: 10.1038/nature04997.

Anonymous (2006). Peer review and fraud. *Nature*, **444**: 971–972.

Atkins, D., Borgman, C., Bindoff, N., et al. (2010). *Building a UK Foundation for the transformative enhancement of research and innovation. Report of the International Panel for the 2009 Review of the UK Research Councils e-Science Programme*. London: Research Council.

Benkler, Y. (2006). *The wealth of networks*, New Haven, CT: Yale University Press.

Bourne, P. (2005). Will a biological database be different from a biological journal? *PLoS Computational Biology*, **1**: e34.

Boyle, J. (2009). *The public domain: enclosing the commons of the mind*. New Haven, CT: Yale University Press.

Brown, D. J. (2008). *The impact of electronic publishing: the future for libraries and publishers*. München: K G Saur Verlag.

Clark, T., Martin, S. and Liefeld, T. (2004). Globally distributed object identification for biological knowledge bases. *Briefings in Bioinformatics*, **5**: 59–70.

Constable, H., Guralnick, R., Wieczorek, J., Spencer, C. and Peterson, A. T. (2010). VertNet: a new model for biodiversity data sharing. *PLoS Biology*, **8**: e1000309.

Dallwitz, M. J. (1980). A general system for coding taxonomic descriptions. *Taxon*, **29**: 41–46.

DCMS-and-BIS (2009). *Digital Britain*. London: The Stationery Office.

Duckworth, W. D., Genoways, H. H. and Rose, C. L. (1993). *Preserving natural science collections: chronicle of our environmental heritage*. Washington D.C.: National Institute for the Conservation of Cultural Property.

Electronic Publishing Services and Oppenheim, C. (2006). *2006 baseline report: an evidence-based analysis of data concerning scholarly journal publishing*. Research Information Network, Research Councils UK and the Department of Trade and Industry. Available at: http://www.rin.ac.uk/our-work/communicating-and-disseminating-research/uk-scholarly-journals-2006-baseline-report.

GBIF-Statistics (2010). *GBIF statistics*. Accessed 1 March 2010 from http://vocabularies.gbif.org.

Ginsparg, P. (2008). The global-village pioneers. *Physics World*, October 2008: 22–26.

Godfray, H. C. J., Clark, B. R., Kitching, I. J., Mayo, S. J. and Scoble, M. J. (2007).

The web and the structure of taxonomy. *Systematic Biology*, **56**: 943–955.

Grayson, L. (2002). *Evidence based policy and the quality of evidence: rethinking peer review*. London: ESRC UK Centre for Evidence Based Policy and Practice.

Hall, M. B. (2002). *Henry Oldenburg: shaping the Royal Society*. Oxford: Oxford University Press.

Hanken, J. (2010). The *Encyclopedia of Life*: a new digital resource for taxonomy. In *Systema naturae 250 – the Linnaean ark*, A. Polaszek (ed). Boca Raton, FL: CRC Press, pp. 127–135.

Harling, P. and Bisby, F. (2004). *Species 2000 Europa IPR licence and access agreements*. Reading: The University of Reading.

Hull, D. L. (1991). *Science as a process: an evolutionary account of the social and conceptual development of science*. Chicago, IL: University of Chicago Press.

IWGSC (2008). *Mission-critical infrastructure for federal science agencies. A report by the Interagency Working Group on Scientific Collections*. Washington D.C.: National Science and Technology Council.

Jefferson, T. (2006). Models of quality control for scientific research. *Nature (online edition)*. DOI: 10.1038/nature05031.

Johnson, N. F. (2010). Future taxonomy today: new tools applied to accelerate the taxonomic process. In *Systema naturae 250 – the Linnaean ark*, A. Polaszek (ed). Boca Raton, FL: CRC Press, pp. 137–147.

Krishtalka, L. and Humphrey, P. S. (2000). Can natural history museums capture the future? *BioScience*, **50**: 611–617.

Lessig, L. (2008). *Remix – making art and commerce thrive in the hybrid economy*. New York, NY: Penguin.

Merton, R. (1942). Science and technology in a democratic order. *Journal of Legal and Political Sociology*, **1**: 115–126.

Nentwich, M. (2006). Cyberinfrastructure for next generation scholarly publishing. In *New infrastructures for knowledge production*, C. M. Hine (ed.). London: Information Science Publishing, pp. 189–205.

Page, L., Brin, S., Motwani, R. and Winograd, T. (1999). *The PageRank citation ranking: bringing order to the Web. Technical report*. Stanford, CA: Stanford InfoLab.

Page, R. D. M. (2008). Biodiversity informatics: the challenge of linking data and the role of shared identifiers. *Briefings in Bioinformatics*, **9**: 345–354.

Penev, L., Erwin, T., Miller, J., et al. (2009). Publication and dissemination of datasets in taxonomy: *ZooKeys* working example. *ZooKeys*, **11**: 1–8.

Procter, R., Williams, R. and Steward, J. (2010). *Use and relevance of Web 2.0 resources for researchers*. London: Research Information Network.

Pruitt, K. D., Tatusova, T., Klimke, W. and Maglott, D. R. (2009). NCBI reference sequences: current status, policy and new initiatives. *Nucleic Acids Research*, **37**: D32–6.

Rinaldo, C. (2009). The Biodiversity Heritage Library: exposing the taxonomic literature. *Journal of Agricultural and Food Information*, **10**: 259–265.

Smith, V. S., Rycroft, S. D., Harman, K. T., Scott, B. and Roberts, D. (2009). Scratchpads: a data-publishing framework to build, share and manage information on the diversity of life. *BMC Bioinformatics*, **10**(Suppl. 14): S6. DOI: 10.1186/1471-2105-10-S14-S6.

TDWG-Statistics (2010). *TDWG biodiversity information projects of the world.* Accessed 1 March 2010 from http://www.tdwg.org/about-tdwg.

Velterop, J. (2004). Open Access: science publishing as science publishing should be. *Serials Review,* **30**: 308–309.

Walter, D. E. and Winterton, S. (2007). Keys and the crisis in taxonomy: extinction or reinvention? *Annual Review of Entomology,* **52**: 193–208.

22

DNA barcoding in floral and faunal research

S. E. MILLER

22.1 Introduction

As I write this chapter in mid 2012, the context in which floral and faunal research is done is changing rapidly. Demand for biodiversity information, especially to understand global change, is increasing. The technologies that are available for carrying out biodiversity research and for disseminating the results are changing dramatically. The funding processes and organisational cultures of the institutions that have been the traditional homes of such research are evolving. This creates new challenges and opportunities for floral and faunal research. This chapter will focus on the intersection of DNA barcoding with floral and faunal research, the opportunities that DNA barcoding offers for increasing the quality and quantity of such work, and its connectivity with related activities. I will discuss the opportunities for DNA barcoding and then provide an example from my own research. The essay focuses on plants and animals, but will include some reference to other organisms. Because of the rapid evolution of the underlying technologies, and the related social changes, this essay represents a 'slice of time', and I expect some of the conclusions will be out of date before it is published. While challenges remain, I believe this is an exciting time of renaissance for taxonomy (Miller, 2007).

A DNA barcode is a short gene sequence taken from standardised portions of the genome, used to identify species. Being DNA based, it can be used for specimens

Descriptive Taxonomy: The Foundation of Biodiversity Research, eds M. F. Watson, C. H. C. Lyal and C. A. Pendry. Published by Cambridge University Press.

without morphological characters necessary for traditional identifications, such as roots or immature insects. Being a short sequence, it can be extracted from material that has not been specially preserved, and can often be extracted from standard museum or herbarium specimens. Being from a standardised region allows the use of universal primers for unknown taxa and allows rapid compilation of a global reference library. The choice of gene regions has focused on species level identification. While barcoding is not intended as a tool for higher classification research or for population genetics research, sometimes the barcoding gene regions have useful information at those levels (Craft et al., 2010).

22.2 The present status of DNA barcoding

While molecular diagnostics have been used for many years, DNA barcoding as a global initiative started by Hebert et al. (2003), who, among other things, pointed out that a standardised choice of gene region for species-level diagnosis allows individual projects of whatever scale to contribute to a global reference library that becomes increasingly more powerful over time. Mitochondrial Cytochrome c oxidase I (COI) had been widely used in animals since Folmer et al. (1994) and was quickly adopted as a community standard following Hebert et al. (2003). Standardised gene regions for plants proved more challenging for technical reasons, but are now designated as rbcL and matK, with additional research on trnH-psbA (Hollingsworth et al., 2009). The nuclear ribosomal internal transcribed spacer (ITS) region has been selected as a universal DNA barcode marker for Fungi (Schoch et al., 2012). Explorations are under way in other taxa for appropriate standardised gene regions. The Consortium for the Barcode of Life (CBOL) was established in 2004 as an international membership organisation to help develop barcoding methodology and set standards, such as the 'barcode' reserved keyword in GenBank (Benson et al., 2012). GenBank[1] and its international partner databases, the European Molecular Biology Laboratory (EMBL) and the DNA Data Bank of Japan (DDBJ), provide the archival database for barcode data, and the Barcode of Life Database[2] (BOLD) at the University of Guelph, Ontario, provides an informatics workbench aiding the acquisition, storage, analysis and publication of DNA barcode records, as well as providing public identification tools and other services (Ratnasingham and Hebert, 2007, 2013). At this time, BOLD includes over 1 700 000 barcode sequences from 160 000 named species and many as yet unidentified species, and growing rapidly. Recent reviews of the state of development of barcoding include Waugh (2007), Valentini et al. (2008), Casiraghi et al. (2010), Teletchea (2010), and Kato et al. (2012).

[1] http://www.ncbi.nlm.nih.gov/genbank/   [2] http://www.barcodeoflife.org/

22.3 How does barcoding change the approach to an inventory?

DNA barcoding provides an important tool to improve the quality or speed of floral and faunal studies, while, at the same time, such studies contribute to development of the global sequence library that is becoming an important community resource. The large-scale inventory of caterpillars, their hosts and their parasites in Costa Rica has provided an excellent example of how barcoding has changed the basic approach to an inventory project, starting with sampling, processing, identification, analysis, and even changing the approach to publication of results (Janzen et al., 2009; Janzen and Hallwachs 2011a, 2011b; see also Strutzenberger et al., 2010). In addition to the changes in work flow there have been significant impacts, from finding cryptic species to matching dimorphic males and females, which have substantially improved the quality and depth of the inventory, but also greatly multiplied the number of situations requiring further taxonomic work for resolution. Although the workflow issues differ between different habitats and taxa, other studies have demonstrated the use of barcoding in inventories of diverse taxa, including poorly known freshwater invertebrates (Zhou et al., 2009; Laforest et al., 2013), tropical sand flies (Azpurua et al., 2010; Krüger et al., 2011), bats in Southeast Asia (Francis et al., 2010), difficult to distinguish agricultural pest moths (Roe et al., 2006), pollinating insects in Africa (Nzeduru et al., 2012), diverse radiations of tropical weevils (Pinzón-Navarro et al., 2010a, 2010b; Tänzler et al., 2012), freshwater fishes in Africa (Swartz et al., 2008; Lowenstein et al., 2011), butterflies at country scales (Dinca et al., 2011; Hausmann et al., 2011), amphibians in Panama (Crawford et al., 2010) and trees in forest plots (Kress et al., 2009, 2010; Costion et al., 2011). Perhaps even greater opportunities for improving the speed and quality of inventories exist in the marine realm, where poorly known larval stages exist in vast quantities, and species concepts must be compared across vast oceanic distances (Goetze, 2010; Heimeier et al., 2010; Hubert et al., 2010; Stern et al., 2010; Plaisance et al., 2011; Ranasinghe et al., 2012). But for most efficient use of DNA barcoding, the appropriate sampling and data management needs to be incorporated from the beginning of the fieldwork (Leponce et al., 2010; Dick and Webb, 2012; Puillandre et al., 2012).

22.4 How does barcoding change the use of morphospecies?

Even in floral and faunal studies, in which most identifications are well-resolved to named species, there are usually a few species designated as informal morphospecies, because the samples available lack the diagnostic characters for morphological identification or the state of taxonomic knowledge does not allow identification. Traditionally, these informal designations are useful only within the local study, cannot be verified except for examination of voucher specimens and cannot be compared in a regional or temporal context. Regional and continental-scale comparisons are starting to become routine with DNA barcodes (see examples below), and Fernandez-Triana et al. (2011) recently used barcoding to compare changes in a local wasp community over 70 years using museum specimens.

DNA barcoding provides new tools for dealing with morphospecies, beyond the obvious facilitation of matches of unidentified specimens with named specimens (e.g. matching immature specimens with adults, or matching males and females). DNA barcoding provides a character-based diagnosis of the morphospecies (the DNA sequence) that can be made public (through GenBank) and can be compared with other species, whether identified or not. Pinzón-Navarro et al. (2010a, 2010b) were able to integrate historic knowledge of a diverse weevil group with larvae and adults reared from fruit in Panama, even though most of the species lacked taxonomic names. DNA barcoding can also provide an interim taxonomic designation, by way of the sequence, the GenBank accession number or the BOLD cluster reference number (BIN) (Schindel and Miller, 2010; Ratnasingham and Hebert, 2013).

22.5 Contribution of barcoding to quality control

The DNA barcode standard (and the restricted keyword barcode in GenBank, EMBL and DDBJ) bring a new standard of documentation and transparency to taxonomy, placing not only the sequence, but the metadata about the sequence and the voucher specimen, in the public record. This will become increasingly important in meeting standards of national and international regulation in fields such as agriculture, forestry and fisheries (Jones, F. C., 2008; de Waard et al., 2010; Floyd et al., 2010; Boykin et al., 2012), as well as emerging rules for access and benefit sharing under the Convention on Biological Diversity (Schindel, 2010). Newmaster and Ragupathy (2010) have applied DNA barcoding to quality control on traditional knowledge in ethnobotany, to test identifications of plants and to explore the presence of cryptic species.

22.6 Value added from the ability to compare regional biotas

DNA barcode data allows comparison of species concepts across geographical boundaries. For example, the taxonomy of the insect faunas of Australia and New Guinea were traditionally studied independently, but extensive DNA barcode surveys of Lepidoptera in both places are now allowing comparisons of the biogeo-graphical relationships in new depth (Holloway et al., 2009). It has always been challenging to assess small morphological variations across geographical barriers, such as defining the boundaries of species across islands. This was the case in the moth *Homona salaconis* (Meyrick), described from the Philippines but found on nearby islands including New Guinea (Hulcr et al., 2007), where addition of DNA data made the difference between the species as found in the Philippines and New Guinea clear, resulting in the recognition of the New Guinea species as *Homona auriga* (Durrant) (Miller et al., 2010). The Center for Tropical Forest Science's (CTFS's) global network of forest dynamic plots is now implementing barcoding across all the tree species in the plots (early results have been reported by Kress et al., 2009, 2010, 2012) and the National Ecological Observatory Network (NEON) is implementing the barcoding of selected insect groups across North America (Gibson et al., 2012).

Benefits go both ways between floral and faunal work and DNA barcoding. The 18-volume faunal work *The moths of Borneo* completed in 2011 (Holloway, 2011), while based on morphology, began to use DNA data to resolve some taxonomic problems and also pointed out taxonomic and biogeographical problems to which others have started to apply DNA barcode data. The existence of *The moths of Borneo* series itself encouraged Erik Van Nieukerken to undertake a faunal study on moths in Borneo testing the application of DNA barcoding (E. Van Nieukerken, pers. comm.).

While many barcoding studies to date have focused on patterns of local diversity, including recognition of cryptic species, barcoding shows great promise for the analysis of supposedly widespread species, and the identification of invasive spe-cies (Smith and Fisher, 2009; Hulcr et al., 2007; Floyd et al., 2010). One of the great values of the creation of global DNA barcode libraries is the opportunity for unexpected matches across the world.

22.7 Opportunities for meta-analysis: phylogeography and community phylogenies

Floral and faunal studies have always provided the raw data for biogeographical studies, and increasingly provide the raw data for the coalescence of the fields of ecology and evolution in phylogeography. While phylogeography might often best be done with longer sequences and more genes, DNA barcode data offer distinct advantages in many cases, being relatively inexpensive to produce with high throughput methods and having the benefit of large comparative libraries for many taxa (Craft et al., 2010). For example, Craft et al. (2010) were able to sample COI haplotypes from 28 Lepidoptera species and 1359 individuals across 4 host plant genera and 8 sites in New Guinea to estimate population divergence in relation to host specificity and geography, a much larger dataset than most previously published phylogeographical analyses, which had tended to focus on single species. The possibilities for community phylogenetic analyses using large quantities of DNA barcode data are exciting, especially in organisms such as hosts and their parasites, and herbivorous insects and their host plants (Kress et al., 2009, 2010; Emerson et al., 2011).

22.8 Comparing trophic interactions across multiple levels

Traditionally, understanding ecological relationships across multiple trophic levels required time-consuming and expensive rearing or field observations. DNA barcoding is now being used to characterise food items from insect guts (Greenstone et al., 2005; Jurado-Rivera et al., 2009), fish stomachs (Valdez-Moreno et al., 2012) or mammal faeces (Bohmann et al., 2011; Clare et al., 2011; Pompanon et al., 2012), dead hosts of parasites from their larval remains (Hrcek et al., 2011), insect parasitoids dissected from caterpillars (Hrcek et al., 2011), hosts from DNA remaining in parasites (Rougerie et al., 2011) and bloodmeals in ticks (Gariepy et al., 2012). Kaartinen et al. (2010), Hrcek et al. (2011) and Smith et al. (2012) have applied DNA barcoding to the analysis of complex insect food webs. As techniques for handling degraded DNA improve and DNA libraries expand, we can expect these techniques to be widely used. In the near future, I expect that a single caterpillar can be sampled and, in addition to identification of the caterpillar itself, DNA barcoding will allow identification of its plant diet, its insect parasites, and its microbial symbionts.

22.9 Identification of immature and dimorphic stages

As noted above, faunal and floral studies are plagued by specimens in immature stages that lack the characters necessary for identification, or sexes that cannot be matched, especially if they are dimorphic such as some insects in which the sexes vary dramatically in size or colour (Pinzón-Navarro et al., 2010a, 2010b). Richard et al. (2010) have used barcoding to identify earthworm juveniles in soil ecology studies. Plants sampled only in 'vegetative' stages are a widespread problem in floral studies. Even long-term studies of forest tree plots often have individual trees that remain unidentified for years because of the duration between flowering in many tropical trees (e.g. Lafrankie et al., 2005). The ability to identify plant roots and shoots using DNA will dramatically change the depth of ecological analysis that is possible (Jones, F. A., et al., 2011).

22.10 Environmental samples

One of the exciting horizons for expansion of DNA barcoding is the application of DNA barcode libraries to the identification and quantification of species in environmental samples that have been sequenced using next-generation sequencing techniques (Pfrender et al., 2010; Hajibabaei et al., 2011; Baird and Hajibabaei, 2012). Although the technique has not yet been applied widely, interesting demonstrations are being published, such as the identification of frog DNA in water samples (Ficetola et al., 2008), phylogeography of soil invertebrates (Emerson et al., 2011) and the interesting case of insect DNA from alcohol preservative (the 'worm' in mescal liquor) (Shokralla et al., 2010). Related research is finding that, in many cases, sequences that are shorter than the standard 648 base-pair animal barcodes have almost as much information content as the full-length barcodes, still allowing species identifications (Meusnier et al., 2008; Lees et al., 2010) and opening greater opportunities for the use of next-generation sequencing.

22.11 An example of the impact of DNA barcoding in insect faunistic studies

For many years I have been involved in local inventories of Lepidoptera (butterflies and moths), especially in Papua New Guinea (PNG) and Kenya. The work in PNG involves the large-scale rearing of caterpillars to adults, as part of the analysis of ecological and biogeographical patterns among host plants, caterpillars and their parasites (e.g. Miller et al., 2003, 2013; Craft et al., 2010; Novotny et al., 2012). The PNG research started in 1994 with parataxonomists taking the first pass at morpho-species identifications, with the aid of a database with images as a working identification tool (Basset et al., 2000, 2004), then a review in my laboratory based on external morphology and then extensive dissection of genitalia, to purify species concepts and to associate the species concepts with species names based on published revisions or type specimens. This process worked well, but involved the preparation of large quantities of genitalic dissections and, thus, was relatively expensive and time-consuming. I started collaborating with Paul Hebert in DNA barcoding in 2003, but did not start processing large quantities of DNA barcode samples until 2005. In the early stages, we used DNA barcoding to solve problems that morphology alone could not resolve, such as matching males and females, and clarifying species limits in polymorphic species. Adamski et al. (2010) is an example of a hybrid product during this transitional period – we did a traditional morphology-based analysis of African Blastobasinae moths in the early 2000s, then tested it with DNA barcodes in the mid 2000s and then eventually published the joint results.

In recent years we have shifted the work process to put the emphasis on DNA barcodes, because of their accuracy and cost-effectiveness. We still use genitalic dissections, both for delimiting species concepts and for matching with names, but use the barcode analysis to guide which specimens should be dissected. This has reversed the relative importance of barcodes and genitalic morphology in our work process, allowing faster and higher quality results. Because we are able to do DNA barcodes for more specimens than were dissected under the old system, we have more data for species concept delimitation, and we catch more errors in association of individuals with species concepts (for example, poor quality specimens). Similar projects in Costa Rica and Canada have gone through a similar transition in work process (de Waard et al., 2009; Janzen et al., 2009; Janzen and Hallwachs 2011a, 2011b).

A collection of Lepidoptera reared from native fruits in PNG in 2008–2009 provides an example of the new process of using barcoding. While there are some lineages of Lepidoptera that specialise in using fruit as larval hosts, rearing Lepidoptera from fruit is a time-consuming, messy and relatively low-yield activity, so it is rarely done on a mass scale, but the results are interesting. In addition to the ecology of fruit feeding, Lepidoptera in PNG being poorly known, many of the Microlepidoptera that are fruit specialists are very poorly known globally and the PNG fauna is almost unknown. While a few of the butterflies are well-known, even family-level identifications prove challenging for some of the tiny moths. Thus, I was both delighted and daunted to receive the first instalment of Lepidoptera reared from about 4000 lots of native fruit in PNG, in a programme organised by Richard Ctvrtecka.

The collection had been sorted into 70 morphospecies by the parataxonomists in PNG, and included between 1 and 20 specimens for each of the morphospecies, with many morphospecies represented by only a few specimens. After an initial assessment by external morphology (including a few splits in morphospecies), we sent up to five individuals per morphospecies to the University of Guelph for sequencing using their standard protocols (Craft et al., 2010; Wilson, 2012). This yielded 227 sequences, covering all morphospecies, deposited in GenBank as accession numbers GU695412–5, GU695431–2, GU695434–66, GU695468–9, GU695504–46, GU695548–58, GU695561, GU695575–80, GU695623–36, GU695639–701, GU695716–7, GU695720–1, GU695745, HM376367–75, HM376381–4, HM422448–56, HM902704–15, HQ947496–7, HQ956600–1 and HQ956613–4. The result of barcoding, confirmed by genitalic morphology, is 79 species. Two morphospecies were represented by unique individuals in poor condition that were shown by barcoding to belong to existing morphospecies. Eleven morphospecies were split, in seven cases because of unique individuals in poor condition that were incorrectly identified based on external morphology. This confirms the high quality of the sorting of our PNG parataxonomists, given that they are using only external morphology.

The barcode library in BOLD is becoming rich enough in many parts of the Lepidoptera to be useful in identification of unknowns, especially North America (Hebert et al., 2010), but also other regions such as Costa Rica and Australia. For example, one of the species was identified as the cosmopolitan tineid pest *Phereoeca uterella*, and several Phycitinae, a very difficult group taxonomically, were immediately identified to genus because of samples from Australia that Marianne Horak had provided to BOLD. By contrast, BOLD has been less useful for associating weevils reared from the same fruit, because the taxonomic sampling in BOLD remains small (some 13 000 sequences of Curculionidae in BOLD in July 2012 compared to 114 000 sequences of Geometridae, for example). But this shows how increasingly useful BOLD will become as more projects contribute reference sequences.

Following purification of species concepts, we have targeted genitalic dissections to confirm the barcoding results and to allow comparison with type specimens. About two-thirds of the species have been positively identified (either as known taxa or as new species) through consultation with literature, the collections in Washington, D.C. and London and assistance from colleagues. The identification process will continue for some time, because many of the Microlepidoptera types have never been dissected and properly placed in modern generic concepts.

22.12 Conclusions

DNA barcoding builds on the best of the traditional strengths of floral and faunal research based on morphological identifications of voucher specimens, especially in enhancing the quality of identifications for named species and in enhancing the information associated with informal morphospecies designations. While DNA barcoding can be applied 'after the fact,' it is most cost-effective to plan the appropriate sampling and data management from the beginning of fieldwork. Floristic and faunistic works have traditionally been descriptions of areas at a given point in time, limited by the species concepts available at the time. DNA barcodes, along with modern information management systems for other characters, allow the local species (or morphospecies) concepts to be seen as part of a dynamic global taxonomy that can be repeatedly queried in the context of changing questions.

Acknowledgements

I thank many colleagues and funding agencies, especially the Sloan Foundation, for the opportunity to be part of the development of DNA barcoding through the Consortium for the Barcode of Life and the International Barcode of Life. David

Schindel and other Consortium for the Barcode of Life colleagues helped develop many of the ideas discussed here. The barcode library of Papua New Guinea Lepidoptera was built from US National Science Foundation-funded research since 1995 (including DEB 0841885) in collaboration with Vojtech Novotny, George Weiblen and Yves Basset, and also supported by the Czech Science Foundation, the Czech Ministry of Education, and the Grant Agency of the University of South Bohemia. The Papua New Guinea fruit Lepidoptera fieldwork was coordinated by Richard Ctvrtecka, and the DNA barcoding was undertaken with assistance of Lauren Helgen and Margaret Rosati, with sequencing provided through the Biodiversity Institute of Ontario with funding from Genome Canada and the Ontario Genomics Institute (2008-0GI-ICI-03). The Natural History Museum, London, provided access to type specimens. Chris Lyal provided helpful editorial comments and tolerated my distractions.

References

Adamski, D., Copeland, R. S., Miller, S. E., Hebert, P. D. N., Darrow, K. and Luke, Q. (2010). A review of African Blastobasinae (Lepidoptera: Gelechioidea: Coleophoridae), with new taxa reared from native fruits in Kenya. *Smithsonian Contributions to Zoology*, **630**: vi + 68.

Azpurua, J., De La Cruz, D., Valderama, A. and Windsor, D. (2010). *Lutzomyia* Sand Fly diversity and rates of infection by *Wolbachia* and an exotic *Leishmania* species on Barro Colorado Island, Panama. *PLoS Neglected Tropical Diseases*, **4**(3): e627.

Baird, D. J. and Hajibabaei, M. (2012). Biomonitoring 2.0: a new paradigm in ecosystem assessment made possible by next-generation DNA sequencing. *Molecular Ecology*, **21**: 2039-2044.

Basset, Y., Novotny, V., Miller, S. E. and Pyle, R. (2000). Quantifying biodiversity: experience with parataxonomists and digital photography in Papua New Guinea and Guyana. *BioScience*, **50**: 899-908.

Basset, Y., Novotny, V., Miller, S. E., Weiblen, G. D., Missa, O. and Stewart, A. J. A. (2004). Conservation and biological monitoring of tropical forests: the role of parataxonomists. *Journal of Applied Ecology*, **41**: 163-174.

Benson, D. A., Karsch-Mizrachi, I., Clark, K., Lipman, D. J., Ostell, J. and Sayers, E. W. (2012). GenBank. *Nucleic Acids Research*, **40**(D1): D48-D53.

Bohmann, K., Monadjem, A., Lehmkuhl Noer, C., Rasmussen, M., Seale, M. R., Clare, E., Jones, G., Willerslev, E. and Gilbert, M. T. (2011). Molecular diet analysis of two African free-tailed bats (Molossidae) using high throughput sequencing. *PLoS ONE*, **6**(6): e21441.

Boykin, L. M., Armstrong, K. F., Kubatko, L. and De Barro, P. (2012). Species delimitation and global biosecurity. *Evolutionary Bioinformatics Online*, **8**: 1-37.

Casiraghi, M., Labra, M., Ferri, E., Galimberti, A. and De Mattia, F. (2010). DNA barcoding: a six-question tour to improve users' awareness about the method. *Briefings in Bioinformatics*, **11**: 440–453.

Clare, E. L., Barber, B. R., Sweeney, B. W., Hebert, P. D. N. and Fenton, M. B. (2011). Eating local: influences of habitat on the diet of little brown bats (*Myotis lucifugus*). *Molecular Ecology*, **20**: 1772–1780.

Costion, C., Ford, A., Cross, H., Crayn, D., Harrington, M. and Lowe, A. (2011). Plant DNA barcodes can accurately estimate species richness in poorly known floras. *PloS ONE*, **6**(11): e26841.

Craft, K. J., Pauls, S. U., Darrow, K., Miller, S. E., Hebert, P. D. N., Helgen, L. E., Novotny, V. and Weiblen, G. D. (2010). Population genetics of ecological communities with DNA barcodes: an example from New Guinea Lepidoptera. *Proceedings of the National Academy of Science U S A*, **107**: 5041–5046.

Crawford, A. J., Lips, K. R. and Bermingham, E. (2010). Epidemic disease decimates amphibian abundance, species diversity, and evolutionary history in the highlands of central Panama. *Proceedings of the National Academy of Sciences U S A*, **107**: 13777–13782.

de Waard, J. R., Landry, J. F., Schmidt, B. C., Derhousoff, J., McLean, J. A. and Humble, L. M. (2009). In the dark in a large urban park: DNA barcodes illuminate cryptic and introduced moth species. *Biodiversity and Conservation*, **18**: 3825–3839.

de Waard, J. R., Mitchell, A., Keena, M. A., Gopurenko, D., Boykin, L. M., Armstrong, K. F., Pogue, M. G., Lima, J., Floyd, R., Hanner, R. M. and Humble, L. M. (2010). Towards a global barcode library for *Lymantria* (Lepidoptera: Lymantriinae) tussock moths of biosecurity concern. *PLoS ONE*, **5**(12): e14280.

Dick, C. W. and Webb, C. O. (2012). Plant DNA barcodes, taxonomic management, and species discovery in tropical forests. In *DNA barcodes: methods and protocols*, W. J. Kress and D. L. Erickson (eds). New York, NY: Springer, pp. 379–393.

Dinca, V., Zakharov, E. V., Hebert, P. D. N. and Vila, R. (2011). Complete DNA barcode reference library for a country's butterfly fauna reveals high performance for temperate Europe. *Proceedings of the Royal Society B*, **278**: 347–355.

Emerson, B. C., Cicconardi, F., Fanciulli, P. P. and Shaw, P. J. (2011). Phylogeny, phylogeography, phylobetadiversity and the molecular analysis of biological communities. *Philosophical Transactions of the Royal Society of London B*, **366**: 2391–2402.

Fernandez-Triana, J., Smith, M. A., Boudreault, C., Goulet, H., Hebert, P. D. N., Smith, A. C. and Roughley, R. (2011). A poorly known high-latitude parasitoid wasp community: unexpected diversity and dramatic changes through time. *PloS ONE*, **6**(8): e23719.

Ficetola, G. F., Miaud, C., Pompanon, F. and Taberlet, P. (2008). Species detection using environmental DNA from water samples. *Biology Letters*, **4**: 423–425.

Floyd, R., Lima, J., de Waard, J., Humble, L. and Hanner, R. (2010). Common goals: policy implications of DNA barcoding as a protocol for identification of arthropod pests. *Biological Invasions*, **12**: 2947–2954.

Folmer, O., Black, M., Hoeh, W., Lutz, R. and Vrijenhoek, R. (1994). DNA primers for amplification of mitochondrial cytochrome c oxidase subunit I from diverse metazoan invertebrates. *Molecular Marine Biology and Biotechnology*, **3**: 294–299.

Francis, C. M., Borisenko, A. V,
Ivanova, N. V., Eger, J. L., Lim, B. K.,
Guillen-Servent, A., Kruskop, S. V.,
Mackie, I. and Hebert, P. D. N. (2010).
The role of DNA barcodes in
understanding and conservation of
mammal diversity in Southeast Asia.
PLoS ONE, **5**(9): e12575.

Gariepy, T. D., Lindsay, R., Ogden, N. and
Gregory, T. R. (2012). Identifying the last
supper: utility of the DNA barcode
library for bloodmeal identification in
ticks. *Molecular Ecology Resources*,
12: 646–652.

Gibson, C. M., Kao, R. H., Blevins, K. K.
and Travers, P. D. (2012). Integrative
taxonomy for continental-scale
terrestrial insect observations. *PLoS
ONE*, **7**(5): e37528.

Goetze, E. (2010). Species discovery in
marine planktonic invertebrates
through global molecular screening.
Molecular Ecology, **19**: 952–967.

Greenstone, M. H., Rowley, D. L.,
Heimbach, U., Lundgren, J. G.,
Pfannenstiel and R. S., Rehner, S. A.
(2005). Barcoding generalist predators
by polymerase chain reaction: carabids
and spiders. *Molecular Ecology*,
14: 3247–3266.

Hajibabaei, M., Shokralla, S., Zhou, X.,
Singer, G. A. and Baird, D. J. (2011).
Environmental barcoding: a next-
generation sequencing approach for
biomonitoring applications using river
benthos. *PLoS ONE*, **6**(4): e17497.

Hausmann, A., Haszprunar, G.,
Segerer, A. H., Speidel, W., Behounek, G.
and Hebert, P. D. N. (2011). Now DNA-
barcoded: the butterflies and larger
moths of Germany. *Spixiana*, **34**: 47–58.

Hebert, P. D. N, Cywinska, A., Ball, S. L. and
de Waard, J. R. (2003). Biological
identifications through DNA barcodes.
Proceedings of the Royal Society B,
270: 313–321.

Hebert, P. D. N., de Waard, R. J. and
Landry, J. F. (2010). DNA barcodes for
1/1000 of the animal kingdom. *Biology
Letters*, **6**: 359–362.

Heimeier, D., Lavery, S. and Sewell, M. A.
(2010). Using DNA barcoding and
phylogenetics to identify Antarctic
invertebrate larvae: lessons from
a large scale study. *Marine Genomics*,
3: 165–177.

Hollingsworth, P. M., Forrest, L. L.,
Spouge, J. L., Hajibabaei, M.,
Ratnasingham, S., van der Bank, M.,
Chase, M. W., Cowan, R. S.,
Erickson, D. L., Fazekas, A. J.,
Graham, S. W., James, K. E., et al. (2009).
A DNA barcode for land plants.
*Proceedings of the National Academy
of Sciences U S A*, **106**: 12794–12797.

Holloway, J. D. (2011). The moths of Borneo:
Families Phaudidae, Himantopteridae
and Zygaenidae; revised and annotated
checklist. *Malayan Nature Journal*,
63: 1–548.

Holloway, J. D., Miller, S. E., Pollock, D. M.,
Helgen, L. and Darrow, K. (2009).
GONGED (Geometridae of New Guinea
Electronic Database): a progress report
on development of an online facility of
images. *Spixiana*, **32**: 122.

Hrcek, J., Miller, S. E., Quicke, D. L. J. and
Smith, M. A. (2011). Molecular detection
of trophic links in a complex insect
host–parasitoid food web. *Molecular
Ecology Resources*, **11**: 786–794.

Hubert, N., Delrieu-Trottin, E., Irisson, J. O.,
Meyer, C. and Planes, S. (2010).
Identifying coral reef fish larvae through
DNA barcoding: a test case with the
families Acanthuridae and
Holocentridae. *Molecular Phylogenetics
and Evolution*, **55**: 1195–1203.

Hulcr, J., Miller, S. E, Setliff, G. P.,
Darrow, K., Mueller, N. D.,
Hebert, P. D. N., Weiblen, G. D. (2007).
DNA barcoding confirms polyphagy in a

generalist moth, *Homona mermerodes* (Lepidoptera: Tortricidae). *Molecular Ecology Notes*, **7**: 549–557.

Janzen, D. H., Hallwachs, W., Blandin, P., Burns, J. M., Cadiou, J. M., Chacon, I., Dapkey, T., Deans, A. R., Epstein, M., Espinoza, B., Franclemont, J., Haber, W., et al. (2009). Integration of DNA barcoding into an ongoing inventory of complex tropical biodiversity. *Molecular Ecology Resources*, **9** (Suppl 1): 1–26.

Janzen, D. H. and Hallwachs, W. (2011a). Joining inventory by parataxonomists with DNA Barcoding of a large complex tropical conserved wildland in Northwestern Costa Rica. *PLoS ONE*, **6**(8): e18123.

Janzen, D. H, Hallwachs, W., Burns, J. M., Hajibabaei, M., Bertrand, C., Hebert, P. D. N. (2011b). Reading the complex Skipper butterfly fauna of one tropical place. *PLoS ONE*, **6**(8): e19874.

Jones, F. A., Erickson, D. L., Bernal, M. A, Bermingham, E., Kress, W. J., Herre, E. A., Muller-Landau, H. C. and Turner, B. L. (2011). The roots of diversity: below ground species richness and rooting distributions in a tropical forest revealed by DNA barcodes and inverse modeling. *PLoS ONE*, **6**(9): e24506.

Jones, F. C. (2008). Taxonomic sufficiency: the influence of taxonomic resolution on freshwater bioassessments using benthic macroinvertebrates. *Environmental Reviews*, **16**: 45–69.

Jurado-Rivera, J. A., Vogler, A. P., Reid, C. A. M., Petitpierre, E. and Gómez-Zurita, J. (2009). DNA barcoding insect–host plant associations. *Proceedings of the Royal Society B*, **276**: 639–648.

Kaartinen, R., Stone, G. N., Hearn, J., Lohse, K. and Roslin, T. (2010). Revealing secret liaisons: DNA barcoding changes our understanding of food webs. *Ecological Entomology*, **35**: 623–638.

Kato, T., Jinbo, U. and Ito, M. (2012). DNA barcoding: a novel tool for observation of biodiversity. In *The biodiversity observation network in the Asia–Pacific region: toward further development of monitoring*, S.-I. Nakano (ed.). Japan: Springer, pp. 259–266.

Kress, W. J., Erickson, D. L., Jones, F. A., Swenson, N. G., Perez, R., Sanjur, O. and Bermingham, E. (2009). Plant DNA barcodes and a community phylogeny of a tropical forest dynamics plot in Panama. *Proceedings of the National Academy of Science U S A*, **106**: 18621–18626.

Kress, W. J., Erickson, D. L., Swenson, N. G., Thompson, J., Uriarte, M. and Zimmerman, J. K. (2010). Advances in the use of DNA barcodes to build a community phylogeny for tropical trees in a Puerto Rican forest Dynamics Plot. *PLoS ONE*, **5**(11): e15409.

Kress, W. J., Lopez, I. C. and Erickson, D. L. (2012). Generating plant DNA barcodes for trees in long-term forest Dynamics Plots. In *DNA barcodes: methods and protocols*, W. J. Kress and D. L. Erickson (eds). New York: Springer, pp. 441–458.

Krüger, A., Strüven, L., Post, R. L. and Faulde, M. (2011). The sandflies (Diptera: Psychodidae, Phlebotominae) in military camps in northern Afghanistan (2007–2009), as identified by morphology and DNA 'barcoding'. *Annals of Tropical Medicine and Parasitology*, **105**: 163–176.

Laforest, B. J., Winegardner, A. K., Zaheer, O. A., Jeffery, N. W., Boyle, E. E. and Adamowicz, S. J. (2013). Insights into biodiversity sampling strategies for freshwater microinvertebrate faunas through bioblitz campaigns and DNA barcoding. *BMC Ecology*, **13**(1): 13.

Lafrankie, J. V., Davies, S. J., Wang, L. K., Lee, S. K and Lum, S. K. Y. (2005). *Forest trees of Bukit Timah: population ecology in a tropical forest fragment.* Singapore: Simply Green.

Lees, D. C., Rougerie, R., Zeller-Lukashort, C. and Kristensen, N. P. (2010). DNA mini-barcodes in taxonomic assignment: a morphologically unique new homoneurous moth clade from the Indian Himalayas described in *Micropterix* (Lepidoptera, Micropterigidae). *Zoologica Scripta*, **39**: 642–661.

Leponce, M., Meyer, C., Haeuser, C. L., Bouchet, P., Delabie, J. H. C., Weigt, L. and Basset, Y. (2010). Challenges and solutions for planning and implementing large-scale biotic inventories. In *Manual on field recording techniques and protocols for all taxa biodiversity inventories and monitoring*, J. Eymann, J. Degreef, C. Häuser, J. C. Monje, Y. Samyn and D. VandenSpiegel (eds). Brussels: Belgian Development Cooperation, pp. 18–48.

Lowenstein, J. H., Osmundson, T. W., Becker, S., Hanner, R. and Stiassny, M. L. (2011). Incorporating DNA barcodes into a multi-year inventory of the fishes of the hyperdiverse Lower Congo River, with a multi-gene performance assessment of the genus *Labeo* as a case study. *Mitochondrial DNA*, **22** (Suppl 1): 52–70.

Meusnier, I., Singer, G. A. C., Landry, J. F., Hickey, D. A., Hebert, P. D. N. and Hajibabaei, M. (2008). A universal DNA mini-barcode for biodiversity analysis. *BMC Genomics*, **9**: 214.

Miller, S. E. (2007). DNA barcoding and the renaissance of taxonomy. *Proceedings of the National Academy of Science U S A*, **104**: 4775–4776.

Miller, S. E., Novotny, V. and Basset, Y. (2003). Studies on New Guinea moths. 1. Introduction (Lepidoptera). *Proceedings of the Entomological Society of Washington*, **105**: 1035–1043.

Miller, S. E., Helgen, L. E. and Hebert, P. D. N. (2010). Clarification of the identity of *Homona salaconis* (Lepidoptera: Tortricidae). *Molecular Ecology Resources*, **10**: 580.

Miller, S. E., Hrcek, J., Novotny, V., Weiblen, G. D. and Hebert, P. D. N. (2013). DNA barcodes of caterpillars (Lepidoptera) from Papua New Guinea. *Proceedings of the Entomological Society of Washington*, **115**: 107–109.

Newmaster, S. G. and Ragupathy, S. (2010). Ethnobotany genomics – discovery and innovation in a new era of exploratory research. *Journal of Ethnobiology and Ethnomedicine*, **6**: 2.

Novotny, V., Miller, S. E., Hrcek, J., Baje, L., Basset, Y., Lewis, O. T., Stewart, A. J. A. and Weiblen, G. D. (2012). Insects on plants: explaining the paradox of low diversity within specialist herbivore guilds. *American Naturalist*, **179**: 351–362.

Nzeduru, C. V., Ronca, S. and Wilkinson, M. J. (2012). DNA barcoding simplifies environmental risk assessment of genetically modified crops in biodiverse regions. *PLoS ONE*, **7**(5): e35929.

Pfrender, M. E., Hawkins, C. P., Bagley, M., Courtney, G. W., Creutzburg, B. R., Epler, J. H., Fend, S., Schindel, D., Ferrington, L. C. Jr, Hartzell, P. L., Jackson, S., Larsen, D. P., et al. (2010). Assessing macroinvertebrate biodiversity in freshwater ecosystems: advances and challenges in DNA-based approaches. *Quarterly Review of Biology*, **85**: 319–340.

Pinzón-Navarro, S., Barrios, H., Múrria, C., Lyal, C. H. C. and Vogler, A. P. (2010a).

DNA-based taxonomy of larval stages reveals huge unknown species diversity in Neotropical seed weevils (genus *Conotrachelus*): relevance to evolutionary ecology. *Molecular Phylogenetics and Evolution*, **56**: 281–293.

Pinzón-Navarro, S., Jurado-Rivera, J. A., Gomez-Zurita, J., Lyal, C. H. C. and Vogler, A. P. (2010b). DNA profiling of host–herbivore interactions in tropical forests. *Systematic Entomology*, **35** (Suppl 1): 18–32.

Plaisance, L., Caley, M. J., Brainard, R. E. and Knowlton, N. (2011). The diversity of coral reefs: what are we missing? *PLoS ONE*, **6**(10): e25026.

Pompanon, F., Deagle, B. E., Symondson, W. O. C., Brown, D. S., Jarman, S. N. and Taberlet, P. (2012). Who is eating what: diet assessment using next generation sequencing. *Molecular Ecology*, **21**: 1931–1950.

Puillandre, N., Bouchet, P., Boisselier-Dubayle, M. C., Brisset, J., Buge, B., Castelin, M., Chagnoux, S., Christophe, T., Corbari, L., Lambourdière, J., Lozouet, P., Marani, G., et al. (2012). New taxonomy and old collections: integrating DNA barcoding into the collection curation process. *Molecular Ecology Resources*, **12**: 396–402.

Ranasinghe, J. A., Stein, E. D., Miller, P. E. and Weisberg, S. B. (2012). Performance of two southern California benthic community condition indices using species abundance and presence-only data: relevance to DNA barcoding. *PLoS ONE*, **7**(8): e40875.

Ratnasingham, S. and Hebert, P. D. N. (2007). BOLD: the barcode of life data system (http://www.barcodinglife.org). *Molecular Ecology Notes*, **7**: 355–364.

Ratnasingham, S. and Hebert, P. D. N. (2013). A DNA-based registry for all animal species: the barcode index number (BIN) system. *PLoS ONE*, **8**(7): e66213.

Richard, B., Decaens, T., Rougerie, R., James, S. W., Porco, D. and Hebert, P. D. N. (2010). Re-integrating earthworm juveniles into soil biodiversity studies: species identification through DNA barcoding. *Molecular Ecology Resources*, **10**: 606–614.

Roe, A. D., Stein, J. D., Gillette, N. E. and Sperling, F. A. H. (2006). Identification of *Dioryctria* (Lepidoptera: Pyralidae) in a seed orchard at Chico, California. *Annals of the Entomological Society of America*, **99**: 433–448.

Rougerie, R., Smith, M. A., Fernandez-Triana, J., Lopez-Vaamonde, C., Ratnasingham, S. and Hebert, P. D. N. (2011). Molecular analysis of parasitoid linkages (MAPL): gut contents of adult parasitoid wasps reveal larval host. *Molecular Ecology*, **20**: 179–186.

Schindel, D. E. (2010). Biology without borders. *Nature*, **467**: 779–781.

Schindel, D. E. and Miller, S. E. (2010). Provisional nomenclature: the on-ramp to taxonomic names. In *Systema naturae 250: the Linnaean ark*, A. Polaszek (ed.). Boca Raton, FL: CRC Press, pp. 109–115.

Schoch, C. L., Seifert, K. A., Huhndorf, S., Robert, V., Spouge, J. L., Levesque, C. A., Chen, W. and the Fungal Barcoding Consortium. (2012). Nuclear ribosomal internal transcribed spacer (ITS) region as a universal DNA barcode marker for Fungi. *Proceedings of the National Academy of Science U S A*, **109**: 6241–6246.

Shokralla, S., Singer G. A. C. and Hajibabaei, M. (2010). Direct PCR amplification and sequencing of specimens' DNA from preservative ethanol. *BioTechniques*, **48**: 233–234.

Smith, M. A. and Fisher, B. L. (2009). Invasions, DNA barcodes, and rapid biodiversity assessment using ants of Mauritius. *Frontiers in Zoology*, **6**(1): 31.

Smith, M. A., Bertrand, C., Crosby, K., Eveleigh, E. S., Fernandez-Triana, J., Fisher, B. L., Gibbs, J., Hajibabeaei, M., Hallwachs, W., Hind, K., Hrcek, J., Huang, D.-W., et al. (2012). Wolbachia and DNA barcoding insects: patterns, potential and problems. *PloS ONE*, **7**(5): e36514.

Stern, R. F., Horak, A., Andrew, R. L., Coffroth, M. A., Andersen, R. A., Küpper, F. C., Jameson, I., Hoppenrath, M., Véron, B., Kasai, F., Brand, J., James, E. R. et al. (2010). Environmental barcoding reveals massive dinoflagellate diversity in marine environments. *PLoS ONE*, **5**(11): e13991.

Strutzenberger, P., Brehm, G. and Fiedler, K. (2010). DNA barcoding-based species delimitation increases species count of *Eois* (Geometridae) moths in a well-studied tropical mountain forest by up to 50%. *Insect Science*, **18**: 349–362.

Swartz, E. R., Mwale, M., Hanner, R. (2008). A role for barcoding in the study of African fish diversity and conservation. *South African Journal of Science*, **104**: 293–298.

Tänzler, R., Sagata, K., Surbakti, S., Balke, M. and Riedel, A. (2012). DNA barcoding for community ecology – how to tackle a hyperdiverse, mostly undescribed Melanesian fauna. *PLoS ONE*, **7**(1): e28832.

Teletchea, F. (2010). After 7 years and 1000 citations: Comparative assessment of the DNA barcoding and the DNA taxonomy proposals for taxonomists and non-taxonomists. *Mitochondrial DNA*, **21**: 206–226.

Valdez-Moreno, M., Quintal-Lizama, C., Gómez-Lozano, R. and García-Rivas, M. del C. (2012). Monitoring an alien invasion: DNA barcoding and the identification of lionfish and their prey on coral reefs of the Mexican Caribbean. *PLoS ONE*, **7**(6): e36636.

Valentini, A. Pompanon, F. and Taberlet, P. (2008). DNA barcoding for ecologists. *Trends in Ecology and Evolution*, **24**: 110–117.

Waugh, J. (2007). DNA barcoding in animal species: progress, potential and pitfalls. *BioEssays*, **29**: 188–197.

Wilson, J. J. (2012). DNA barcodes for insects. In *DNA barcodes: methods and protocols*, W. J. Kress and D. L. Erickson (eds). New York, NY: Springer, pp. 17–46.

Zhou, X., Adamowicz, S. J., Jacobus, L. M., Dewalt, R. E. and Hebert, P. D. N. (2009). Towards a comprehensive barcode library for arctic life – Ephemeroptera, Plecoptera, and Trichoptera of Churchill, Manitoba, Canada. *Frontiers in Zoology*, **6**(1): 30.

Index

Systematics Association Publications

1. Bibliography of Key Works for the Identification of the British Fauna and Flora, 3rd edition (1967)[†]
   Edited by G. J. Kerrich, R. D. Meikie and N. Tebble

2. The Species Concept in Palaeontology (1956)[†]
   Edited by P. C. Sylvester-Bradle

3. Function and Taxonomic Importance (1959)[†]
   Edited by A. J. Cain

4. Taxonomy and Geography (1962)[†]
   Edited by D. Nichols

5. Speciation in the Sea (1963)[†]
   Edited by J. P. Harding and N. Tebble

6. Phenetic and Phylogenetic Classification (1964)[†]
   Edited by V. H. Heywood and J. McNeill

7. Aspects of Tethyan Biogeography (1967)[†]
   Edited by C. G. Adams and D. V. Ager

8. The Soil Ecosystem (1969)[†]
   Edited by H. Sheals

9. Organisms and Continents through Time (1973)[*]
   Edited by N. F. Hughes

10. Cladistics: A Practical Course in Systematics (1992)[‡]
    P. L. Forey, C. J. Humphries, I. J. Kitching, R. W. Scotland, D. J. Siebert and D. M. Williams

11. Cladistics: The Theory and Practice of Parsimony Analysis, 2nd edition (1998)[‡]
    I. J. Kitching, P. L. Forey, C. J. Humphries and D. M. Williams

---

[†] Published by the Systematics Association (out of print)
[*] Published by the Palaeontological Association in conjunction with the Systematics Association
[‡] Published by Oxford University Press for the Systematics Association

Systematics Association Special Volumes

15. The Terrestrial Environment and the Origin of Land Vertebrates (1980)[*]
    Edited by A. L. Panchen

16. Chemosystematics: Principles and Practice (1980)[*]
    Edited by F. A. Bisby, J. G. Vaughan and C. A. Wright

17. The Shore Environment: Methods and Ecosystems (2 volumes) (1980)[*]
    Edited by J. H. Price, D. E. C. Irvine and W. F. Farnham

18. The Ammonoidea (1981)[*]
    Edited by M. R. House and J. R. Senior

19. Biosystematics of Social Insects (1981)[*]
    Edited by P. E. House and J.-L. Clement

20. Genome Evolution (1982)[*]
    Edited by G. A. Dover and R. B. Flavell

21. Problems of Phylogenetic Reconstruction (1982)[*]
    Edited by K. A. Joysey and A. E. Friday

22. Concepts in Nematode Systematics (1983)[*]
    Edited by A. R. Stone, H. M. Platt and L. F. Khalil

23. Evolution, Time and Space: The Emergence of the Biosphere (1983)[*]
    Edited by R. W. Sims, J. H. Price and P. E. S. Whalley

24. Protein Polymorphism: Adaptive and Taxonomic Significance (1983)[*]
    Edited by G. S. Oxford and D. Rollinson

25. Current Concepts in Plant Taxonomy (1983)[*]
    Edited by V. H. Heywood and D. M. Moore

26. Databases in Systematics (1984)[*]
    Edited by R. Allkin and F. A. Bisby

27. Systematics of the Green Algae (1984)[*]
    Edited by D. E. G. Irvine and D. M. John

28. The Origins and Relationships of Lower Invertebrates (1985)[‡]
    Edited by S. Conway Morris, J. D. George, R. Gibson and H. M. Platt

29. Infraspecific Classification of Wild and Cultivated Plants (1986)[‡]
    Edited by B. T. Styles

30. Biomineralization in Lower Plants and Animals (1986)[‡]
    Edited by B. S. C. Leadbeater and R. Riding

31. Systematic and Taxonomic Approaches in Palaeobotany (1986)[‡]
    Edited by R. A. Spicer and B. A. Thomas

32. Coevolution and Systematics (1986)[‡]
    Edited by A. R. Stone and D. L. Hawksworth

33. Key Works to the Fauna and Flora of the British Isles and Northwestern Europe, 5th edition (1988)[‡]
    Edited by R. W. Sims, P. Freeman and D. L. Hawksworth

34. Extinction and Survival in the Fossil Record (1988)[‡]
    Edited by G. P. Larwood

---

[a] Published by Clarendon Press for the Systematics Association
[*] Published by Academic Press for the Systematics Association
[‡] Published by Oxford University Press for the Systematics Association
[**] Published by Chapman & Hall for the Systematics Association
[‡‡] Published by CRC Press for the Systematics Association